C. Bathurst an others

The New English Theatre

Vol VI: Oroonoko, George Barnwell, Venice Preserved, Tamerlane, Distrest Mothers

C. Bathurst an others

The New English Theatre
Vol VI: Oroonoko, George Barnwell, Venice Preserved, Tamerlane, Distrest Mothers

ISBN/EAN: 9783743394896

Manufactured in Europe, USA, Canada, Australia, Japa

Cover: Foto ©Thomas Meinert / pixelio.de

Manufactured and distributed by brebook publishing software (www.brebook.com)

C. Bathurst an others

The New English Theatre

THE
NEW ENGLISH THEATRE
VOL. VI.

Oroonoko, George Barnwell,
Venice Preserved,
Tamerlane, Distrest. Mother.

Angelica Kauffman inv. Fra. Bartolozzi Sculp.

LONDON.

4292
3. 11.

Printed for J. Rivington & Sons, W. Strahan & Co. Johnston,
C. Bathurst, T. Davies, L. Davis, J. Dodsley, T. Longman,
T. Lowndes, B. Law, T. Caslon, T. Becket, W. Nicoll, R. Horsfield,
J. Bladon, B. White, E. Dilly, R. Baldwin, G. Robinson &
T. Cadell, W. Flexney, W. Woodfull & J. Bew 1776.

OROONOKO

A

TRAGEDY.

WRITTEN BY

THOMAS SOUTHERN.

Marked with the VARIATIONS in the

MANAGER's BOOK,

AT THE

Theatre-Royal in Drury-Lane.

LONDON:

Printed for C. BATHURST, W. LOWNDES, W. NICOLL
T. WHIELDON, and W. FOX,

M.DCC.LXXXV.

☞ The Reader is defired to obferve, that the Paffages omitted in the Reprefentation at the Theatres are here preferved, and marked with inverted Commas; as in the Whole of Page 6.

PROLOGUE.

AS when in hostile times two neighbouring states
Strive by themselves and their confederates :
The war at first is made with awkward skill,
And soldiers clumsily each other kill,
Till time at length their untaught fury tames,
And into rules their heedless rage reclaims :
Then ev'ry science by degrees is made
Subservient to the man-destroying trade :
Wit, wisdom, reading, observation, art ;
A well-turn'd head to guide a generous heart.
So it may prove with our contending stages,
If you will kindly but supply their wages :
Which you with ease may furnish, by retrenching
Your superfluities of wine and wenching.
Who'd grudge to spare from riot and hard drinking,
To lay it out on means to mend his thinking ?
To follow such advice you should have leisure,
Since what refines your sense refines your pleasure.
Women grown tame by use each fool can get,
But cuckolds all are made by men of wit.
To virgin favours fools have no pretence ;
For maidenheads were made for men of sense.
'Tis not enough to have a horse well bred,
To shew his mettle he must be well fed ;
Nor is it all in provender and breed,
He must be try'd and strain'd to mend his speed.
A favour'd poet, like a pamper'd horse,
Will strain his eye-balls out to win the course.
Do you but in your wisdom vote it fit
To yield due succours to this war of wit,
The buskins with more grace should tread the stage,
Love sigh in softer strains, heroes less rage ;
Satire shall shew a triple row of teeth,
And comedy shall laugh your fops to death :
Wit shall refine, and Pegasus shall foam,
And soar in search of ancient Greece and Rome.
And since the nation's in the conquering fit,
As you by arms, we'll vanquish France in wit.
The works were over, cou'd our poets write
With half the spirit that our soldiers fight.

A 2   Dramatis

Dramatis Personæ, 1785.

M E N.

	Drury-Lane.	Covent-Garden.
Aboan,	Mr. PALMER.	Mr. AICKIN.
Lieutenant Governor,	Mr. FARREN.	Mr. DAVIES.
Oroonoko,	Mr. BANNISTER, jun.	Mr. POPE.
Blandford,	Mr. J. AICKIN.	Mr. HULL.
Hotman,	Mr. WILLIAMS.	Mr. THOMPSON.
Stanmore,	Mr. R. PALMER.	Mr. CUBITT.
J. Stanmore,	Mr. NORRIS.	Mr. HELME.
Daniel,	Mr. SUETT.	Mr. QUICK.
Captain Driver,	Mr. WRIGHTEN.	Mr. FEARON.

W O M E N.

Widow Lackitt,	Mrs. HOPKINS.	Mrs. WEBB.
Charlotte Weldon,	Mifs COLLET.	Mrs. BATES.
Lucy Weldon,	Mifs SIMSON.	Mrs. INCHBALD.
Imoinda,	Mifs KEMBLE.	Mifs YOUNGE.

Planters, Indians, Negroes, Men, Women, and Children.

The SCENE *Surinam*, a Colony in the *Weſt-Indies*, at the Times of the Action of this Tragedy in the Poſſeſſion of the *Engliſh*.

A C T I.

Enter Charlotte Weldon, *in Man's Cloaths, following Lucy.*

Luc. WHAT will this come to? what can it end in? you have perfuaded me to leave dear *England*, and dearer *London*, the place of the world moft worthy living in, to follow you a hufband hunting into *America*: I thought hufbands grew in thefe plantations.

Weld. Why fo they do, as thick as oranges ripening one under another. Week after week they drop into fome woman's mouth: 'Tis but a little patience, fpreading your apron in expectation, and one of 'em will fall into your lap at laft.

Luc. Ay, fay you fo, indeed.

Weld. But you have left dear *London*, you fay: Pray what have you left in *London* that was very dear to you, that had not left you before.

Luc. Speak for yourfelf, fifter.

Weld. Nay, I'll keep you in countenance. The young fellows, you know, the deareft part of the town, and without whom *London* had been a wildernefs to you and me, had forfaken us a great while.

Luc. Forfaken us! I don't know that ever they had us.

Weld. Forfaken us the worft way, child; that is, did not think us worth having; they neglected us, no longer defign'd upon us, they were tir'd of us. Women in *London* are like the rich filks, they are out of fafhion, a great while before they wear out——

Luc. The devil take the fafhion, I fay.

Weld. You may tumble them over and over at their firft coming up, and never difparage their price; but they fall upon wearing immediately, lower and lower in their value, till they come to the broker at laft.

' *Luc.*

' *Luc.* Ay, aye, that's the merchant they deal with.
' The men would have us at their own fcandalous
' rates; their plenty makes them wanton, and in a
' little time, I fuppofe, they wont know what they
' would have of the women themfelves.

' *Weld.* O yes, they know what they would have.
' They would have a woman give the town a pattern
' of her perfon and beauty, and not ftay in it fo long
' to have the whole piece worn out. They would
' have the good face only difcover'd, and not the folly
' that commonly goes along with it. They fay there
' is a va" ftock of beauty in the nation, but a great
' part of it lies in unprofitable hands; therefore, for
' the good of the public, they would have a draught
' made once a quarter, fend the decaying beauties for
' breeders into the country, to make room for new
' faces to appear, to countenance the pleafures of the
' town.

' *Luc.* 'Tis very hard, the men muft be young as
' long as they live, and poor women be thought de-
' caying and unfit for the town at one and twenty.
' I'm fure we were not feven years in *London*.

' *Weld.* Not half the time taken notice of, fifter.
' The two or three laft years we could make nothing of
' it, even in a vizard-mafk; not in a vizard-mafk, that
' has cheated many man into an old acquaintance.
' Our faces began to be as familiar to the men of in-
' trigue as their duns, and as much avoided. We durft
' not appear in public places, and were almoft grudg'd
' a gallery in the churches: Even there they had their
' jefts upon us, and cry'd, fhe's in the right on't, good
' gentlewoman, fince no man confiders her body, fhe
' does very well indeed to take care of her foul.

' *Luc.* Such unmannerly fel'ows there will always be.

' *Weld.* Then you may remember we were reduc d
' to the laft neceffity, the neceffity of making filly
' vifits to our civil acquaintance, to bring us into toler-
' able company. Nay, the young inns-of-court beaus,
' of but one term's ftanding in the fafhion, who knew
' nobody, but as they were fhewn them by the orange-
woman,

' woman, had nick-names for us: How often have
' they laughed out, there goes my landlady; is she not
' come to let lodgings yet?
    ' *Luc.* Young coxcombs that knew no better.
    ' *Weld.* And that we mult have come to. For your
' part, what trade could you set up in? you would
' never arrive at the trust and credit of a guinea-bawd:
' You would have too much bufinefs of your own ever
' to mind other people's.
    ' *Luc.* That is true, indeed.
    ' *Weld.* Then, as a certain fign that there was no-
' thing more to be hop'd for, the maids of the choco-
' late-houfes found us out, and laugh'd at us: Our
' billet-doux lay there neglected for wafte-paper: We
' were cry'd down fo low, we could not pafs upon the
' city; and became fo notorious in our galloping way,
' from one end of the town to t'other, that at laft we
' could hardly compafs a competent change of petti-
' coats to difguife us to the hackney-coachmen: And
' then it was near walking a-foot indeed.
    ' *Luc.* Nay, that I began to be afraid of.
    • *Weld.*' To prevent which, with what youth and beauty
were left, fome experience, and the fmall remainder of
fifteen hundred pounds a-piece, which amounted to
bare two hundred between us both, I perfuaded you to
bring your perfon for a venture to the *Indies.* Every
thing has fucceeded in our voyage: I pafs for your
brother: One of the richeft planters here happening
to die juft as we landed, I have claimed kindred with
him: So, without making his will, he has left us the
credit of his relation to trade upon: ' We pafs for his
' coufins, coming here to *Surinam* chiefly upon his in-
' vitation:' We live in reputation; have the beft acquaintance in the place; and we fhall fee our accoun:
in't, I warrant you.
    Luc. I muft rely upon you.——
             Enter Widow Lackitt.
    Wid. Mr. *Welden*, your fervant. Your fervant, Mrs.
Lucy, I am an ill vifitor, but 'tis not too late, I hope, to
bid you welcome to this fide of the world. [*Salutes* Lucy.
               A 4   *Well.*

Weld. Gad fo, I beg your pardon, Widow, I fhould
have done the civilit'es of my houfe before: But, as
you fay, 'tis not too late, I hope— [*Going to kifs her.*

Wid. What! you think now this was a civil way of
begging a kifs; and by my troth, if it were, I fee no
harm in't; 'tis a pitiful favour indeed that is not
wo th afking for: Tho' I have known a woman fpeak
plainer before now, and not underftood neither.

Weld. Not under my rcof. Have at you, Widow—

Wid. Why that's well faid, fpcke like a younger brother, that deferves to have a widow.——[*He kiffes her.*]
You're a younger brother, I know by your kiffing.

Weld. How fo, pray?

Wid. Why, you kifs as if ycu expected to be paid
for't. You have bird-lime upon your lips. You ftick
fo clofe, thei e's no getting rid of you.

Weld. I am a-kin to a younger brother.

Wid. So much the better: We widows are commonly the better for younger brothers.

Luc. Better cr worfe, mcft of ycu. But you won't
be much the better for him, I can tell you. —— [*Afide.*

Weld. I was a younger brother; but an uncle of my
mother's has malicioufly left me an eftate, and, I'm
afraid, fpoil'd my fortune.

Wid. No, no; an eftate will never fpoil your fortune; I have a good eftate myfelf, thank Heaven, and
a kind hufband that left it behind him.

Weld. Thank Heaven, that took him away from it,
Widow, and left you behind him.

Wid. Nay, Heaven's will muft be done; he's in a
better place.

Weld. A better place for you, no doubt on't: Now
you may look about you; chufe for yourfelf, Mrs.
Lackitt, that's your bufinefs; for I know you defign to
marry again.

Wid. O dear! not I, I proteft and fwear; I don't
defign it: But I won't fwear neither; one does not
know what may happen to tempt one.

Weld. Why a lufty young fellow may happen to
tempt you.

Wid.

Wid. Nay, I'll do nothing rafhly : I'll refolve againft nothing. The devil, they fay, is very bufy upon thefe occafions, efpecially with the widows. But, if I am to be tempted, it muft be with a young man, I promife you—Mrs. *Lucy*, your brother is a very pleafant gentleman : I came about bufinefs to him, but he turns every thing into merriment.

Weld. Bufinefs, Mrs. *Lackitt ?* Then I know you would have me to yourfelf. Pray, leave us together, fifter.   [*Exit* Lucy.
What am I drawing upon myfelf here ?   [*Afide.*

Wid. You have taken a very pretty houfe here ; every thing fo neat about you already. I hear you are laying out for a plantation.

Wild. Why, yes truly, I like the country, and would buy a plantation, if I could reafonably.—

Wid. O! by all means reafonably.

Wild. If I could have one to my mind, I would think of fettling among you.

Wid. O! you can't do better. Indeed we can't pretend to have fo good company for you as you had in *England*; but we fhall make very much of you. For my own part, I affure you, I fhall think myfelf very happy to be more particularly known to you.

Weld. Dear Mrs. *Lackitt*, you do me too much honour.

Wid. Then as to a plantation, Mr. *Weldon*, you know I have feveral to difpofe of. Mr. *Lackit*, I thank him, has left, tho' I fay it, the richeft widow upon the place ; therefore I may afford to ufe you better than other people can. You fhall have one upon any reafonable terms.

Weld. That's a fair offer indeed.

Wid. You fhall find me as eafy as any body you can have to do with, I affure you. Pray try me, I would have you try me, Mr. *Weldon*. Well, I like that name of your's exceedingly, Mr. *Weldon*.

Weld. My name!

Wid. O exceedingly ! If any thing could perfuade me to alter my own name, I verily believe nothing in the world would do it fo foon, as to be called Mrs. *Weldon*.

Weld. Why, indeed *Weldon* doth found fomething better than *Lackitt.*

Wid. O! a great deal better. Not that there is fo much in the name neither. But, I don't know, there is fomething; I fhould like mightily to be called Mrs. *Weldon.*

Weld. I'm glad you like my name.

Wid. Of all things. But then there's the misfortune, one cannot change one's name without changing one's condition.

Weld. You hardly think it worth that, I believe.

Wid. Think it worth what, Sir? changing my condition! indeed, Sir, I think it worth every thing. But alas! Mr. *Weldon,* I have been a widow but fix weeks; 'tis too foon to think of changing one's condition yet: indeed it is: pray don't defire it of me: not but that you may perfuade me to any thing, fooner than any perfon in the world.———

Weld. Who, I, Mrs. *Lackitt?*

Wid. Indeed you may, Mr. *Weldon,* fooner than any man living. Lord, there's a great deal in faving a decency: I never minded it before: Well, I am glad you fpoke firft, to excufe my modefty. But, what? modefty means nothing, and is the virtue of a girl, that does not know what fhe would be at: A widow fhould be wifer. Now I will own to you, (but I won't confefs neither) I have had a great refpect for you a great while. I beg you pardon, Sir, and I muft declare to you, indeed I muft, if you defire to difpofe of all I have in the world, in an honourable way, which I don't pretend to be any way deferving your confideration, my fortune and perfon, if you won't underftand me without telling you fo, are both at your fervice, gad fo! another time———

Enter Stanmore.

Stan. So, Mrs. *Lackitt,* your widowhood's weaning a-pace; I fee which way 'tis going. *Weldon,* you're a happy man. The women and their favours come home to you.

Wid. A fiddle of favour, Mr. *Stanmore:* I am a lone woman, you know it, left in a great deal of bufinefs, and bufinefs muft be followed, or loft. I have feveral

ftocks

ſtocks and plantations upon my hands, and other things to diſpoſe of, which Mr. *Weldon* may have occaſion for.

Weld. We were juſt upon the brink of a bargain, as you came in.

Stan. Let me drive it on for you.

Weld. So you muſt, I believe, you or ſomebody for me.

Stan. I'll ſtand by you : I underſtand more of this buſineſs than you can pretend to.

Weld. I don't pretend to it ; 'tis quite out of my way indeed.

Stan. If the widow gets you to herſelf, ſhe will cer-tainly be too hard for you : I know her of old : She has no conſcience in a corner ; a very *Jew* in a bar-gain, and would circumciſe you to get more of you

Weld. Is this true, Widow ?

Wid. Speak as you find, Mr. *Weldon*, I have offer'd you very fair ! think upon't, and let me hear of you ; the ſooner the better, Mr. *Weldon*.   [*Exit.*

Stan. I aſſure you, my friend, ſhe'll cheat you if ſhe can.

Weld. I don't know that; but I can cheat her, if I will.

Stan. Cheat her ! how ?

Weld. I can marry her; and then I am ſure I have it in my power to cheat her.

Stan. Can you marry her ?

Weld. Yes, faith, ſo ſhe ſays : Her pretty perſon and fortune, (which, one with the other, you know are not contemptible) are both at my ſervice.

. *Stan.* Contemptible ! very conſiderable, egad ; very deſirable ; why ſhe's worth ten thouſand pounds, man ;, a clear eſtate : No charge upon't, but a boobily ſon : He indeed was to have half; but his father begot him, and ſhe breeds him up not to know or have more than ſhe has a mind to : And ſhe has a mind to ſomething elſe, it ſeems.

Weld There's a great deal to be made of this—[*Muſing*

Stan. A handſome fortune may be made on't ; and I adviſe you to't by all means,

Weld. To marry her ! an old wanton witch ! I hate her.

Stan. No matter for that : Let her go to the devil for you. She'll cheat her ſon of a good eſtate for you : that's a perquiſite of a widow's portion always.

                                        Weld.

Weld. I have a defign, and will follow her at leaft,
till I have a pennyworth of the plantation.

Stan. I fpeak as a friend, when I advife you to marry
her, for 'tis directly againft the intereft of my own family. My coufin *Jack* has belabour'd her a good while
that way.

Weld. What! honeft *Jack!* I'll not hinder him. I'll
give over the thoughts of her.

Stan. He'll make nothing on't; fhe does not care
for him. I'm glad you have her in your power.

Weld. I may be able to ferve him.

Stan. Here's a fhip come into the river; I was in
hopes it had been from *England.*

Weld. From *England!*

Stan. No. I was difappointed; I long to fee this
handfome coufin of your's: The picture you gave me
of her has charm'd me.

Weld. You'll fee whether it has flatter'd her or no,
in a little time. If fhe recover'd of that illnefs that
was the reafon of her ftaying behind us, I know fhe
will come with the firft opportunity. We fhall fee her,
or hear of her death.

Stan. We'll hope the beft. The fhips from *England*
are expected every day.

Weld. What fhip is this?

Stan. A rover, a buccaneer, a trader in flaves:
That's the commodity we deal in, you know. If you
have a curiofity to fee our manner of marketing, I'll
wait upon you.

Weld. We'll take my fifter with us.—   [*Exeunt.*

S C E N E, *An open Place.*

Enter Lieutenant-Governor *and* Blandford.

Gov. There's no refifting your fortune, *Blandford;*
you draw all the prizes.

Bland. I draw for our lord governor; you know his
fortune favours me.

Gov. I grudge him nothing this time; but if fortune had favour'd me in the laft fale, the fair flave had
been mine; *Clemene* had been mine.

Bland.

Bland. Are you still in love with her?

Gov. Every day more in love with her?

Enter Capt. Driver, *teazed and pulled about by* Widow Lackitt, *and several* Planters. *Enter, at another Door,* Weldon, Lucy, *and* Stanmore.

Wid. Here have I six slaves in my lot, and not a man among them; all women and children; what can I do with 'em, Captain? Pray consider I am a woman myself, and can't get my own slaves, as some of my neighbours do.

1st Plant. I have all men in mine: Pray, Captain, let the men and women be mingled together, for procreation sake, and the good of the plantation.

2d Plant. Ay, ay, a man and a woman, Captain, for the good of the plantation.

Capt. Let them mingle together, and be damn'd, what care I? would you have me a pimp for the good of the plantation?

1st Plant. I am a constant customer, Captain.

Wid. I am always ready money to you, Captain.

1st Plant. For that matter, mistress, my money is as ready as yours.

Wid. Pray hear me, Captain.

Cap. Look you, I have done my part by you; I have brought the number of slaves I bargain'd for; if your lots have not pleas'd you, you must draw again among yourselves.

3d Plant. I am contented with my lot.

4th Plant. I am very well satisfied.

3d Plant. We'll have no drawing again.

Cap. Do you hear, mistress? you may hold your tongue: For my part I expect my money.

Wid. Captain, nobody questions or scruples the payment: but I won't hold my tongue; 'tis too much to pray and pay too: One may speak for one's own I hope.

Capt. Well, what would you say?

Wid. I say no more than I can make out.

Capt. Out with it then.

Wid. I say things have not been so fair carried as

they

they might have been. How do I know but you have juggled together in my abfence? You drew the lots before I came, I'm fure.

Capt. That's your own fault, miftrefs, you might have come fooner.

Wid. Then here's a prince, as they fay, among the flaves, and you let him down to go as a common man.

Capt. Have you a mind to try what a man he is? You'll find him no more than a common man at your bufinefs.

Wid. Sir, you're a fcurvy fellow to talk at this rate to me: If my hufband were alive, gadfbodykins you would not ufe me fo.

Capt. Right, miftrefs, I would not ufe you at all.

Wid. Not ufe me! your betters every inch of you, I would have you to krow, would be glad to ufe me, firrah. Marry come up here, who are you I tiow? You begin to think yourfelf a Captain, forfooth, becaufe we call you fo. You forget yourfelf as faft as you can; but I remember you; I know you fo a pitiful paltry fellow as you are, an upftart to profperity; one that is but juft come acquainted with cleanlinefs, and that never faw five fhillings of your own without deferving to be hang'd for 'em.

Gov. She has given you a broadfide, Captain; you'll ftand up to her.

Capt. Hang her, ' ftink-pot,' I'll come no nearer.

Wid. By this good light it would make a woman do a thing fhe never defigned; marry again, though fhe were fure to repent it, and be revenged of fuch a——

J. Stan. What's the matter, Mrs. *Lackitt*, can I ferve you?

Wid. No, no, you can't ferve me: You are for ferving yourfelf, I'm fure. Pray go about your bufinefs, I have none for you: You know, I have told you fo. Lord! how can you be fo troublefome; nay, fo unconfcionable, to think that every rich widow muft throw herfelf away upon a young fellow that has nothing?

Stan. *Jack*, you are anfwer'd, I fuppofe.

J. Stan. I'll have another pluck at her.

Wid.

3

Wid. Mr. *Weldon,* I am a little out of order; but
pray bring your fifter to dine with me. Gad's my life,
I'm out of all patience with that piiful fellow: My
flefh rifes at him; I can't ftay in the place where he
is.   [*Exit.*

Bland. Captain, you have ufed the widow very fa-
miliarly.

Capt. This is my way; I have no defign, and therefore am not over civil. If fhe had ever a handfome
daughter to wheedle her out of; or if I could make
any thing of her booby fon——

Weld. I may improve that hint, and make fomething
of him.   [*Afide.*

Gov. She's very rich.

Capt. I'm rich myfelf. She has nothing that I
want; I have no leaks to ftop. Old women are for-
tune-menders. I have made a good voyage, and would
reap the fruits of my labour. We plow the deep, my
mafters, but our harveft is on fhore. I am for a young
woman.

Stan. Look about, Captain, there's one ripe, and
ready for the fickle.

Capt. A woman indeed: I will be acquainted with
her: Who is fhe?

Weld. My fifter, Sir.

Capt. Would I were a-kin to her: If fhe were my
fifter, fhe fhould never go out of the family. What fay
you, miftrefs? You expect I fhould marry you, I fuppofe?

Luc. I fhan't be difappointed if you don't.
                                                [*Turning away.*

Weld. She won't break her heart, Sir.

Capt. But I mean——   [*Following her.*

Weld. And I mean -- [*Going between him and* Lucy]
That you muft not think of her without marrying.

Capt. I mean fo too.

Weld. Why then your meaning's out.

Capt. You're very fhort.

Weld. I will grow, and be taller for you.

Capt. I fhall grow angry, and fwear.

Weld. You'll catch no fifh then.

                                                   Capt.

Capt. I don't well know whether he defigns to affront me or no.

Stan. No, no, he's a little familiar; 'tis his way.

Capt. Say you fo? nay, I can be as familiar as he, if that be it. Well, Sir, look upon me full. What fay you? how do you like me for a brother-in-law?

Wild. Why yes, faith, you'll do my bufinefs, [*turning him about*] if we can agree about my filter's.

Capt. I don't know whether your filter will like me or not: I can't fay much to her; but I have money enough : And if you are her brother, as you feem to be a-kin to her, I know that will recommend me to you.

Weid. This is your market for flaves; my filter is a free woman, and mult not be difpofed of in public. You fhall be welcome to my houfe, if you pleafe : and, upon better acquaintance, if my filter likes you, and I like your offers ——

Capt. Very well, Sir, I'll come and fee her.

Gov. Where are the flaves, Captain? they are long a-coming.

Bland. And who is this prince that's fall'n to my lot for the lord governor? Let me know fomething of him, that I may treat him accordingly : Who is he?

Capt. He's the devil of a fellow, I can tell you? a prince every inch of him : You have paid dear enough for him for all the good he'll do you : I was forc'd to clap him in irons, and did not think the fhip fafe neither. You are in hoftility with the *Indians*, they fay; they threaten you daily : You had beft have an eye upon him.

Bland. But who is he?

Gov. And how do you know him to be a prince?

Capt. He is fon and heir to the great king of *Angola*, a mifchievous monarch in thofe parts, who, by his good will, would never let any of his neighbours be in quiet. This fon was his general, a plaguy fighting fellow. I have formerly had dealings with him for flaves, which he took prifoners, and have got pretty roundly by him. But the wars being at an end, and nothing more to be got by the trade of that country, I made bold to bring the prince along with me.

Gov.

Gov. How could you do that?

Bland. What! steal a prince out of his own country! impossible!

Capt. 'Twas hard indeed; but I did it. You must know this *Oroonoko*——

Bland. Is that his name?

Capt. Ay, *Oroonoko.*

Gov. *Oroonoko.*

Capt. Is naturally inquisitive about the men and manners of the white nations. Because I could give him some account of the other parts of the world, I grew very much into his favour: In return of so great an honour, you know, I could do no less, upon my coming away, than invite him on board me. Never having been in a ship, he appointed his time, and I prepared my entertainment. He came the next evening, as private as he could, with about some twenty along with him. The punch went round; and as many of his attendants as would be dangerous, I sent dead drunk on shore; the rest we secured; and so you have the prince *Oroonoko.*

1st Plant. Gad-a-mercy, Captain, there you were with him, i'faith.

2d Plant. Such men as you are fit to be employed in public affairs: The plantation will thrive by you.

3d Plant. Industry ought to be encouraged.

Capt. There's nothing done without it, boys. I have made my fortune this way.

Bland. Unheard of villainy!

Stan. Barbarous treachery!

Bland. They applaud him for't.

Gov. But, Captain, methinks you have taken a great deal of pains for this prince *Oroonoko*; why did you part with him at the common rate of slaves?

Capt. Why, Lieutenant-Governor, I'll tell you, I did design to carry him to *England*, to have show'd him there; but I found him troublesome upon my hands, and I'm glad I'm rid of him——Oh, oh, hark, they come.

Black Slaves, Men, Women, and Children, pass across the Stage by two and two; Aboan, and others of Oroonoko's noko's *Attendants, two and two :* Oroonoko *last of all in Chains.*

Luc. Are all these wretches slaves?

Stan. All sold, they and their posterity, all slaves.

Luc. O miserable fortune !

Bland. Most of them know no better; they were born so, and only change their masters. But a prince, born only to command, betray'd and sold! my heart drops blood for him.

Capt. Now, Governor, here he comes, pray observe him.

Oço. So, Sir, you have kept your word with me?

Capt. I am a better Christian, I thank you, than to keep it with a Heathen.

Oro. You are a Christian ; be a Christian still ;
If you have any God that teaches you
To break your word, I need not curse you more :
Let him cheat you, as you are false to me.
You faithful followers of my better fortune,
We have been fellow-soldiers in the field ;

      [Embracing his friends.
Now we are fellow-slaves. This last farewel.
Be sure of one thing that will comfort us,
Whatever world we are next thrown upon
Cannot be worse than this.

     [All slaves go off but Oroonoko.

Capt. You see what a bloody Pagan he is, Governor ; but I took care that none of his followers should be in the same lot with him, for fear they should undertake some desperate action, to the danger of the colony.

Oro. Live still in fear ; it is the villain's curse,
And will revenge my chains ; fear even me,
Who have no power to hurt thee. Nature abhors,
And drives thee out from the society
And commerce of mankind, for breach of faith.
Men live and prosper but in mutual trust,
A confidence of one another's truth :
That thou hast violated. I have done ;
I know my fortune, and submit to it.

Gov. Sir, I am sorry for your fortune, and would help it, if I could.

          Bland.

Bland. Take off his chains. You know your condition; but you are fal'en into honourable hands : You are the Lord Governor's flave, who will ufe you nobly : In his abfence it fhall be my care to ferve you.

[*Blandford applying to him.*

Oro. I hear you, but I can believe no more.

Gov. Captain, I'm afraid the world wont fpeak fo honouiable of this action of yours, as you would have them.

Capt. I have the money, let the world fpeak and be damn'd, I care not.

Oro. I would forget myfelf. Be fatisfied [*To Bland.* I am above the rank of common flaves. Let that content you. The Chriftian there that knows me, For his own fake will not difcover more.

Capt. I have other matters to mind. You have him, and much good may do you with your prince. [*Exit.*

The Planters pulling and ftaring at Oroonoko.

Bland. What would you have there ? you ftare as if you never faw a man before. Stand farther off.

[*Turns 'em away.*

Oro. Let 'em ftare on.
I am unfortunate, but not afham'd
Of being fo. No, let the guilty blufh,
The white man that betray'd me. Honeft black
Difdains to change its colour. I am ready :
Where muft I go ? Difpofe me as you pleafe ;
I am not well acquainted with my fortune,
But muft learn to know it better : So I know, you fay,
Degrees make all things eafy.

Bland. All things fhall be eafy.

Oro. Tear off this pomp, and let me know myfelf:
The flavifh habit beft becomes me now.
Hard fate, and whips, and chains may overpow'r
The frailer flefh, and bow my body down :
But there's another, nobler part of me,
Out of your reach, which you can never tame.

- *Bland.* You fhall find nothing of this wretchednefs
You apprehend. We are not monfters all.
You feem unwilling to difclofe yourfelf:
Therefore, for fear the mentioning your name

Should

Should give you new difquiets, I prefume
To call you *Cæfar.*

Oro. I am myfelf; but call me what you pleafe.

Stan. A very good name *Cæfar.*

Gov. And very fit for his character.

Oro. Was *Cæfar* then a flave?

Gov. I think he was; to pirates too? he was a great
conqueror, but unfortunate in his friends——

Oro. His friends were Chriftians?

Bland. No.

Oro. No! that's ftrange.

Gov. And murder'd by 'em.

Oro. I would be *Cæfar* then. Yet I will live.

Bland. Live to be happier.

Oro. Do what you will with me.

Bland. I will wait upon you, attend, and ferve you.
                    [*Exit with* Oroonoko.

Luc. Well, if the Captain had brought this Prince's
country along with him, and would make me queen of
it, I would not have him, after doing fo bafe a thing.

Weld. He's a man to thrive in the world, fifter:
He'll make you the better jointure.

Luc. Hang him, nothing can profper with him.

Stan. Enquire into the great eftates, and you'll find
moft of them depend upon the fame title of honefty:
The men who raife 'em firft are much of the Captain's
principles.

Weld. Ay, ay, as you fay, let him be damn'd for the
good of his family. Come, fifter, we are invited to
dinner.

Gov. Stanmore, you dine with me.   [*Exeunt.*

A C T II.

S C E N E, Widow Lackitt's *Houfe.*

Enter Widow Lackitt *and* Weldon.

Weld. THIS is fo great a favour, I don't know how
to receive it.

Wid. O dear Sir! you know how to receive, and how
                                                    to

to return a favour as well as any body, I don't doubt it:
'Tis not the first you have had from our sex, I suppose.

Weld. But this is so unexpected.

Wid. Lord, how can you say so, Mr. *Weldon?* I
won't believe you.   Don't I know you handsome
gentlemen expect every thing a woman can do for you?
and by my troth you're in the right on't.   I think one
can't do too much for a handsome gentleman; and so
you shall find it.

Weld. I shall never have such an offer again, that's
certain: What shall I do?   I am mightily divided—

[*Pretending a concern.*

Wid. Divided: O dear, I hope not so, Sir: If I
marry, truly I expect to have you to myself.

Weld. There's no danger of that, Mrs. *Lackitt.* I am
divided in my thoughts: My father upon his deathbed
obliged me to see my sister disposed of, before I married
myself. 'Tis that sticks upon me.   They say, indeed,
promises are to be broken or kept; and I know 'tis a
foolish thing to be tied to a promise; but I can't help
it.   I don't know how to get rid of it.

Wid. Is that all?

Weld. All in all to me.   The commands of a dying
father, you know, ought to be obey'd.

Wid. And so they may.

Weld. Impossible to do me any good.

Wid. They shan't be your hindrance.   You wou'd
have a husband for your sister, you say: He must be
very well to pass too in the world, I suppose.

Weld. I would not throw her away.

Wid. Then marry her out of hand to the sea-cap-
tain you were speaking of.

Weld. I was thinking of him, but 'tis to no purpose; she hates him.

Wid. Does she hate him? nay, 'tis no matter, an
impudent rascal as he is, I would not advise her to
marry him.

Weld. Can you think of nobody else?

Wid. Let me see.

Weld.

Weld. Ay, pray do, I should be loth to part with my good fortune in you for so small a matter as a sister : But you find how it is with me.

Wid. Well remember'd, i'faith : Well, if I thought you would like of it, I have a husband for her : What do you think of my son ?

Weld. You don't think of it yourself.

Wid. I protest but I do : I am in earnest, if you are, he shall marry her within this half hour, if you'll give your consent to it.

Weld. I give my consent ! I'll answer for my sister, she shall have him : You may be sure I shall be glad to get over the difficulty.

Wid. No more to be said then, that difficulty is over : But I vow and swear you frighten'd me, Mr. *Weldon.* If I had not had a son now for your sister, what must I have done, do you think ? Were not you an ill-natur'd thing to boggle at a promise ? I could break twenty for you.

Weld. I am the more obliged to you ; but this son will save all.

Wid. He's in the house ; I'll go and bring him my-self., [*Going.*] You would do well to break the business to your sister. She's within, I'll send her to you—

                                   [*Going again, comes back.*
Weld. Pray do.

Wid. But d'you hear ? perhaps she may stand upon her maidenly behaviour, and blush, and play the fool, and delay : But don't be answer'd so : What ! she is not a girl at these years : Shew your authority, and tell her roundly, she must be married immediately. I'll manage my son, I warrant you——   [*Gets out in haste.*

Weld. The widow's in haste, I see : I thought I had laid a rub in the road, about my sister : But she has stepp'd over that. She's making way for herself as fast as she can ; but little thinks where she is going : I could tell her she is going to play the fool : But people don't love to hear of their faults : Besides, that is not my business at present.

Enter Lucy.

So, sister, I have a husband for you——

                                            Luc.

Luc. With all my heart. I don't know what confinement marriage may be to the men, but I'm sure the women have no liberty without it. I'm for any thing that will deliver me from the care of a reputation, which I begin to find impossible to preserve.

Weld. I'll ease you of that care: You must be married immediately.

Luc. The sooner the better; for I am quite tir'd of setting up for a husband. The widow's foolish son is the man, I suppose.

Weld. I consider'd your constitution, sister; and, finding you would have occasion for a fool, I have provided accordingly.

Luc. I don't know what occasion I may have for a fool when I'm married; but I find none but fools have occasion to marry.

Weld. Since he is to be a fool then, I thought it better for you to have one of his mother's making than your own; 'twill save you the trouble.

Luc. I thank you; you take a great deal of pains for me; but pray tell me what you are doing for yourself all this while?

Weld. You are never true to your own secrets, and therefore I won't trust you with mine. Only remember this, I am your eldest sister, and, consequently, laying my breeches aside, have as much occasion for a husband as you can have. I have a man in my eye, be satisfy'd.

Enter Widow Lackitt, *with her son* Daniel.

Wid. Come *Daniel,* hold up thy head, child; look like a man: You must not take it as you have done Gad's my life! there's nothing to be done with twirling your hat, man.

Dan. Why mother, what's to be done then?

Wid. Why, look me in the face, and mind what I say to you.

Dan. Marry, who's the fool then? What shall I get by minding what you say to me?

Wid. Mrs. *Lucy,* the boy is bashful, don't discourage him; pray come a little forward, and let him salute you.

[*Going between* Lucy *and* Daniel.

Luc.

Luc. A fine hufband I am to have truly. [*To* Weldon.

Wid. Come *Daniel*, you mult be acquainted with this gentlewoman.

Dan. Nay I'm not proud, that is not my fault : I am prefently acquainted when I know the company; but this gentlewoman is a ftranger to me.

Wid. She is your miftrefs, I have fpoke a good word for you; make her a bow, and go and kifs her.

Dan. Kifs her ! have a care what you fay ; I warrant fhe fcorns your words. Such fine folks are not us'd to be flopp'd and kifs'd. Do you think I don't know that, mother !

Wid. Try her, try her man : [Daniel *bows, fhe thrufts him forward*] Why that's well done; go nearer her.

Dan. Is the devil in the woman ? Why fo I can go nearer her, if you would let a body alone. [*To his Mother.*] Cry your mercy, forfooth ; my mother is always fhaming one before company ; fhe would have me as unmannerly as herfelf, and offer to kifs you. [*To* Lucy.

Weld. Why won't you kifs her ?

Dan. Why, pray may I.

Weld. Kifs her, kifs her man.

Dan. Marry, and I will ; [*Kiffes her.*] gadfooks, fhe kiffes rarely : An' pleafe you, miftrefs, and feeing my mother will have it fo, I don't much care if I kifs you again, forfooth. [*Kiffes her again.*

Luc. Well, how do you like me now ?

Dan. Like you ? marry I don't know, you have bewitched me, I think : I was never fo in my born days before.

Wid. You muft marry this fine woman, *Daniel.*

Dan. Hey day ! marry her ! I was never married in all my life. What muft I do with her then, mother ?

Wid. You muft live with her, eat and drink with her, go to bed with her, and fleep with her.

Dan. Nay, marry, if I muft go to bed with her, I fhall never fleep, that's certain ; fhe'll break me of my reft, quite and clean, I tell you before hand. As for eating and drinking with her, why I have a good ftomach, and can play my part in any company. But how do you think I can go to bed to a woman I don't know ?

Weld.

Weld. You fhall know her better.

Dan. Say you fo, Sir?

Weld. Kifs her again.   [*Daniel kiſſes Lucy.*

Dan. Nay, kiffing I find will make us prefently acquainted. We'll fteal into a corner to practice a little, and then I fhall be able to do any thing.—

Weld. The young man mends a-pace.

Wid. Pray don't baulk him.

Dan. Mother, mother, if you'll ftay in the room by me, and promife not to leave me, I don't care for once if I venture to go to bed with her.

Wid. There's a good child, go in and put on thy beft cloaths; pluck up a fpirit, I'll ftay in the room by thee. She won't hurt thee, I warrant thee.

Dan. Nay, as to that matter, I am not afraid of her: I'll give her as good as fhe brings. I have a *Rowland* for her *Oliver*, and fo thou may tell her.   [*Exit.*

Wid. Mrs. *Lucia*, we fhan't ftay for you: You are in readinefs I fuppofe.

Weld. She is always ready to do what I would have her, I muft fay that for my fifter.

Wid. 'Twill be her own another day, Mr. *Weldon*, we'll marry 'em out of hand, and then——

Weld. And then, Mrs. *Lackitt*, look to yourfelf——
                                              [*Exeunt.*

Enter Oroonoko *and* Blandford.

' *Oro.* You grant I have good reafon to fufpect
' All the profeffions you can make to me.

' *Bland.* Indeed you have.

' *Oro.* The dog that fold me did profefs as much
' As you can do—but yet, I know not why—
' Whether it is becaufe I'm fall'n fo low,
' And have no more to fear—that is not it:
' I am a flave no longer than I pleafe.
' 'Tis fomething nobler—being juft myfelf,
' I am inclining to think others fo:
' 'Tis that prevails upon me to believe you.

' *Bland.* You may believe me.

' *Oro.* I do believe you.

B   ' From

' From what I know of you, you are no fool :
' Fools only are the knaves, and live by tricks :
' Wife-men may thrive without 'em, and be honeſt.
 ' *Bland.* They won't all take your counſel. [*Aſide.*'
 Oro. ' You know my ſtory, and' you ſay you are
A friend to my misfortunes : That's a name
Will teach you what you owe yourſelf and me.
 Brand. I'll ſtudy to deſerve to be your friend.
When once our noble governor arrives,
With him you will not need my intereſt :
He is too generous not to feel your wrongs.
But be aſſur'd I will employ my pow'r,
And find the means to ſend you home again.
 Oro. I thank you, Sir.—My honeſt, wretched friends !
           [*Sighing.*
Their chains are heavy : They have hardly found
So kind a maſter. May I aſk you, Sir,
What is become of them : Perhaps I ſhould not.
You will forgive a ſtranger.
 Bland. I'll enquire.
And uſe my beſt endeavours, where they are,
To have 'em gently us'd.
 Oro. Once more I thank you.
You offer every cordial that can keep
My hopes alive, to wait a better day.
What friendly care can do, you have apply'd :
But oh ! I have a grief admits no cure.
 Bland. You do not know, Sir——
 Oro. Can you raiſe the dead ?
Purſue and overtake the wings of Time ?
And bring about again the hours, the days,
The years that made me happy ?
 Bland. That is not to be done.
 Oro. No, there is nothing to be done for me.
      [*Kneeling and kiſſing the earth.*
Thou God ador'd ! thou ever-glorious ſun !
If ſhe be yet on earth, ſend me a beam
Of thy all-ſeeing pow'r to light me to her :
Or, if thy ſiſter goddeſs has preferr'd
Her beauty to the ſkies, to be a ſtar ;
             O tell

O tell me where she shines, that I may stand
Whole nights, and gaze upon her.

   Bland. I am rude, and interrupt you.

   Oro. I am troublesome:
But pray give me your pardon. My swoll'n heart
Burst out its passage, and I must complain.
O! can you think of nothing dearer to me?
Dearer than liberty, my country, friends,
Much dearer than my life, that I have lost
The tend'rest best belov'd, and loving wife.

   Bland. Alas! I pity you.

   Oro. Do pity me:
Pity's a-kin to love; and every thought
Of that soft kind is welcome to my soul.
I would be pity'd here.

   Bland. I dare not ask
More than you please to tell me: But, if you
Think it convenient to let me know
Your story, I dare promise you to bear
A part in your distress, if not assist you.

   Oro. Thou honest-hearted man! I wanted such,
Just such a friend as thou art, that would sit
Still as the night, and let me talk whole days
Of my *Imoinda.* O! I'll tell thee all
From first to last; and pray observe me well.

   Bland. I will most heedfully.

   Oro. There was a stranger in my father's court,
Valu'd and honour'd much: He was a white,
The first I ever saw of your complexion.
He chang'd his God for ours, and so grew great;
Of many virtues, and so fam'd in arms,
He still commanded all my father's wars.
I was bred under him. One fatal day,
The armies joining, he before me stepp'd,
Receiving in his breast a poison'd dart
Levell'd at me; he dy'd within my arms.
I've tir'd you already.

   Bland. Pray go on.

   Oro. He left an only daughter, whom he brought
An infant to *Angola.* When I came

            Back

Back to the Court, a happy conqueror,
Humanity oblig'd me to condole
With this sad virgin for a father's lofs,
Loft for my fafety.   I prefented her
With all the flaves of battle, to atone
Her father's ghoft.   But, when I faw her face,
And heard her fpeak, I offer'd up myfelf
To be the facrifice.   She bow'd and blufh'd :
I wonder'd and ador'd.   The facred pow'r,
That had fubdu'd me, then infpir'd my tongue,
Inclin'd her heart, and all our talk was love.
 Bland. Then you were happy.
 Oro. O! I was too happy.
I marry'd her : And, though my country's cuftom
Indulg'd the privilege of many wives,
I fwore myfelf never to know but her.
She grew with child, and I grew happier ftill.
O my *Imoinda!* But it could not laft.
Her fatal beauty reach'd my father's ears :
He fent for her to court, where, curfed court!
No woman comes but for his amorous ufe.
He raging to poffefs her, fhe was forc'd
To own herfelf my wife.   The furious king
Started at inceft ; but, grown defperate,
Not daring to enjoy what he defir'd,
In mad revenge (which I could never learn)
He poifon'd her, or fent her far, far off,
Far from my hopes ever to fee her more.
 Bland. Moft barbarous of fathers ! the fad tale
Has ftruck me dumb with wonder.
 Oro. I have done.
I'll trouble you no farther : Now and then
A figh will have its way : That fhall be all.
    Enter Stanmore.
 Stan. *Blandford*, the Lieutenant-Governor is gone
to your plantation.   He defires you would bring the
Royal Slave with you.   The fight of his fair miftrefs,
he fays, is an entertainment for a Prince; he would
have his opinion of her.
 Oro. Is he a lover !

          Bland.

Bland. So he fays himfelf: He flatters a beautiful.
flave that I have, and calls her miftrefs.

Oro. Muft he then flatter her to call her miftrefs?
I pity the proud man, who thinks himfelf
Above being in love: What, tho' fhe be a flave,
She may deferve him.

Bland. You fhall judge of that when you fee her, Sir.

Oro. I go with you.   [*Exeunt.*

SCENE, *a Plantation.*

Lieut. Governor *following* Imoinda.

Gov. I have difturb'd you, I confefs my faults,
My fair *Clemene*; ' but begin again,
' And I will liften to your mournful fong,
' Sweet as the foft complaining nightingale's.
' While every note calls out my trembling foul,
' And leaves me filent, as the midnight groves,
' Only to fhelter you;' fing, fing again,
And let me wonder at the many ways
You have to ravifh me.

Imo. O I can weep
Enough for you and me, if that will pleafe you.

Gov. You muft not weep: I come to dry your tears,
And raife you from your forrow.   Look upon me:
' Look with the eyes of kind indulging love,
' That I may have full caufe for what I fay:'
I came to offer you your liberty,
And be myfelf the flave. You turn away: [*Following her.*
But every thing become you.   I may take
This pretty hand: I know your modefty
Would draw it back: But you would take it ill
If I fhould let it go, I know ye wou'd.
You fhall be gently forc'd to pleafe yourfelf;
That you will thank me for.

> [*She ftruggles, and gets her hand from him, then
>   he offers to kifs her.*

Nay, if you ftruggle with me, I muft take—

Imo. You may my life, that I can part with freely.

[*Exit.*

B 3   *Enter*

Enter Blandford, Stanmore, *and* Oroonoko.

Bland. So, Governor, we don't difturb you, I hope:
Your miftrefs has left you: You were making love:
She's thankful for the honour, I fuppofe.

Gov. Quite infenfible to all I fay, and do:
When I fpeak to her, fhe fighs, or weeps,
But never anfwers me as I would have her.

Stan. There's fomething nearer than her flavery, that
touches her.

Bland. What do her fellow flaves fay of her? can't
they find the caufe?

Gov. Some of them, who pretend to be wifer than
the reft, and hate her, I fuppofe for being us'd better
than they are, will needs have it that fhe is with child.

Bland. Poor wretch! if it be fo, I pity her:
She has loft a hufband, that perhaps was dear
To her, and then you cannot blame her.

Oro. If it be fo, indeed you cannot blame her,
                              [*Sighing.*

Gov. No, no, it is not fo: If it be fo,
I muft ftill love her: And, defiring ftill,
I muft enjoy her.

Bland. Try what you can do with fair means, and
welcome.

Gov. I'll give you ten flaves for her.

Bland. You know fhe is our Lord Governor's: But,
if I could difpofe of her, I would not now, efpecially
to you.

Gov. Why not to me?

Bland. I mean againft her will. You are in love
        with her;
And we all know what your defires would have:
Love ftops at nothing but poffeffion.
' Were fhe within your pow'r, you do not know
' How foon you would be tempted to forget
' The nature of the deed, and, may be, act
' A violence, you after would repent.'

Oro. 'Tis godlike in you to protect the weak.

Gov. Fie, fie, I would not force her. Tho' fhe be
A flave, her mind is free, and fhould confent.

                                        Oro.

Oro. Such honour will engage her to confent :
And then, if you're in love, fhe's worth the having.
Shall we not fee the wonder?

Gov. Have a care;
You have a heart, and fhe has conqu'ring eyes.

Oro. I have a heart; but, if it could be falfe
To my firft vows, ever to love again,
Thefe honeft hands fhould tear it from my breaft,
And throw the traitor from me. O! *Imoinda!*
Living or dead, I can be only thine.

Bland. *Imoinda* was his wife: She's either dead,
Or living, dead to him; forc'd from his arms
By an inhuman father. Another time
I'll tell you all.   [*To the* Gov. *and* Stan.

Stan. Hark! the flaves have done their work;
And now begins their evening merriment.

Bland. The men are all in love with fair *Clemene*
As much as you are: And the women hate her,
From an inftinct of natural jealoufy.
They fing, and dance, and try their little tricks
To entertain her, and divert her fadnefs.
May be fhe is among them: Shall we fee?   [*Exeunt.*

The SCENE *drawn fhews the Slaves, Men, Women,
and Children, upon the Ground; fome rife and dance.*

'A S O N G by a B O Y.

' *A* Lafs there lives upon the green,
    ' Could I her picture draw;
' A brighter nymph was never feen,
' That looks, and reigns a little queen,
    ' And keeps the fwains in awe.

II.

' Her eyes are Cupid's darts and wings,
    ' Her eye-brows are his bow:
' Her filken hair the filver ftrings,
' Which fure and fwift deftruction brings
    ' To all the world below.

III. *If*

III.

' *If* Paftorella'*s dawning light*
' *Can warm and wound us fo* ;
' *Her noon will fhine fo piercing bright,*
' *Each glancing beam will kill outright,*
' *And every fwain fubdue.*

'·A SONG by a MAN.

' *B*Right Cynthia'*s power divinely great,*
  ' *What heart is not obeying ?*
' *A thoufand* Cupids *on her wait,*
 ' *And in her eyes are playing.*

II.

' *She feems the queen of love to reign,*
' *For fhe alone difpenfes*
' *Such fweets, as beft can entertain*
 ' *The guft of all the fenfes.*

III.

' *Her face a charming profpect brings* ;
' *Her breath gives balmy bliffes* ;
' *I hear an angel when fhe fings,*
 ' *And tafte of Heav'n in kiffes.*

IV.

' *Four fenfes thus fhe feafts with joy,*
' *From Nature's richeft treafure:*
' *Let me the other fenfe employ,*
 ' *And I fhall die with pleafure.*'

During the Entertainment, the Governor, Blandford,
Stanmore, Oroonoko, *enter as Spectators; that ended,*
Captain Driver, Jack Stanmore, *and feveral* Plant-
ers, *enter with their fwords drawn.* [*Drum beats.*
         [*A bell rings.*

Capt. Where are you, Governor ? Make what hafte
 • you can
To fave yourfelf and the whole colony.
I bid 'em ring the bell.

        Go: .

Gov. What's the matter?

J. Stan. The *Inaïans* are come down upon us; they have plundered fome of the plantations already, and are marching this way as faft as they can.

Gov. What can we do againft them?

Bland. We fhall be able to make a ftand, till more planters come into us.

J. Stan. There are a great many more without, if you would fhew yourfelf, and put us in order.

Gov. There's no danger of the white flaves, they'll not ftir. *Blandford* and *Stanmore*, come you along with me. Some of you ftay here to look after the black flaves.

        [*All go out but the* Captain *and fix* Planters, *who all at once feize* Oroonoko.

1ft Plant. Ay, ay, let us alone.

Capt. In the firft place, we fecure you, Sir, As an enemy to the government.

Oro. Are you there, Sir? you are my conftant friend.

1ft Plant. You will be able to do a great deal of mifchief.

Capt. But we fhall prevent you: Bring the irons hither. He has the malice of a flave in him, and would be glad to be cutting his mafters throats. I know him. Chain his hands and feet, that he may not run over to 'em. If they have him, they'll carry him on their backs, that I can tell 'em.

    [*As they are chaining him,* Blandford *enters, runs to 'em.*

Bland. What are you doing there?

Capt. Securing the main chance: This is a bofom enemy.

Bland. Away, you brutes: I'll anfwer with my life for his behaviour; fo tell the Governor.

Capt. and Plant. Well, Sir, fo we will.

        [*Exeunt Captain and Planters.*

Oro. Give me a fword, and I'll deferve your truft.

[*A party of* Indians *enter, hurrying* Imoinda *among the flaves; another party of* Indians *juftains 'em retreating, followed at a diftance by the Governor with the Planters:* Blandford, Oroonoko, *join 'em.*]

Bland. Hell and the devil! they drive away our flaves
before

before our faces. Governor, can you ſtand tamely by,
and ſuffer this? C'emene, Sir, your miſtreſs, is among 'em.

Gov. We throw ourſelves away, in the attempt to
reſcue 'em.

Oro. A lover cannot fall more glorious,
Than in the cauſe of love. He that deſerves
His miſtreſs's favour, wo'not ſtay behind:
I'll lead you on, be bold, and follow me.

[Oroonoko, at the head of the Planters, falls upon
the Indians with a great ſhout, and beats 'em off.
Enter Imoinda.

Imo. I'm toſt about by my tempeſtuous fate,
And no-where muſt have reſt: Indians, or Engliſh!
Whoever has me, I am ſtill a ſlave.
No matter whoſe I am, ſince I'm no more
My royal maſter's; ſince I'm his no more.
O I was happy! nay, I will be happy,
In the dear thought that I am ſtill his wife,
Tho' far divided from him. [Draws off to a cor-
ner of the ſtage.

Enter the Governor, with Oroonoko, Blandford, Stanmore, and the Planters.

Gov. Thou glorious man! thou ſomething greater ſure
Than Cæſar ever was! that ſingle arm
Has ſav'd us all: Accept our general thanks.
[All bow to Oroonoko.
And what can we do more to recompenſe
Such noble ſervices, you ſhall command.
Clemene too ſhall thank you —— ſhe is ſafe ——
Look up, and bleſs your brave deliverer.
[Brings Clemene forward, looking down on the ground.

Oro. Bleſs me indeed!

Bland. You ſtart!

Oro. O all you gods,
Who govern this great world, and bring about
Things ſtrange and unexpected! can it be?

Gov. What is't you ſtare at ſo?

Oro. Anſwer me ſome of you, you who have pow'r,
And have your ſenſes free: Or are you all
Struck thro' with wonder too? [Looking ſtill fix'd on her.

Bland

Bland. What would you know?

Oro. My foul fteals from my body thro' my eyes;
All that is left of life I'll gaze away,
And die upon the pleafure.

Gov. This is ftrange!

Oro. If you but mock me with her image here:
If fhe be not *Imoinda* ——

[*She looks upon him, and falls into a fwoon;* he runs to her.
Ha! She faints!
Nay, then it muft be fhe: It is *Imoinda:*
My heart confeffes her, and leaps for joy,
To welcome her to her own empire here.
' I feel her all, in ev'ry part of me.
' O! let me prefs her in my eager arms,
' Wake her to life, and with this kindling kifs
' Give back that foul, fhe only lent to me. [*Kiffes her.*
  ' *Gov.* I am amaz'd!
  ' *Bland.* I am as much as you.'

Oro. Imoinda! Oh! thy *Oroonoko* calls.
                              [Imoinda *coming to life.*

Imo. My *Oroonoko!* Oh! I can't believe
What an, man can fay. But, if I am
To be deceiv'd, there's fomething in that name,
That voice, that face—— [*Staring on him.*
O! if I know myfelf, I cannot be miftaken.
                    [*Runs and embraces* Oroonoko.

Oro. Never here:
You cannot be miftaken: I am your's,
Your *Oroonoko,* all that you would have,
Your tender loving hufband.

Imo. All indeed
That I would have: My hufband! then I am
Alive, and waking to the joys I feel:
They were fo great, I could not think 'em true;
But I believe all that you fay to me:
For truth itfelf, and everlafting love
Grows in this breaft, and pleafure in thefe arms.

Oro. Take, take me all: Enquire into my heart,
(You know the way to ev'ry fecret there)
My heart, the facred treafury of love:

And

And if, in abfence, I have mifemploy'd
A mite from the rich ftore ; if I have fpent
A wifh, a figh, but what I fent to you ;
May I be curs'd to wifh, and figh in vain,
And you not pity me.

Imo. O ! I believe,
And know you by myfelf. If thefe fad eyes,
Since laft we parted, have beheld the face
Of any comfort, or once wifh'd to fee
The light of any other Heav'n but you,
May I be ftruck this moment blind, and lofe
Your bleffed fight, never to find you more.

Oro. Imoinda ! O ! this feparation
Has made you dearer, if it can be fo,
Than you ever were to me. You appear
Like a kind ftar to my benighted fteps,
To guide me on my way to happinefs :
I cannot mifs it now. Governor, friend,
You think me mad : But let me blefs you all,
Who, any ways, have been the inftruments
Of finding her again. *Imoinda's* found !
And every thing that I would have in her.

[*Embracing her in the moft paffionate fondnefs.*

Stan. Where's your miftrefs now, Governor ?

Gov. Why, where moft men's miftreffes are forced
to be fometimes,
With her hufband, it feems : But I won't lofe her fo.

[*Afide.*

Stan. He has fought luftily for her, and deferves
I'll fay that for him. [her.

Bland. Sir, we congratulate your happinefs : I do
moft heartily.

Gov. And all of us ; but how it comes to pafs——

' *Oro.* That will require
' More precious time than I can fpare you now.
' I have a thoufand things to afk of her,
' And fhe as many more to know of me.
' But you have made me happier, I confefs,
' Acknowledge it, much happier than I
' Have words or pow'r to tell you. Captain, you,
' Ev'n

‘ Ev'n you, who moſt have wrong'd me, I forgive.
‘ I wo'not ſay you have betray'd me now :
‘ I'll think you but the miniſter of fate,
‘ To bring me to my lov'd *Imoinda* here.'
   Imo. How, how, ſhall I receive you; how be worthy
Of ſuch endearments, all this tendernefs?
Theſe are the tranſports of proſperity,
When Fortune ſmiles upon us.
   Oro. Let the fools
Who follow Fortune live upon her ſmiles ;
All our proſperity is plac'd in love,
We have enough of that to make us happy.
This little ſpot of earth you ſtand upon,
Is more to me than the extended plains
Of my great father's kingdom.   Here I reign
In full delights, in joys to pow'r unknown :
Your love my empire, and your heart my throne.
                                        [*Exeunt.*

A C T   III.

Enter Aboan, *with ſeveral Slaves, and* Hotman.

Hot. **W**HAT ! to be ſlaves to cowards ! Slaves to
         rogues ! who can't defend themſelves !
   Abo. Who is this fellow? He talks as if he were ac-
quainted with our deſign : Is he one of us ?
                              [*Aſide to his own gang.*
   Slav. Not yet; but he will be glad to make one, I
believe.
   Abo. He makes a mighty noiſe.
   Hot. Go, ſneak in corners, whiſper out your griefs,
For fear your maſters hear you : Cringe and crouch
Under the bloody whip, like beaten curs,
That lick their wounds, and know no other cure,
All, wretches all ! you feel their cruelty,
As much as I can feel, but dare not groan.
For my part, while I have a life and tongue,
I'll cuiſe the authors of my ſlavery.
                                        Abo.

Abo. Have you been long a flave?

Hot. Yes, many years.

Abo. And do you only curfe?

Hot. Curfe! only curfe! I cannot conjure,
To raife the fpirits up of other men :
I am but one. O! for a foul of fire,
To warm and animate our common caufe,
And make a body of us; then I would
Do fomething more than curfe.

Abo. That body fet on foot, you would be one,
A limb, to lend it motion?

Hot. I would be
The heart of it; the head, the hand, and heart :
Would I could fee the day.

Abo. You will do all yourfelf.

Hot. I would do more
Than I fhall fpeak, but I may find a time——

Abo. The time may come to you; be ready for't.
Methinks he talks too much; I'll know him more
Before I truft him farther.   [*Afide.*

Slav. If he dares
Half what he fays, he'll be of ufe to us.

Enter Blandford.

Bland. If there be any one among you here
That did belong to *Oroonoko*, fpeak,
I come to him.

Abo. I did belong to him; *Aboan* my name.

Bland. You are the man I want; pray come with me.
                                               [*Exeunt.*

Enter Oroonoko *and* Imoinda.

Oro. I do not blame my father for his love :
(Tho' that had been enough to ruin me.)
' 'Twas Nature's fault that made you, like the fun,
' The reafonable worfhip of mankind :
' He could not help his adoration.
' Age had not lock'd his fenfes up fo clofe,
' But he had eyes, that open'd to his foul,
' And took your beauties in : He felt your pow'r,
' And therefore I forgive his loving you :'
But, when I think on his barbarity,

                                               That

That could expofe you to fo many wrongs ;
Driving you out to wretched flavery,
Only for being mine ; then I confefs
I wifh I could forget the name of fon,
That I might curfe the tyrant.

Imo. I will blefs him,
For I have found you here : Heav'n only knows
What is referv'd for us : But, if we guefs
The future by the paft, our fortune muft
Be wonderful, above the common fize
Of good or ill; it muft be in extremes :
Extremely happy, or extremely wretched.

Oro. 'Tis in our pow'r to make it happy now..

Imo. But not to keep it fo.

        Enter Blandford *and* Aboan.

Bland. My royal lord !
I have a prefent for you.

Oro. Aboan !

Abo. Your loweft flave.

Oro. My try'd and valued friend !
This worthy man always prevents my wants : ,
I only wifh'd, and he has brought thee to me.
Thou art furpriz'd : Carry thy duty there ;

        [Aboan *goes to* Imoinda, *and falls at her feet.*
While I acknowledge mine, how fhall I thank you ?

Bland. Believe me honeft to your intereft,
And I am more than paid. I have fecur'd
That all your followers fhall be gently us'd.
Shall wait upon your perfon, while you ftay
Among us.

Oro. I owe every thing to you.

Bland. You muft not think you are in flavery.

Oro. I do not find I am.

Bland. Kind Heav'n has miraculoufly fent
Thofe comforts, that may teach you to expect
Its farther care, in your deliverance.

Oro. I fometimes think, myfelf, Heav'n is con-
    cern'd
For my deliverance.

                     Bland.

Bland. It will be foon ;
You may expect it. Pray, in the mean time,
Appear as chearful as you can among us.
You have fome enemies, that reprefent
You dangerous, and would be glad to find
A reafon, in your difcontent, to fear :
They watch your looks. But there are honeft men,
Who are your friends : You are fecur'd in them.

   Oro. I thank you for your caution.

   Bland. I will leave you :
And be affur'd, I with your liberty.   [*Exit.*

   Abo. He fpeaks you very fair.

   Oro. He means me fair.

   Abo. If he fhould not, my lord ?

   Oro. If he fhould not ?
I'll not fufpect his truth : But, if I did,
What fhall I get by doubting ?

   Abo. You fecure
Not to be difappointed : But, befides,
There's this advantage in fufpecting him :
When you put off the hopes of other men,
You will rely upon your god-like felf ;
And then you may be fure of liberty.

   Oro. Be fure of liberty ! what doft thou mean ;
Advifing to rely upon myfelf ?
I think I may be fure on't : We muft wait :
'Tis worth a little patience.   [*Turning to* Imoinda.

   Abo. O my lord !

   Oro. What doft thou drive at ?

   Abo. Sir, another time
You would have found it fooner : But I fee
Love has your heart, and takes up all your thoughts.

   Oro. And can't thou blame me ?

   Abo. Sir, I muft not blame you.
But, as our fortune ftands, there is a paffion
(Your pardon, royal miftrefs, I muft fpeak)
That would become you better than your love :
A brave refentment ; which, infpir'd by you,
Might kindle and diffufe a gen'rous rage
Among the flaves, to roufe and fhake our chains.

                        And

And ſtruggle to be free.

Oro. How can we help ourſelves?

Abo. I knew you when you would have found a way.
How help ourſelves! the very *Indians* teach us:
We need but to attempt our liberty,
And we carry it. We have hands ſufficient,
Double the number of our maſter's force,
Ready to be employ'd. ' What hinders us
' To ſet 'em at work?' We want but you,
To head our enterprize, and bid us ſtrike.

Oro. What would you do?

Abo. Cut our oppreſſors throats.

Oro. And you would have me join in your deſign of
murder?

Abo. It deſerves a better name:
But, be it what it will, 'tis juſtify'd
By ſelf-defence, and natural liberty.

Oro. I'll hear no more on't.

Abo. I'm ſorry for't.

Oro. Nor ſhall you think of it!

Abo. Not think of it!

Oro. No, I command you not.

Abo. Remember, Sir,
You are a ſlave yourſelf, and to command
Is now another's right. Not think of it!
Since the firſt moment they put on my chains,
I've thought of nothing but the weight of 'em,
And how to throw 'em off: Can your's ſit eaſy?

Oro. I have a ſenſe of my condition,
As painful, and as quick, as your's can be.
I feel for my *Imoinda* and myſelf;
Imoinda! much the tendereſt part of me.
But tho' I languiſh for my liberty,
I would not buy it at the Chriſtian price
Of black ingratitude: They ſha'not ſay,
That we deſerv'd our fortune by our crimes.
Murder the innocent!

Abo. The innocent!

Oro. Theſe men are ſo, whom you would riſe againſt;
If we are ſlaves, they did not make us ſlaves.

But

But bought us in an hon' ft way of trade :
As we have done b fore 'em, bought and fold
Many a wretch, and never thought it wrong.
' They paid our price for us, and we are now
' Their property, a part of their eftate,
' To manage as they pleafe. Miftake me not,'
I do not tamely fay, that we fhould bear
All they could lay upon us : But we find
The load fo light, fo little to be felt,
(Confidering they have us in their pow'r,
And may inflict what grievances they pleafe)
We ought not to complain.

Abo. My royal lord!
You do not know the heavy grievances,
The toils, the labours, weary drudgeries,
Which they impofe ; burdens more fit for beafts,
For fenfelefs beafts to bear, than thinking men.
Then if you faw the bloody cruelties
They execute on every flight offence ;
Nay, fometimes in their proud, infulting fport,
How worfe than dogs they lafh their fellow-creatures ;
Your heart would bleed for 'em. Oh! could you know
How many wretches lift their hands and eyes
To you for their relief!

Oro. I pity 'em,
And with I could with honefty do more.

Abo. You muft do more, and may, with honefty.
O royal Sir, remember who you are,
A prince, born for the good of other men :
Whofe god-like office is to draw the fword
Againft oppreffion, and fet free mankind :
And this I m fure you think oppreffion now.
What tho' you have not felt thefe miferies,
Never believe you are oblig'd to them :
They have their felfifh reafons, may be, now,
For ufing of you well : But there will come
A time, when you muft have your fhare of 'em.

Oro. You fee how little caufe I have to think fo :
Favou:'d in my own perfon, in my friends ;
Indulg'd in all that can concern my care,

In my *Imoinda*'s foft fociety. [*Embracing her.*
Abo. And, therefore, would you lie contented down
In the forgetfulnefs, and arms of love,
To get young princes for 'em?
  Oro. Say it thou! ha!
  Abo. Princes, the heirs of empire, and the laft
Of your illuftrious lineage, to be born
To pamper up their pride, and be their flaves?
  Oro. Imoinda! fave me, fave me from that thought.
  '*Imo.* There is no fafety from it: I have long
' Suffer'd it with a mother's labouring pains;
' And can no longer. Kill me, kill me now,
' While I am blefs'd, and happy in your love;
' Rather than let me live to fee you hate me:
' As you muft hate me; me, the only caufe,
' The fountain of thefe flowing miferies:
' Dry up the fpring of life, this pois'nous fpring,
' That fwells fo faft, to overwhelm us all.
  ' *Oro.*' Shall the dear babe, the eldeft of my hopes,
Whom I begot a prince, be born a flave?
The treafure of this temple was defign'd
T' enrich a kingdom's fortune: Shall it here
Be feiz'd upon by vile unhallow'd hands,
To be employ'd in ufes moft profane?
  Abo. In moft unworthy ufes; think of that;
And, while you may, prevent it. ' O my lord,
' Rely on nothing that they fay to you.
' They fpeak you fair, I know, and bid you wait:
' But think what 'tis to wait on promifes,
' And promifes of men who know no tie
' Upon their words, againft their intereft:
' And where's their intereft in freeing you?
  ' *Imo.* O! where indeed, to lofe fo many flaves?
  ' *Abo.* Nay, grant this man, you think fo much
        ' your friend,
' Be honeft, and intends all that he fays;
' He is but one; and in a government,
· Where, he confeffes, you have enemies,
' That watch your looks. What looks can you put on,
' To pleafe thefe men, who are before refolv'd
' To read 'em their own way? Alas! my lord,
                                    ' If

‘ If they incline to think you dangerous,
‘ They have their knavish arts to make you fo :
‘ And then who knows how far their cruelty
‘ May carry their revenge !
 ‘ *Imo.* To every thing
‘ That does belong to you, your friends, and me ;
‘ I shall be torn from you, forced away,
‘ Helpless and miferable : Shall I live
‘ To fee that day again ?
 ‘ *Oro.* That day shall never come.’
 Abo. I know you are perfuaded to believe
The governor’s arrival will prevent
Thefe mifchiefs, and beftow your liberty :
But who is fure of that ? I rather fear
More mifchiefs from his coming. He is young,
Luxurious, paffionate, and amorous :
Such a complexion, and made bold by pow’r,
To countenance all he is prone to do,
Will know no bounds, no law againft his lufts.
If, in a fit of his intemperance,
With a ftrong hand he shall refolve to feize,
And force my royal miftrefs from your arms,
How can you help yourfelf ?
 Oro. Ha ! thou haft rous’d
The lion in his den, he ftalks abroad,
And the wide foreft trembles at his roar.
I find the danger now. My fpirits ftart
At the alarm, and from all quarters come
To man my heart, the citadel of love.
Is there a pow’r on earth to force you from me ?
And shall I not refill it ? ‘ nor ftrike firft,
‘ To keep, to fave you : to prevent that curfe ?
‘ This is your caufe, and shall it not prevail ?’
Oh ! you were born always to conquer me.
Now I am fashion’d to thy purpofe : Speak,
What combination. what confpiracy,
Would’ft thou engage me in ? I’ll undertake
All thou would’ft have me now for liberty,
For the great caufe of love and liberty.
 Abo. Now, my great mafter, you appear yourfelf.
           And,

And, fince we have you join'd in our defign,
It cannot fail us. I have mufter'd up
The choiceft flaves, men who are fenfible
Of their condition, and feem moft refolv'd:
They have their feveral parties.
  Oro. Summon 'em,
Affemble 'em : I will come forth and fhew
Myfelf among 'em : If they are refolv'd,
I'll lead their foremoft refolutions.
  Abo. I have provided thofe will follow you.
  Oro. With this referve in our proceedings ftill,
The means that lead us to our liberty
Muft not be bloody.
  ' *Abo.* You command in all.
' We fhall expect you, Sir :
  ' *Oro.* You fha'not long.'
  [*Exeunt* Oro. *and* Imo. *at one door,* Aboan *at another.*
    Weldon *coming in before Mrs.* Lackitt.
  Wid. Thefe unmannerly *Indians* were fomething un-
reafonable to difturb us juft in the nick, Mr *Weldon* ;
but I have the Parfon within call ftill, to do us the
good turn.
  Weld. We had beft ftay a little I think, to fee things
fettled again, had not we ? Marriage is a ferious thing
you know.
  Wid. What do you talk of a ferious thing, Mr. *Weldon ?* I think you have found me fufficiently ferious : I
have married my fon to your fifter, to pleafure you :
And now I come to claim your promife to me, you tell
me marriage is a ferious thing.
  Weld. Why, is it not ?
  Wid. Fiddle, faddle, I know what it is : 'Tis not
the fift time I have been marry'd, I hope : But I fhall
begin to think you don't defign to do fairly by me, fo
I fhall.
  Weld. Why indeed, Mrs. *Lackitt,* I'm afraid I can't
do fo fairly as I would by you. 'Tis what you muft
know firft or laft ; and I fhould be the worft man in the
world to conceal it any longer ; therefore I muft own
to you that I am married already.
  Wid. Married ? You don't fay fo, I hope ! how have
                                                        you

you the confcience to tell me fuch a thing to my face. Have you abus'd me then, fool'd and cheated me ? what do you take me for, Mr. *Weldon ?* Do you think I am to be ferv'd at this rate ? But you fhan't find me the filly creature you think me : I would have you to know I underftand better things than to ruin my fon without a valuable confideration. If I can't have you, I can keep my money. Your fifter fhan't have the catch of him fhe expected : I won't part with a fhilling to 'em.

Weld. You made the match yourfelf, you know, you can't blame me

Wid. Yes, yes, I can, and do blame you : you might have told me before, you were marry'd.

Weld. I would not have told you now ; but you fol-low'd me fo clofe, I was forc'd to it : Indeed I am marry'd in *England* ; but 'tis as if I were not ; for I have been parted from my wife a great while, and, to do reafon on both fides, we hate one another heartily. Now I did defign, and will marry you ftill, if you'll have a little patience.

Wid. A likely bufinefs truly.

Weld. I have a friend in *England* that I will write to, to poifon my wife, and then I can marry you with a good confcience ; if you love me, as you fay you do, you'll confent to that, I'm fure.

Wid. And will he do it, do you think ?

Weld. At the firft word, or he is not the man I take him to be.

Wid. Well, you are a dear devil, Mr. *Weldon :* And would you poifon your wife for me ?

Weld. I would do any thing for you.

Wid. Well, I am mightily oblig'd to you. But 'twill be a great while before you can have an anfwer of your letter.

Weld. 'Twill be a great while indeed.

Wid. In the mean time, Mr. *Weldon* ————

Weld. Why in the mean time ——— Here's company. We'll fettle that within ; I ll follow you. [*Exit* Wid.

Enter Stanmore.

Stan. So, Sir, you carry on your bufinefs fwimming-ly : You have ftolen a wedding I hear.

Weld.

Weld. Ay, my fifter is marry'd: And I am very near being run away with myfelf.

Stan. The widow will have you then?

Weld. You come very feafonably to my refcue: *Jack Stanmore* is to be had, I hope?

Stan. At half an hour's warning.

Weld. I muft advife with you. [*Exeunt.*

' SCENE, *The Country.*

' *Enter* Oroonoko, *with* Aboan, Hotman, *and* Slaves.

' *Oro.* Impoffible! nothing's impoffible:
' We know our ftrength only by being try'd.
' If you objeft the mountains, rivers, woods
' Unpaffable, that lie before our march:
' Woods we can fet on fire: We fwim by nature:
' What can oppofe us then but we may tame?
' All things fubmit to virtuous induftry:
' That we carry with us, that is ours.
    ' *Slav.* Great Sir, we have attended all you faid,
' With filent joy and admiration:
' And, were we only men, would follow fuch,
' So great a leader, thro' the untry'd world.
' But, oh! confider we have other names,
' Hufbands and fathers, and have things more dear
' To us than life, our children and our wives,
' Unfit for fuch an expedition:
' What muft become of them?
    ' *Oro.* We wo'not wrong
' The virtue of our women, to believe
' There is a wife among them would refufe
' To fhare her hufband's fortune. What is hard,
· We muft make eafy to 'em in our love: While we live,
' And have our limbs, we can take care of them;
' Therefore I ftill propofe to lead our march
' Down to the fea, and plant a colony;
' Where, in our native innocence, we fhall live
' Free, and be able to defend ourfelves;
' Till ftrefs of weather, or fome accident,
' Provide a fhip for us.

' *Abo.*

' *Abo.* An accident!
' The luckieft accident prefents itfelf;
' The very fhip that brought and made us flaves,
' Swims in the river ftill.   I fee no caufe
' But we may feize on that.
      ' *Oro.* It fhall be fo:
' There is a juftice in it pleafes me:
' Do you agree to it?   [*To the* Slaves.
        ' *Omnes.* We follow you.
        ' *Oro.* You do not relifh it.   [*To* Hotman.
        ' *Hot.* I am afraid
' You'll find it difficult and dangerous.
        ' *Abo.* Are you the man to find the dangers firft?
' You fhould have giv'n example.   Dangerous!
' I thought you had not underftood the word;
' You, who would be the head, the hand and heart;
' Sir, I remember you, you can̄ talk well;
' I wo'not doubt but you'll maintain your word.
        ' *Oro.* This fellow is not right; I'll try him further;
                                     [*To* Aboan.
' The danger will be certain to us all,
' And Death moft certain in mifcarrying.
' We muft expect no mercy, if we fail:
' Therefore our way muft be not to expect:
' We'll put it out of expectation,
' By death upon the place, or liberty.
' There is no mean, but death, or liberty.
' There's no man here I hope, but comes prepar'd
' For all that can befal him.
        ' *Abo.* Death is all:
' In moft conditions of humanity
' To be defir'd, but to be fhunn'd by none:
' The remedy of many, wifh of fome,
' And certain end of all.
' If there be one among us, who can fear
' The face of death appearing like a friend,
' As in this caufe of honour death muft be:
' How will he tremble when he fees him drefs'd
' In the wild fury of our enemies,
· In all the terrors of their cruelty!

                                      · For

‘ For now, if we fhould fall into their hands,
‘ Could they invent a thoufand murd'ring ways,
‘ By racking torments, we fhould feel 'em all.
  ‘ *Hot.* What will become of us ?
  ‘ *Oro.* Obferve him now. [*To* Abo. *concerning* Hot.
‘ I could die, altogether, like a man ;
‘ As you, and you, and all of us, muft do.
‘ But who can promife for his bravery
‘ Upon the rack ? where fainting, weary life,
‘ Hunted thro' ev'ry limb, is forc'd to feel
‘ An agonizing death of all its parts ?
‘ Who can bea this ? refolve to be empal'd ?
‘ His fkin flead off, and roafted yet alive ?
‘ The quivering flefh torn from his broken bones
‘ By burning pincers ? Who can bear thefe pains ?
  ‘ *Hot.* They are not to be borne.
          [*Difcovering all the confufion of fear.*
  ‘ *Oro.* You fee him now, this man of mighty words !
  ‘ *Abo.* How his eyes roll !
  ‘ *Oro.* He cannot hide his fear :
‘ I ry'd him this way, and have found him out.
  ‘ *Abo.* I could not have believ'd it. Such a blaze,
‘ And not a fpark of fire !
  ‘ *Oro.* His violence
‘ Made me fufpect : Now I'm convinc'd.
  ‘ *Abo.* What fhall we do with him ?
  ‘ *Oro.* He is not fit——
  ‘ *Abo.* Fit ! hang him, he is only fit to be
‘ Juft what he is, to live and die a flave :
‘ The bafe companion of his fervile fears.
  ‘ *Oro.* We are not fafe with him.
  ‘ *Abo.* Do you think fo ?
  ‘ *Oro.* He'll certainly betray us.
  ‘ *Abo.* That he fhan't :
‘ I can take care of that : I have a way
‘ To take him off his evidence.
  ‘ *Oro.* What way ?
  ‘ *Abo.* I'll ftop his mouth before you, ftab him here,
‘ And then let him inform.
     ‘ [*Going to ftab* Hotman, Oroonoko *holds him.*
        C   ‘ *Oro.*

' *Oro.* Thou art not mad ?

' *Abo.* I would fecure ourfelves.

' *Oro.* It fha'not be this way ; nay cannot be :
' His murder will alarm all the reft,
' Make 'em fufpect us of barbarity,
' And, may be, fall away from our defign.
' We'll not fet out in blood.   We have, my friends,
' This night to furnifh what we can provide
' For our fecurity and juft defence.
' If there be one among us we fufpect
' Of bafenefs, or vile fear, it will become
' Our common care to have an eye on him :
' I wo'not name the man.

  ' *Abo.* You guefs at him.   [*To* Hotman.

  ' *Oro.* To-morrow, early as the breaking day,
' We rendezvous behind the citron grove.
' That fhip fecur'd, we may tranfport ourfelves
' To our refpective homes : My father's kingdom
' Shall open her wide arms to take you in,
' And nurfe you for her own, adopt you all,
' All, who will follow me.

  ' *Omnes.* All, all follow you.

  ' *Oro.* There I can give you all your liberty :
' Beftow its bleffings, and fecure 'em yours.
' There you fhall live with honour, as becomes
' My fellow-fufferers and worthy friends.
' Thus, if we do fucceed : But, if we fall
' In our attempt, 'tis nobler ftill to die,
' Than drag the galling yoke of flavery.'

         [*Exeunt.*

A C T   IV.

Enter Weldon *and* Jack Stanmore.

' *Weld.* YOU fee, honeft *Jack*, I have been in-
   ' duftrious for you : You muft take fome
' pains now to ferve yourfelf.

        ' *J. Stan.*

' *J. Stan.* Gad, Mr *Wildon*, I have taken a great
' deal of pains; and, if the Widow fp ak honeftly, faith
' and troth fhe'll tell you what a pains-taker I am.

' *Weld.* Fie, fie, not me; I am her hufband you
' know. She won't tell me what pains you have taken
' with her: Befides, fhe takes you for me.

' *J. Stan.* That's true: I forgot you had married
' her. But if you knew all——

' *Weld.* 'Tis no matter for my knowing all, if fhe does.

' *J. Stan.* Ay, ay, fhe does know, and more than
' ever fhe knew fince fhe was a woman, for the time,
' I will be bold to fay; for I have done ——

' *Weld.* The devil take you, for you'll never have done.

' *J. Stan.* As old as fhe is, fhe has a wrinkle behind
' more than fhe had, I believe; for I have taught her
' what fhe never knew in her life before.

' *Weld.* What care I what wrinkles fhe has? or what
' you have taught her? If you'll let me advife you, you
' may: If not, you may prate on, and ruin the whole
' defign.

' *J. Stan.* Well, well, I have done.

' *Weld.* Nobody but your coufin, and you, and I,
' know any thing of this matter. I have marry'd Mrs.
' *Lackitt*, and put you to bed to her, which fhe knows
' nothing of, to ferve you: In two or three days I ll
' bring it about fo, to refign up my claim, and with
' her confent, quietly to you.

' *J. Stan.* But how will you do it?

' *Weld.* That muft be my bufinefs: In the mean time,
' if you fhould make any noife, 'twill come to her ears,
' and be impoffible to reconcile her.

' *J. Stan.* Nay, as for that, I know the way to re-
' concile her, I warrant you.

' *Weld.* But how will you get her money? I am mar-
' ry'd to her.

' *J. Stan.* That I don't know, indeed.

' *Weld.* You muft leave it to me, you find; all the
' pains I fhall put you to, will be to be filent: You
' can hold your tongue for two or three days?

' *J. Stan.* Truly not well, in a matter of this nature:

' I fhould

'I fhould be very unwilling to lofe the reputation of
'this night's work, and the pleafure of telling it.

'*Weld.* You muft mortify that vanity a little : You
'will have time enough to brag and li- of your man-
'hood, when you have her in a bare-fac'd condition to
'di prove you.

'*J. Stan.* Well, I'll try what I can do : The hopes
'of her money muft do it.

'*Weld.* You'll come at night again ? 'Tis your own
'bufinefs.

'*J. Stan.* But you have the credit on't.

'*Weld.* 'Twill be our own another day, as the widow
'fays. Send your coufin to me : I want his advice.

'*J. Stan.* I want to be recruited, I'm fure ; a good
'breakfaft, and to bed : She has rock'd my cradle fuf-
'ficiently.   [*Exit.*

'*Weld.* She would have a hufhand ; and, if all be as
'he fays, fhe has no reafon to complain : But there's no
'relying on what men fay upon thefe occafions : They
'have the benefit of their bragging, by recommending
'their abilities to other women : Their's is a trading
'eftate, that lives upon credit, and increafes by removing
'it out of one bank into another. Now poor women have
'not thefe opportunities We muft keep our ftocks
'dead by us, at home, to be ready for a purchafe, when
'it comes, a hufband, let him be never fo dear, and be
'glad of him : Or venture our fortunes abroad on fuch
'rotten fecurity, that the principal and intereft, nay,
'very often, our perfons are in danger. If the wo en
'would agree (which they never will) to call home their
'effects, how many proper gentlemen would fneak into
'another way of living, for want of being refponfible
'in this ! then hufbands would be cheaper. Here comes
'the widow, fhe'll tell truth ; fhe'll not bear falfe wit-
'nefs againft her own intereft, I know.'

         Enter Widow Lackitt.

Weld. Now, Mrs. *Lackitt.*

Wid. Well, well, *Lackitt*, or what you will now;
now I am marry'd to you : I am very well pleas'd with
what I have done, I affure you.

                                Weld.

Weld. And with what I have done too, I hope.

Wid. Ah! Mr. *Weldon!* I fay nothing, but you're a dear man, and I did not think it had been in you.

Weld. I have more in me than you imagine.

Wid. No no, you can't have more than I imagine. 'Tis impoffible to have more: You have enough for any woman, in an honeft way, that I will fay for you.

‘ *Weld.* Then I find you are fatisfied.

‘ *Wid.* Satisfied! No indeed: I'm not to be fatisfied ‘ with you or without you: To be fatisfied is to have ‘ enough of you. Now, 'tis a folly to lie, I fhall never ‘ think I can have enough of you. I fhall be very fond ‘ of you. Would you have me fond of you? What do ‘ you do to me, to make me love you fo well?

‘ *Weld.* Can't you tell what?

‘ *Wid.* Go, there's no fpeaking to you: You bring ‘ all the blood of one's body into one's face, fo you do: ‘ Why do you talk fo?

‘ *Weld.* Why, how do I talk?

‘ *Wid.* You know how: But a little colour becomes ‘ me, I believe: How do I look to-day?

‘ *Weld.* O! moft lovingly, moft amiably.

‘ *Wid.* Nay, this can't be long a fecret, I find, I fhall ‘ difcover it by my countenance.

‘ *Weld.* The women will find you out, you look fo chearfully.

‘ *Wid.* But do I, do I really look fo chearfully, fo ami- ‘ ably? There's no fuch paint in the world as the natu- ‘ ral glowing of a complexion. Let 'em find me out if ‘ they pleafe, poor creatures, I pity 'em: They envy ‘ me, I'm fure, and would be glad to mend their looks ‘ upon the fame occafion. The young jill-flirting girls, ‘ forfooth, believe no body muft have a hufband but them- ‘ felves: but I would have them to know there are other ‘ things to be taken care of, befides their green-ficknefs.

‘ *Weld.* Ay, fure, or the phyficians would have but ‘ little practice.

‘ *Wid.*’ Mr. *Weldon,* what muft I call you? I muft have fome pretty fond name or other for you. What fhall I call you?

Will.

Weld. I thought you lik'd my own name.

Wid. Yes, yes, I like it, but I muſt have a nick-name for you : moſt women have nick-names for their huſbands.

Weld. Cuckold.

Wid. No, no, but 'tis very pretty before company ; it looks negligent, and is the faſhion, you know.

Weld. To be negligent of their huſbands, it is, indeed.

Wid. Nay then, I won't be in the faſhion ; for I can never be negligent of dear Mr. *Weldon :* And, to convince you, here's ſomething to encourage you not to be negligent of me, [*Gives him a purſe and a little caſket.* five hundred pounds in gold in this ; and jewels to the value of five hundred pounds more in this.

[Weldon *opens the caſket.*

We'd. Ay, marry, this will encourage me indeed.

Wid. There are comforts in marrying an elderly woman, Mr. *Weldon.* Now a young woman would have fancy'd ſhe had paid you with her perſon, or had done you the favour.

Weld. What do you talk of young women : You are as young as any of 'em, in every thing but their folly and ignorance.

Wid. And do you think me ſo ? But I have reaſon to ſuſpect you. Was not I ſeen at your houſe this morning, do you think ?

Weld. You may venture again : You'll come at night, I ſuppoſe.

Wid. O dear! at night ? ſo ſoon ?

Weld. Nay, if you think it ſo ſoon—

Wid. O! no, 'tis not for that, Mr. *Weldon*, but——

Weld. You won't come then ?

Wid. Won't! I don't ſay I won't : That is not a word for a wife : If you command me——

Weld. To pleaſe yourſelf.

Wid. I will come to pleaſe you.

Weld. To pleaſe yourſelf, own it.

Wid. Well, well, to pleaſe myſelf then. You're the ſtrangeſt man in the world, nothing can 'ſcape you ; you'll to the bottom of ev'ry thing.

Enter

Enter Daniel, Lucy *following.*

Dan. What would you have? what do you follow me for?

Luc. Why mayn't I follow you? I muſt follow you now all the world over.

Dan. Hold you, hold you there: Not ſo far by a mile or two; I have enough of your company already, by'r lady, and ſomething to ſpare: You may go home to your brother, an you will; I have no farther to do with you.

Wid. Why, 'Daniel, child, thou art not out of thy wits, ſure, art thou?

Dan. Nay, marry, I don't know; but I am very near, I believe: I am alter'd for the worſe mightily ſince you ſaw me; and ſhe has been the cauſe of it there.

Wid. How ſo, child?

Dan. I told you before what wou'd come on't of putting me to bed to a ſtrange woman; but you would not be ſaid nay.

Wid. She is your wife now, child, you muſt love her.

Dan. Why, ſo I did, at firſt.

Wid. But you muſt love her always.

Dan. Always! I lov'd her as long as I could, mother, and as long as loving was good, I believe; for I find now I don't care a fig for her.

Luc. Why, you lubberly, ſlovenly, miſbegotten blockhead——

Wid. Nay, Miſtreſs *Lucy*, ſay any thing elſe, and ſpare not: But, as to his begetting, that touches me: He is as honeſtly begotten, tho' I ſay it, that he is the worſe again.

Luc. I ſee all good nature is thrown away upon you——

Wid. It was ſo with his father before him: He takes after him.

Luc. And therefore I will uſe you as you deſerve, you tony.

Wid. Indeed he deſerves bad enough; but don't call him out of his name: His name is *Daniel*, you know.

Dan. She may call me hermaphrodite if ſhe will; for I hardly know whether I'm a boy or girl.

' *Wid.* A boy, I warrant thee, as long as thou liv'ſt.

' *Dan.*

' *Dan.* Let her call me what she pleases, mother,
' 'tis not her tongue that I'm afraid of.

' *Luc.* I will make such a beast of thee, such a cuckold!

' *Wid.* O, pray, no I hope; do nothing rashly Mrs.
' *Lucy.*

' *Luc.* Such a cuckold I will make of thee.

' *Dan.* I had rather be a cuckold than what you would
' make of me in a week, I'm sure; I have no more man-
' hood left in me already, than there is, saving the mark,
' in one of my mother's old under petticoats here.

' *Wid.* Sirrah, sirrah, meddle with your wife's petti-
' coats, and let your mother's alone, you ungracious
' bird you.   [*Beats him.*

' *Dan.* Why, is the devil in the woman? What have I
' said now? Do you know, if you were ask'd, I trow?
' But you are all of a bundle; ev'n hang together: He
' that unties you, makes a rod for his own tail; and so
' he will find it that has any thing to do with you.

' *Wid.* Ay, rogue enough, you shall find it: I have
' a rod for your tail still.

' *Dan.* No wife, and I care not.'

Wid. I'll swinge you into better manners, you booby.
                          [*Beats him off, and exit.*

Weld. You have consummated our project upon him.

Luc. Nay, if I have a limb of the fortune, I care
not who has the whole body of the fool.

Weld. That you shall, and a large one I promise you.

Luc. Have you heard the news? They talk of an
English ship in the river.

Weld. I have heard on't; and am preparing to receive it, as fast as I can.

Luc. There's something the matter too with the slaves,
some disturbance or other, I don't know what 'tis.

Weld. So much the better still: We fish in troubled
waters: We shall have fewer eyes upon us. Pray go
you home, and be ready to assist me in your part of the
design.

Luc. I can't fail in mine.   [*Exit.*

Weld. The widow has furnish'd me, I thank her, to
carry it on. Now I have got a wife, 'tis high time to
think of getting a husband. I carry my fortune about
                                                   me

me—a thoufand pounds in gold and jewels. Let me
fee—'twill be a confiderable truft : And I think I fhall
lay it out to advantage.

Enter Stanmore.

Stan. So, *Welden*, *Jack* has told me his fuccefs; and
his hopes of marrying the Widow by your means.

Weld. I have ftrain'd a point, *Stanmore*, upon your
account, to be ferviceable to your family.

Stan. I take it upon my account ; and am very much
obliged to you. But here we are all in an uproar.

Weld. So they fay; what's the matter ?

Stan. A mutiny among the flaves : *Oroonoko* is at the
head of 'em. Our Governor is gone out with his rafcally
militia againft 'em. What it may come to no body knows.

Weld. For my part, I fhall do as well as the reft : But
I'm concerned for my fifter and coufin, whom I expect
in the fhip from *England*.

Stan. There's no danger of 'em

Weld. I have a thoufand pounds here, in gold and
jewels, for my coufin's ufe, that I would more particularly take care of: 'Tis too great a fum to venture at
home ; and I would not have her wrong'd of it : therefore, to fecure it, I think my beft way will be to put
it into your own keeping.

Stan. You have a very good opinion of my honefty.

[*Takes the purfe and casket.*

Weld. I have, indeed ; if any thing fhould happen to
me, in this baftle, as no body is fecure of accidents, I
know you will take my coufin into your protection and
care ; and

' *Stan.* You may be fure on't.

Weld. If you hear fhe is dead, as fhe may be, then I
' defire you to accept of the thoufand pounds as a legacy,
' and token of my friendfhip ; my fifter is provided for.

' *Stan.* Why, you amaze me ; but you are never the
' nearer dying, I hope, for making your will ?

' *Weld.* Not a jot ; but I love to be before-hand with
' fortune. If fhe comes fafe, this is not a place for a
' fingle woman, you know ;' pray fee her married as
foon as you can.

Stan. If she be as handsome as her picture, I can promise her a husband.

Weld. If you like her when you see her, I wish nothing so much as to have you marry her yourself.

' *Stan.* From what I have heard of her, and my en-
' gagements to you, it must be her fault if I don't: I
' hope to have her from your own hand.

' *Weld.* And I hope to give her to you, and all this.

' *Stan.* Ay, ay, hang these melancholy reflections:
' Your generosity has engaged all my services.'

Weld. I always thought you worth making a friend.

Stan. You shan't find your good opinion thrown away upon me: I am in your debt, and shall think so as long as I live.   [*Exeunt.*

SCENE, *The Country.*

Enter on one side of the stage Oroonoko, Aboan, *with the* Slaves. Imoinda *with a bow and quiver; the women, some leading, others carrying their children upon their backs.*

Oro. The women with their children fall behind.
Imoinda, you must not expose yourself;
Retire, my love: I almost fear for you.

Imo. I fear no danger; life, or death, I will
Enjoy with you.

Oro. My person is your guard.

Abo. ' Now, Sir, blame yourself:' If you had not prevented my cutting his throat, that coward there had not discovered us; he comes now to upbraid you.

Enter on the other side the Governor, *talking to* Hotman, *with his* rabble.

Gov. This is the very thing I would have wish'd.
Your honest service to the government   [*To* Hotman.
Shall be rewarded with your liberty.

Abo. His honest service! call it what it is,
His villainy, the service of his fear:
If he pretends to honest services,
Let him stand out, and meet me like a man.
         [*Advancing.*

Oro. Hold, you: and you who come against us, hold:
I charge you in a general good to all.

                   And

And wiſh I could command you, to prevent
The bloody havock of the murd'ring ſword.
I would not urge deſtruction uncompell'd :
But, if you follow fate, you find it here.
The bounds are ſet, the limits of our lives :
Between us lies the gaping gulph of death,
To ſwallow all : Who firſt advances——
    Enter the Captain, *with his* Crew.
 Capt. Here, here, here they are, Governor :
What, ſeize upon my ſhip !
Come, boys, fall on——
    [*Advancing firſt,* Oroonoko *kills him.*
 Oro. Thou art fall'n indeed ;
Thy own blood be upon thee.
 Gov. Reſt it there.
He did deſerve his death. ' Take him away.'
     [*The body remov'd.*
You ſee, Sir, you and thoſe miſtaken men
Muſt be our witneſſes, we do not come
As enemies, and thirſting for your blood.
If we deſir'd your ruin, the revenge
Of our companion's death had puſh'd it on.
But that we overlook, in a regard
To common ſafety, and the public good.
 Oro. Regard that public good ; draw off your men,
And leave us to our fortune : We're reſolv'd.
 Gov. Reſolv'd ! on what ? your reſolutions
Are broken, overturn'd, prevented, loſt :
' What fortune now can you raiſe out of 'em ?
' Nay, grant we ſhould draw off, what can you do ?
' Where can you move ? What more can you reſolve ?
' Unleſs it be to throw yourſelves away.'
Famine muſt eat you up, if you go on.
You ſee our numbers could with eaſe compel
What we requeſt : And what do we requeſt ?
Only to ſave yourſelves.
 [*The women with their children gathering about the men.*
 Oro. I'll hear no more.
 ' *Women.* Hear him, hear him, he takes no care of us.'
 Gov. To thoſe poor wretches, who have been ſeduc'd
          And

And led away, to all, and ev'ry one,
We offer a full pardon——

 Oro. Then fall on.   [*Preparing to engage.*

 Gov. Lay hold upon't, before it be too late,
Pardon and mercy.

[*The women clinging about the men, they leave* Oroonoko,
 and fall upon their faces, crying out for pardon.

 Slaves. Pardon, mercy, pardon.

 Oro. Let them go all. Now, Governor, I see,
I own the folly of my enterprife,
The rafhnefs of this action; and muft blufh,
Quite through this veil of night, a whitely fhame,
To think I could defign to make thofe free,
Who were by nature flaves; wretches defign'd
To be their mafters' dogs, and lick their feet.
' Whip, whip 'em to the knowledge of your gods,
' Your Chriftian gods, who fuffer you to be
' Unjuft, difhoneft, cowardly, and bafe :
' And give 'em your excufe for being fo.'
I would not live on the fame earth with creatures,
That only have the faces of their kind :
Why fhould they look like men, who are not fo ?
When they put off their noble natures, for
The grov'ling qualities of downcaft beafts,
' I wifh they had their tails.

  ' *Abo.* Then we fhould know 'em.'

 Oro. We were too few before for victory.
We're ftill enow to die.   [*To* Imoinda *and* Aboan.

    Enter Blandford.

 Gov. Live, Royal Sir :
Live, and be happy long on your own terms;
Only confent to yield, and you fhall have
What terms you can propofe for you and yours.

 Oro. Confent to yield ! fhall I betray myfelf ?

 ' *Gov.* Alas ! we cannot fear that your fmall force,
' The force of two, with a weak woman's arms,
' Should conquer us. I fpeak, in the regard
' And honour of your worth, in my defire
' And forwardnefs to ferve fo great a man.
' I would not have it lie upon my thoughts,

         ' That

' That I was the occafion of the fall
' Of fuch a prince, whofe courage, carried on
' In a more noble caufe, would well deferve
' The empire of the world.
  ' *Oro.* You can fpeak fair.
  ' *Gov.* Your undertaking, tho' it would have brought
' So great a lofs to us, we muft all fay
' Was generous, and noble ; and fhall be
' Regarded only as the fire of youth,
' That will break out fometimes in gallant fouls ;
' We'll think it but the natural impulfe,
' A rafh impatience of liberty :
' No otherwife.
  ' *Oro.* Think it what you will.
' I was not born to render an account
' Of what I do, to any but myfelf.'
               [Bland. *comes forward.*
Bland. I'm glad you have proceeded by fair means.
               [*To the* Governor.
I came to be a mediator.
  Gov. Try what you can work upon him.
  Oro. Are you come againft me too ?
  Bland. Is this to come againft you ?
          [*Offering his fword to* Oroonoko.
Unarm'd to put myfelf into your hands ?
I come, I hope, to ferve you.
  Oro. You have ferv'd me ;
I thank you for't : And I am pleas'd to think
You were my friend, while I had need of one :
But now 'tis paft ; this farewel, and be gone.
               [*Embraces him.*
  Bland. It is not paft, and I muft ferve you ftill.
' I would make up thefe breaches which the fword
' Will widen more, and clofe us all in love.'
  Oro. I know what I have done, and I fhould be
A child to think they ever can forgive.
Forgive ! were there but that, I would not live
To be forgiven : Is there a Power on earth,
That I can ever need forgivenefs from ?
  Bland. You fha'not need it.
  Oro. No, I wo'not need it.
                      Bland.

Bland. You fee he offers you your own conditions,
For you and yours.

Oro. Muſt I capitulate ?
Precariouſly compound, on ſtinted terms,
To fave my life ?

Bland. Sir, he impofes none.
You make 'em for your own fecurity.
' If your great heart cannot d fcend to treat,
' In adverfe fortune, with an enemy,
' Yet fure your honour's fafe, you may accept
' Offers of peace and fafety from a friend.'

Gov. He will rely on what you fay to him. [*To* Bland.
Offer him what you can; I will confirm
And make all good : Be you my pledge of truſt.

Bland. I'll anfwer with my life for all he fays.

Gov. Ay, do, and pay the forfeit if you pleafe. [*Aſide.*

Bland. Confider, Sir, can you confent to throw ·
That bleffing from you ? you fo hardly found, [*Of* Imo.
And fo much valu'd once ?

Oro. Imoinda ! Oh !
'Tis fhe that holds me on this argument
Of tedious life : I could refolve it foon,
Were this curſt being only in debate.
But my *Imoinda* ſtruggles in my foul :
She makes a coward of me, I confefs :
I am afraid to part with her in death ;
And more afraid of life to lofe her here.

Bland. This way you muſt lofe her: Think upon
The weaknefs of her fex, made yet more weak
With her condition, requiring jeſt,
And foft indulging eafe, to nurfe your hope,
And make you a glad father.

Oro. There I feel
A father's fondnefs, and a hufband's love.
They feize upon my heart, ſtrain all its ſtrings,
To pull me to 'em from my ſtern refolve.
Hufband and father ! all the melting art
Of eloquence lives in thofe foft'ning names.
Methinks I fee the babe, with infant hands,.
Pleading for life, and begging to be born.

' Shall

' Shall I forbid its birth; deny him light?
' 'The heavenly comforts of all-chearing light?
' And make the womb the dungeon of his death?
' His bleeding mother his sad monument?'
These are the calls of nature, that call loud;
They will be heard, and conquer in their cause :
He must not be a man who can resist 'em.
No, my *Imoinda!* I will venture all
To save thee, and that little innocent :
The world may be a better friend to him
Than I have found it. Now I yield myself:
                    [*Gives up his sword.*
The conflict's past, and we are in your hands.
          [*Several men get about* Oroonoko *and* Aboan,.
             and seize them.
  Gov. So you shall find you are. Dispose of them
As I commanded you.
  Bland. Good Heav'n forbid! you cannot mean ——
  Gov. This is not your concern.
                 [*To* Blandford, *who goes to* Oroonoko.
I must take care of you.   [*To* Imoinda..
  Imo. I'm at the end
Of all my care : Here will I die with him. [*Holding* Oro.
  Oro. You shall not force her from me. [*He holds her.*
  Gov. Then I must   [*They force her from him.*
Try other means, and conquer force by force :
Break, cut off his hold, bring her away.
  Imo. I do not ask to live, kill me but here.
  Oro. O bloody dogs! inhuman murderers!
     [Imoinda *forc'd out of one door by the* Governor *and*
       others. Oroonoko *and* Aboan *hurried out of an-*
       other.   [*Exeunt.*

A C T V.

Enter Stanmore, Lucy, *and* Charlotte.

' *Stan.* 'TIS strange we cannot hear of him : Can
          ' no-body give an account of him?
  ' *Luc.* Nay, I begin to despair : I give him for gone.
                              ' *Stan.*

' *Stan.* Not so, I hope.

' *Luc.* There are so many disturbances in this devilish
' country! Would we had never seen it!

' *Stan.* This is but a cold welcome for you, Madam,
' after so troublesome a voyage.

' *Char.* A cold welcome indeed, Sir, without my
' cousin *Weldon:* He was the best friend I had in the
' world.

' *Stan.* He was a very good friend of yours, indeed,
' Madam.

' *Luc.* They have made him away, murder'd him
' for his money, I believe; he took a considerable sum
' out with him, I know that has been his ruin.

' *Stan.* That has done him no injury, to my know-
' ledge: for this morning he put into my custody what
' you speak of, I suppose—a thousand pounds for the
' use of this lady.

' *Char.* I was always oblig'd to him; and he has
' shewn his care of me, in placing my little affairs in
' such honourable hands.

' *Stan.* He gave me a particular charge of you, Ma-
' dam, very particular, so particular, that you will be
' surpriz'd when I tell you.

' *Char.* What, pray, Sir?

' *Stan.* I am engag'd to get you a husband; I pro-
' mised that before I saw you; and, now I have seen
' you, you must give me leave to offer you myself.

' *Luc.* Nay, cousin, never be coy upon the matter;
' to my knowledge, my brother always design'd you
' for this gentleman.

' *Stan.* You hear, Madam, he has given me his in-
' terest, and 'tis the favour I would have begg'd of
' him. Lord! you are so like him——

' *Char.* That you are oblig'd to say you like me for
' his sake.

' *Stan.* I should be glad to love you for your own.'

Char. If I should consent to the fine things you can
say to me, how would you look at last, to find 'em
thrown away on an old acquaintance?

Stan. An old acquaintance!

Char.

Char. Lord, how eafily are you men to be impos'd upon! I am no coufin newly arriv'd from *England*, not I; but the very *Weldon* you wot of.

Stan. Weldon!

Char. Not murder'd, nor made away, as my fifter would have you believe; but am in very good health, your old friend in breeches that was, and now your humble fervant in petticoats.

Stan. I am glad we have you again. But what fervice can you do me in petticoats, pray?

Char. Can't you tell what?

Stan. Not I, by my troth: I have found my friend and loft my miftrefs, it feems, which I did not expect from your petticoats.

Char. Come, come, you have had a friend of your miftrefs long enough; 'tis high time now to have a miftrefs of your friend.

Stan. What do you fay?

Char. I am a woman, Sir.

Stan. A woman!

Char. As arrant a woman as you would have had me but now, I affure you.

Stan. And at my fervice?

Char. If you have any for me in petticoats.

Stan. Yes, yes, I fhall find you employment.

' *Char.* You wonder at my proceeding, I believe.

' *Stan.* 'Tis a little extraordinary, indeed.

' *Char.* I have taken fome pains to come into your
' favour.

' *Stan.* You might have had it cheaper a great deal.

' *Char.* I might have married you in the perfon of
' my *Englifh* coufin, but could not confent to cheat
' you, even in the thing I had a mind to.

' *Stan.* 'Twas done as you do every thing.'

Char. I need not tell you, I made that little plot, and carry d it on only for this opportunity. I was refolv'd to fee whether you lik'd me as a woman, or not: If I had found you indifferent, I would have endeavour'd to have been fo too: But you fay you like me, and therefore I have ventur'd to difcover the truth.

Stan.

Stan. Like you! I like you fo well, that I am afraid
you won't think marriage a proof on't: Shall I give
you any ether?

Char. No, no, I'm inclin'd to believe you, and that
fhall convince me. At more leifure I'll fatisfy you how
I came to be in man's cloaths; for no ill, I affure you,
tho' I have happen'd to play the rogue in 'em. ' They
' have afiifted me in marrying my fifter, and have gone a
' great way in befriending your coufin *Jack* with the Wi-
' dow. Can you forgive me for pimping for your family?'

Enter Jack Stanmore.

Stan. So, *Jack*, what news with you?

J. Stan. I am the forepart of the Widow you know;
fhe's coming after with the body of the family, the
young 'fquire in her hand, my fon-in-law that is to be,
with the help of Mr. *Weldon.*

Char. Say you fo, Sir? [*Clapping* Jack *upon the back.*

Enter Widow Lackitt *with her fon* Daniel.

Wid. So, Mrs. *Lucy*, I have brought him about
again; I have chaftis'd him, I have made him as fupple
as a glove for your wearing, to pull on, or throw off,
at your pleafure. Will you ever rebel again? will
you, firrah? But come, come, down on your marrow-
bones, and afk her forgivenefs. [Daniel *kneels.*] Say
after me: Pray forfooth wife.

Dan. Pray forfooth wife.

Luc. Well, well, this is a day of good-nature, and
fo I take you into favour: But firft take the oath of
allegiance; [*He kiffes her hand, and rifes.*] If ever you
do fo again——

Dan. Nay, marry if I do, I fhall have the worft on't.

Luc. Here's a ftranger, forfooth, would be glad to
be known to you, a fifter of mine, pray falute her.

[*Starts at* Charlotte.

Wid. Your fifter, Mrs. *Lucy*! What do you mean?
This is your brother, Mr. *Weldon:* Do you think I do
not know Mr. *Weldon?*

Luc. Have a care what you fay: This Gentleman's
about marrying her: You may fpoil all.

Wid. Fiddle, faddle; what! You would put a trick
upon me.

Char.

Char. No faith, Widow, the trick is over; it has taken fufficiently; and now I will teach you the trick, to prevent your being cheated another time.

Wid. How! cheated, Mr. *Weldon!*

Char. Why, aye, you will always take things by the wrong handle: I fee you will have me Mr. *Weldon*: I grant you I was Mr. *Weldon* a little while to pleafe you or fo: But Mr. *Stanmore* here has perfuaded me into a woman again.

Wid. A woman! pray let me fpeak with you [*Drawing her afide.*] You are not in earneft, I hope? a woman!

Char. Really a woman.

Wid. Gads my life! I could not be cheated in every thing: I know a man from a woman at thefe years, or the devil is in't. Pray, did not you marry me?

Char. You would have it fo.

Wid. And did not I give you a thoufand pounds this morning?

Char. Yes, indeed, 'twas more than I deferv'd: But you had your penny-worth for your penny, I fuppofe: You feem'd to be pleas'd with your bargain.

Wid. A rare bargain I have made on't truly! I have laid out my money to a fine purpofe upon a woman.

Char. You would have a hufband, and I provided for you as well as I could.

Wid. Yes, yes, you have provided for me.

Char. And you have paid me very well for't; I thank you.

Wid. 'Tis very well: I may be with child too, for aught I know, and may go look for the father.

Char. Nay, if you think fo, 'tis time to look about you, indeed. ' Ev'n make up the matter as well as you ' can, I advife you as a friend, and let us live neigh- ' bourly and lovingly together.

' *Wid.* I have nothing elfe for it that I know of now.'

Char. For my part, Mrs. *Lackitt*, your thoufand pounds will engage me not to laugh at you. Then my fifter is marry'd to your fon; he is to have half your eftate, I know; and indeed they may live upon it very comfortably to themfelves, and very creditably to you.

Wid.

Wid. Nay, I can blame no body but myself.

Char. You have enough for a hufband ftill, and that you may beftow upon honeft *Jack Stanmore*.

Wid. Is he the man then?

Char. He is the man you are oblig'd to.

J. Stan. Yes faith, Widow, I am the man: I have done fairly by you, you find; you know what you have to truft to before hand.

Wid. Well, well, I fee you will have me, ev'n marry me, and make an end of the bufinefs.

Stan. Why that's well faid, now we are all agreed, and all well provided for.

Enter a fervant to Stanmore.

Serv. Sir, Mr. *Blandford* defires you to come to him, and bring as many of your friends as you can with you.

Stan. I come to him. You fhall all go along with me. Come, young Gentleman, marriage is the fafhion, you fee, you muft like it now.

Dan. If I don't, how fhall I help myfelf?

Luc. Nay, you may hang yourfelf in the noofe, if you pleafe, but you'll never get out on't with ftruggling.

Dan. Come then, let's e'en jog on in the old road. Cuckold, or worfe, I muft now be contented: I'm not the firft has marry'd and repented.   [*Exeunt.*

Enter Governor, *with* Blandford *and* Planters.

Bland. Have you no reverence of future fame?
No awe upon your actions, from the tongues,
The cens'ring tongues of men, that will be free?
' If you confefs humanity, believe
' There is a God, or devil, to reward
' Our doings here; do not provoke your fate.
' The hand of Heav'n is arm'd againft thefe crimes,
' With hotter thunderbolts, prepar'd to fhoot,
' And nail you to the earth, a fad example;
' A monument of faithlefs infamy.'

Enter Stanmore, J. Stanmore, Charlotte, Lucy,
Widow, *and* Daniel.

So, *Stanmore*, you, I know, the women too,
Will join with me: 'Tis *Oroonoko's* caufe,

A lover's

A lover's caufe, a wretched woman's caufe,
That will become your interceffion. [*To the* Women.

1ʃt Plant. Never mind 'em, Governor; he ought to
be made an example for the good of the plantation.

2d Plant. Ay, ay, 'twi l frighten the negroes from
attempting the like again.

1ʃt Plant. What, rife gainſt their lords and maſters!
at this rate no man is fafe from his own ſlaves.

2d Plant. No, no more he iⸯ. Therefore, one and
all, Governor, we declare for hanging.

Omn. Plant. Ay, ay, hang him, hang him.

Wid What! hano him? O forbid it, Governor.

Char. Luc. We all petition for him.

J. Stan. They are for a holiday; guilty, or not, is
not the bufinefs, hanging is their ſport.

Bland. We a e not fure, fo wretched, to have thefe,
The rabble. judge for us: The hanging croud,
The arbitrary guard of Fortune's power,
Who wait to catch the fentence of her frowns,
And hurry all to ruin fhe condemns.

Stan. So far from farther wrong, that 'tis a fhame
He fhould be where he is. Good Governor,
Order his liberty: He yielded up
Himfelf, his all, at your difcretion.

Bland. Difcretion! no, he yielded on your word;
And I am made the cautionary pledge,
The gage and hoftage of your keeping it.
Remember, Sir, he yielded on your word;
Your word! which honeſt men will think fhould be
The laſt refort of truth, and truſt on earth:
There's no appeal beyond it but to Heav'n:
' An oath is a recognizance to Heav'n,
' Binding us over in the courts above,
' To plead to the indictment of our crimes,
' That thofe who 'fcape this world fhould fuffer there.
' But in the common intercourfe of men,
' (Where the dread Majefty is not invok'd,
' His honour not immediately concern'd,
' Not made a party in our interefts),
' Our word is all to be rely'd upon.'

Wid.

Wid. Come, come, you'll be as good as your word, we know.

Stan. He's out of all power of doing any harm now, if he were disposed to it.

Char. But he is not disposed to it.

Bland. To keep him where he is, will make him soon Find out some desperate way to liberty:
He'll hang himself, or dash out his mad brains.

Char. Pray try him by gentle means: We'll all be sureties for him.

Omn. All, all.

' *Luc.* We will all answer for him now.'

Gov. Well, you will have it so, do what you please, just what you will with him, I give you leave.

[*Exit.*

Bland. We thank you, Sir; this way, pray come with me. [*Exeunt.*

The SCENE *drawn shews* Oroonoko *upon his back, his legs and arms stretch'd out, and chain'd to the ground.*

Enter Blandford, Stanmore, *&c.*

Bland. O miserable sight! help every one,
Assist me all to free him from his chains.

[*They help him up and bring him forward, looking down.*
Most injur'd prince! how shall we clear ourselves?
We cannot hope you will vouchsafe to hear,
Or credit what we say in the defence
And cause of our suspected innocence.

Stan. We are not guilty of your injuries,
No way consenting to 'em; but abhor,
Abominate, and loath this cruelty.

' *Bland.* It is our curse, but make it not our crime;
' A heavy curse upon us, that we must
' Share any thing in common, ev'n the light,
' The elements and seasons, with such men,
' Whose principles, like the fam'd dragons teeth,
' Scatter'd and sown, would shoot a harvest up
' Of fighting mischiefs to confound themselves,
' And ruin all about 'em.

' *Stan.*

‘ *Stan.* Profligates!
‘ Whofe bold *Titanian* impiety
‘ Would once again pollute their mother earth,
‘ Force her to teem with her old monftrous brood
‘ Of giants, and forget the race of men.
‘ *Bland.* We are not fo : Believe us innocent,
‘ We come prepar’d with all our fervices,
‘ To offer a redrefs of your bafe wrongs.
‘ Which way fhall we employ ’em ?
‘ *Stan.* Tell us, Sir ?
‘ If there is any thing that can atone ?
‘ But nothing can : that may be fome amends’——

Oro. If you would have me think you are not all
Confederates, all acceffary to
The bafe injuftice of your Governor ;
If you would have me live, as you appear
Concern’d for me ; if you would have me live
To thank, and blefs you, there is yet a way
To tie me ever to your honeft love ;
Bring my *Imoinda* to me ; give me her,
To charm my forrows, and, if poffible,
I’ll fit down with my wrongs, never to rife
Againft my fate, or think of vengeance more.

Bland. Be fatisfy’d, you may depend upon us,
We’ll bring her fafe to you, and fuddenly.

Char. We will not leave you in fo good a work.

Wid. No, no, we’ll go with you.

Bland. In the mean time
Endeavour to forget, Sir, and forgive ;
And hope a better fortune.   [*Exeunt.*

Oroonoko *alone.*

Oro. Forget ! forgive ! I muft indeed forget
When I forgive : But while I am a man,
In flefh, that bears the living marks of fhame,
The print of his difhonourable chains,
My memory ftill roufing up my wrongs,
I never can forgive this Governor,
This villain ; the difgrace of truft, and place,
And juft contempt of delegated power.
What fhall I do ? If I declare myfelf,

         I know

I know him, he will fneak behind his guard
Of followers, and brave me in his fears.
Elfe, lion-'ike, with my devouring ra; e,
I would rufh on him, faften on his throat,
Tear a wide paffage to his treacherous heart,
And that way lay him open to the world.   [*Paufing.*
If I fhou'd turn his Chriftian arts on him,
Promife him, fpeak him fair, flatter and creep
With fawning fteps, to get within his faith,
I could betray him then, as he has me.
But am I fure I y that to right myfelf?
Lying's a certain mark of cowardice:
And, when the tongue forgets its honefty,
The heart and hand may drop their functions too,
And nothing worthy be refolv'd or done.
‘ The man muft go together, bad, or good:
‘ In one part frail, he foon grows weak in all.
‘ Honour fhould be concern'd in honour's caufe,
‘ That is not to be cur'd by contraries,
‘ As bodies are, whofe health is often drawn
‘ From rankeft poifons.’   I et me but find out
An honeft remedy, I have the hand,
A minift'ring hand, that will apply it home.   [*Exit.*

S C E N E, *The* Governor's *Houfe.*

Enter Governor.

Gov. I would not have her tell me, fhe confents;
In favour of the fex's modefty,
That ftill fhould be prefum'd; becaufe there is
A greater impudence in owning it,
Than in allowing all that we can do.
‘ This truth I know, and yet againft myfelf
‘ (So unaccountable are lovers ways)
‘ I talk, and lofe the opportunities,
‘ Which love, and fhe, expects I fhould employ.
‘ Ev'n fhe expects:’ For when a man has faid
All that is fit, to fave the decency,
The women know the reft is to be done.
I wo'not difappoint her.   [*Going.*
                                            Enter

Enter Blandford, *the* Stanmores, Daniel, *Mrs.*
Lackitt, Charlotte, *and* Lucy.

Wid. O Governor! I'm glad we've lit upon you.

Gov. Why! what's the matter?

Char. Nay, nothing extraordinary. But one good
action draws on another. You have given the prince
his freedom: now we come a begging for his wife:
you won't refuse us.

Gov. Refuse you! No, no, what have I to do to
refuse you?

Wid. You won't refuse to send her to him, she
means.

Gov. I send her to him!

Wid. We have promis'd him to bring her.

Gov. You do very well; 'tis kindly done of you;
Ev'n carry her to him, with all my heart.

Luc. You must tell us where she is.

Gov. I tell you! why, don't you know?

Bland. Your servant says she's in the house.

Gov. No, no, I brought her home at first, indeed;
but I thought it would not look well to keep her here;
I remov'd her in the hurry only to take care of her.
What! she belongs to you: I have nothing to do with
her.

Char. But where is she now, sir?

Gov. Why, faith, I can't say certainly: you'll hear
of her at *Parham* house, I suppose: there or there-
abouts: I think I sent her there.

Bland. I'll have an eye on him   [*Aside.*

[*Exeunt all but the Governor.*

Gov. I have ly'd myself into a little time,
And must employ it: ' they'll be here again;
' But I must be before 'em.'

[*Going out, he meets* Imoinda, *and seizes her.*
Are you come?
I'll court no longer for a happiness
That is in my own keeping: you may still
Refuse to grant, so I have power to take.
The man that asks deserves to be deny'd.

[*She disengages one hand, and draws his sword from his
side upon him: Governor starts and retires;* Blandford
enters behind him.   D   *Imo.*

Imo. He does indeed, that aſks unworthily.

Bland. You hear her, ſir, that aſks unworthily.

Gov. You are no judge.

Bland. I am of my own ſlave.

Gov. Be gone and leave us.

Bland When you let her go.

Gov. To faſten upon you.

Bland. I muſt defend myſelf.

Imo. Help, murder, help!

[Imoinda *retreats towards the door, favour'd by* Blandford; *when they are cloſed, ſhe throws down the
ſword, and runs out. Governor takes up his ſword,
they fight, cloſe, and fall,* Blandford *upon him. Servants enter, and part them.*

Gov. She ſha'not 'ſcape me ſo. I've gone too far,
Not to go farther. Curſe on my delay:
But yet ſhe is, and ſhall be in my power.

Bland. Nay, then it is the war of honeſty;
I know you, and will ſave you from yourſelf.

Gov. All come along with me. [*Exeunt.*

S C E N E *the laſt.*

Enter Oroonoko.

Oro. To honour bound! and yet a ſlave to love!
I am diſtracted by their rival powers,
And both will be obey'd. O great revenge!
Thou raiſer and reſtorer of fall'n fame!
Let me not be unworthy of thy aid,
For ſtopping in thy courſe: I ſtill am thine;
But can't forget I am *Imoinda's* too.
She calls me from my wrongs to reſcue her.
No man condemn me, who has never felt
A woman's power, or try'd the force of love:
‘ All tempers yield and ſoften in thoſe fires:
‘ Our honours, intereſts reſolving down,
‘ Run in the gentle current of our joys;
‘ But not to ſink, and drown our memory;
‘ We mount again to action, like the ſun,
‘ That riſes from the boſom of the ſea,

‘ To

' To run his glorious race of light a-new,
' And carry on the world.' Love, love will be
My first ambition, and my fame the next.

Enter Aboan *bloody.*

My eyes are turn'd against me and combine
With my sworn enemies, to represent
This spectacle of horror. *Aboan!*
' My ever faithful friend!'

Abo. I have no name
That can distinguish me from the vile earth,
To which I'm going: a poor abject worm,
That crawl'd awhile upon the bustling world,
And now am trampled to my dust again.

Oro. I see thee gash'd and mangled.

Abo. Spare my shame.
To tell how they have us'd me: but believe
The hangman's hand would have been merciful.
Do not you scorn me, sir, to think I can
Intend to live under this infamy.
I do not come for pity, to complain.
I've spent an honourable life with you.
The earliest servant of your rising fame,
And would attend it with my latest care:
My life was yours, and so shall be my death.
You must not live,
Bending and sinking, I have dragg'd my steps
Thus far to tell you that you cannot live:
To warn you of those ignominious wrongs,
Whips, rods, and all the instruments of death,
Which I have felt, and are prepar'd for you.
This was the duty that I had to pay.
Tis done, and now I beg to be discharg'd.

Oro. What shall I do for thee?

Abo. My body tires,
And wo'not bear me off to liberty:
I shall again be taken, made a slave.
A sword, a dagger yet would rescue me.
I have not strength to go and find out death,
You must direct him to me.

Oro. Here he is,   [*Gives him a dagger.*

The

The only prefent I can make thee now:
And, next the honourable means of life,
I would beftow the honeft means of death.
   Abo. I cannot ftay to thank you.   If there is
A being after this, I fhall be yours
In the next world, your faithful flave again.
This is to try. [*Stabs himfelf.*] I had a living fenfe
Of all your royal favours, but this laft
Strikes through my heart.   I wo'not fay farewel,
For you muft follow me.   [*Dies.*
      Oro. In life and death,
The guardian of my honour! Follow thee!
I fhould have gone before thee: then perhaps
Thy fate had been prevented.   All his care
Was to preferve me from the barbarous rage
That worry'd him, only for being mine.
Why, why, you Gods! why am I fo accus'd,
That it muft be a reafon of your wrath,
A guilt, a crime fufficient to the fate
Of any one, but to belong to me?
My friend has found it out, and my wife will foon:
My wife! the very fear's too much for life.
I can't fupport it. Where? *Imoinda!* Oh!
         [*Going out, fhe meets him, running into his arms.*
Thou bofom foftnefs! Down of all my cares!
I could recline my thoughts upon this breaft
To a forgetfulnefs of all my griefs,
· And yet be happy: but it wo'not be,
Thou art diforder'd, pale, and out of breath!
If fate purfues thee, find a fhelter here.
What is it thou would'ft tell me?
      Imo. 'Tis in vain to call him villain.
      Oro. Call him Governor: is it not fo?
      Imo. There's not another fure.
      Oro. Villain's the common name of mankind here,
But his moft properly. What! what of him?
I fear to be refolv'd, and muft enquire.
He had thee in his power.
      Imo. I blufh to think it.
      Oro. Blufh! to think what?

                                              Imo.

Imo. That I was in his power.

Oro. He cou'd not ufe it?

Imo. What can't fuch men do?

Oro. But did he, durft he?

Imo. What he cou'd, he dar'd.

Oro. His own Gods damn him then? For ours have none,

No punifhment for fuch unheard of crime.

Imo. This monfter, cunning in his flatteries,

When he had weary'd all his ufelefs arts,

Leap'd out, fierce as a beaft of prey, to feize me.

I trembled, fear'd.

Oro. I fear and tremble now.

What could preferve thee? What deliver thee?

Imo. That worthy man, you us'd to call your friend.

Oro. Blandford?

Imo. Came in, and fav'd me from his rage.

Oro. He was a friend indeed, to refcue thee!

And, for his fake, I'll think it poffible

A Chriftian may be yet an honeft man.

Imo. O did you know what I have ftruggled thro',

To fave me yours, fure you would promife me

Never to fee me forc'd from you again.

Oro. To promife thee! O! do I need to promife?

But there is now no farther ufe of words.

Death is fecurity for all our fears.

[*Shews* Aboan's *body on the floor.*

And yet I cannot truft him.

Imo. Aboan!

Oro. Mangled and torn, refolv'd to give me time

'To fit myfelf for what I muft expect,

Groan'd out a warning to me, and expir'd.

Imo. For what you muft expect?

Oro. Would that were all!

Imo. What to be butcher'd thus ——

O o. Juft as thou feeft.

Imo. By barb'rous hands to fall at laft their prey?

Oro. I have run the race with honour, fhall I now

Lag, and be overtaken at the goal?

Imo. No.

Oro.

Oro. I muſt look back to thee.   *[Tenderly.*

Imo. You ſha'not need.

I am always preſent to your purpoſe, ſay,

Which way would you diſpoſe me?

  ' *Oro.* Have a care.

' Thou'rt on a precipice, and doſt not ſee

' Whither that queſtion leads thee. O! too ſoon

• Thou doſt enquire what the aſſembled Gods

' Have not determin'd, and will lateſt doom.

' Yet this I know of fate, this is moſt certain,

' I cannot, as I would, diſpoſe of thee;

' And, as I ought, I dare not. O *Imoinda!*

  ' *Imo.* Alas! that ſigh! why do you tremble ſo!'

' Nay, then 'tis bad indeed, if you can weep.

  ' *Oro.* My heart runs over, if my guſhing eyes

' Betray a weakneſs which they never knew.

' Believe, thou only, thou couldſt cauſe theſe tears:

' The Gods themſelves conſpire with faithleſs men

' To our deſtruction.

  ' *Imo.* Heav'n and earth our foes!

  ' *Oro.* It is not always granted to the great

' To be moſt happy: if the angry pow'rs

' Repent their favours, let 'em take 'em back:

' The hopes of empire, which they gave my youth,

' By making me a prince, I here reſign.

' Let 'em quench in me all thoſe glorious fires,

• Which kindled at their beams: that luſt of fame,

' That fever of ambition, reſtleſs ſtill,

' And burning with the ſacred thirſt of ſway,

• Which they inſpir'd, to qualify my fate,

' And makes me fit to govern under them,

' Let 'em extinguiſh. I ſubmit myſelf

' To their high pleaſure, and devoted bow

' Yet lower, to continue ſtill a ſlave;

' Hopeleſs of liberty: and, if I could

' Live after it, would give up honour too,

' To ſatisfy their vengeance, to avert

' This only curſe, the curſe of loſing thee.

  ' *Imo.* If Heav'n could be appeaſ'd, theſe cruel

    ' men·

                       ' Atc

    I

' Are not to be intreated or believ'd :
' O ! think on that, and be no more deceiv'd.
 ' *Oro.* What can we do ?
 ' *Imo.* Can I do any thing ?
 ' *Oro.* But we were born to fuffer.
 ' *Imo.* Suffer both,
' Both die, and fo prevent 'em.
 ' *Oro.* By thy death !
' O ! let me hunt my travell'd thoughts again ;
' Range the wide wafte of defolate defpair ;
· Start any hope. Alas ! I lofe myfelf,
' 'Tis pathlefs, dark, and barren all to me.
' Thou art my only guide, my light of life,
' And thou art le ving me : Send out thy beams
' Upon the wing ; let 'em fly all around,
' Difcover every way : Is there a dawn,
' A glimmering of comfort ? The great God,
' That rifes on the world, muft fhine on us.
 ' *Imo.* And fee us fet before him.
 ' *Oro.* Thou befpeak'ft,
' And goeft before me.
 ' *Imo.* So I would in love,
' In the dear unfufpected part of life,
' In death for love. Alas ! what hopes for me ?
' I was preferv'd but to acquit myfelf,
' To beg to die with you.
 ' *Oro.* And can'ft thou afk it ?
' I never durft enquire into myfelf
' About thy fate, and thou refolv'ft it all. ..
 ' *Imo.* Alas ! my lord ! my fate's refolv'd in yours.
 ' *Oro.* O ! keep thee there : Let not thy virtue fhrink
' From my fupport, and I will gather ftrength,
' Faft as I can, to tell thee ——
 · *Imo.* I muft die :
' I know 'tis fit, and I can die with you.
 ' *Oro.* O ! thou haft banifh'd hence a thoufand fears,
' Which ficken'd at my heart, and quite unmann'd me.
 ' *Imo.* Your fears for me ; I know you fear my ftrength,
' And could not overcome your tendernefs,
' To pafs this fentence on me : And indeed .
          There

'There you were kind, as I have always found you;
'As you have e er been: For tho' I am
'Relign'd, and ready to obey y doom,
'Methinks it fhould not be pronounc'd by you.
'   'Oro. O! that was all the labour of my grief.
'My heart and tongue forfook me in the ftrife;
'I never could pronounce it.
'   'Imo. I have for you, for both of us.
'   'Oro. Alas! for me! my death
'I could regard as the laft fcene of life,
'And act it thro' with joy, to have it done.
'But then to part with thee——
'   'Im. 'Tis hard to part.
'But parting thus, as the moft happy muft,
'Parting in death, makes it the eafier.
'You might have thrown me off, forfaken me,
'And my misfortunes: That had been a death
'Indeed of terror, to have trembled at.
'   'Oro. Forfaken! thrown thee off!
'   'Imo. But 'tis a pleafure more than life can give,
'That with unconquer'd paffion, to the laft,
'You ftruggle ftill, and fain would hold me to you.
'   'Oro. Ever, ever, and let thofe ftars, which are my
'   'enemies,
'Witnefs againft me in the other world,
'If I would leave this manfion of my blifs,
''To be the brighteft ruler of their fkies.
'O! that we could incorporate, be one, [Embracing her.
'One body, as we have been long one mind;
'That, blended fo, we might together mix,
'And, lofing thus our being to the world,
'Be only found to one another's joys.
'   'Imo. Is this the way to part?
'   'Oro. Which is the way?
'   'Imo. The god of love is blind, and cannot find it.
'But quick make hafte, our enemies have eyes,
'To find us out, and fhew us the worft way
'Of parting. Think on them.
'   'Oro. Why doft thou wake me?
'   'Imo. O! no more of love.

For,

' For, if I liften to you, I fhall quite
' Forget my dangers, and defire to live.
' I can't live yours.   *[Takes up the dagger.*

   Oro. ' There all the ftings of death
' Are fhot into my heart'—what fhall I do ?

   Imo. This dagger will inftruct you.   *[Gives it him.*

   Oro. Ha! this dagger!
Like fate, it points me to the horrid deed.

   Imo. Strike, ftrike it home, and bravely fave us both.
There is no other fafety.

   Oro. It muft be——
But firft a dying kifs——   *[Kiffes her.*
This laft embrace——   *[Embracing her.*
And now——

   Imo. I'm ready.

   Oro. O! where fhall I ftrike ?
Is there a fmalleft grain of that lov'd body
That is not dearer to me than my eyes,
My bofom'd heart, and all the life blood there ?
Bid me cut off thefe limbs, hew off thefe hands,
Dig out thefe eyes, tho' I would keep them laft
To gaze upon thee : But to murder thee !
The joy, and charm of ev'ry ravifh'd fenfe,
My wife! forbid it, nature.

   Imo. 'Tis your wife,
Who on her knees conjures you. O! in time
Prevent thofe mifchiefs that are falling on us.
You may be hurry'd to a fhameful death,
And I too dragg'd to the vile governor;
Then I may cry aloud : When you are gone,
Where fhall I find a friend again to fave me ?

   Oro. It will be fo. Thou unexampled virtue !
Thy refolution has recover'd mine :
And now prepare thee.

   Imo. Thus, with open arms,
I welcome you and death.

     [He drops his dagger, as he looks on her, and throws
      himfelf on the ground.

   Oro. I cannot bear it.
' O let me dafh againft the rock of fate,

Dig up this earth, tear her bowls out,
To make a grave, deep as the center down,
To swallow wide and bury us together,
It wo'not be. O! then some pitying god
(If there be one, a friend to innocence)
Find yet a way to lay her beauties down
Gently in death, and save me from her blood.

Imo. O rise, 'tis more than death to see you thus,
I'll ease your love, and do the deed myself—
[*She takes up the aagger, he rises in haste to take it from
    her.*

Oro. O! hold, I charge thee, hold.

Imo. Tho' I must own
It would be nobler for us both from you.

Oro. O! for a whirlwind's wing to hurry us
To yonder cliff, which frowns upon the flood;
That in embraces lock'd we might plunge in,
And perish thus in one another's arms.

Imo. Alas! what shout is that?

Oro. I see 'em coming.
They sha'not overtake us. This last kiss,
And now farewel.

Imo. Farewel, farewel for ever.

Oro. I'll turn my face away, and do it so.
Now, are you ready?

Imo. Now. But do n't grudge me
The pleasure in my death of a last look ;
Pray look upon me.—Now I'm satisfied.

Oro. So fate must be by this.
[*Going to stab her, he stps short ; she lays her hand on
    his, in order to give the blow.*

Imo. Nay, then I must assist you.
And, since it is the common cause of both,
'Tis just that both should be employ'd in it.
Thus, thus 'tis finish'd, and I bless my fate, [*Stabs herself.*
That, where I liv'd, I die in these lov'd arms.   [*Dies.*

Oro. She's gone. And now all's at an end with me,
Soft, lay her down, O we will part no more.
                              [*Then throws himself by her.*
But let me pay the tribute of my grief,

A

OROONOKO.

Mr. SAVIGNY in the Character of OROONOKO.

Oro. I'll turn my Face away, and do it so.

Published Nov.r 23, 1776 by J. Lowndes & Partners

A few fad tears to thy lov'd memory,
And then I follow —— [*bouts*]   [*Weeps over her.*
But I ftay too long.   [*A noife again.*
The noife comes nearer. Hold, before I go,
There's fomething would be done. It fhall be fo,
And then, *Imoinda*, I'll come all to thee.   [*Rifes.*
[Blandford *and his party enter before the* Governor *and his*
party; fwords drawn on both fides.
Gov. You ftrive in vain to fave him, he fhall die.
Bland. Not while we can defend him with our lives.
Gov. Where is he?
Oro. Here is the wretch whom you would have.
Put up your fwords, and let not civil broils
Engage you in the curfed caue of one
Who cannot live, and now intreats to die.
This object will convince you
    Bland. 'Tis his wife.   [*They gather about the body.*
Alas! there was no other remedy.
Gov. Who did th bloody deed?
Oro. The deed was mine:
Bloody I know it is, and I expect
Your laws fhould tell me fo. Thus, felf-condemn'd,
I do refign myfelf into your hands,
The hands of juftice —— But I hold the fword
For you —— and for myfelf.
    [*Stabs the* Governor *and himfelf, then throws himfelf*
    by Imoinda's *body.*
' *Stan.* He has kill'd the Governor and ftabb'd him-
    ' felf.'
Oro. 'Tis as it fhould be now, I have fent his ghoft
To be a witnefs of that happinefs
In the next world, which he deny'd us here.   [*Dies.*
    Bland. I hope there is a place of happinefs
In the next world for fuch exalted virtue.
Pagan or unbeliever, yet he liv'd
To all he knew: And, if he went aftray,
There's mercy ftill above to fet him right.
But Chriftians, guided by the heav'nly ray,
Have no excufe if we miftake our way. [*Exeunt Omnes.*

E P I-

EPILOGUE.

YOU see we try all shapes, and shifts, and arts,
    To tempt your favours, and regain your hearts.
We weep and laugh, join mirth and grief together,
Like rain and sunshine mix'd, in April weather.
Your diff'rent tastes divide our poet's cares;
One foot the sock, t'other the buskins wears.
Thus, while he strives to please, he's forc'd to do't,
Like Volscius, hip hop, in a single boot.
Critics, he knows, for this may damn his books:
But he makes feasts for friends, and not for cooks.
    Tho' errant knights of late no favour find,
Sure you will be to ladies errant kind.
To follow fame, knight errants make profession:
We damsels fly to save our reputation:
So they their valour shew, we our discretion.
To lands of monsters and fierce beasts they go:
We, to these islands, where rich husbands grow:
Tho' they're no monsters, we may make them so.
If they're of English growth, they'll bear't with patience:
But save us from a spouse of Oroonoko's nations:
Then bless your stars, you happy London wives,
Who love at large, each day, yet keep your lives:
Nor envy poor Imoinda's doating blindness,
We thought her husband kill'd her out of kindness.
Death with a husband ne'er had shewn such charms,
Had she once dy'd within a lover's arms.
Her error was from ignorance proceeding;
Poor soul! she wanted some of our town-breeding.
Forgive this Indian fondness of her spouse;
Their law no Christian liberty allows:
Alas! they make a conscience of their vows!
If virtue in a Heathen be a fault;
Then damn the Heathen school where she was taught.
She might have learn'd to cuckold, jilt, and sham,
Had Covent-Garden been in Surinam.

THE
LONDON MERCHANT;

OR, THE

HISTORY

OF

GEORGE BARNWELL.

A

TRAGEDY,

WRITTEN

By Mr. LILLO.

MARKED WITH THE

VARIATIONS IN THE MANAGER's BOOK,

AT THE

Theatre-Royal, in Drury-Lane.

LEARN TO BE WISE BY OTHERS HARM,
AND YOU SHALL DO FULL WELL.
Old Ballad of the Lady's Fall.

LONDON:

PRINTED FOR S. BLADON, W. NICOLL, AND
W. LOWNDES.

M,DCC,LXXXVIII.

⁎ The Reader is defired to obferve, that the Paffages omitted in the Reprefentation at the Theatres are here preferved, and marked with inverted Commas; as at Line 16 to 26, in Page 6.

PROLOGUE.

THE Tragic Muse, sublime, delights to shew
    Princes distress'd, and scenes of Royal woe;
In awful pomp, majestic, to relate
The fall of nations, or some hero's fate:
That scepter'd chiefs may, by example, know
The strange vicissitudes of things below;
What dangers on security attend;
How pride and cruelty in ruin end:
Hence Providence supreme to know, and own
Humanity adds glory to a throne.

In ev'ry former age, and foreign tongue,
With native grandeur thus the goddess sung.
Upon our stage, indeed, with wish'd success,
You've sometimes seen her in an humbler dress;
Great only in distress. When she complains
In Southern's, Rowe's, or Otway's moving strains,
The brilliant drops that fall from each bright eye,
The absent pomp, with brighter gems, supply.

Forgive us, then, if we attempt to shew,
In artless strains, a tale of private woe.
A London 'prentice ruin'd is our theme,
Drawn from the fam'd old song that bears his name.
We hope your taste is not so high, to scorn
A moral tale esteem'd ere you were born;
Which, for a century of rolling years,
Has fill'd a thousand thousand eyes with tears.

If thoughtless youth to warn, and shame the age
From vice destructive, well becomes the stage;
If this example innocence ensures,
Prevents our guilt, or by reflection cures;
If Millwood's dreadful crimes, and sad despair,
Commend the virtue of the good and fair;
Tho' art be wanting, and our numbers fail,
Indulge the attempt, in justice to the tale.

DRAMATIS

DRAMATIS PERSONÆ.

MEN.

	At Drury Lane.	At Covent Garden.
Thorowgood		Mr. HULL.
Barnwell, Uncle to George,		Mr. FEARON.
George Barnwell,	Mr. PACKER.	Mr. FARREN.
Trueman,	Mr. CHAPLIN.	Mr. DAVIS.
Blunt,	Mr. BANNISTER.	Mr. THOMPSON.
	Mr. BARRYMORE.	
	Mr. BURTON.	

WOMEN.

	At Drury Lane.	At Covent Garden.
Maria,	Mrs. KEMBLE.	Mrs. T. KENNEDY.
Millwood,	Mrs. WILSON.	Mrs. BATES.
Lucy,	Mrs. WARD.	Mrs. WILSON.

Officers, with their Attendants, Keeper, and Footmen.

SCENE LONDON, and an adjacent Village.

GEORGE BARNWELL.

ACT I. SCENE, *a room in* Thorowgood's *house.*

Enter Thorowgood *and* Trueman.

Trueman. SIR, the packet from Genoa is arrived.
[*Gives letters.*

Thor. Heaven be praised! The storm that threaten-
ed our royal mistress, pure religion, liberty, and laws,
is for a time diverted. The haughty and revengeful
Spaniard, disappointed of the loan on which he depended from Genoa, must now attend the flow returns
of wealth from his new world, to supply his empty
coffers, ere he can execute his proposed invasion of
our happy island. By this means time is gained to
make such preparations on our part, as may, Heaven
concurring, prevent his malice, or turn the meditated
mischief on himself.

Tr. He must be insensible indeed, who is not affected
when the safety of his country is concerned. Sir, may
I know by what means? —— If I am too bold—

Thor. Your curiosity is laudable; and I gratify it
with the greater pleasure, because from thence you
may learn how honest merchants, as such, may sometimes contribute to the safety of their country, as they
do at all times to its happiness; that if hereafter you
should be tempted to any action that has the appearance
of vice or meanness in it, upon reflecting on the dig-
nity of our profession, you may, with honest scorn,
reject whatever is unworthy of it.

Tr. Should Barnwell, or I, who have the benefit of
your example, by our ill conduct bring any imputation on that honourable name, we must be left without
excuse.

Thor. You compliment, young man. [Tr. *bows
respectfully.*] Nay, I'm not offended. As the name
of merchant never degrades the gentleman, so by no
means does it exclude him; only take heed not to
purchase the character of complaisant at the expence
of your sincerity. But to answer your question: The
A 3   bank

bank of Genoa had agreed, at an exceſſive intereſt, and on good ſecurity, to advance the king of Spain a ſum of money ſufficient to equip his vaſt armada; of which our peerleſs Elizabeth (more than in name the mother of her people) being well informed, ſent Walſingham, her wife and faithful ſecretary, to con- ſult the merchants of this loyal city; who all agreed, to direct their ſeveral agents to influence, if poſſible, the Genoeſe to break their contract with the Spaniſh court. 'Tis done; the ſtate and bank of Genoa hav- ing maturely weighed, and rightly judged of their true intereſt, prefer the friendſhip of the merchants of London to that of the monarch, who proudly ſtiles himſelf king of both Indies.

Tr. Happy ſucceſs of prudent counſels! What an expence of blood and treaſure is here ſaved! ' Excel- ' lent queen; Oh, how unlike thoſe princes, who ' make the danger of foreign enemies a pretence to op- ' preſs their ſubjects by taxes great, and grievous to ' be borne.

' *Thor.* Not ſo our gracious queen! whoſe richeſt ' exchequer is her people's love, as their happineſs her ' greateſt glory.

' *Tr.* On theſe terms to defend us, is to make our ' protection a benefit worthy her who confers it, and ' well worth our acceptance.' Sir, have you any commands for me at this time?

Thor. Only look carefully over the files, to ſee whe- ther there are any tradeſmen's bills unpaid; if there are, ſend and diſcharge 'em. We muſt not let artifi- cers loſe their time, ſo uſeful to the public and their families, in unneceſſary attendance.   [*Exit* Trueman.

Enter Maria.

Well, Maria, have you given orders for the entertain- ment? I would have it in ſome meaſure worthy the gueſts. Let there be plenty, and of the beſt, that the courtiers may at leaſt commend our hoſpitality.

Ma. Sir, I have endeavoured not to wrong your well-known generoſity by an ill-timed parſimony.

Thor. Nay, 'twas a needleſs caution: I have no cauſe to doubt your prudence.

Ma.

Ma. Sir, I find myfelf unfit for converfation. I fhould but increafe the number of the company, without adding to their fatisfaction.

Thor. Nay, my child, this melancholy muft not be indulged.

Ma. Company will but increafe it. I wifh you would difpenfe with my prefence. Solitude beft fuits my prefent temper.

Thor. You are not infenfible, that it is chiefly on your account thefe noble lords do me the honour fo frequently to grace my board. Should you be abfent, the difappointment may make them repent of their condefcenfion, and think their labour loft.

Ma. He that fhall think his time or honour loft in vifiting you, can fet no real value on your daughter's company, whofe only merit is, that fhe is your's. The man of quality who chufes to converfe with a gentleman and merchant of your worth and character, may confer honour by fo doing, but he,lofes none.

Thor. Come, come, Maria, I need not tell you, that a young gentleman may prefer your converfation to mine, and yet intend me no difrefpect at all; for though he may lofe no honour in my company, 'tis very natural for him to expect more pleafure in your's. I remember the time when the company of the greateft and wifeft man in the kingdom would have been infipid and tirefome to me, if it had deprived me of an opportunity of enjoying your mother's

Ma. Your's, no doubt, was as agreeable to her; for generous minds know no pleafure in fociety but where 'tis mutual.

Thor. Thou knoweft I have no heir, no child, but thee; the fruits of many years fuccefsful induftry muft all be thine. Now it would give me pleafure, great as my love, to fee on whom you will beftow it. I am daily folicited by men of the greateft rank and merit for leave to addrefs you; but I have hitherto declined it, in hopes that, by obfervation, I fhould learn which way your inclination tends; for, as I know love to be effential to happinefs in the marriage ftate, I had rather my approbation fhould confirm your choice than direct it.

Ma.

Ma. What can I fay? How fhall I anfwer as I ought, this tendernefs, fo uncommon even in the beft of parents? But you are without example; yet, had you been lefs indulgent, I had been moft wretched. That I look on the crowd of courtiers that vifit here, with equal efteem, but equal indifference, you have obferved, and I muft needs confefs; yet, had you afferted your authority, and infifted on a parent's right to be obeyed, I had fubmitted, and to my duty facrificed my peace.

Thor. From your perfect obedience in every other inftance, I feared as much; and therefore would leave you without a bias in an affair wherein your happinefs is fo immediately concerned.

Ma. Whether from a want of that juft ambition that would become your daughter, or from fome other caufe, I know not; but I find high birth and titles don't recommend the man who owns them to my affections.

Thor. I would not that they fhould, unlefs his merit recommends him more. A noble birth and fortune, though they make not a bad man good, yet they are a real advantage to a worthy one, and place his virtues in the faireft light.

Ma. I cannot anfwer for my inclinations; but they fhall ever be fubmitted to your wifdom and authority. And as you will not compel me to marry where I cannot love, love fhall never make me act contrary to my duty. Sir, have I your permiffion to retire?

Thor. I'll fee you to your chamber. [*Exeunt.*

SCENE, *a room in* Millwood's *houfe.*

Enter Millwood *and* Lucy.

Mill. How do I look to-day, Lucy?

Lucy. O, killingly, madam! A little more red, and you'll be irrefiftible!———But why this more than ordinary care of your drefs and complexion? What new conqueft are you aiming at?

Mill. A conqueft would be new indeed!

Lucy. Not to you, who make 'em every day----but

to me ——— Well, 'tis what I'm never to expect ———
unfortunate as I am ——— But your wit and beauty----

Mill. First made me a wretch, and still continue me
so. Men, however generous and sincere to one another, are all selfish hypocrites in their affairs with
us; we are no otherwise esteemed or regarded by them,
but as we contribute to their satisfaction.

Lucy. You are certainly, madam, on the wrong side
in this argument. Is not the expence all theirs? And
I am sure, it is our own fault if we han't a share of
the pleasure.

Mill. We are but slaves to men.

Lucy. Nay, 'tis they that are slaves, most certainly,
for we lay them under contribution.

Mill. Slaves have no property; no, not even in
themselves: all is the victor's.

Lucy. You are strangely arbitrary in your principles, madam.

Mill. I would have my conquests complete, like
those of the Spaniards in the new world; who first
plundered the natives of all the wealth they had, and
then condemned the wretches to the mines for life, to
work for more.

Lucy. Well, I shall never approve of your scheme of
government: I should think it much more politic, as
well as just, to find my subjects an easier employment.

Mill. It is a general maxim among the knowing part
of mankind, that a woman without virtue, like a man
without honour or honesty, is capable of any action,
though never so vile: and yet what pains will they not
take, what arts not use, to seduce us from our innocence, and make us contemptible and wicked, even in
their own opinion? Then, is it not just the villains,
to their cost, should find us so? But guilt makes them
suspicious, and keeps them on their guard; therefore
we can take advantage only of the young and innocent
part of the sex, who, having never injured women,
apprehend no danger from them.

Lucy. Aye, they must be young indeed!

Mill. Such a one, I think, I have found. As I have
passed through the city, I have often observed him re-

ceiving

ceiving and paying confiderable fums of money; from thence I conclude he is employed in affairs of confe-quence.

Lucy. Is he handfome?

Mil. Aye, aye, the ftripling is well made, and has a good face.

Lucy. About———

Mill. Eighteen.

Lucy. Innocent, handfome, and about eighteen! You'll be vaftly happy. Why, if you manage well, you may keep him to yourfelf thefe two or three years.

Mill. If I manage well, I fhall have done with him much fooner. Having long had a defign on him, and meeting him yefterday, I made a full ftop, and gazing wifhfully on his face, afked his name. He blufhed, and, bowing very low, anfwered, George Barnwell. I begged his pardon for the freedom I had taken, and told him that he was the perfon I had long wifhed to fee, and to whom I had an affair of importance to communicate, at a proper time and place. He named a tavern: I talked of honour and reputation, and in-vited him to my houfe. He fwallowed the bait, pro-mifed to come, and this is the time I expect him. [*Knocking at the door.*] Somebody knocks. D'ye hear, I'm at home to nobody to-day but him. [*Exit Lucy.*] Lefs affairs muft give way to thofe of more confequence; and I am ftrangely miftaken, if this does not prove of great importance to me, and him too, before I have done with him. Now, after what manner fhall I receive him? Let me confider—What manner of perfon am I to receive? He is young, in-nocent, and bafhful; therefore I muft take care not to put him out of countenance at firft. ' But then, if ' I have any fkill in phyfiognomy, he is amorous, and ' with a little affiftance will foon get the better of his ' modefty.' I'll e'en truft to nature, who does won-ders in thefe matters. ' If to feem what one is not, ' in order to be the better liked for what one really is; ' if to fpeak one thing, and mean the direct con- ' trary, be art in woman———I know nothing of ' nature.'

Enter

Enter Barnwell, *bowing very low*, Lucy *at a diſtance*.

Mill. Sir, the ſurpriſe and joy!

Barn. Madam!

Mill. This is ſuch a favour———   [*Advancing:*

Barn. Pardon me, madam!

Mill. So unhoped for!   [*Still advances.*

[Barnwell *ſalutes her, and retires in confuſion.*

To ſee you here——Excuſe the confuſion——

Barn. I fear I am too bold.

Mill. Alas, Sir, I may juſtly apprehend you think me ſo. Pleaſe, Sir, to ſit. I am as much at a loſs how to receive this honour as I ought, as I am ſurpriſed at your goodneſs in conferring it.

Barn. I thought you had expected me: I promiſed to come.

Mill. That is the more ſurpriſing: few men are ſuch religious obſervers of their word.

Barn. All who are honeſt are.

Mill. To one another; but we ſimple women are ſeldom thought of conſequence enough to gain a place in their remembrace.

[*Laying her hand on his, as by accident.*

Barn. Her diſorder is ſo great, ſhe don't perceive ſhe has laid her hand on mine. Heavens! how ſhe trembles! What can this mean ?   [*Aſide.*

Mill. The intereſt I have in all that relates to you (the reaſon of which you ſhall know hereafter) excites my curioſity; and were I ſure you would pardon my preſumption, I ſhould deſire to know your real ſentiments on a very particular ſubject.

Barn. Madam, you may command my poor thoughts on any ſubject. I have none that I would conceal.

Mill. You'll think me bold.

Barn. No, indeed.

Mill. What then are your thoughts of love ?

Barn. If you mean the love of women, I have not thought of it at all. My youth and circumſtances make ſuch thoughts improper in me yet. But if you mean the general love we owe to mankind, I think no one has more of it in his temper than myſelf. I don't know that perſon in the world, whoſe happineſs I don't wiſh.

and

and wou'dn't promote, were it in my power. In so especial manner I love my uncle, and my mafter; but above all, my friend.

Mill. You have a friend then, whom you love?

Barn. As he does me, fincerely.

Mill. He is, no doubt, often blefs'd with your company and converfation.

Barn. We live in one houfe, and both ferve the fame worthy merchant.

Mill. Happy, happy youth! Whoe'er thou art, I envy thee; ' and fo muft all who fee and know this ' youth.' What have I loft by being formed a woman! I hate my fex, myfelf. Had I been a man, I might, perhaps, have been as happy in your friendfhip, as he who now enjoys it is: but as it is----Oh!----

Barn. I never obferved woman before; or this is, fure, the moft beautiful of her fex. [*Afide.*] You feem difordered, madam!---May I know the caufe?

Mill. Do not afk me---I can never fpeak it, whatever is the caufe. I wifh for things impoffible. I would be a fervant, bound to the fame mafter, to live in one houfe with you.

Barn. How ftrange, and yet how kind, her words and actions are! and the effect they have on me is as ftrange. I feel defires I never knew before. I muft be gone, while I have power to go. [*Afide.*] Madam, I humbly take my leave.

Mill. You will not, fure, leave me fo foon!

Barn. Indeed I muft.

Mill. You cannot be fo cruel! I have prepared a poor fupper, at which I promifed myfelf your company.

Barn. I am forry I muft refufe the honour you defigned me: but my duty to my mafter calls me hence. I never yet neglected his fervice. He is fo gentle, and fo good a mafter, that fhould I wrong him, though he might forgive me, I fhould never forgive myfelf.

Mill. Am I refufed by the firft man, the fecond favour I ever ftooped to afk? Go then, thou proud hard-hearted youth; but know, you are the only man that could be found, who would let me fue twice for greater favours.

Barn.

Barn. What fhall I do! How fhall I go, or ftay!

Mill. Yet do not, do not leave me. I with my fex's pride would meet your fcorn; but when I look upon you, when I behold thofe eyes---Oh! fpare my tongue, and let my blufhes----this flood of tears too, that will force its way, declare-----what woman's modefty fhould hide.

Barn. Oh, Heavens! fhe loves me, worthlefs as I am. Her looks, her words, her flowing tears confefs it. And can I leave her then? Oh, never, never! Madam, dry up your tears: you fhall command me always. I will ftay here for ever, if you would have me.

Lucy. So; fhe has wheedled him out of his virtue of obedience already, and will ftrip him of all the reft, one after another, till fhe has left him as few as her ladyfhip, or myfelf.

Mill. Now you are kind, indeed; but I mean not to detain you always: I would have you fhake off all flavifh obedience to your mafter; but you may ferve him ftill.

Lucy. Serve him ftill! Aye, or he'll have no opportunity of fingering his cafh; and then he'll not ferve your end, I'll be fworn. [*Afide.*

Enter Blunt.

Blunt. Madam, fupper's on the table.

Mill. Come, Sir; you'll excufe all defects. My thoughts were too much employed on my gueft to obferve the entertainment. [*Exeunt* Barn. *and* Mill.

Blunt. What! is all this preparation, this elegant fupper, variety of wines, and mufic, for the entertainment of that young fellow?

Lucy. So it feems.

Blunt. How! Is our miftrefs turned fool at laft? She's in love with him, I fuppofe.

Lucy. I fuppofe not. But fhe defigns to make him in love with her, if fhe can.

Blunt. What will fhe get by that? He feems under age, and can't be fuppofed to have much money.

Lucy. But his mafter has, and that's the fame thing, as fhe'll manage it.

Blunt.

Blunt. I don't like this fooling with a handsome young fellow: while she's endeavouring to ensnare him she may be caught herself.

Lucy. Nay, were she like me, that would certainly be the consequence; for, I confess, there is something in youth and innocence that moves me mightily.

Blunt. Yes, so does the smoothness and plumpness of a partridge move a mighty desire in the hawk to be the destruction of it.

Lucy. Why, birds are their prey, and men ours; though, as you observed, we are sometimes caught ourselves. But that, I dare say, will never be the case of our mistress.

Blunt. I wish it may prove so; for you know we all depend upon her. Should she trifle away her time with a young fellow that there's nothing to be got by, we must all starve.

Lucy. There's no danger of that; for I am sure she has no view in this affair but interest.

Blunt. Well, and what hopes are there of success in that?

Lucy. The most promising that can be. 'Tis true the youth hath his scruples; but she'll soon teach him to answer them, by stifling his conscience. Oh, the lad is in a hopeful way, depend upon't.   [*Exeunt.*

SCENE *draws, and discovers* Barnwell *and* Millwood *at supper. An entertainment of music and singing. After which they come forward,*

Barn. What can I answer? All that I know is, that you are fair, and I am miserable.

Mill. We are both so; and yet the fault is in ourselves.

Barn. To ease our present anguish by plunging into guilt, is to buy a moment's pleasure with an age of pain.

Mill. I should have thought the joys of love as lasting as they are great; if ours prove otherwise, 'tis your inconstancy must make them so.

Barn. The law of Heaven will not be reversed, and that requires us to govern our passions.

Mill.

Mill. To give us fenfe of beauty and defires, and yet forbid us to tafte and be happy, is a cruelty to nature. Have we paffions only to torment us?

Barn. To hear you talk, though 'i the caufe of vice; to gaze upon your beauty, prefs your hand, ' and fee your fnow-white bofom heave and fall,' inflames my wifhes; my pulfe beats high, ' my fenfes ' are all in a hurry,' and I am on the rack of wild defire. Yet, for a moment's guilty pleafure, fhall I lofe my innocence, my peace of mind, and hopes of folid happinefs?

Mill. Chimæras all!

Barn. I would not-----yet muft on----

  . ' Reluctant thus the merchant quits his eafe,

    ' And trufts to rocks and fands, and ftormy feas;

    ' In hopes fome unknown golden coaft to find,

    ' Commits himfelf, tho' doubtful, to the wind,

    ' Longs much for joys to come, yet mourns thofe

      ' left behind.'

Mill. Along with me, and prove

    No joys like woman-kind, no Heaven like love.

                            [*Exeunt.*

ACT II. SCENE *a room in* Thorowgood's *houfe.*

Enter Barnwell.

Barn. HOW ftrange are all things round me! Like fome thief who treads forbidden ground, and fain would lurk unfeen, fearful I enter each apartment of this well-known houfe. To guilty love, as if that were too little, already have I added breach of truft. A thief! Can I know myfelf that wretched thing, and look my honeft friend and injured mafter in the face? Though hypocrify may awhile conceal my guilt, at length it will be known, and public fhame and ruin muft enfue. In the mean time, what muft be my life? Ever to fpeak a language foreign to my heart; hourly to add to the number of my crimes, in order to conceal 'em. Sure fuch was

                                the

the condition of the grand apoſtate, when firſt he loſt his purity. Like me, diſconſolate he wandered; and while yet in Heaven, bore all his future hell about him.

Enter Truemen.

Tr. Barnwell, Oh, how I rejoice to ſee you ſafe! So will our maſter, and his gentle daughter; who, during your abſence, often enquired after you.

Barn. Would he were gone! His officious love will pry into the ſecrets of my ſoul. —   [*Aſide.*

Tr. Unleſs you knew the pain the whole family has felt on your account, you can't conceive how much you are beloved. But why thus cold and ſilent?——— When my heart is full of joy for your return, why do you turn away----why thus avoid me? What have I done? How am I altered ſince you ſaw me laſt? Or rather, what have you done----and why are you thus changed? for I am ſtill the ſame.

Barn. What have I done, indeed!   [*Aſide.*

Tr. Not ſpeak!----nor look upon me!----

Barn. By my face he will diſcover all I would conceal. Methinks already I begin to hate him.   [*Aſide.*

Tr. I cannot bear this uſage from a friend; one whom till now I ever found ſo loving; whom yet I love; though his unkindneſs ſtrikes at the root of friendſhip, and might deſtroy it in any breaſt but mine.

Barn. I am not well. [*Turning to him.*] Sleep has been a ſtranger to theſe eyes ſince you beheld 'em laſt.

Tr. Heavy they look, indeed, and ſwol'n with tears;---now they overflow. Rightly did my ſympathizing heart forebode laſt night, when thou waſt abſent, ſomething fatal to our peace.

Barn. Your friendſhip engages you too far. My troubles, whate'er they are, are mine alone: you have no intereſt in them, nor ought your concern for me to give you a moment's pain.

Tr. You ſpeak, as if you knew of friendſhip nothing but the name. Before I ſaw your grief, I felt it. ‘ Since we parted laſt, I have ſlept no more than ‘ you; but penſive in my chamber ſat alone, and ‘ ſpent the tedious night in wiſhes for your ſafety,
‘ and

ᵗ and return;' e'en now, though ignorant of the caufe,
your forrow wounds me to the heart.

Barn. 'Twill not be always thus. Friendfhip and
all engagements ceafe as circumftances and occafions
vary; and fince you once may hate me, perhaps it
might be better for us both that now you loved me
lefs.

Tr. Sure I but dream! Without a caufe would
Barnwell ufe me thus? Ungenerous, and ungrateful
youth, farewell: I fhall endeavour to follow your
advice. [*Going.*] Yet ftay; perhaps I am too rafh
and angry, when the caufe demands compaffion. Some
unforefeen calamity may have befallen him, too great
to bear.

Barn. What part am I reduced to act? 'Tis vile
and bafe to move his temper thus, the beft of friends
and men.

Tr. I am to blame; pr'ythee forgive me, Barnwell.
Try to compofe your ruffled mind; and let me know
the caufe that thus tranfports you from yourfelf; my
friendly counfel may reftore your peace.

Barn. All that is poffible for man to do for man,
your generous friendfhip many effect; but here, even
that's in vain.

Tr. Something dreadful is labouring in your breaft;
Oh, give it vent, and let me fhare your grief; 'twill
eafe your pain, fhould it admit no cure, and make it
lighter, by the part I bear.

Barn. Vain fuppofition! My woes increafe by being obferved: fhould the caufe be known, they would
exceed all bounds.

Tr. So well I know thy honeft heart, guilt cannot
harbour there.

Barn. Oh, torture infupportable.!   [*Afide.*

Tr. Then why am I excluded? Have I a thought
I would conceal from you?

Barn. If ftill you urge me on this hated fubject,
I'll never enter more beneath this roof, nor fee your
face again.

Tr. 'Tis ftrange-----but I have done-----fay but you
hate me not.

Barn.

Barn. Hate you!   I am not that monfter yet.

Tr. Shall our friendſhip ſtill continue?

Barn. It's a bleſſing I never was worthy of; yet now muſt ſtand on terms, and but upon conditions can confirm it.

Tr. What are they?

Barn. Never hereafter, though you ſhould wonder at my conduct, deſire to know more than I am willing to reveal.

Tr. 'Tis hard; but upon any conditions I muſt be your friend.

Barn. Then, as much as one loſt to himſelf can be another's, I am your's   [*Embracing.*

Tr. Be ever ſo; and may Heaven reſtore your peace!

' *Barn.* Will yeſterday return?   We have heard the
' glorious ſun, that till then inceſſant roll'd, once
' ſtopp'd his rapid courſe, and once went back.   The
' dead have riſen, and parch'd rocks pour'd forth a
' liquid ſtream, to quench a people's thirſt.   The ſea
' divided, and formed walls of water, while a whole
' nation paſſed in ſafety through its ſandy bottom.
' Hungry lions have refuſed their prey; and men,
' unhurt, have walked amidſt conſuming flames; but
' never yet did time, ence paſt, return.

' *Tr.* Though the continued chain of time has
' never once been broke, nor ever will, but uninter-
' rupted muſt keep on its courſe, till loſt in eternity,
' it ends where it firſt began: yet as Heaven can re-
' pair whatever evils time can bring upon us, we
' ought never to deſpair.'   But buſineſs requires our
attendance: buſineſs, the youth's beſt preſervative
from ill, as idleneſs his worſt of ſnares.   Will you go
with me?

Barn. I'll take a little time to reflect on what has
paſt, and follow you. [*Exit* Trueman.]   I might have
truſted Trueman, and engaged him to apply to my
uncle, to repair the wrong I have done my maſter;---
but what of Millwood? ' Muſt I expoſe her too?
' Ungenerous and baſe!   Then Heaven requires it not?
' But Heaven requires that I forſake her.   What!
' never to ſee her more?   Does Heaven require that?
                                                ' I hope

‘ I hope I may fee her, and Heaven not be offended.
‘ Prefumptuous hope! Dearly already have I proved
‘ my frailty. Should I once more tempt Heaven, I
‘ may be left to fail, never to rife again. Yet,’ fhall
I leave her, for ever leave her, and not let her know
the caufe? She who loves me with fuch a boundlefs
paffion! Can cruelty be duty? I judge of what fhe
then muft feel, by what I now endure. The love of
life, and fear of fhame, oppofed by inclination ftrong
as death or fhame, like wind and tide in raging conflict met, when neither can prevail, keep me in doubt.
How then can I determine?

Enter Thorowgood.

Thor. Without a caufe affigned, or notice given, to
abfent yourfelf laft night was a fault, young man, and
I came to chide you for it, but hope I am prevented.
That modeft blufh, the confufion fo vifible in your
face, fpeak grief and fhame. When we have offended
Heaven, it requires no more: and fhall man, who
needs himfelf to be forgiven, be harder to appeafe?
If my pardon, or love, be of moment to your peace,
look up fecure of both.

Barn. This goodnefs has o’ercome me. [*Afide.*] Oh,
Sir, you know not the nature and extent of my offence, and I fhould abufe your miftaken bounty to receive it. Though I had rather die than fpeak my
fhame, though racks could not have forced the guilty
fecret from my breaft, your kindnefs has.

Thor. Enough, enough; whate’er it be, this concern fhews you’re convinced, and I am fatisfied. How
painful is the fenfe of guilt to an ingenuous mind?
Some youthful folly, which it were prudent not to enquire into. ‘ When we confider the frail condition
‘ of humanity, it may raife our pity, not our won-
‘ der, that youth fhould go aftray; when reafon,
‘ weak at the beft, oppofed to inclination, fcarce
‘ formed, and wholly unaffifted by experience, faintly
‘ contends, or willingly becomes the flave of fenfe,
‘ The ftate of youth is much to be deplored; and the
‘ more fo, becaufe they fee it not; being then to dan-
‘ ger moft expofed, when they are leaft prepared for
‘ their defence.’ [*Afide.*
Barn.

Barn. It will be known, and you'll recall your pardon, and abhor me.

Thor. I never will. Yet be upon your guard in this gay, thoughtless season of your life; ' when the ' sense of pleasure's quick, and passion's high, the ' voluptuous appetites, raging and fierce, demand ' the strongest curb; take heed of a relapse:' when vice becomes habitual, the very power of leaving it is lost.

Barn. Hear me, on my knees, confess————

Thor. Not a syllable more upon this subject; it were not mercy, but cruelty, to hear what must give you such torment to reveal.

Barn. This generosity amazes and distracts me!

Thor. This remorse makes thee dearer to me, than if thou hadst never offended. Whatever is your fault, of this I am certain, 'twas harder for you to offend, than me to pardon.   [*Exit* Thorowgood.

Barn. Villain! villain! villain! basely to wrong so excellent a man. Should I again return to folly! -----Detested thought!-----But what of Millwood then? -------Why, I renounce her------I give her up------The struggle's over, and virtue has prevailed. Reason may convince, but gratitude compels. This unlooked-for generosity has saved me from destruction. [*Going.*

Enter a Footman.

Foot. Sir, two ladies, from your uncle in the country, desire to see you.

Barn. Who should they be? [*Aside.*] Tell them I'll wait upon 'em. [*Exit Footman.*] Methinks I dread to see 'em ———— Now, every thing alarms me! ———— Guilt, what a coward hast thou made me.   [*Exit.*

SCENE *another room in* Thorowgood's *house.*

Enter Millwood, Lucy, *and a Footman.*

Foot. Ladies, he'll wait upon you immediately.

Mill. 'Tis very well-----I thank you.   [*Exit. Foot.*

Enter Barnwell.

Barn. Confusion! Millwood!

Mill. That angry look tells me, that here I am an unwelcome guest: I feared as much: the unhappy are so every where.

Barn.

Barn. Will nothing but my utter ruin content you?

Mill. Unkind and cruel! Loft myfelf, your happinefs is now my only care.

Barn. How did you gain admiffion?

Mill. Saying we were defired by your uncle to vifit and deliver a meffage to you, we were received by the family without fufpicion, and with much refpect conducted here.

Barn. Why did you come at all?

Mill. I never fhall trouble you more. I'm come to take my leave for ever. Such is the malice of my fate: I go hopelefs, defpairing ever to return. This hour is all I have left; one fhort hour is all I have to beftow on love and you, for whom I thought the longeft life too fhort.

Barn. Then we are met to part for ever.

Mill. It muft be fo. Yet think not that time or abfence fhall ever put a period to my grief, or make me love you lefs. Though I muft leave you, yet condemn me not.

Barn. Condemn you! No; I approve your refolution, and rejoice to hear it: 'tis juft, 'tis neceffary;--- I have well weighed, and found it fo.

Lucy. I am afraid the young man has more fenfe than fhe thought he had.   [*Afide.*

Barn. Before you came, I had determined never to fee you more.

Mill. Confufion!   [*Afide.*

Lucy. Aye, we are all out; this is a turn fo unexpected, that I fhall make nothing of my part; they muft e'en play the fcene betwixt themfelves.   [*Afide.*

Mill. 'Twas fome relief to think, though abfent, you would love me ftill; but to find, ' though fortune ' had been indulgent, that you, more cruel and in- ' conftant,' *you* had refolvrd to caft me off----This, as I never could expect, I have not learnt to bear.

Barn. I am forry to hear you blame me in a refolution that fo well becomes us both.

Mill. I have reafon for what I do, but you have none.

Barn. Can we want a reafon for parting, who have fo many to wifh we never had met?

Mill.

Mill. Look on me, Barnwell. Am I deformed, or old, that fatiety fo foon fucceeds enjoyment? Nay, look again: am I not fhe whom yefterday you thought the faireft and the kindeft of her fex; whofe hand, trembling with extafy, you preffed and moulded thus, while on my eyes you gazed with fuch delight, as if defire increafed by being fed.

Barn. No more; let me repent my former follies, if poffible, without remembering what they were.

Mill. Why?

Barn. Such is my frailty, that 'tis dangerous.

Mill. Where is the danger, fince we are to part?

Barn. The thought of that already is too painful.

Mill. If it be painful to part, then I may hope, at leaft, you do not hate me?

Barn. No —— No —— I never faid I did —— Oh, my heart!

Mill. Perhaps you pity me?

Barn. I do------I do------Indeed I do.

Mill. You'll think upon me?

Barn. Doubt it not, while I can think at all.

Mill. You may judge an embrace at parting too great a favour, though it would be the laft. [*He draws back.*] A look fhall then fuffice-------Farewell-----for ever. [*Exeunt* Millwood *and* Lucy.

Barn. If to refolve to fuffer be to conquer-----I have conquered —— Painful victory!

Re-enter Millwood *and* Lucy.

Mill. One thing I had forgot----I never muft return to my own houfe again. This I thought proper to let you know, left your mind fhould change, and you fhould feek in vain to find me there. Forgive me this fecond intrufion; I only came to give you this caution, and that, perhaps, was needlefs.

Barn. I hope it was; yet it is kind, and I muft thank you for it.

Mill. My friend, your arm. [*To Lucy.*] Now, I am gone for ever. [*Going.*

Barn. One thing more-----Sure there's no danger in knowing where you go? If you think otherwife----

Mill. Alas! [*Weeping.*
Lucy.

Lucy. We are right, I find; that's my cue. [*Afide.*] Ah, dear Sir, fhe's going fhe knows not whither; but go fhe muft.

Barn. Humanity obliges me to wifh you well: why will you thus expofe yourfelf to needlefs troubles?

Lucy. Nay, there's no help for it: fhe muft quit the town immediately, and the kingdom as foon as poffible. It was no fmall matter, you may be fure, that could make her refolve to leave you.

Mill. No more, my friend; fince he for whofe dear fake alone I fuffer, and am content to fuffer, is kind, and pities me; where'er I wander, through wilds and defarts, benighted and forlorn, that thought fhall give me comfort.

Barn. For my fake!-----Oh, tell me how, which way I am fo curfed to bring fuch ruin on thee?

Mill. No matter: I am contented with my lot.

Barn. Leave me not in this uncertainty.

Mill. I have faid too much.

Barn. How, how am I the caufe of your undoing?

Mill. To know it will but increafe your troubles.

Barn. My troubles can't be greater than they are.

Lucy. Well, well, Sir, if fhe won't fatisfy you, I will.

Barn. I am bound to you beyond expreffion.

Mill. Remember, Sir, that I defired you not to hear it.

Barn. Begin, and eafe my racking expectation.

Lucy. Why, you muft know, my lady here was an only child, and her parents dying while fhe was young, left her and her fortune (no inconfiderable one, I affure you) to the care of a gentleman, who has a good eftate of his own.

Mill. Aye, aye, the barbarous man is rich enough; but what are riches, when compared to love!

Lucy. For a while he performed the office of a faithful guardian, fettled her in a houfe, hired her fervants -------But you have feen in what manner fhe has lived, fo I need fay no more of that.

Mill. How I fhall live hereafter, Heaven knows!

Lucy. All things went on as one could wifh; till fome time ago, his wife dying, he fell violently in

love

love with his charge, and would fain have married her. Now the man is neither old nor ugly, but a good perfonable fort of a man; but, I don't know how it was, fhe could never endure him. In fhort, her ill ufage fo provoked him, that he brought in an account of his executorfhip, wherein he makes her debtor to him————

Mill. A trifle in itfelf, but more than enough to ruin me, whom, by this unjuft account, he had ftripped of all before.

Lucy. Now, fhe having neither money nor friend, except me, who am as unfortunate as herfelf, he compelled her to pafs his account, and give bond for the fum he demanded; but ftill provided handfomely for her, and continued his courtfhip, till being informed by his fpies (truly I fufpect fome in her own family) that you were entertained in her houfe, and ftaid with her all night, he came this morning raving and ftorming like a mad-man; talks no more of marriage, (fo there's no hope of making up matters that way) but vows her ruin, unlefs fhe'll allow him the fame favour that he fuppofes fhe granted you.

Barn. Muft fhe be ruined, or find a refuge in another's arms?

Mill. He gave me but an hour to refolve in: that's happily fpent with you——And now I go————

Barn. To be expofed to all the rigours of the various feafons; the fummer's parching heat, and winter's cold; unhoufed, to wander friendlefs through the unhofpitable world, in mifery and want; attended with fear and danger, and purfued by malice and revenge. Would'ft thou endure all this for me, and can I do nothing, nothing to prevent it?

Lucy. 'Tis really a pity there can be no way found out.

Barn. Oh, where are all my refolutions now? ' Like ' early vapours, or the morning dew, chafed by the fun's warm beams, they're vanifhed and loft, as though ' they had never been.'

Lucy. Now, I advifed her, Sir, to comply with the geatleman; ' that would not only put an end to her trou-' bles, but make her fortune at once.'

Barn.

Barn. Tormenting fiend, away! I had rather perish, nay, see her perish, than have her saved by him. I will, myself, prevent her ruin, though with my own. A moment's patience; I'll return immediately.

[*Exit* Barnwell.

Lucy. 'Twas well you came, or, by what I can perceive, you had lost him.

Mill. That, I must confess, was a danger I did not foresee: I was only afraid he should have come without money. You know, a house of entertainment, like mine, is not kept without expence.

Lucy. That's very true; but then you should be reasonable in your demands; 'tis pity to discourage a young man.

Mill. Leave that to me.

Re-enter Barnwell *with a bag of money.*

Barn. What am I about to do?——Now you, who boast your reason all-sufficient, suppose yourselves in my condition, and determine for me; whether 'tis right to let her suffer for my faults, or, by this small addition to my guilt, prevent the ill effects of what is past?

Lucy. These young sinners think every thing in the ways of wickedness so strange!——But I could tell him that this is nothing but what's very common; for one vice as naturally begets another, as a father a son. But he'll find out that himself, if he lives long enough. [*Aside.*

Barn. Here, take this, and with it purchase your deliverance; return to your house, and live in peace and safety.

Mill. So, I may hope to see you there again?

Barn. Answer me not, but fly—lest, in the agonies of my remorse, I again take what is not mine to give, and abandon thee to want and misery.

Mill. Say but you'll come.

Barn. You are my fate—my Heaven, or my hell; only leave me now—dispose of me hereafter as you please. [*Exeunt* Millwood *and* Lucy.] What have I done? Were my resolutions founded on reason, and sincerely made? Why then has Heaven suffered me to fall? I fought not the occasion; and, if my heart deceives me not, compassion and generosity were my motives. ' Is virtue inconsistent with itself, or are ' vice and virtue only empty names; or do they de- ' pend on accidents, beyond our power to produce or ' to prevent, wherein we have no part, and yet must ' be determined by the event?' —— But why should I attempt to reason? All is confusion, horror, and re- morse. I find I am lost, cast down from all my late- erected hope, and plunged again in guilt, yet scarce know how or why—

Such undistinguish'd horrors make my brain,
Like hell, the seat of darkness, and of pain.

[*Exit.*

ACT III.   SCENE *a room in* Thorowgood's
house.

Thorowgood *and* Trueman *discovered (with account-
books) sitting at a table.*

' *Thor.* METHINKS I would not have you only
' learn the method of merchandize, and
' practise it hereafter merely as a means of getting
' wealth: it will be well worth your pains to study it
' as a science, to see how it is founded in reason, and
' the nature of things; how it promotes humanity, as
' it has opened, and yet kept up, an intercourse be-
' tween nations, far remote from one another in
' situation, customs, and religion; promoting arts,
' industry, peace, and plenty; by mutual benefits dif-
' fusing mutual love from pole to pole.

' *Tr.* Something of this I have considered, and
' hope, by your assistance, to extend my thoughts
' much farther.   I have observed those countries,
' where trade is promoted and encouraged, do not
' make discoveries to destroy, but to improve mankind
' by love and friendship; to tame the fierce, and po-
' lish the most savage; to teach them the advantage
' of honest traffic, by taking from them, with their
' own consent, their useless superfluities, and giving
' them, in return, what, from their ignorance in
' manual

' manual arts, their situation, or some other accident,
' they stand in need of.'

Thor. ' 'Tis justly observed: the populous East,
' luxuriant, abounds with glittering gems, bright
' pearls, aromatic spices, and health-restoring drugs:
' the late-found Western world's rich earth glows with
' unnumbered veins of gold and silver ore. On every
' climate, and on every country, Heaven has bestowed
' some good, peculiar to itself. It is the industrious
' merchant's business to collect the various blessings of
' each soil and climate, and, with the product of the
' whole, to enrich his native country.'————Well, I
have examined your accounts; they are not only just,
as I have always found them, but regularly kept, and
fairly entered. I commend your diligence. Method
in business is the surest guide: ' he who neglects it
' frequently stumbles, and always wanders perplexed,
' uncertain, and in danger.' Are Barnwell's accounts
ready for my inspection? He does not use to be the
last on those occasions.

Tr. Upon receiving your orders he retired, I
thought, in some confusion. If you please, I'll go
and hasten him. I hope he has not been guilty of any
neglect.

Thor. I'm now going to the Exchange: let him
know, at my return I expect to find him ready.

[*Exeunt.*

Enter Maria *with a book. Sits and reads.*

Ma. How forcible is truth? The weakest mind,
inspired with love of that, fixed and collected in itself,
with indifference beholds the united force of earth
and hell opposing. Such souls are raised above the
sense of pain, or so supported that they regard it not.
The martyr cheaply purchases his Heaven; small are
his sufferings, great is his reward. Not so the wretch
who combats love with duty; whose mind, weakened
and dissolved by the soft passion, feeble and hopeless,
opposes his own desires——What is an hour, a day,
a year of pain, to a whole life of tortures such as
these?

Enter

Enter Trueman.

Tr. Oh, Barnwell! Oh, my friend! how art thou fallen!

Ma. Ha! Barnwell! What of him? Speak, say, what of Barnwell?

Tr. 'Tis not to be concealed: I've news to tell of him that will afflict your generous father, yourself, and all who know him.

Ma. Defend us, Heaven!

Tr. I cannot speak it. See there.

[Trueman *gives a letter,* Maria *reads.*

" I know my absence will surprize my honoured master and yourself; and the more, when you shall understand, that the reason of my withdrawing is, my having embezzled part of the cash with which I was entrusted. After this, 'tis needless to inform you, that I intend never to return again. Though this might have been known by examining my accounts; yet to prevent that unnecessary trouble, and to cut off all fruitless expectations of my return, I have left this from the lost   GEORGE BARNWELL."

Tr. Lost indeed! Yet how he should be guilty of what he here charges himself withal, raises my wonder equal to my grief. Never had youth a higher sense of virtue. Justly he thought, and as he thought he practised; never was life more regular than his. An understanding uncommon at his years; an open, generous, manliness of temper; his manners easy, unaffected, and engaging.

Ma. This, and much more, you might have said with truth. He was the delight of every eye, and joy of every heart that knew him.

Tr. Since such he was, and was my friend, can I support his loss? See, the fairest, happiest maid this wealthy city boasts, kindly condescends to weep for thy unhappy fate, poor, ruined Barnwell!

Ma. Trueman, do you think a soul so delicate as his, so sensible of shame, can e'er submit to live a slave to vice?

Tr. Never, never. So well I know him, I'm sure this act of his, so contrary to his nature, must have been caused by some unavoidable necessity.

Ma.

Ma. Is there no means yet to preserve him?

Tr. Oh, that there were! But few men recover their reputation lost, a merchant never. Nor would he, I fear, though I should find him, ever be brought to look his injured master in the face.

Ma. I fear as much, and therefore would never have my father know it.

Tr. That's impossible.

Ma. What's the sum?

Tr. 'Tis considerable. I've marked it here, to shew it, with the letter, to your father, at his return.

Ma. If I should supply the money, could you so dispose of that and the account, as to conceal this unhappy mismanagement from my father?

Tr. Nothing more easy. But can you intend it? Will you save a helpless wretch from ruin? Oh, 'twere an act worthy such exalted virtue as Maria's! Sure Heaven, in mercy to my friend, inspired the generous thought.

Ma. Doubt not but I would purchase so great a happiness at a much dearer price. But how shall he be found?

Tr. Trust to my diligence for that. In the mean time I'll conceal his absence from your father, or find such excuses for it, that the real cause shall never be suspected.

Ma. In attempting to save from shame, one whom we hope may yet return to virtue, to Heaven, and you, the only witnesses of this action, I appeal, whether I do any thing misbecoming my sex and character.

Tr. Earth must approve the deed, and Heaven, I doubt not, will reward it.

Ma. If Heaven succeeds it I am well rewarded. A virgin's fame is sullied by suspicion's lightest breath; and, therefore, as this must be a secret from my father and the world, for Barnwell's sake, for mine, let it be so to him. [*Exeunt.*

SCENE *a room in* Millwood's *house.*

Enter Lucy *and* Blunt.

Lucy. Well, what do you think of Millwood's conduct now?

Blunt.

Blunt. I own it is furprifing. I don't know which
to admire moft, her feigned, or his real paffion; though
I have fometimes been afraid that her avarice would
difcover her. But his youth and want of experience
make it the eafier to impofe on him.

Lucy. No, it is his love. To do him juftice, not-
withftanding his youth, he don't want underftanding.
But you men are much eafier impofed on in thefe affairs, than your vanity will allow you to believe. Let
me fee the wifeft of you all as much in love with me
as Barnwell is with Millwood, and I'll engage to make
as great a fool of him.

Blunt. And, all circumftances confidered, to make
as much money of him too.

Lucy. I can't anfwer for that. Her artifice in making him rob his mafter at firft, and the various ftrata-
gems by which fhe has obliged him to continue that
courfe, aftonifh even me, who know her fo well.

Blunt. But then you are to confider that the money
was his mafter's.

Lucy. There was the difficulty of it. Had it been
his own, it had been nothing. Were the world his,
fhe might have it for a fmile. But thofe golden days
are gone; he's ruined, and Millwood's hopes of farther profits there are at an end.

Blunt. That's no more than we all expected.

Lucy. Being called by his mafter to make up his accounts, he was forced to quit his houfe and fervice, and
wifely flies to Millwood for relief and entertainment.

Blunt. I have not heard of this before. How did
fhe receive him?

Lucy. As you would expect. She wondered what
he meant, was aftonifhed at his impudence, and, with
an air of modefty peculiar to herfelf, fwore fo heartily
that fhe never faw him before, that fhe put me out of
countenance.

Blunt. That's much, indeed! But how did Barnwell
behave?

Lucy. He grieved; and, at length, enraged at this
barbarous treatment, was preparing to be gone; and
making towards the door, fhewed a fum of money,

which

which he had brought from his master's, the last he is ever likely to have from thence.

Blunt. But then, Millwood——

Lucy. Aye, she, with her usual address, returned to her old arts of lying, swearing, and dissembling; hung on his neck, wept, and swore 'twas meant in jest. The amorous youth melted into tears, threw the money into her lap, and swore he had rather die than think her false.

Blunt. Strange infatuation!

Lucy. But what ensued was stranger still. As doubts and fears, followed by reconcilement, ever increase love, where the passion is sincere, so in him it caused so wild a transport of excessive fondness, such joy, such grief, such pleasure, and such anguish, that nature seemed sinking with the weight, and his charmed soul disposed to quit his breast for her's. Just then, when every passion with lawless anarchy prevailed, and reason was in the raging tempest lost, the cruel, artful Millwood prevailed upon the wretched youth to promise—what I tremble but to think on.

Blunt. I am amazed! What can it be?

Lucy. You will be more so to hear---it is to attempt the life of his nearest relation, and best benefactor.

Blunt. His uncle! whom we have often heard him speak of, as a gentleman of a large estate, and fair character, in the country where he lives.

Lucy. The same. She was no sooner possessed of the last dear purchase of his ruin, but her avarice, infatiate as the grave, demanded this horrid sacrifice. Barnwell's near relation, ' and unsuspected virtue, ' must give too easy means to seize this good man's ' treasure;' whose blood must seal the dreadful secret, and prevent the terrors of her guilty fears.

Blunt. Is it possible she could persuade him to do an act like that? He is by nature honest, grateful, compassionate, and generous; ' and though his love, and ' her artful persuasions, have wrought him to practise ' what he most abhors, yet we all can witness for him, ' with what reluctance he has still complied: so many ' tears he shed o'er each offence, as might, if possible, ' sanctify theft, and make a merit of a crime.'

Lucy.

Lucy. 'Tis true, at the raming of the murder of his uncle he started into rage, and, breaking from her arms, (where she till then had held him with well-diffembled love, and falfe endearments) called her cruel, monfter, devil, and told her fhe was born for his deftruction. She thought it not for her purpofe to meet his rage with her rage, but affected a moft paffionate fit of grief, railed at her fate, and curfed her wayward ftars, that ftill her wants fhould force her to prefs him to act fuch deeds, as fhe muft needs abhor as well as he. She told him neceffity had no law, and love no bounds; that therefore he never truly loved, but meant, in her neceffity, to forfake her. Then fhe kneeled, and fwore, that fince by his refufal he had given her caufe to doubt his love, fhe never would fee him more, unlefs, to prove it true, he robbed his uncle to fupply her wants, and murdered him to keep it from difcovery.

Blunt. I am aftonifhed! What faid he?

Lucy. Speechlefs he ftood; but in his face you might have read, that various paffions tore his very foul. Oft he in anguifh threw his eyes towards Heaven, ' and " then as often bent their beams on her;' then wept and groaned, and beat his troubled breaft: at length, with horror not to be expreffed, he cried, 'Thou curfed fair, have I not given dreadful proofs of love? What drew me from my youthful innocence, and ftained my then unfpotted foul, but love? What caufed me to rob my worthy, gentle mafter, but curfed love? What makes me now a fugitive from his fervice, loathed by myfelf, and fcorned by all the world, but love? What fills my eyes with tears, my foul with torture never felt on this fide death before? Why love! love! love! And why, above all, do I refolve (for, tearing his hair, he cried, I do refolve) to kill my uncle?

Blunt. Was fhe not moved? It makes me weep to hear the fad relation.

Lucy. Yes——with joy, that fhe had gain'd her point. She gave him no time to cool, but urged him to attempt it inftantly. He's now gone. If he performs it, and efcapes, there's more money for her; if not, he'll ne'er return, and then fhe's fairly rid of him,

Blunt.

Blunt- 'Tis time the world were rid of such a monster.

Lucy. If we don't use our endeavours to prevent the murder, we are as bad as she.

Blunt. I'm afraid it is too late.

Lucy. Perhaps not. Her barbarity to Barnwell makes me hate her. We have run too great a length with her already. I did not think her or myself so wicked as I find, upon reflection, we are.

Blunt. 'Tis true, we have all been too much so. But there is something so horrid in murder, that all other crimes seem nothing, when compared to that; I would not be involved in the guilt of it for all the world.

Lucy. Nor I, Heaven knows. Therefore let us clear ourselves, by doing all that's in our power to prevent it. I have just thought of a way, that to me seems probable. Will you join with me to detect this cursed design?

Blunt. With all my heart. He who knows of a murder intended to be committed, and does not discover it, in the eye of the law and reason, is a murderer.

Lucy. Let us lose no time. I'll acquaint you with the particulars as we go.   [*Exeunt.*

SCENE *a walk, at some distance from a country seat.*

Enter Barnwell.

Barn. A dismal gloom obscures the face of day. Either the sun has slipped behind a cloud, or journies down the west of Heaven with more than common speed, to avoid the sight of what I am doomed to act. Since I set forth on this accursed design, where'er I tread, methinks the solid earth trembles beneath my feet. " *Murder my uncle!*" ' Yonder limpid stream, ' whose hoary fall has made a natural cascade, as I ' passed by, in doleful accents seemed to murmur—— ' murder! The earth, the air, and water seemed con- ' cerned. But that's not strange: the world is punished, ' and nature feels a shock, when Providence permits a ' good man's fall. Just Heaven! then what should ' I feel for him that was my father's only brother,

‘ and, since his death, has been to me a father; that
‘ took me up an infant and an orphan, reared me with
‘ tenderest care, and still indulged me with most
‘ paternal fondness!   Yet here I stand his destined mur-
‘ derer.’——I stiffen with horror at my own impiety—
’Tis yet unperformed——What if I quit my bloody
purpose, and fly the place? [*Going, then stops.*]——But
whither, Oh, whither shall I fly?   My master’s once
friendly doors are ever shut against me, and without
money Millwood will never see me more; and she has
got such firm possession of my heart, and governs there
with such despotic sway, that life is not to be endured
without her.   Aye, there’s the cause of all my sin and·
sorrow: ’tis more than love; it is the fever of the soul,
and madness of desire.   In vain does nature, reason,
conscience, all oppose it; the impetuous passion bears
down all before it, and drives me on to lust, to theft,
and murder.   Oh, conscience, feeble guide to virtue,
thou only shewest us when we go astray, but wantest
power to stop us in our course!—Ha! in yonder shady
walk I see my uncle———He’s alone——Now for my
disguise. [*Plucks out a vizor.*] —— This is his hour of
private meditation.   Thus daily he prepares his soul
for Heaven, while I———But what have I to do with
Heaven?—Ha! no struggles, conscience——

Hence, hence remorse, and ev’ry thought that’s good;
The storm that lust began must end in blood.

    [*Puts on the vizor, draws a pistol, and exit.*

    S C E N E *a close walk, in a wood.*

Enter Uncle.

Un. If I were superstitious, I should fear some danger lurked unseen, or death were nigh.   A heavy melancholy clouds my spirits.   My imagination is filled
with ghastly forms of dreary graves, and bodies changed
by death; when the pale length’n’d visage attracts each
weeping eye, and fills the musing soul at once with
grief and horror, pity and aversion.   I will indulge
the thought.   The wise man prepares himself for
death by making it familiar to his mind.   When
               strong

GEORGE BARNWELL.

M.r BRERETON in the Character of BARNWELL.

—————————— Let Heaven from its high
Throne, in justice or in Mercy now look down,
on that dear Murthered Saint, & me the Murtherer:

Act 3 Sc last.

Published Dec.r 1776 by I. Lowndes & Partners.

ſtrong reflections hold the mirror near, and the living in the dead behold their future ſelf: how does each inordinate paſſion and deſire ceaſe, or ſicken at the view! The mind ſcarce moves; the blood curdling and chilled, creeps ſlowly through the veins; fixed, ſtill, and motionleſs we ſtand, ſo like the ſolemn ob-ject of our thoughts. we are almoſt at preſent what we muſt be hereafter; till curioſity awakes the ſoul, and ſets it on enquiry.

Enter George Barnwell, *at a diſtance.*

Oh, death! thou ſtrange, myſterious power, ſeen every day, yet never underſtood, but by the incommunica-tive dead, what art thou? The extenſive mind of man, that with a thought circles the earth's vaſt globe, ſinks to the centre, or aſcends above the ſtars; that worlds exotic finds, or thinks it finds, thy thick clouds attempts to paſs in vain; loſt and bewildered in the horrid gloom, defeated, ſhe returns more doubtful than be-fore, of nothing certain but of labour loſt.

[*During this ſpeech* Barnwell *ſometimes preſents the piſtol, and draws it back again.*]

Barn. Oh, 'tis impoſſible! [*Throwing down the piſtol.*
[*Uncle ſtarts, and attempts to draw his ſword.*]

Uncle. A man ſo near me! armed and maſqued——

Barn. Nay, then there's no retreat.

[*Plucks a poignard from his boſom, and ſtabs him.*

Uncle. Oh, I am ſlain! All gracious Heaven, regard the prayer of thy dying ſervant: bleſs, with the choiceſt bleſſings, my deareſt nephew; forgive my murderer, and take my fleeting ſoul to endleſs mercy!

[Barnwell *throws off his maſk, runs to him, and kneeling by him, raiſes and chafes him.*

Barn. Expiring faint! Oh, murdered, martyred un-cle! lift up your dying eyes, and view your nephew in your murderer.————Oh, do not look ſo tenderly upon me——Let indignation lighten from your eyes, and blaſt me ere you die.——By Heaven, he weeps, in pity of my woes. ———Tears, tears for blood.——— The murdered, in the agonies of death, weeps for his murderer ———Oh, ſpeak your pious purpoſe; pro-nounce my pardon then, and take me with you ———

He would, but cannot.-----Oh, why with such fond af-
fection do you prefs my murdering hand?-----[*Uncle
sighs and dies.*] ‘ What, will you kifs me?’ Life,
that hovered on his lips but till he had fealed my pardon, in that figh expired! – He’s gone for ever---‘ and,
‘ Oh! I follow----[*Swoons away upon his uncle's dead
body.*]’ Do I ftill breathe, and taint with my infectious
breath the wholefome air? Let Heaven from its high
throne, in juftice or in mercy, now look down on that
dear murdered faint, and me the murderer, and if his
vengeance fpares, let pity ftrike, and end my wretched
being.———Murder the worft of crimes, and parricide
the worft of murders, and this the worft of parricides.
‘ Cain, who ftands on record from the birth of time,
‘ and muft to its laft final period, as accurfed, flew a
‘ brother favoured above him: detefted Nero, by an-
‘ other's hand, difpatched a mother that he feared and
.‘ hated: but I, with my own hand, have murdered a
‘ brother, mother, father, and a friend, moft loving
‘ and beloved.—This execrable act of mine is without
‘ a parallel.—Oh, may it ever ftand alone, the laft of
‘ murders as it is the worft!
    ‘ The rich man thus, in torment and defpair,
    ‘ Preferr’d his vain, his charitable prayer.
    ‘ The fool, his own foul loft, would fain be wife
    ‘ For others good; but Heaven his fuit denies.
    ‘ By laws and means well-known we ftand or fall,
    ‘ And one eternal rule remains for all.’
      “ *Oh, may it ever ftand alone accurft,*
      “ *The laft of murders as it is the worft.*”

ACT IV. SCENE *a room in* Thorowgood's *houfe.*

Enter Maria, *meeting* Trueman.

‘ *Maria.* HOW falfely do they judge, who cenfure
      ‘ or applaud, as we’re afflicted or re-
‘ warded here? I know I am unhappy; yet cannot
‘ charge myfelf with any crime, more than the com-
‘ mon frailties of our kind, that fhould provoke juft
‘ Heaven to mark me out for fufferings fo uncommon
‘ and fevere. Falfely to accufe ourfelves, Heaven muft
                  ‘ abhor.

' abhor. Then it is juſt and right that innocence
' ſhould ſuffer; for Heaven muſt be juſt in all its ways.
' Perhaps by that we are kept from moral evils much
' worſe than-penal, or more improved in virtue. Or
' may not the leſſer ills that we ſuſtain, be made the
' means of greater good to others? Might all the joy-
' leſs days and ſleepleſs nights that I have paſſed, but
' purchaſe peace for thee,

    ' Thou dear, dear cauſe of all my grief and pain,

     ' Small were the loſs, and infinite the gain ;

     ' Though to the grave in ſecret love I pine,

     ' So life, and fame, and happineſs were thine.'

What news of Barnwell?

Tr. None; I have ſought him with the greateſt diligence, but all in vain.

Ma. Does my father yet ſuſpect the cauſe of his
abſence?

Tr. All appeared ſo juſt and fair to him, it is not
poſſible he ever ſhould. But his abſence will no longer be concealed. Your father is wiſe; and though
he ſeems to hearken to the friendly excuſes I would
make for Barnwell, yet I am afraid he regards 'em
only as ſuch, without ſuffering them to influence his
judgment.

' *Ma.* How does the unhappy youth defeat all our
' deſigns to ſerve him! yet I can never repent what
' we have done. Should he return, 'twill make his
' reconciliation with my father eaſier, and preſerve
' him from future reproach of a malicious and unfor-
' giving world.'

     Enter Thorowgood *and* Lucy.

Thor. This woman here has given me a ſad, and,
bating ſome circumſtances, too probable an account of
Barnwell's defection.

Lucy. I am ſorry, Sir, that my frank confeſſion of
my former unhappy courſe of life ſhould cauſe you to
ſuſpect my truth on this occaſion.

Thor. It is not that ; your confeſſion has in it all
the appearance of truth. Among many other particulars, ſhe informs me, that Barnwell has been influenced to break his truſt, and wrong me, at ſeveral
times, of conſiderable ſums of money. Now, as I
know

know this to be falfe, I would fain doubt the whole of her relation, too dreadful to be willingly believed.

Ma. Sir, your pardon: I find myfelf on a fudden fo indifpofed, that I muft retire. ' Providence oppofes ' all attempts to fave him.' Poor, ruined Barnwell! Wretched, loft Maria!   [*Afide. Exit* Maria.

Thor. How am I diftreffed on every fide! Pity for that unhappy youth, fear for the life of a much valuable friend----and then my child----the only joy and hope of my declining life!------Her melancholy increafes hourly, and gives me painful apprehenfions of her lofs------Oh, Trueman, this perfon informs me that your friend, at the inftigation of an impious woman, is gone to rob and murder his venerable uncle.

Tr. Oh, execrable deed! I'm biafted with the horror of the thought!

Lucy. This delay may ruin all.

Thor. What to do, or think, I know not. That he ever wronged me, I know is falfe: the reft may be fo too; there's all my hope.

Tr. Truft not to that; rather fuppofe all true, than lofe a moment's time. Even now the horrid deed may be doing---dreadful imagination!----or it may be done, and we be vainly debating on the means to prevent what is already paft.

Thor. This earneftnefs convinces me that he knows more than he has yet difcovered. What, ho! without there, who waits?

Enter a Servant.

Order the groom to faddle the fwifteft horfe, and prepare to fet out with fpeed; an affair of life and death demands his diligence. [*Exit Servant.*] For you, whofe behaviour on this occafion I have no time to commend as it deferves, I muft engage your further affiftance. Return, and obferve this Millwood till I come. I have your directions, and will follow you as foon as poffible. [*Exit* Lucy.] Trueman, you, I am fure, will not be idle on this occafion.   [*Exit* Thorowgood,

Tr. He only who is a friend, can judge of my diftrefs.   [*Exit.*

SCENE

SCENE Millwood's *house*.

Enter Millwood.

Mill. I wish I knew the event of his design. The attempt without success would ruin him.———Well, what have I to apprehend from that? I fear too much. The mischief being only intended, his friends, through pity of his youth, turn all their rage on me. I should have thought of that before. Suppose the deed done; then, and then only, I shall be secure— Or what if he returns without attempting it at all ——— [*Enter* Barnwell *bloody*.] But he is here, and I have done him wrong. His bloody hands shew he has done the deed, but shew he wants the prudence to conceal it.

Barn. Where shall I hide me? Whither shall I fly to avoid the swift unerring hand of justice?

Mill. Dismiss your fears: though thousands had pursued you to the door, yet being entered here, you are as safe as innocence. I have a cavern, by art so cunningly contrived, that the piercing eyes of jealousy and revenge may search in vain, nor find the entrance to the safe retreat. There will I hide you, if any danger's near.

Barn. Oh, hide me ——— from myself, if it be possible; for while I bear my conscience in my bosom, though I were hid where man's eye never saw, nor light ere dawned, 'twere all in vain. For, Oh, that inmate, that impartial judge, will try, convict, and sentence me for murder, and execute me with never-ending torments. Behold these hands all crimsoned o'er with my dear uncle's blood. Here's a sight to make a statue start with horror, or turn a living man into a statue!

Mill. Ridiculous! Then it seems you are afraid of your own shadow, or, what is less than a shadow, your conscience.

Barn. Though to man unknown I did the accursed act, what can hide me from Heaven's all-seeing eye?

Mill. No more of this stuff! What advantage have
you

you made by his death; or what advantage may yet be made of it? Did you secure the keys of his treasure, which, no doubt, were about him? What gold, what jewels, or what else of value have you brought me?

Barn. Think you I added sacrilege to murder! Oh, had you seen him as his life flowed from him in a crimson flood, and heard him praying for me by the double name of nephew and of murderer; (alas, alas, he knew not then that his nephew was his murderer!) how would you have wished, as I did. though you had a thousand years of life to come, to have given them all to have lengthened his one hour. But being dead, I fled the sight of what my hands had done; nor could I, to have gained the empire of the world, have violated, by theft, his sacred corpse.

Mill. Whining, preposterous, canting villain! to murder your uncle, rob him of life, nature's first, last, dear prerogative, after which there's no injury, then fear to take what he no longer wanted, and bring to me your penury and guilt. Do you think I'll hazard my reputation, nay, my life, to entertain you?

Barn. Oh, Millwood!——this from thee?——— But I have done—If you hate me, if you wish me dead, then are you happy; for, Oh, 'tis sure my grief will quickly end me.

Mill. In this madness he will discover all, and involve me in his ruin. We are on a precipice, from whence there's no retreat for both. Then to preserve myself———[*Pauses.*]———There is no other way. 'Tis dreadful; but reflection comes too late when danger's pressing, and there's no room for choice. It must be done. [*Aside. Rings a bell; enter a Servant.*]— Fetch me an officer, and seize this villain, He has confess'd himself a murderer. Should I let him escape, I might justly be thought as bad as he.

[*Exit Servant.*

Barn. Oh, Millwood! sure you do not, you cannot mean it. Stop the messenger; upon my knees, I beg you'd call him back. 'Tis fit I die, indeed,
but

but not by you.   I will this inftant throw myfelf into the hands of juftice, indeed I will; for death is all
I wifh.   But thy ingratitude fo tears my wounded
foul, 'tis worfe ten thoufand times than death with
torture.

Mill. Call it what you will: I am willing to live,
and live fecure, which nothing but your death can
warrant.

Barn. If there be a pitch of wickednefs that fets
the author beyond the reach of vengeance, you muft
be fecure.   But what remains for me, but a difmal
dungeon, hard galling fetters, an awful trial, and
an ignominious death, juftly to fall unpitied and ab-
horred?   ' After death to be fufpended between Hea-
' ven and earth, a dreadful fpectacle, the warning
''and horror of a gaping crowd!'   This I could bear,
nay, wifh not to avoid, had it but come from any
hand but thine.

Enter Blunt, *Officer, and Attendants.*

Mill. Heaven defend me!   Conceal a murderer!
Here, Sir, take this youth into your cuftody, I accufe
him of murder, and will appear to make good my
charge,   *[They feize him.*

Barn. To whom, of what, or how fhall I complain?
I'll not accufe her.   The hand of Heaven is in it, and
this the punifhment of luft and parricide.   ' Yet Hea-
' ven, that juftly cuts me off, ftill fuffers her to live;
' perhaps to punifh others.   Tremendous mercy!   So
' fiends are curfed with immortality, to be the execu-
' tioners of Heaven.'

Be warn'd ye youths, who fee my fad defpair;
Avoid lewd women, falfe as they are fair.
' By reafon guided, honeft joys purfue;   ⎫
' The fair to honour and to virtue true,   ⎬
' Juft to herfelf, will ne'er be falfe to you.'   ⎭
By my example learn to fhun my fate,
(How wretched is the man who's wife too late!)
Ere innocence, and fame, and life be loft,
Here purchafe wifdom cheaply at my coft.

[Exeunt Barnwell, *Officer, and Attendants.*

Mill. Where's Lucy?   Why is fhe abfent at fuch a
time?

Blunt.

Blunt. Would I had been fo too! Lucy will foon be here; and I hope to thy confufion, thou devil!

Mill. Infolent! This to me!

Blunt. The worft that we know of the devil is, that he firft feduces to fin, and then betrays to punifhment.

[*Exit* Blunt.

Mill. They difapprove of my conduct then, ' and ' mean to take this opportunity to fet up for them- ' felves.' My ruin is refolved. I fee my danger, but fcorn both it and them. I was not born to fall by fuch weak inftruments.

[*Going.*

Enter Thorowgood.

Thor. Where is the fcandal of her own fex, and curfe of ours?

Mill. What means this infolence? Whom do you feek for?

Thor. Millwood.

Mill. Well, you have found her then. I am Millwood.

Thor. Then you are the moft impious wretch that e'er the fun beheld.

Mill. From your appearance I fhould have expected wifdom and moderation; but your manners belie your afpect. What is your bufinefs here? I know you not.

Thor. Hereafter you may know me better. I am Barnwell's mafter.

Mill. Then you are mafter to a villain; which, I think, is not much to your credit.

Thor. Had he been as much above thy arts, as my credit is fuperior to thy malice, I need not have blufh-ed to own him.

Mill. My arts! I don't underftand you, Sir. If he has done amifs, what's that to me? Was he my fer-vant, or yours? You fhould have taught him better.

Thor. Why fhould I wonder to find fuch uncommon impudence in one arrived to fuch a heighth of wicked-nefs? ' When innocence is banifh'd, modefty foon ' follows.' Know, forcerefs, I'm not ignorant of any of the arts by which you firft deceived the unwary youth. I know how, ftep by ftep, you've led him on, reluctant and unwilling, from crime to crime, to this laft horrid act, which you contrived, and by your curfed wiles even forced him to commit.

Mill.

Mill. Ha! Lucy has got the advantage, and accused me first. Unless I can turn the accusation, and fix it upon her and Blunt, I am lost.   [*Aside.*

Thor. Had I known your cruel design sooner, it had been prevented. To see you punished, as the law directs, is all that now remains. Poor satisfaction! For he, innocent as he is, compared to you, must suffer too. ' But Heaven, who knows our frame, and graciously ' distinguishes between frailty and presumption, will ' make a difference, though man cannot, who sees ' not the heart, but only judges by the outward ac- ' tion.'

Mill. I find, Sir, we are both unhappy in our servants. I was surprized at such ill treatment without cause, from a gentleman of your appearance, and therefore too hastily returned it, for which I ask your pardon. I now perceive you have been so far imposed on, as to think me engaged in a former correspondence with your servant, and some way or other accessary to his undoing.

Thor. I charge you as the cause, the sole cause of all his guilt, and all his suffering, of all he now endures, and must endure, till a violent and shameful death shall put a dreadful period to his life and miseries together.

Mill. 'Tis very strange? But who's secure from scandal and detraction? So far from contributing to his ruin, I never spoke to him till since this fatal accident, which I lament as much as you. 'Tis true I have a servant, on whose account he hath of late frequented my house. If she has abused my good opinion of her, am I to blame? Has not Barnwell done the same by you?

Thor. I hear you. Pray go on.

Mill. I have been informed he had a violent passion for her, and she for him; but till now I always thought it innocent. I know her poor, and given to expensive pleasures. Now, who can tell but she may have influenced the amorous youth to commit this murder, to supply her extravagances.————It must be so. I now recollect a thousand circumstances that confirm it. I'll have her, and a man-servant
whom

whom I fufpect as an accomplice, fecured immediately. I hope, Sir, you will lay afide your ill-grounded fufpicions of me, and join to punifh the real contrivers of this bloody deed, [*Offers to go.*

Thor. Madam, you pafs not this way. I fee your defign, but fhall protect them from your malice.

Mill. I hope you will not ufe your influence, and the credit of your name, to fcreen fuch guilty wretches. Confider, Sir, the wickednefs of perfuading a thoughtlefs youth to fuch a crime!

Thor. I do ———and of betraying him when it was done.

Mill. That which you call betraying him may convince you of my innocence. She who loves him, though fhe contrived the murder, would never have delivered him into the hands of juftice, as I, ftruck with horror at his crimes, have done.

Thor. How fhould an unexperienced youth efcape her fnares? ' The powerful magic of her wit and ' form might betray the wifeft to fimple dotage, and ' fire the blood that age hal froze long fince.' Even I, that with juft prejudice came prepared, had by her artful ftory been deceived, but that my ftrong conviction of her guilt makes even a doubt impoffible. [*Afide.*
Thofe whom fubtilly you would accufe, you know are your accufers; and, which proves unanfwerably their innocence, and your guilt, they accufed you before the deed was done, and did all that was in their power to prevent it.

Mill. Sir, you are very hard to be convinced; but I have a proof, which, when produced, will filence all objection. [*Exit* Millwood.

Enter Lucy, Trueman, Blunt, *Officers, &c.*

Lucy. Gentlemen, pray place yourfelves, fome on one fide of that door, and fome on the other; watch her entrance, and act as your prudence fhall direct you. This way, [*To* Thorowgood.] and note her behaviour. I have obferved her; fhe's driven to the laft extremity, and is forming fome defperate refolution. I guefs at her defign.

Re-enter Millwood *with a piftol,* Trueman *fecures her.*

                                        Tr.

Tr. Here thy power of doing mischief ends, deceitful, cruel, bloody woman!

Mill. Fool, hypocrite, villain, man! Thou can'st not call me that.

Tr. To call thee woman were to wrong thy sex, thou devil!

Mill. That imaginary being is an emblem of thy cursed sex collected. A mirror, wherein each particular man may see his own likenefs, and that of all mankind.

Thor. Think not by aggravating the faults of others to extenuate thy own, of which the abuse of such uncommon perfections of mind and body is not the least.

Mill. If such I had, well may I curse your barbarous sex, who robbed me of 'em ere I knew their worth; then left me, too late, to count their value by their lofs.— Another, and another spoiler came, and all my gain was poverty and reproach. My soul difdained, and yet difdains, dependance and contempt. Riches, no matter by what means obtained, I saw secured the worst of men from both; I found it therefore neceffary to be rich, and to that end I summoned all my arts. You call 'em wicked; be it so; they were such as my conversation with your sex had furnished me withal.

Thor. Sure none but the worst of men conversed with thee!

Mill. Men of all degrees, and all professions, I have known, yet found no difference, but in their several capacities; all were alike, wicked to the utmost of their power, ‘ In pride, contention, avarice, cruelty, and ‘ revenge, the reverend priesthood were my unerring ‘ guides. From fuburb magistrates, who live by ruined ‘ reputations, as the unhofpitable natives of Cornwall ‘ do by shipwreck, I learned, that to charge my inno- ‘ cent neighbours with my crimes, was to merit their ‘ protection: for, to screen the guilty, is the lefs scanda- ‘ lous, when many are fufpected; and detraction, like ‘ darkness and death, blackens all objects, and levels all ‘ diftinction. Such are your venal magistrates, who fa- ‘ vour none but such as by their office they are sworn ‘ to punish. With them, n t the guilty, is the worst ‘ of crimes; and large fees, privately paid, are every • needful virtue.

Thor.

' *Thor.* Your practice has sufficiently discovered your
' contempt of laws, both human and divine; no wonder
' then that you should have the officers of both.

' *Mill.*' I know you, and I hate you all. I expect no
mercy, and I ask for none. I follow my inclinations,
and that the best of you do every day. ' All actions
' seem alike natural and indifferent to man and beast,
' who devour, or are devoured, as they meet with
' others weaker or stronger than themselves.

' *Thor.* What pity it is a mind so comprehensive,
' daring, and inquisitive, should be a stranger to re-
' ligion's sweet and powerful charms!

' *Mill.* I am not fool enough to be an atheist, though
' I have known enough of men's hypocrisy to make a
' thousand simple women so. Whatever religion is in
' itself, as practised by mankind, it has caused the
' evils you say it was designed to cure. War, plague,
' and famine, have not destroyed so many of the hu-
' man race as this pretended piety has done; and with
' such barbarous cruelty, as if the only way to honour
' Heaven were to turn the present world into hell.

' *Thor.* Truth is truth, though from an enemy, and
' spoken in malice. You bloody, blind, and super-
' stitious bigots, how will you answer this?

' *Mill.*' What are your laws, of which you make your
boast, but the fool's wisdom, and the coward's valour,
the instrument and screen of all your villainies? By
them you punish in others what you act yourselves, or
would have acted, had you been in their circumstances.
The judge, who condemns the poor man for being a
thief, had been a thief himself had he been poor.—
Thus you go on deceiving and being deceived, harras-
sing, plaguing, and destroying one another. But women are your universal prey:

Women, by whom you are, the source of joy,
With cruel arts you labour to destroy:
A thousand ways our ruin you pursue,
Yet blame in us those arts first taught by you.
Oh, may from hence each violated maid,
By flattering, faithless, barb'rous man betray'd,
When robb'd of innocence and virgin fame,
From your destruction raise a nobler name,

To

To avenge their sex's wrongs devote their mind,
And future Millwoods prove to plague mankind.

                           [Exeunt.

'ACT V. SCENE *a room in a prison.*

'*Enter* Thorowgood, Blunt. *and* Lucy.

'*Thor.* I Have recommended to Barnwell a reverend
'   divine, whose judgment and integrity I am
' well acquainted with. Nor has Millwood been ne-
' glected; but she, unhappy woman, still obstinate,
' refuses his assistance.

' *Lucy.* This pious charity to the afflicted well be-
' comes your character: yet pardon me, Sir, if I won-
' der you were not at their trial.

' *Thor.* I knew it was impossible to save him; and I
' and my family bear so great a part in his distress,
' that to have been present would but have aggravated
' our sorrows, without relieving his.

' *Blunt.* It was mournful indeed. Barnwell's youth
' and modest deportment, as he passed, drew tears from
' every eye. When placed at the bar, and arraigned
' before the reverend judges, with many tears and inter-
' rupting sobs, he confessed and aggravated his of-
' fences, without accusing, or once reflecting on Mill-
' wood, the shameless author of his ruin. But she,
' dauntless and unconcerned, stood by his side, view-
' ing with visible pride and contempt the vast assembly,
' who all with sympathizing sorrow wept for the
' wretched youth. Millwood, when called upon to an-
' swer, loudly insisted upon her innocence, and made
' an artful and a bold defence; but finding all in vain,
' the impartial jury and the learned bench concurring
' to find her guilty, how did she curse herself, poor
' Barnwell, us, her judges, and all mankind. But
' what could that avail? She was condemned, and is
' this day to suffer with him.

' *Thor.* The time draws on. I am going to visit
' Barnwell, as you are Millwood.

' *Lucy.* We have not wronged her, yet I dread this
                         ' interview.

' interview. She's proud, impatient, wrathful, and
' unforgiving.   To be the branded inſtruments of
' veageance, to ſuffer in her ſhame, and ſympathize
' with her in all ſhe ſuffers, is the tribute we muſt pay
' for our former ill-ſpent lives, and long confederacy
' with her in wickedneſs.

' *Thor.* Happy for you it ended when it did. What
' you have done againſt Millwood I know proceeded
' from a juſt abhorrence of her crimes, free from in-
' tereſt, malice, or revenge. Proſelytes to virtue ſhould
' be encouraged: purſue your propoſed reformation,
' and know me hereafter for your friend.

' *Lucy.* This is a bleſſing as unhoped for as unme-
' rited. But Heaven, that ſnatched us from impend-
' ing ruin, ſure intends you as its inſtrument to ſecure
' us from apoſtacy.

' *Thor.* With gratitude to impute your deliverance
' to Heaven is juſt. Many, leſs virtuouſly diſpoſed than
' Barnwell was, have never fallen in the manner he has
' done. May not ſuch owe their ſafety rather to Pro-
' vidence than to themſelves? With pity and compaſ-
' ſion let us judge him. Great were his faults, but
' ſtrong was the temptation. Let his ruin teach us dif-
' fidence, humanity, and circumſpection; for if we,
' who wonder at his fate, had like him been tried,
' like him perhaps we had fallen.'   [*Exeunt.*

SCENE *a dungeon, a table, and a lamp.*   Barnwell
reading.

Enter Thorowgood, *at a diſtance.*

Thor. There ſee the bitter fruits of paſſion's deteſted
reign, and ſenſual appetite indulged; ſevere reflections,
penitence, and tears,

Barn. My honoured, injured maſter, whoſe goodneſs
has covered me a thouſand times with ſhame, forgive
this laſt unwilling diſreſpect. Indeed I ſaw you not.

Thor. 'Tis well: I hope you are better employed in
viewing of yourſelf; ' your journey's long, your time
' for preparation almoſt ſpent.' I ſent a reverend divine to teach you to improve it, and ſhould be glad
to hear of his ſucceſs.

Barn. The word of truth, which he recommended
for

for my conſtant companion in this my ſad retirement,
has at length removed the doubts I laboured under.
From thence I have learned the infinite extent of heavenly mercy; that my offences, though great, are not
unpardonable; and that 'tis not my intereſt only, but
my duty, to believe and to rejoice in my hope. So
ſhall Heaven receive the glory, and future penitents
the profit of my example.

Thor. Proceed.

Barn. 'Tis wonderful that words ſhould charm deſpair, ſpeak peace and pardon to a murderer's conſcience; but truth and mercy flow in every ſentence, attended with force and energy divine. How ſhall I
deſcribe my preſent ſtate of mind? I hope in doubt,
and trembling I rejoice; I feel my grief increaſe, even
as my fears give way. Joy and gratitude now ſupply
more tears than the horror and anguiſh of deſpair before.

Thor. Theſe are the genuine ſigns of true repentance;
the only preparatory, the certain way to everlaſting
peace. ‘ Oh, the joy it gives to ſee a ſoul formed and
‘ prepared for Heaven! For this the faithful miniſter
‘ devotes himſelf to meditation, abſtinence, and prayer,
‘ ſhunning the vain delights of ſenſual joys, and daily
‘ dies, that others may live for ever. For this he turns
‘ the ſacred volumes o'er, and ſpends his life in pain-
‘ ful ſearch of truth. The love of riches, and the luſt
‘ of power, he looks upon with juſt contempt and de-
‘ teſtation; he only counts for wealth the ſouls he wins,
‘ and his higheſt ambition is to ſerve mankind. If
‘ the reward of all his pains be to preſerve one ſoul
‘ from wandering, or turn one from the error of his
‘ ways, how does he then rejoice, and own his little
‘ labours overpaid!’

Barn. What do I owe for all your generous kindneſs?
But though I cannot, Heaven can and will reward you.

Thor. To ſee thee thus, is joy too great for words.
Farewell.—Heaven ſtrengthen thee!—Farewell.

Barn. Oh, Sir, there's ſomething I would ſay, if
my ſad ſwelling heart would give me leave.

Thor. Give it vent awhile, and try.

Barn. I had a friend—'tis true I am unworthy——

C   yet

yet methinks your generous example might perfuade——
Could I not fee him once, before I go from whence
there's no return?

Thor. He's coming, and as much thy friend as ever.
I will not anticipate his forrow; too foon he'll fee the
fad effects of this contagious ruin.—This torrent of
domeftic mifery bears too hard upon me. I muft retire, to indulge a weaknefs I find impoffible to overcome. [*Afide.*] Much loved——and much lamented
youth!———Farewell. ——— Heaven ftrengthen thee!
———Eternally farewell.

Barn. The beft of mafters, and of men——Farewell.
While I live let me not want your prayers.

Thor. Thou fhalt not. Thy peace being made with
Heaven, death is already vanquifhed. Bear a little
longer the pains that attend this tranfitory life, and
ceafe from pain for ever. [*Exit* Thorowgood.

Barn. Perhaps I fhall. I find a power within, that
bears my foul above the fears of death; and, fpite of
confcious fhame and guilt, gives me a tafte of pleafure
more than mortal.

Enter Trueman *and Keeper.*

Keep. Sir, there's the prifoner. [*Exit Keeper.*
Barn. Trueman!—My friend, whom I fo wifhed to
fee; yet, now he's here, I dare not look upon him.
[*Weeps.*

Tr. Oh, Barnwell! Barnwell!

Barn. Mercy! Mercy! gracious Heaven! For
death, but not for this, I was prepared.

Tr. What have I fuffered fince I faw thee laft!—
What pain has abfence given me!———But, Oh, to
fee thee thus!———

Barn. I know it is dreadful! I feel the anguifh of
thy generous foul:———But I was born to murder
all who love me. [*Both weep.*

Tr. I came not to reproach you; I thought to bring
you comfort; but I'm deceived, for I have none to give.
I came to fhare thy forrow, but cannot bear my own.

Barn. My fenfe of guilt indeed you cannot know;
'tis what the good and innocent, like you, can ne'er
conceive: but other griefs at prefent I have none, but
what

what I feel for you. In your sorrow I read you love me still; but yet, methinks, 'tis strange, when I consider what I am.

Tr. No more of that. I can remember nothing but thy virtues, thy honest, tender friendship, our former happy state, and present misery. Oh, had you trusted me, when first the fair seducer tempted you, all might have been prevented.

Barn. Alas, thou knowest not what a wretch I've been. Breach of friendship was my first, and least offence. So far was I left to goodness, so devoted to the author of my ruin, that had she insisted on my murdering thee,————I think————I should have done it.

Tr. Pr'ythee aggravate thy faults no more.

Barn. I think I should! Thus good and generous as you are, I should have murdered you!

Tr. We have not yet embraced, and may be interrupted. Come to my arms.

Barn. Never, never will I taste such joys on earth; never will I soothe my just remorse. Are those honest arms and faithful bosom fit to embrace and to support a murderer? These iron fetters only shall clasp, and flinty pavement bear me [*throwing himself on the ground*]; even these too good for such a bloody monster.

Tr. Shall fortune sever those whom friendship joined? Thy miseries cannot lay thee so low, but love will find thee. Here will we offer to stern calamity; this place the altar, and ourselves the sacrifice. Our mutual groans shall echo to each other through the dreary vault; our sighs shall number the moments as they pass; and mingling tears communicate such anguish, as words were never made to express.

Barn. Then be it so [*Rising*]. Since you propose an intercourse of woe, pour all your griefs into my breast, and in exchange take mine [*Embracing*]. Where's now the anguish that you promised? You've taken mine, and make me no return. Sure peace and comfort dwell within these arms, and sorrow can't approach me while I am here. ' This too is the work of Heaven; which ' having before spoke peace and pardon to me, now

C 2 ' sends

' sends thee to confirm it.' Oh, take, take some of
the joy that overflows my breast!

Tr. I do, do. Almighty power! how hast thou
made us capable to bear at once the extremes of pleasure and of pain!

Enter Keeper.

Keep. Sir.

Tr. I come. *[Exit Keeper.*

Barn. Must you leave me? Death would soon have
parted us for ever,

Tr. Oh, my Barnwell! there's yet another task behind. Again your heart must bleed for others woes.

Barn. To meet and part with you, I thought was
all I had to do on earth. What is there more for me to
do or suffer?

Tr. I dread to tell thee, yet it must be known!—
Maria——

Barn. Our master's fair and virtuous daughter?

Tr. The same.

Barn. No misfortune, I hope, has reached that
maid! Preserve her, Heaven, from every ill, to shew
mankind that goodness is your care!

Tr. Thy, thy misfortunes, my unhappy friend,
have reached her ear. Whatever you and I have felt,
and more, if more be possible, she feels for you.

Barn. ' I know he doth abhor a lie, and would not
' trifle with his dying friend.' This is indeed the bitterness of death. *[Aside.*

Tr. You must remember (for we all observed it) for
some time past, a heavy melancholy weighed her down.
Disconsolate she seemed, and pined and languished
from a cause unknown; till, hearing of your dreadful
fate, the long-stifled flame blazed out; ' she wept and
' wrung her hands, and tore her hair,' and in the
transport of her grief discovered her own lost state,
while she lamented yours.

Barn. ' Will all the pain I feel restore thy ease,
' lovely unhappy maid! [*Weeping*]' Why did you
not let me die, and never know it?

Tr. It was impossible. She makes no secret of her
passion

paſſion for you; ſhe is determined to ſee you ere you die, and waits for me to introduce her.

[Exit Trueman.

Barn. Vain, buſy thoughts, be ſtill! What avails it to think on what I might have been! I now am what I've made myſelf.

Enter Trueman *and* Maria.

Tr. Madam, reluctant I lead you to this diſmal ſcene. This is the ſeat of miſery and guilt. Here awful juſtice reſerves her public victims. This is the entrance to a ſhameful death.

Ma. To this ſad place then no improper gueſt, the abandoned loſt Maria brings deſpair, and ſees the ſubject and the cauſe of all this world of woe. Silent and motionleſs he ſtands, as if his ſoul had quitted her abode, and the lifeleſs form alone was left behind, ' yet that ' ſo perfect, that beauty and death, ever at enmity, ' now ſeem united there.'

Barn. ' I groan, but murmur not.' Juſt Heaven! I am your own; do with me what you pleaſe.

Ma. Why are your ſtreaming eyes ſtill fix'd below, as though thou'dſt give the greedy earth thy ſorrows, and rob me of my due? Were happineſs within your power, you ſhould beſtow it where you pleaſed; but in your miſery I muſt and will partake.

Barn. Oh, ſay not ſo, but fly, abhor, and leave me to my fate. Conſider what you are, ' how vaſt your ' fortune, and how bright your fame. Have pity on ' your youth, your beauty, and unequalled virtue; for ' which ſo many noble peers have ſigh'd in vain.' Bleſs with your charms ſome honourable lord. ' Adorn with ' your beauty, and by your example improve the Engliſh ' court that juſtly claims ſuch merit:' ſo ſhall I quickly be to you———as though I had never been.

Ma. When I forget you, I muſt be ſo indeed. Reaſon, choice, virtue all forbid it. Let women, like Millwood, if there are more ſuch women, ſmile in proſperity, and in adverſity forſake. Be it the pride of virtue to repair, or to partake, the ruin ſuch have made.

C 3 *Tr.*

Tr. Lovely, illfated maid! ' Was there ever such
' generous diftrefs before! How muft this pierce his
' grateful heart, and aggravate his woes.

Barn. Ere I knew guilt or fhame, when fortune
fmiled, and when my youthful hopes were at the higheft ;
if then to have raifed my thoughts to you, had been
prefumption in me never to have been pardoned, think
how much beneath yourfelf you condefcend to regard
me now.

' *Ma.* Let her blufh, who, proffering love, invades
' the freedom of your fex's choice, and meanly fues
' in hopes of a return. Your inevitable fate hath ren-
' dered hope impoffible as vain. 'Then why fhould I
' fear to avow a paffion fo juft and fo difinterefted?

' *Tr.* If any fhould take occafion from Millwood's
' crimes to libel the beft and faireft part of the crea-
' tion, here let them fee their error. The moft diftant
' hopes of fuch a tender paffion from fo bright a maid,
' might add to the happinefs of the moft happy, and
' make the greateft proud ; yet here 'tis lavifhed in vain.
' Though by the rich prefent the generous donor is un-
' done, he on whom it is beftowed receives no benefit.

' *Barn.* So the aromatic fpices of the eaft, which
' all the living covet and efteem, are with unavailing
' kindnefs wafted on the dead.'

Ma. Yes, fruitlefs is my love, and unavailing all
my fighs and tears. Can they fave thee from approaching death?————from fuch a death? ———— " Oh for-
" row infupportable!"————' Oh, terrible idea!————
' What is her mifery and diftrefs, who fees the firft, laft
' object of her love, for whom alone fhe'd live, for
' whom fhe'd die a thoufand thoufand deaths, if it
' were poffible, expiring in her arms! Yet fhe is
' happy, when compared to me. Were millions of
' worlds mine, I'd gladly give them in exchange for
' her condition. The moft confummate woe is light
' to mine. The laft of curfes to other miferable
' maids is all I afk for my relief, and that's denied
' me.

' *Tr.* Time and reflection cure all ills.

' *Ma.* All but this. His dreadful cataftrophe vir-

' tue

' tue herself abhors. To give a holiday to suburb
' slaves, and passing entertain the savage herd, who,
' elbowing each other for a sight, pursue and press
' upon him like his fate!———A mind with piety and
' resolution armed may smile on death:———But
' public ignominy, everlasting shame, shame the death
' of souls, to die a thousand times, and yet survive
' even death itself in never-dying infamy——Is this
' to be endured?——Can I who live in him, and must
' each hour of my devoted life feel all these woes re-
' newed——Can I endure this?

' *Tr.* Grief has so impaired her spirits, she pants,
' as in the agonies of death.'

Barn. Preserve her, Heaven, and restore her peace,
nor let her death be added to my crimes! [*Bell tolls.*]
I am summoned to my fate.

Enter Keeper.

Keep. Sir, the officers attend you. Millwood is
already summoned.

Barn. Tell 'em, I am ready. And now, my friend,
farewell [*Embracing*]. Support and comfort, the best
you can, this mourning fair,———No more——
Forget not to pray for me. •[*Turning to* Maria.]
Would you, bright excellence, permit me the honour
of a chaste embrace, the last happiness this world
could give were mine. [*She inclines towards him; they
embrace.*] Exalted goodness! Oh, turn your eyes from
earth and me to Heaven, where virtue, like yours, is
ever heard. Pray for the peace of my departing soul!
Early my race of wickedness began, and soon I reached the summit. ' Ere nature has finished her work,
' and stamped me man, just at the time when others
' begin to stray, my course is finished. Though short
' my span of life, and few my days, yet count my
' crimes for years, and I have lived whole ages.'——
Thus justice, in compassion to mankind, cuts off a
wretch like me; by one such example to secure thousands from future ruin. ' Justice and mercy are in
' Heaven the same: its utmost severity is mercy to the
' whole; thereby to cure man's folly and presumption,
' which else would render even infinite mercy vain and
' ineffectual.'

If

If any youth, like you, in future times
Shall mourn my fate, tho' he abhors my crimes;
Or tender maid, like you, my tale shall hear,
And to my sorrows give a pitying tear;
To each such melting eye and throbbing heart,
Would gracious Heaven this benefit impart,
Never to know my guilt, nor feel my pain,
Then must you own you ought not to complain,
Since you nor weep, nor I shall die in vain.

[*Exeunt.*

' SCENE, *the place of execution. The gallows and*
' *ladder at the farther end of the stage. A crowd of*
' *spectators,* Blunt *and* Lucy.

' *Lucy.* Heavens! what a throng!
' *Blunt.* How terrible is death, when thus prepared!
' *Lucy.* Support them, Heaven! thou only can'st
support them; all other help is vain.
' *Officer.* [*Within.*] Make way there; make way,
' and give the prisoners room.
' *Lucy.* They are here. Observe them well. How
' humble and composed young Barnwell seems; but
' Millwood looks wild, ruffled with passion, confound-
' ed and amazed.
Enter Barnwell, Millwood, *Officers, and Executioner.*
' *Barn.* See, Millwood, see, our journey's at an
' end. Life, like a tale that's told, is passed away.
' That short, but dark and unknown passage, death,
' is all the space between us and endless joys, or woes
' eternal.
' *Mill.* Is this the end of all my flattering hopes?
' Were youth and beauty given me for a curse, and
' wisdom only to insure my ruin? They were, they
' were! Heaven, thou hast done thy worst. Or, if
' thou hast in store some untried plague, somewhat
' that's worse than shame, despair, and death, un-
' pitied death, confirmed despair, and soul-confound-
' ing shame; something that men and angels can't
' describe, and only fiends, who bear it, can con-
' ceive; now, pour it on this devoted head, that I
may

' may feel the worſt thou can'ſt inflict, and bid defi-
' ance to thy utmoſt power.

' *Barn.* Yet ere we paſs the dreadful gulph of death,
' yet ere you're plunged in everlaſting woe, Oh, bend
' your ſtubborn knees and harder heart, humbly to
' deprecate the wrath divine. Who knows but Hea-
' ven, in your dying moments, may beſtow that grace
' and mercy which your life defpiſed!

' *Mill.* Why name you mercy to a wretch like me?
' Mercy is beyond my hope, almoſt beyond my wiſh.
' I can't repent, nor aſk to be forgiven.

' *Barn.* Oh, think what 'tis to be for ever, ever
' miſerable, nor with vain pride oppoſe a power that's
' able to deſtroy you.

' *Mill.* That will deſtroy me; I feel it will. A de-
' luge of wrath is pouring on my ſoul. Chains,
' darkneſs, wheels, racks, ſharp-ſtinged ſcorpions,
' molten lead, and whole ſeas of ſulphur, are light to
' what I feel.

' *Barn.* Oh, add not to your vaſt account deſpair;
' a ſin more injurious to Heaven, than all you've yet
' committed.

' *Mill.* Oh, I have ſinned beyond the reach of
' mercy!

' *Barn.* Oh, ſay not ſo; 'tis blaſphemy to think it.
' As yon bright roof is higher than the earth, ſo and
' much more does Heaven's goodneſs paſs our appre-
' henſion. Oh, what created being ſhall preſume to
' circumſcribe mercy that knows no bounds?

' *Mill.* This yields no hope. Though pity may
' be boundleſs, yet 'tis free. I was doomed before
' the world began to endleſs pains, and thou to joy
' eternal.

' *Barn.* Oh, gracious Heaven! extend thy pity to
' her; let thy rich mercy flow in plenteous ſtreams, to
' chace her fears, and heal her wounded ſoul.

' *Mill.* It will not be: your prayers are loſt in air,
' or elſe returned, perhaps, with double bleſſings to
' your boſom: they help not me.

' *Barn.* Yet hear me, Millwood.

' *Mill.* Away, I will not hear thee: I tell thee,
' youth,

' youth, I am by Heaven devoted a dreadful inſtance
'. of its power to puniſh. [Barnwell *ſeems to pray.*] If
' theu wilt pray, pray for thyſelf, not for me. How
' doth his fervent ſoul mount with his words, and
' both aſcend to Heaven!—that Heaven, whoſe gates
' are ſhut with adamantine bars againſt my prayers,
' had I the will to pray. I cannot bear it! Sure 'tis
' the worſt of torments to behold others enjoy that
' bliſs which we muſt never taſte.

' *Officer.* The utmoſt limit of your time's expired.

' *Mill.* Encompaſſed with horror, whither muſt I
' go? I would not live—nor die ——That I could
' ceaſe to be —— or ne'er had been!

' *Barn.* Since peace and comfort are denied her
' here, may ſhe find mercy where ſhe leaſt expects it,
' and this be all her hell! From our example may all
' be taught to fly the firſt approach of vice; but if
' o'ertaken

' By ſtrong temptation, weakneſs, or ſurprize,
' Lament their guilt, and by repentance riſe;
' Th' impenitent alone die unforgiven:
' To ſin's like man, and to forgive like Heaven.

' *Enter* Trueman.

' *Lucy.* Heart-breaking ſight!———Oh, wretched,
' wretched Millwood!

' *Tr.* How is ſhe diſpoſed to meet her fate?

' *Blunt.* Who can deſcribe unutterable woe?

' *Lucy.* She goes to death encompaſſed with horror,
' loathing life, and yet afraid to die. No tongue can
' tell her anguiſh and deſpair.

' *Tr.* Heaven be better to her than her fears! May
' ſhe prove a warning to others, a monument of mercy
' in herſelf.

' *Lucy.* Oh, ſorrow inſupportable! Break, break,
' my heart.

Tr. In vain
With bleeding hearts, and weeping eyes, we ſhow
A humane, gen'rous ſenſe of others woe,
Unleſs we mark what drew their ruin on,
And, by avoiding that, prevent our own.

EPILOGUE.

EPILOGUE.

Spoken by MARIA.

SINCE Fate has robb'd me of the hapless youth,
  For whom my heart had hoarded up its truth,
By all the laws of love and honour, now,
I'm free again to choose-------and one of you.
  But soft------with caution first I'll round me peep:
Maids in my case should look before they leap.
Here's choice enough, of various sorts and hue,
The cit, the wit, the rake cock'd up in cue,
The fair spruce mercer, and the tawny Jew.
  Suppose I search the sober gallery?-----No;
There's none but 'prentices, and cuckolds all-a-row;
And these, I doubt, are those that make 'em so.
                [Pointing to the boxes.
'Tis very well, enjoy the jest:-----but you
Fine powdered sparks------nay, I'm told 'tis true,
Your happy spouses-----can make cuckolds too.
'Twixt you and them the diff'rence this, perhaps,
The cit's asham'd whene'er his duck he traps;
But you, when madam's tripping, let her fall,
Cock up your hats, and take no shame at all.
  What if some favoured poet I could meet,
Whose love would lay his laurels at my feet:
No-------painted passion real love abhors-------
His flame would prove the suit of creditors.
  Not to detain you then with longer pause,
In short my heart to this conclusion draws----
I yield it to the hand that's loudest in applause.

Just published, making 12 *handsome Volumes, Ducdecimo, neatly bound, Price* Two Guineas.

THE ENGLISH THEATRE, containing sixty of the best Tragedies and Comedies in the English Language; each Volume has an elegant Vignette Title, and every Play a Frontispiece, representing a striking Likeness of the most favourite Actors and Actresses, designed and engraved by the best Artists.

⁎ Any of the above Plays may be had separate, Price 6d, although the Frontispieces are worth the Money.

VENICE PRESERV'D;

OR,

A PLOT DISCOVER'D.

A

T R A G E D Y.

WRITTEN BY

Mr. O T W A Y.

Marked with the Variations in the

M A N A G E R's B O O K,

AT THE

Theatre-Royal in Covent-Garden.

LONDON:

PRINTED FOR C. BATHURST, W. LOWNDES, AND
W. NICOLL.

M.DCC,LXXXV.

☞ The Reader is defired to obferve, that the Paffages omitted in the Reprefentation at the Theatres are here preferved, and marked with inverted Commas; as in Line 18, Page 8, to the Middle of Page 9.

Dramatis Personæ.

MEN.

		At DRURY-LANE.
Duke of Venice	-	Mr. CHAPLIN.
Priuli, *father of Belvidera*	-	Mr. AICKIN.
Bedamar, *the Spanish ambaffador*		Mr R. PALMER.
Jaffier, *married to Belvidera*		Mr. BRERETON.
Pierre, *friend to Jaffier*		Mr. BENSLEY.
Renault,		Mr. PACKER.
Elliot, } *Confpirators*		Mr. FAWCET.
Spinofa,		Mr. WRIGHT.
Officer,	-	Mr. PHILLIMORE.

WOMEN.

Belvidera, *daughter to Priuli, married to Jaffier*	-	Mrs. SIDDONS.

Two Women, Attendants on Belvidera.
The Council of Ten.
Officer, Guard, Friar, Executioner, and Rabble.

PROLOGUE.

IN these distracted times, when each man dreads
  The bloody stratagems of busy heads:
When we had fear'd three years we know not what,
'Till witnesses began to die o'th' rot ;
What made our poet meddle with a plot?
Was't that he fancy'd for the very sake,
And name of plot, his trifling play might take?
For there's not in't one inch-board evidence ;
But 'tis, he says, to reason plain and sense ;
And that he thinks a plausible defence.
Were truth by sense and reason to be try'd,
Sure all our swearers might be laid aside.
No ; of such tools our author has no need,
To make his plot, or make his play succeed ;
He of black bills has no prodigious tales,
Or Spanish pilgrims cast ashore in Wales :
Here's not one murder'd magistrate, at least,
Kept rank, like ven'son for a city feast,
Grown four days stiff, the better to prepare
And fit his pliant limbs to ride in chair.
Yet here's an army rais'd, tho' under ground,
But no man seen, nor one commission found :
Here is a traitor too, that's very old,
Turbulent, subtle, mischievous, and bold,
Bloody, revengeful, and—to crown his part,
Loves fumbling with a wench with all his heart :
'Till, after having many changes past,
In spite of age (thanks t'heav'n) is hang'd at last ;
Next is a senator that keeps a whore,
In Venice none a higher office bore,
To lewdness ev'ry night the letcher ran ;
Shew me, all London, such another man ;
Match him at mother Creswell's, if you can.
O Poland ! Poland ! had it been thy lot
T'have heard in time of this Venetian plot,
Thou surely chosen hadst one king from thence,
And honour'd them, as thou hast England since.

A 2   VENICE

A PLOT DISCOVER'D.

ACT I.

SCENE, a *Street in* Venice.

Enter Priuli *and* Jaffier.

Pri. NO more! I'll hear no more! begone and leave
    me.

Jaff. Not hear me! by my fufferings but you fhall!
My lord! my lord! I'm not that abject wretch
You think me. Patience! where's the diftance throws
Me back fo far, but I may boldly fpeak
In right, tho' proud oppreffion will not hear me?

  Pri. Have you not wrong'd me?

  Jaff. Could my nature e'er •
Have brook'd injuftice, or the doing wrong,
I need not now thus low have bent myfelf
To gain a hearing from a cruel father.
Wrong'd you!

  Pri. Yes, wrong'd me! in the niceft point,
The honour of my houfe, you've done me wrong.
You may remember (for now I will fpeak,
And urge its bafenefs) when you firft came home
From travel, with fuch hopes as made you look'd on
By all men's eyes, a youth of expectation;
Pleas'd with your growing virtue, I receiv'd you;
Courted, and fought to raife you to your merits;
My houfe, my table, nay, my fortune too,
My very felf was yours; you might have us'd me
To your beft fervice; like an open friend
I treated, trufted you, and thought you mine:
When, in requital of my beft endeavours,
You treacheroufly practis'd to undo me;
Seduc'd the weaknefs of my age's darling,
My only child, and ftole her from my bofom.
O! *Belvidera!*

                          Jaff.

Jaff. 'Tis to me you owe her:
Childless you had been else, and in the grave
Your name extinct; no more *Priuli* heard of.
You may remember, scarce five years are past,
Since in your brigantine you sail'd to see
The *Adriatic* wedded by our duke;
And I was with you: your unskilful pilot
Dash'd us upon a rock; when to your boat
You made for safety: enter'd first yourself;
Th' affrighted *Belvidera*, following next,
As she stood trembling on the vessel's side,
Was by a wave wash'd off into the deep:
When instantly I plung'd into the sea,
And buffeting the billows to her rescue,
Redeem'd her life with half the loss of mine.
Like a rich conquest, in one hand I bore her,
And with the other dash'd the saucy waves,
That throng'd and press'd to rob me of my prize.
I brought her, gave her to your despairing arms:
Indeed you thank'd me; but a nobler gratitude
Rose in her soul; for from that hour she lov'd me,
'Till for her life she paid me with herself.

   Pri. You stole her from me; like a thief you stole her,
At dead of night: that cursed hour you chose
To rifle me of all my heart held dear.
May all your joys in her prove false, like mine;
A sterile fortune, and a barren bed,
Attend you both: continual discord make
Your days and nights bitter and grievous still:
May the hard hand of a vexatious need
Oppress and grind you; till at last you find
The curse of disobedience all your portion.

   Jaff. Half of your curse you have bestow'd in vain;
Heav'n has already crown'd our faithful loves
With a young boy, sweet as his mother's beauty:
May he live to prove more gentle than his grandsire,
And happier than his father.

   Pri. Rather live
To bate thee for his bread, and din your ears
With hungry cries; whilst his unhappy mother
Sits down and weeps in bitterness of want.

   Jaff. You talk as if 'twould please you.
   Pri. 'Twould, by Heav'n!
' Once she was dear indeed; the drops that fell

       * From

' From my sad heart, when she forgot her duty,
' The fountain of my life was not so precious—
' But she is gone, and, if I am a man,
' I will forget her.'

Jaff. Would I were in my grave!

Pri. And the too with thee:
For, living here, you're but my curs'd remembrancer.
I once was happy.

Jaff. You use me thus, because you know my soul
Is fond of *Belvidera*. You perceive
My life feeds on her, therefore thus you treat me.
Oh! could my soul ever have found satiety;
Were I that thief, the doer of such wrongs
As you upbraid me with, what hinders me
But I might send her back to you with contumely,
And court my fortune where she would be kinder?

Pri. You dare not do't.

Jaff. Indeed, my lord, I dare not.
My heart, that awes me, is too much my master:
Three years are past, since first our vows were plighted,
During which time, the world must bear me witness,
I've treated *Belvidera* like your daughter,
The daughter of a senator of *Venice:*
Distinction, place, attendance, and observance,
Due to her birth, she always has commanded.
Out of my little fortune I've done this;
Because (tho' hopeless e'er to win your nature)
The world might see I lov'd her for herself;
Not as the heiress of the great *Priuli.*

Pri. No more.

Jaff. Yes, all, and then adieu for ever.
There's not a wretch, that lives on common charity,
But's happier than me: for I have known
The luscious sweets of plenty; every night
Have slept with soft content about my head,
And never wak'd, but to a joyful morning:
Yet now must fall, like a full ear of corn,
Whose blossom 'scap'd, yet's wither'd in the ripening.

Pri. Home, and be humble; study to retrench;
Discharge the lazy vermin of thy hall,
Those pageants of thy folly:
Reduce the glitt'ring trappings of thy wife
To humble weeds, fit for thy little state:
Then, to some suburb cottage both retire;

Drudge

Drudge to feed loathsome life; get brats and starve ———
Home, home, I say.　　　　　　　　　　　　[*Exit.*

Jaff. Yes, if my heart would let me ———
This proud, this swelling heart: home I would go,
But that my doors are hateful to my eyes,
Fill'd and damm'd up with gaping creditors.
I've now not fifty ducats in the world,
Yet still I am in love, and pleas'd with ruin.
Oh *Belvidera!* Oh! she is my wife ———
And we will bear our wayward fate together,
But ne'er know comfort more.

Enter Pierre.

Pier. My friend, good-morrow,
How fares the honest partner of my heart?
What, melancholy! not a word to spare me!

Jaff. I'm thinking, *Pierre*, how that damn'd starving
Call'd honesty, got footing in the world.　　　[quality,

Pier. Why, powerful villainy first set it up,
For its own ease and safety.　Honest men
Are the soft easy cushions on which knaves
Repose and fatten.　Were all mankind villains,
They'd starve each other; lawyers would want practice,
Cut-throats rewards: each man would kill his brother
Himself; none would be paid or hang'd for murder.
Honesty! 'twas a cheat invented first
To bind the hands of bold deserving rogues,
That fools and cowards might sit safe in power,
And lord it uncontroul'd above their betters.

Jaff. Then honesty is but a notion?

Pier. Nothing else:
Like wit, much talk'd of, not to be defin'd:
He that pretends to most, too, has least share in't,
'Tis a ragged virtue.　Honesty! no more on't.

Jaff. Sure thou art honest?

Pier. So, indeed, men think me;
But they are mistaken, *Jaffier:* I am a rogue
As well as they;
A fine, gay, bold-fac'd villain as thou seest me.
'Tis true, I pay my debts, when they're contracted;
I steal from no man; would not cut a throat
To gain admission to a great man's purse,
Or a whore's bed; I'd not betray my friend
To get his place or fortune; I scorn to flatter

A 4　　　　　　　　　　　A blown-

A blown-up fool above, to crush the wretch beneath me;
Yet, *Jaffier*, for all this I am a villain.

   Jaff. A villain!

   Pier. Yes, and a most notorious villain;
To see the sufferings of my fellow-creatures,
And own myself a man: to see our senators
Cheat the deluded people with a shew
Of liberty, which yet they ne'er must taste of.
They say, by them our hands are free from fetters;
Yet whom they please they lay in basest bonds;
Bring whom they please to infamy and sorrow;
Drive us, like wrecks, down the rough tide of power,
Whilst no hold is to save us from destruction.
All that bear this are villains, and I one,
Not to rouse up at that great call of nature,
And check the growth of these domestic spoilers,
That make us slaves, and tell us, 'tis our charter.

   ' *Jaff.* O *Aquilina!* Friend, to lose such beauty,
' The dearest purchase of thy noble labours!'
' She was thy right by conquest, as by love.

   ' *Pier.* O *Jaffier!* I had so fix'd my heart upon her,
' That wheresoe'er I fram'd a scheme of life,
' For time to come, she was my only joy,
' With which I wish'd to sweeten future cares:
' I fancy'd pleasures, none, but one that loves
' And doats as I did, can imagine like 'em:
' When in the extremity of all these hopes,
' In the most charming hour of expectation,
' Then, when our eager wishes soar the highest,
' Ready to stoop and grasp the lovely game,
' A haggard owl, a worthless kite of prey,
' With his foul wings, sail'd in, and spoil'd my quarry.

   ' *Jaff.* I know the wretch, and scorn him as thou hat'st
      him.

   ' *Pier.* Curse on the common good that's so protected,
' Where every slave, that heaps up wealth enough
' To do much wrong, becomes the lord of right!
' I, who believ'd no ill could e'er come near me,
' Found in the embraces of my *Aquilina*
' A wretched, old, but itching senator;
' A wealthy fool, that had bought out my title:
' A rogue that uses beauty like a lamb-skin,
' Barely to keep him warm; that filthy cuckow too

                     ' Was,

' Was, in my abfence, crept into my neft,
' And fpoiling all my brood of noble pleafure.
  ' *Jaff.* Did'ft thou not chace him thence?
  ' *Pier.* I did, and drove
' The rank old bearded hirco ftinking home.
' The matter was complain'd of in the fenate,
' I fummon'd to appear, and cenfur'd bafely,
' For violating fomething they call'd privilege—
' This was the recompence of all my fervice:
' Would I'd been rather beaten by a coward.
' A foldier's miftrefs, *Jaffier*, is his religion;
' When that's profan'd, all other ties are broken:
' That even diffolves all former bonds of fervice;
' And from that hour I think myfelf as free
' To be the foe, as e'er the friend of *Venice*—
' Nay, dear revenge, whene'er thou call'ft, I'm ready.'

  Jaff. I think no fafety can be here for virtue,
And grieve, my friend, as much as thou, to live
In fuch a wretched ftate as this of *Venice*,
Where all agree to fpoil the public good,
And villains fatten with the brave man's labours.

  Pier. We've neither fafety, unity, nor peace, my friend,
For the foundation's loft of common good;
Juftice is lame, as well as blind, amongft us;
The laws (corrupted to their ends that make 'em)
Serve but for inftruments of fome new tyranny,
That every day ftarts up, t'enflave us deeper.
Now could this glorious caufe but find out friends.
To do it right, O *Jaffier!* then might'ft thou
Not wear thofe feals of woe upon thy face;
The proud *Priuli* fhould be taught humanity,
And learn to value fuch a fon as thou art.
I dare not fpeak, but my heart bleeds this moment.

  Jaff. Curs'd be the caufe, tho' I, thy friend, be part
Let me partake the troubles of thy bofom,   [on't:
For I am us'd to mis'ry, and perhaps
May find a way to fweeten't to thy fpirit.

  Pier. Too foon 'twill reach thy knowledge—

  Jaff. Then from thee
Let it proceed. There's virtue in thy friendfhip,
Would make the faddeft tale of forrow pleafing,
Strengthen my conftancy, and welcome ruin.

  Pier. Then, thou art ruin'd!

  Jaff. That I long fince knew;

        I and

I and ill-fortune have been long acquainted.

Pier. I pafs'd this very moment by thy doors,
And found them guarded by a troop of villains;
The fons of public rapine were deftroying.
They told me, by the fentence of the law,
They had commiffion to feize all thy fortune:
Nay more, *Priuli*'s cruel hand had fign'd it.
Here ftood a ruffian with an horrid face,
Lording it o'er a pile of mafiy plate,
Tumbled into a heap for public fale;
There was another making villainous jefts
At thy undoing: he had ta'en poffeffion
Of all thy ancient moft domeftic ornaments,
Rich hangings intermix'd and wrought with gold;
The very bed, which on thy wedding-night
Receiv'd thee to the arms of *Belvidera*,
The fcene of all thy joys, was violated
By the coarfe hands of filthy dungeon villains,
And thrown amongft the common lumber.

Jaff. Now thank Heaven——

Pier. Thank Heaven! for what?

Jaff. That I'm not worth a ducat.

Pier. Curfe thy dull ftars, and the worfe fate of *Venice*,
Where brothers, friends and fathers are all falfe;
Where there's no truth, no truft; where Innocence
Stoops under vile Oppreffion, and Vice lords it.
Hadft thou but feen, as I did, how at laft
Thy beauteous *Belvidera*, like a wretch
That's doom'd to banifhment, came weeping forth,
' Shining thro' tears, like April-funs in fhowers,
' That labour to o'ercome the cloud that loads 'em;'
Whilft two young virgins, on whofe arm fhe lean'd,
Kindly look'd up, and at her grief grew fad,
As if they catch'd the forrows that fell from her;
Ev'n the lewd rabble, that were gather'd round
To fee the fight, ftood mute when they beheld her;
Govern'd their roaring throats, and grumbled pity;
I could have hugg'd the greafy rogues: they pleas'd me.

Jaff. I thank thee for this ftory, from my foul;
Since now I know the worft that can befall me.
Ah, *Pierre!* I have a heart that could have borne
The rougheft wrong my fortune could have done me;
But when I think what *Belvidera* feels,
The bitternefs her tender fpirits tafte of,

I own

I own myfelf a coward : bear my weaknefs;
If, throwing thus my arms about thy neck,
I play the boy, and blubber in thy bofom.
Oh! I fhall drown thee with my forrows.

Pier. Burn,
Firft, burn and level *Venice* to thy ruin.
What! ftarve, like beggars brats, in frofty weather,
Under a hedge, and whine ourfelves to death!
Thou, or thy caufe, fhall never want affiftance,
Whilft I have blood or fortune fit to ferve thee:
Command my heart, thou'rt every way its mafter.

Jaff. No, there's a fecret pride in bravely dying.
Pier. Rats die in holes and corners, dogs run mad;
Man knows a braver remedy for forrow;
Revenge, the attribute of gods; they ftamp'd it,
With their great image, on our natures. Die!
Confider well the caufe, that calls upon thee:
And, if thou'rt bafe enough, die then. Remember,
Thy *Belvidera* fuffers; *Belvidera!*
Die – damn firft—What! be decently interr'd
In a church-yard, and mingle thy brave duft
With ftinking rogues, that rot in dirty winding-fheets,
Surfeit flain fools, the common dung o'th' foil!

Jaff. Oh!
Pier. Well faid, out with't, fwear a little——
Jaff. Swear! By fea and air; by earth, by Heav'n and
I will revenge my *Belvidera*'s tears.   [hell,
Hark thee, my friend—*Priuli*—is—a fenator.

Pier. A dog.
Jaff. Agreed.
Pier. Shoot him.
Jaff. With all my heart.
No more; where fhall we meet at night?

Pier. I'll tell thee;
On the Rialto, every night at twelve,
I take my evening's walk of meditation:
There we two'll meet, and talk of precious
Mifchief———

Jaff. Farewel.
Pier. At twelve.
Jaff. At any hour; my plagues
Will keep me waking.   [*Exit* Pierre.
Tell me why, good Heaven,
Thou mad'ft me what I am, with all the fpirit,
Afpiring thoughts, and elegant defires,

A 6   That

That fill the happieſt man? Ah rather why
Didſt thou not form me ſordid as my fate,
Baſe-minded, dull, and fit to carry burthens?
Why have I ſenſe to know the curſe that's on me?
Is this juſt dealing, Nature? *Belvidera!*

     Enter Belvidera.

Poor Belvidera!

 Bel. Lead me, lead me, my virgins,
To that kind voice. My lord, my love, my refuge!
Happy my eyes, when they behold thy face!
My heavy heart will leave its doleful beating
At ſight of thee, and bound with ſprightful joys.
Oh ſmile! as when our loves were in their ſpring,
And chear my fainting ſoul.

 Jaff. As when our loves
Were in their ſpring! Has then our fortunes chang'd?
Art thou not, *Belvidera,* ſtill the ſame,
Kind, good, and tender, as my arms firſt found thee?
If thou art alter'd, where ſhall I have harbour?
Where eaſe my loaded heart? Oh! where complain?

 Bel. Does this appear like change, or love decaying,
When thus I throw myſelf into thy boſom,
With all the reſolution of ſtrong truth!
Beats not my heart, as 'twould alarum thine
'To a new charge of bliſs? I joy more in thee, .
Than did thy mother, when ſhe hugg'd thee firſt,
And bleſs'd the gods for all her travail paſt.

 Jaff. Can there in woman be ſuch glorious faith?
Sure all ill ſtories of thy ſex are falſe!
O woman! lovely woman! Nature made thee
To temper man: we had been brutes without you!
Angels are painted fair, to look like you:
There's in you all that we believe of Heaven;
Amazing brightneſs, purity and truth,
Eternal joy, and everlaſting love.

 Bel. If love be treaſure, we'll be wond'rous rich;
I have ſo much, my heart will ſurely break with't:
Vows can't expreſs it. When I would declare
How great's the joy, I'm dumb with the big thought;
I ſwell, I ſigh, and labour with my longing.
O! lead me to ſome deſart wide and wild,
Barren as our misfortunes, where my ſoul
May have its vent, where I may tell aloud
To the high heavens, and ev'ry liſt'ning planet,
With what a boundleſs ſtock my boſom's fraught;

          Where

Where I may throw my eager arms about thee,
Give loose to love, with kisses kindling joy,
And let off all the fire that's in my heart.
　Jaff. O *Belvidera!* doubly I'm a beggar:
Undone by fortune, and in debt to thee.
Want, worldly want, that hungry meagre fiend,
Is at my heels, and chases me in view.
Can'st thou bear cold and hunger? Can these limbs,
Fram'd for the tender offices of love,
Endure the bitter gripes of smarting poverty?
When banish'd by our miseries abroad
(As suddenly we shall be) to seek out
In some far climate, where our names are strangers,
For charitable succour; wilt thou then,
When in a bed of straw we shrink together,
And the bleak winds shall whistle round our heads;
Wilt thou then talk thus to me? Wilt thou then
Hush my cares thus, and shelter me with love?
　Bel. Oh! I will love thee, even in madness love thee;
Tho' my distracted senses should forsake me,
I'd find some intervals when my poor heart
Should 'swage itself, and be let loose to thine.
Tho' the bare earth be all our resting-place,
Its roots our food, some clift our habitation,
I'll make this arm a pillow for thine head;
And as thou sighing ly'st, and swell'd with sorrow,
Creep to thy bosom, pour the balm of love
Into thy soul, and kiss thee to thy rest;
Then praise our gods, and watch thee till the morning.
　Jaff. Hear this, you Heav'ns, and wonder how you
　　　made her!
Reign, reign, ye monarchs that divide the world,
Busy religion ne'er will let you know
'Tranquillity and happiness like mine;
Like gaudy ships, the obsequious billows fall,
And rise again, to lift you in your pride;
They wait but for a storm, and then devour you:
I in my private bark already wreck'd,
Like a poor merchant driven to unknown land,
That had by chance pack'd up his choicest treasure
In one dear casket, and sav'd only that;
Since I must wander farther on the shore,
Thus hug my little, but my precious store,
Resolv'd to scorn, and trust my fate no more.　[*Ex.*

ACT

A C T II.

' *Enter* Pierre *and* Aquilina.

' *Aqui.* BY all thy wrongs, thou'rt dearer to my arms
            ' Than all the wealth of *Venice*. Prithee ftay,
' And let us love to-night.
    ' *Pier.* No : there's fool,
' There's fool about thee.   When a woman fells
' Her flefh to fools, her beauty's loft to me ;
' They leave a tainted fully, where they've pafs'd ;
' There's fuch a baneful quality about 'em,
' E'en fpoils complexions with their naufeoufnefs ;
' They infect all they touch : I cannot think
' Of tafting any thing that a fool has pall'd.   [much
    ' *Aqui.* I loath and fcorn that fool thou mean'ft, as
' Or more than thou can'ft ; but the beaft has gold,
' That makes him neceffary ; power too,
' To qualify my character, and poife me
' Equal with peevifh virtue, that beholds
' My liberty with envy.   In their hearts
' They're loofe as I am ; but an ugly power
' Sits in their faces, and frights pleafures from them.
        ' *Pier.* Much good may't do you, madam, with your
                fenator.
        ' *Aqui.* My fenator ! Why, can'ft thou think that
                wretch
' E'er fill'd thy *Aquilina's* arms with pleafure ?
' Think'ft thou, becaufe I fometimes give him leave
' To foil himfelf at what he is unfit for ;
' Becaufe I force myfelf t'endure and fuffer him,
' Think'it thou I love him ? No, by all the joys
' Thou ever gav'ft me, his prefence is my penance.
' The worft thing an old man can be's a lover,
' A mere *memento mori* to poor woman.
' I never lay by his decrepid fide,
' But all that night I ponder on my grave.
    ' *Pier.* Would he were well fent thither.
    ' *Aqui.* That's my wifh too :   [fure,
' For then, my *Pierre*, I might have caufe, with plea-
' To play the hypocrite.   Oh ! how I could weep
' Over the dying dotard, and kifs him too,
' In hopes to fmother him quite ; then, when the time
' Was come to pay my forrows at his funeral,

                                        ' (For

' (For he has already made me heir to treasures
' Would make me out-act a real widow's whining)
' How could I frame my face to fit my mourning !
' With wringing hands attend him to his grave ;
' Fall swooning on his hearse ; take mad possession
' E'en of the dismal vault where he lay buried ;
' There, like th' *Ephesian* matron, dwell till thou,
' My lovely soldier, com'st to my deliverance ;
' Then throwing up my veil, with open arms
' And laughing eyes, run to new dawning joy.
 ' *Pier.* No more : I've friends to meet me here to-
   night,
' And must be private. As you prize my friendship,
' Keep up your coxcomb ; let him not pry, nor listen,
' Nor frisk about the house, as I have seen him,
' Like a tame mumping squirrel with a bell on :
' Curs will be abroad to bite him, if you do.
 ' *Aqui.* What friends to meet ! Mayn't I be of your
   council ?
 ' *Pier.* How ! a woman ask questions out of bed !
' Go to your senator ; ask him what passes
' Amongst his brethren : he'll hide nothing from you :
' But pump not me for politicks. No more !
' Give order, that whoever in my name
' Comes here, receive admittance. So good night.
 ' *Aqui.* Must we ne'er meet again ! embrace no more ?
' Is love so soon and utterly forgotten ?
 ' *Pier.* As you henceforward treat your fool, I'll
   think on't.
 ' *Aqui.* Curs'd be all fools, and doubly curs'd myself,
' The worst of fools—I die if he forsake me ;
' And how to keep him, Heaven or hell instruct me. [*Ex.*'
  S C E N E, *the* Rialto. *Enter* Jaffier.

 Jaff. I'm here ; and thus, the shades of night around
I look as if all hell were in my heart,   [me,
And I in hell. Nay, surely 'tis so with me !——
For every step I tread, methinks some fiend
Knocks at my breast, and bids it not be quiet.
I've heard how desperate wretches, like myself,
Have wander'd out at this dead time of night,
To meet the foe of mankind in his walk,
Sure I'm so curs'd, that, tho' of Heav'n forsaken,
No minister of darkness cares to tempt me.
Hell, hell ! why sleep'st thou ?

           Enter

Enter Pierre.

Pier. Sure I've ſtaid too long :
The clock has ſtruck, and I may loſe my proſelyte.
Speak, who goes there ?

Jaff. A dog, that comes to howl
At yonder moon. What's he, that aſks the queſtion ?

Pier. A friend to dogs, for they are honeſt creatures,
And ne'er betray their maſters ; never fawn
On any that they love not. Well met, friend *Jaffier !*

Jaff. The ſame. ' O *Pierre,* thou'rt come in ſeaſon,
' I was juſt going to pray.

Pier. ' Ah ! that's mechanic ;
' Prieſts make a trade on't, and yet ſtarve by't, too.
' No praying ; it ſpoils buſineſs, and time's precious.'
Where's *Belvidera ?*——

Jaff. For a day or two
I've lodg'd her privately, till I ſee farther
What Fortune will do with me. Prithee, friend,
If thou would'ſt have me fit to hear good counſel,
Speak not of *Belvidera*——

Pier. Speak not of her ?

Jaff. Oh, no !

Pier. Nor name her ? May be I wiſh her well!

Jaff. Whom well ?

Pier. Thy wife ; thy lovely *Belvidera.*
I hope a man may wiſh his friend's wife well,
And no harm done.

Jaff. Y' are merry, *Pierre.*

Pier. I am ſo :
Thou ſhalt ſmile too, and *Belvidera* ſmile :
We'll all rejoice. Here's ſomething to buy pins ;
Marriage is chargeable. [*Gives him a purſe.*

Jaff. I but half wiſh'd
To ſee the devil, and he's here already. Well !
What muſt this buy ? Rebellion, murder, treaſon ?
Tell me which way I muſt be damn'd for this.

Pier. When laſt we parted, we'd no qualms like theſe,
But entertain'd each other's thoughts like men
Whoſe ſouls were well acquainted. Is the world
Reform'd ſince our laſt meeting ? What new miracles
Have happen'd ? Has *Priuli's* heart relented ?
Can he, be honeſt ?

Jaff. Kind Heav'n, let heavy curſes
Gall his old age ; cramps, aches rack his bones,

And

And bittereſt diſquiet wring his heart.
'Oh! let him live, till life becomes his burden;
'Let him groan under't long. Linger an age
'In the worſt agonies and pangs of death,
'And find its eaſe, but late.'
   Pier. Nay, could'ſt thou not
As well, my friend, have ſtretch'd the curſe to all
The ſenate round, as to one ſingle villain?
   Jaff. But curſes ſtick not; could I kill with curſing,
By Heaven I know not thirty heads in *Venice*
Should not be blaſted. Senators ſhould rot
Like dogs on dunghills: 'But their wives and daughters
'Die of their own diſeaſes.' Oh! for a curſe
To kill with!
   Pier. Daggers, daggers are much better.
   Jaff. Ha!
   Pier. Daggers.
   Jaff. But where are they?
   Pier. Oh! a thouſand
May be diſpos'd of, in honeſt hands in *Venice.*
   Jaff. Thou talk'ſt in clouds.
   Pier. But yet a heart, half wrong'd
As thine has been, would find the meaning, *Jaffier.*
   Jaff. A thouſand daggers, all in honeſt hands!
And have I not a friend will ſtick one here?
   Pier. Yes, if I thought thou wert not to be cheriſh'd
T'a nobler purpoſe, I would be that friend;
But thou haſt better friends; friends whom thy wrongs
Have made thy friends; friends worthy to be call'd ſo.
I'll truſt thee with a ſecret: There are ſpirits
This hour at work.—But as thou'rt a man,
Whom I have pick'd and choſen from the world,
Swear that thou wilt be true to what I utter;
And when I've told·thee that which only gods,
And men like gods, are privy to, then ſwear
No chance or change ſhall wreſt it from thy boſom.
   Jaff. When thou would'ſt bind me, is there need of
        oaths?   [counters;'
'Green-ſickneſs girls loſe maidenheads with ſuch
For thou'rt ſo near my heart, that thou may'ſt ſee
Its bottom, ſound its ſtrength and firmneſs to thee.
Is coward, fool, or villain in my face?
If I ſeem none of theſe, I dare believe
Thou would'ſt not uſe me in a little cauſe;

                                   For

For I am fit for honour's rougheſt taſk ;
Nor ever yet found fooling was my province :
And for a villainous, inglorious enterprize,
I know thy heart ſo well, I dare lay mine
Before thee, ſet it to what poſt thou wilt.

    Pier. Nay, 'tis a cauſe thou wilt be fond of, *Jaffier* ;
For it is founded on the nobleſt baſis ;
Our liberties, our natural inheritance.
There's no religion, no hypocriſy in't ;
We'll do the buſineſs, and ne'er faſt and pray for't ;
Openly act a deed the world may gaze
With wonder at, and envy when 'tis done.

    Jaff. For liberty !
    Pier. For liberty, my friend.
Thou ſhalt be freed from baſe *Priuli*'s tyranny,
And thy ſequeſter'd fortunes heal'd again :
I ſhall be free from thoſe opprobrious wrongs,
That preſs me now, and bend my ſpirit downward ;
All *Venice* free, and every growing merit
Succeed to its juſt rights : fools ſhall be pull'd
From Wiſdom's ſeat ; thoſe baleful unclean birds,
Thoſe lazy owls, who (perch'd near Fortune's top)
Sit only watchful with their heavy wings
To cuff down new-fledg'd virtues, that would riſe
To nobler heights, and make the grove harmonious.

    Jaff. What can I do ?
    Pier. Can'ſt thou not kill a ſenator ?
    Jaff. Were there one wiſe or honeſt, I could kill him,
For herding with that neſt of fools or knaves.
By all my wrongs, thou talk'ſt as if revenge
Were to be had ; and the brave ſtory warms me.

    Pier. Swear then !
    Jaff. I do, by all thoſe glittering ſtars,
And yon great ruling planet of the night ;
By all good powers above, and ill below ;
By love and friendſhip, dearer than my life,
No pow'r or death ſhall make me falſe to thee.

    Pier. Here we embrace, and I'll unlock my heart.
A council's held hard by, where the deſtruction
Of this great empire's hatching : there I'll lead thee.
But be a man ! for thou'rt to mix with men
Fit to diſturb the peace of all the world,
And rule it when 'tis wildeſt———

    Jaff. I give thee thanks

For

For this kind warning. Yes, I'll be a man ;
And charge thee, *Pierre*, whene'er thou fee'ft my fears
Betray me lefs, to rip this heart of mine
Out of my breaft, and fhew it for a coward's.
Come, let's begone, for from this hour I chace
All little thoughts, all tender human follies
Out of my bofom : Vengeance fhall have room :
Revenge !

   Pier. And liberty !

   Jaff. Revenge !

   Pier. And liberty !

   Jaff. Revenge ! revenge !————— [*Exeunt.*

The SCENE *changes to* Aquilina's *houfe, the* Greek
courtezan.

Enter Renault.

   Ren. Why was my choice ambition ? the worft
      ground
A wretch can build on ! 'tis, indeed, at diftance,
A goodly profpect, tempting to the view ;
The height delights us, and the mountain top
Looks beautiful, becaufe 'tis nigh to Heav'n ;
But we ne'er think how fandy's the foundation,
What ftorms will batter, and what tempefts fhake us.
Who's there ?

Enter Spinofa.

   Spin. *Renault*, good-morrow, for by this time
I think the fcale of night has turn'd the balance,
And weighs up morning ? Has the clock ftruck twelve ?

   Ren. Yes ; clocks will go as they are fet : but man,
Irregular man's ne'er conftant, never certain :
I've fpent at leaft three precious hours of darknefs
In waiting dull attendance ; 'tis the curfe
Of diligent virtue to be mix'd, like mine,
With giddy tempers, fouls but half refolv'd.

   Spin. Hell feize that foul amongft us it can frighten.

   Ren. What's then the caufe that I am here alone ?
Why are we not together ?

Enter Elliot.

O, fir, welcome !
You are an Englifhman : when treafon's hatching,
One might have thought you'd not have been behind-
In what whore's lap have you been lolling ?   [hand.
Give but an *Englifhman* his whore and eafe,
Beef and a fea-coal fire, he's your's for ever.

                        Ell.

Ell. *Frenchman*, you are faucy.

Ren. How!

Enter Bedamar *the Ambaffador*, Theodore, Bramveil,
Durand, Brabe, Revillido, Mezzana, Ternon, Re-
trofi, *Confpirators.*

Bed. At difference; fie!
Is this a time for quarrels? Thieves and rogues
Fall out and brawl: fhould men of your high calling,
Men feparated by the choice of Providence
From the grofs heap of mankind, and fet here
In this affembly as in one great jewel,
T' adorn the braveft purpofe it e'er fmil'd on;
Should you, like boys, wrangle for trifles?

Ren. Boys!

Bed. Renault, thy hand.

Ren. I thought I'd given my heart
Long fince to every man that mingles here;
But grieve to find it trufted with fuch tempers,
That can't forgive my froward age its weaknefs.

Bed. *Elliot*, thou once hadft virtue. I have feen
Thy ftubborn temper bend with god-like goodnefs,
Not half thus courted: 'Tis thy nation's glory
To hug the foe that offers brave alliance.
One more embrace, my friends—we'll all take hands.
United thus, we are the mighty engine
Muft twift the rooted empire from its bafis.
Totters it not already?

Ell. Would 'twere tumbling.

Bed. Nay, it fhall down. this night we feal its ruin.

Enter Pierre.

O *Pierre!* thou art welcome.
Come to my breaft, for by its hopes thou look'ft
Lovelily dreadful; and the fate of *Venice*
Seems on thy fword already. O my *Mars!*
The poets that firft feign'd a god of war,
Sure prophefy'd of thee.

Pier. Friend, was not *Brutus*,
(I mean that *Brutus*, who in open fenate
Stabb'd the firft *Cæfar* that ufurp'd the world)
A gallant man?

Ren. Yes, and *Cataline* too;
Tho' ftory wrongs his fame: for he confpir'd
To prop the reeling glory of his country:
His caufe was good.

Bed.

Bed. And ours as much above it,
As *Renault,* thou'rt fuperior to *Cethegus,*
Or *Pierre* to *Caffius.*
    Pier. Then to what we aim at.
When do we ftart? or muft we talk for ever?
    Bed. No, *Pierre,* the deed's near birth; fate feems to
        have fet
The bufinefs up, and given it to our care;
I hope there's not a heart or hand amongft us,
But what is firm and ready.
    All. All.
We'll die with *Bedamar.*
    Bed. O men,
Matchlefs! as will your glory be hereafter:
The game is for a matchlefs prize, if won:
If loft, difgraceful ruin.
    ' *Ren.* Who can lofe it?
' The public ftock's a beggar: one *Venetian*
' Trufts not another. Look into their ftores
' Of general fafety; empty magazines,
' A tatter'd fleet, a murmuring unpaid army,
' Bankrupt nobility, a harrafs'd commonalty,
' A factious, giddy, and divided ferate,
' Is all the ftrength of *Venice:* let's deftroy it:
' Let's fill their magazines with arms to awe them;
' Man out their fleet, and make their trade maintain it;
' Let loofe their murmuring army on their mafters
' To pay themfelves with plunder; lop their nobles
' To the bafe roots whence moft of them firft fprung;
' Enflave the rout, whom fmarting will make humble;
' Turn out that droning fenate, and poffefs
' That feat of empire which our fouls were fram'd for.
    Pier. Ten thoufand men are armed at your nod,
Commanded all by leaders fit to guide
A battle for the freedom of the world:
This wretched ftate has ftarv'd them in its fervice;
And by your bounty quicken'd, they're refolv'd
To ferve your glory, and revenge their own:
They've all their different quarters in this city,
Watch for the alarm, and grumble 'tis fo tardy.
    Bed. I doubt not, friend, but thy unwearied diligence
Has ftill kept waking, and it fhall have eafe;
After this night it is refolv'd we meet
No more, till *Venice* owns us for her lords.

2   *Pier.*

Pier. How lovely the *Adriatic* whore,
Dress'd in her flames, will shine? Devouring flames!
Such as shall burn her to the watery bottom,
And hiss in her foundation.
    Bed. Now if any
Amongst us, that owns this glorious cause,
Have friends or interest he'd wish to save,
Let it be told: the general doom is seal'd;
But I'd forego the hopes of a world's empire,
Rather than wound the bowels of my friend.
    Pier. I must confess, you there have touch'd my
I have a friend; hear it! such a friend,   [weakness.
My heart was ne'er shut to him. Nay, I tell you
He knows the very business of this hour;
But he rejoices in the cause, and loves it:
We've chang'd a vow to live and die together,
And he's at hand to ratify it here.
    Ren. How! all betray'd!
    Pier. No—I've dealt nobly with you,
I've brought my all into the public stock:
I'd but one friend, and him I'll share amongst you:
Receive and cherish him; or if, when seen
And search'd, you find him worthless; as my tongue
Has lodg'd this secret in his faithful breast,
To ease your fears, I wear a dagger here
Shall rip it out again, and give you rest.
Come forth, thou only good I e'er could boast of.
        Enter Jaffier, *with a dagger.*
    Bed. His presence bears the shew of manly virtue.
    Jaff. I know you'll wonder all, that thus uncall'd
I dare approach this place of fatal councils;
But I'm amongst you, and by Heav'n it glads me
To see so many virtues thus united
To restore justice, and dethrone oppression.
Command this sword, if you would have it quiet,
Into this breast; but, if you think it worthy
To cut the throats of reverend rogues in robes,
Send me into the curs'd assembled senate:
It shrinks not, tho' I meet a father there.
Would you behold this city flaming? here's
A hand shall bear a lighted torch at noon
To th' arsenal, and set its gates on fire.
    Ren. You talk this well, sir,
    Jaff. Nay——by Heaven I'll do this.

                             Come,

Come, come, I read diſtruſt in all your faces:
You fear me villain, and indeed it's odd
To hear a ſtranger talk thus, at firſt meeting,
Of matters that have been ſo well debated;
But I come ripe with wrongs, as you with councils.
I hate this ſenate, am a foe to *Venice* ;
A friend to none, but men reſolv'd like me
To puſh on miſchief. Oh! did you but know me,
I need not talk thus !

 Bed. Pierre, I muſt embrace him,
My heart beats to this man, as if it knew him.

 Ren I never lov'd theſe huggers.

 Jaff. Still I ſee
The cauſe delights ye not. Your friends ſurvey me
As I were dangerous ————But I come arm'd
Againſt all doubts, and to your truſts will give
A pledge, worth more than all the world can pay for.
My *Belvidera.* Ho ! my *Belvidera !*

 Bed. What wonder next ?

 Jaff. Let me intreat you,
As I have henceforth hoped to call you friends,
That all but the ambaſſador, and this
Grave guide of councils, with my friend that owns me,
Withdraw a while, to ſpare a woman's bluſhes
     [*Exeunt all but* Bed. Ren. Jaff. Pier.

 Bed. Pierre, whither will this ceremony lead us ?

 Jaff. My *Belvidera ! Belvidera !*
    Enter Belvidera.

 Bel. Who,
Who calls ſo loud at this late peaceful hour ?
That voice was wont to come in gentle whiſpers,
And fill my ears with the ſoft breath of love.
Thou hourly image of my thoughts, where art thou ?

 Jaff. Indeed 'tis late.

 ' *Bel.* Oh ! I have ſlept and dreamt,
' And dreamt again. Where haſt thou been, thou loiterer ?
' Tho' my eyes clos'd, my arms have ſtill been open'd :
' Stretch'd every way betwixt my broken ſlumbers,
' To ſearch if thou wer't come to crown my reſt :
' There's no repoſe without thee . oh ! the day
' Too ſoon will break, and wake us to our ſorrow.
' Come, come to bed, and bid thy cares good night.

 ' *Jaff.* O *Belvidera !* we muſt change the ſcene,
' In which the paſt delights of life were taſted :

        ' The

' The poor sleep little ; we must learn to watch
' Our labours late, and early every morning ;
' 'Midst winter frosts, thin clad and fed with sparing,
' Rise to our toils, and drudge away the day.

Bel. Alas ! where am I ! whither is't you lead me ?
Methinks I read distraction in your face,
Something less gentle than the fate you tell me.
You shake and tremble too ! your blood runs cold !
Heav'ns guard my love, and bless his heart with patience.

Jaff. That I have patience, let our fate bear witness,
Who has ordain'd it so, that thou and I,
(Thou, the divinest good man e'er possess'd,
And I, the wretched'st of the race of man)
This very hour, without one tear, must part.

Bel. Part ! must we part ? Oh, am I then forsaken ?
' Will my love cast me off ? Have my misfortunes
' Offended him so highly, that he'll leave me ?'
Why drag you from me ; whither are you going ?
My dear ! my life ! my love !

Jaff. O, friend !
Bel. Speak to me.
Jaff. Take her from my heart.
She'll gain such hold else, I shall ne'er get loose.
I charge thee take her, but with tender'st care
Relieve her troubles, and assuage her sorrows.

Ren. Rise, madam, and command amongst your servants.

Jaff. To you, sir, and your honour, I bequeath her,
And with her this ; when I prove unworthy—
　　　　　　　　　　　　　　[*Gives a dagger.*
You know the rest ——— Then strike it to her heart ;
And tell her, he who three whole happy years
Lay in her arms, and every night repeated
The passionate vows still of increasing love,
Sent that reward for all her truth and sufferings.

' *Bel.* Nay, take my life, since he has sold it cheaply ;
' Or send me to some distant clime your slave,
' But let it be far off, lest my complainings
' Should reach his guilty ears, and shake his peace.

' *Jaff.* No, *Belvidera,* I've contriv'd thy honour.
' Trust to my faith, and be but fortune kind
' To me, as I'll preserve that faith unbroken ;
' When next we meet, I'll lift thee to a height
' Shall gather all the gazing world about thee,
' To wonder what strange virtue plac'd thee there.
' But, if we ne'er meet more'———
　　　　　　　　　　　　　　　　　　　Bel.

Bel. O! thou unkind one;
Ne'er meet more! have I deserv'd this from you?
Look on me, tell me, speak, thou dear deceiver,
Why am I separated from thy love?
If I am false, accuse me, but if true,
Don't, prithee don't, in poverty forsake me,
But pity the sad heart that's torn with parting.
Yet hear me! yet recall me— [*Ex. Ren. Bed. and Belv.*

Jaff. ' O my eyes, my heart-strings!
' Look not that way, but turn yourselves a while
' Into my heart, and be wean'd altogether.'
My friend, where art thou?
   Pier. Here, my honour's brother.
   Jaff. Is *Belvidera* gone?
   Pier. Renault has led her
Back to her own apartment; but, by Heav'n,
Thou must not see her more, 'till our work's over.
   Jaff. Not see her!
   Pier. Not for your life.
   Jaff. O *Pierre*, were she but here,
How I would pull her down into my heart,
Gaze on her, till my eye-strings crack'd with love;
' Till all my sinews, with its fire extended,
' Fix'd me upon the rack of ardent longing:'
Then, swelling, sighing, raging to be blest,
Come, like a panting turtle, to her breast;
On her soft bosom hovering, bill and play,
Confess the cause why last I fled away;
Own 'twas a fault, but swear to give it o'er,
And never follow false ambition more.   [*Exeunt.*

ACT III.

' *Enter Aquilina and her maid.*

' *Aqui.* TELL him I am gone to bed; tell him I am
' not at home; tell him I've better com-
' pany with me, or any thing; tell him, in short, I will
' not see him, the eternal troublesome vexatious fool:
' he's worse company than an ignorant physician—I'll not
' be disturb'd at these unreasonable hours.

  ' *Maid.* But, Madam! he's here already, just enter'd
' the door.

B   ' *Aqui.*

' *Aqui.* Turn him out again, you unneceffary, ufelefs,
' giddy-brain'd afs : if he will not be gone, fet the houfe a
' fire, and burn us both : I'd rather meet a toad in my difh,
' than an old hideous animal in my chamber to-night.

' *Enter* Antonio.

' *Ant.* Nacky, Nacky, Nacky —— how doft do,
' Nacky? Hurry, durry. I am come, little Nacky :
' paft eleven o'clock, a late hour ; time in all confcience
' to go to bed, Nacky —— Nacky, did I fay? Ah,
' Nacky, Aquilina, lina, lina, quilina, quilina, quilina,
' Aquilina, Naquilina, Naquilina, Acky, Acky, Nacky,
' Nacky, queen Nacky—— come, let's to bed ——
' you fubbs, you pug you—— you little pufs——Puriee,
' Tuzzy—I am a fenator.

' *Aqui.* You are a fool, I am fure.

' *Ant.* May be fo too, fweetheart : never the worfe
' fenator for all that. Come, Nacky, Nacky, let's have
' a game at romps, Nacky.

' *Aqui.* You would do well, fignor, to be troublefome
' here no longer, but leave me to myfelf; be fober, and
' go home, fir.

' *Ant.* Home, Madona !

' *Aqui.* Ay, home, fir. Who am I ?

' *Ant.* Madona, as I take it, you are my —— you are
' ——thou art my little Nicky Nacky —— that's all.

' *Aqui.* I find you are refolv'd to be troublefome ; and
' fo, to make fhort of the matter in few words, I hate you,
' deteft you, loath you, I am weary of you, fick of you
' —hang you, you are an old, filly, impertinent, impo-
' tent, folicitous coxcomb : crazy in your head, and lazy
' in your body; love to be meddling with every thing,
' and, if you had no money, you are good for nothing.

' *Ant.* Good for nothing ! Hurry durry, I'll try that
' prefently. Sixty-one years old, and good for nothing !
' that's brave : [*To the maid.*] Come, come, come Mrs.
' fiddle-faddle, turn you out for a feafon : go, turn out,
' I fay, it is our will and pleafure to be private fome mo-
' ments—out, out, when you are bid to ——[*Puts her out,
' and locks the door*] Good for nothing, you fay ?

' *Aqui.* Why, what are you good for ?

' *Ant.* In the firft place, madam, I am old, and con-
' fequently very wife, very wife, Madona, d'ye mark
' that ? In the fecond place, take notice, if you pleafe,
' that I am a fenator ; and, when I think fit, can make
' fpeeches,

‘ fpeeches, Madona. Hurry durry, I can make a fpeech
‘ in the fenate-houfe, now and then — would make your
‘ hair ftand an end, Madona.

‘ *Aqui.* What care I for your fpeeches in the fenate-
‘ houfe ; if you would but be filent here, I fhould thank
‘ you.

‘ *Ant.* Why I can make fpeeches to thee too, my lovely
‘ Madona ; for example—My cruel fair one, [*Takes out a*
‘ *purfe, and at every paufe fhakes it*] fince it is my fate,
‘ that you fhould, with your fervant, angry prove ; though
‘ late at night—I hope ’tis not too late with this, to gain
‘ reception for my love——There’s for thee, my little
‘ Nicky Nacky—take it, here take it — I fay take it, or
‘ I’ll throw it at your head—how now, rebel ?

‘ *Aqui.* Truly, my illuftrious fenator, I muft confefs
‘ your honour is at prefent moft profoundly eloquent
‘ indeed.

‘ *Ant.* Very well : come, now let’s fit down, and think
‘ upon’t a little—come, fit, I fay—fit down by me a lit-
‘ tle, my Nicky Nacky.—— [*Sits down.*] Hurry durry—
‘ good for nothing—

‘ *Aqui.* No, fir, if you pleafe, I can know my diftance,
‘ and ftand.

‘ *Ant.* Stand ! how, Nacky up, and I down ? Nay
‘ then, let me exclaim with the poet,

‘ Shew me a cafe more pitiful who can,
‘ A ftanding woman and a falling man.

‘ Hurry durry not fit down—fee this, ye gods !
‘ You won’t fit down ?

‘ *Aqui.* No, fir.

‘ *Ant.* Then look you, now ; fuppofe me a bull, a
‘ bafan-bull, the bull of bulls, or any bull. Thus up I
‘ get, and with my brows, thus bent—I broo, I fay,
‘ I broo, I broo, I broo. You won’t fit down, will you ?
‘ —— I broo ——

‘ [*Bellows like a bull, and drives her about.*

‘ *Aqui.* Well, fir, I muft endure this. [*She fits down.*]
‘ Now your honour has been a bull, pray what beaft will
‘ your worfhip pleafe to be next ?

‘ *Ant.* Now I’ll be a fenator again, and thy lover,
‘ little Nicky Nacky. [*He fits by her.*] Ah ! toad, toad,
‘ toad, toad ! fpit in my face a little, Nacky, fpit in
‘ my face, prithee, fpit in my face never fo little : fpit
‘ but a little bit —— fpit, fpit, fpit, fpit, when you are

B 2 ‘ bid,

' bid, I fay; do prithee fpit——now, now, now, fpit;
' what, you won't fpit, will you? then I'll be a dog.

' *Aqui.* A dog, my lord!

' *Ant.* Ay a dog—and I'll give thee this t'other purfe,
' to let me be a dog—and ufe me like a dog a little,
' Hurry durry—I will—here 'tis—   [*Gives the purfe.*

' *Aqui.* Well, with all my heart. But let me befeech
' your dogfhip, to play your tricks over as faft as you can,
' that you may come to ftinking the fooner, and be turn'd
' out of doors, as you deferve.

' *Ant.* Ay, ay—no matter for that—that fhan't move—
' [*He gets under the table.*] Now, bough, waugh, waugh,
' bough, waugh.—   [*Barks like a dog.*

' *Aqui.* Hold, hold, hold, fir, I befeech you: what is't
' you do? If curs bite, they muft be kick'd, fir: Do you
' fee, kick'd thus.

' *Ant.* Ay, with all my heart: do, kick, kick on;
' now I am under the table, kick again, kick harder—
' harder yet, bough, waugh, waugh, waugh, bough. Odd,
' I'll have a fnap at thy fhins—bough, waugh waugh
' waugh, bough——odds, fhe kicks bravely——

' *Aqui.* Nay, then I'll go another way to work with
' you: and I think here's an inftrument fit for the pur-
' pofe.   [*Fetches a whip and a bell.*
' What, bite your miftrefs, firrah? out of doors you dog,
' to kennel, and be hang'd—— bite your miftrefs by the
' legs, you rogue—   [*She whips him.*

' *Ant.* Nay, prithee Nacky, now thou art too loving:
' Hurry durry, odd, I'll be a dog no longer.

' *Aqui.* Nay, none of your fawning and grinning: but
' be gone, or here's the difcipline. What, bite your
' miftrefs by the leg, you mungrel? Out of doors—hout,
' hout, to kennel, firrah, go.

' *Ant.* This is very barbarous ufage, Nacky, very bar-
' barous; look you, I will not go—I will not ftir from
' the door, that I refolve—— hurry durry, what fhut me
' out?   [*She whips him out.*

' *Aqui.* Ay, if you come here any more to-night, I'll
' have my footman lug you, you cur! What, bite your
' poor miftrefs Nacky, firrah?

' *Enter* Maid.

' *Maid.* Heav'ns! madam, what's the matter?
        [*He howls at the door like a dog.*
' *Aqui.* Call my footmen hither prefently.

' *Enter two* Footmen.

' *Maid.* They're here already, madam; all the houfe
' is alarm'd with a ftrange noife, that no-body knows
' what to make of.

' *Aqui.* Go, all of you, and turn that troublefome
' beaft in the next room out of my houfe—If ever I fee
' him within thefe walls again, without my leave for his
' admittance, you fneaking rogues—I'll have you poi-
' fon'd, all poifon'd like rats: every corner of the houfe
' fhall ftink of one of you; go, and learn hereafter to
' know my pleafure. So; now for my *Purre.*

' Thus, when the god-like lover is difpleas'd,
' We facrifice our fool, and he's appeas'd. [*Exeunt.*'

SCENE *a chamber.* Enter Belvidera.

Bel. I'm facrific'd! I'm fold! betray'd to fhame!
Inevitable ruin has inclos'd me!
' No fooner was I to my bed repair'd,
' To weigh and (weeping) ponder my condition;
' But the old hoary wretch, to whofe falfe care
' My peace and honour was entrufted, came,
' (Like *Tarquin*) ghaftly, with infernal luft.
' O thou *Roman Lucrece!*
' Thou could'ft find friends, to vindicate thy wrong?
' I never had but one, and he's prov'd falfe:'
He that fhould guard my virtue, has betray'd it;
Left me! undone me! Oh, that I could hate him!
Where fhall I go? Oh, whither, whither wander?

Enter Jaffier.

Jaff. Can *Belvidera* want a refting-place,
When thefe poor arms are ready to receive her?
' Oh! 'tis in vain to ftruggle with defires.
' Strong is my love to thee; for, every moment
' I'm from thy fight, the heart within my bofom
' Mourns like a tender infant in its cradle,
' Whofe nurfe has left it. Come, and with the fongs
' Of gentle love, perfuade it to its peace.
' *Bel.* I fear the ftubborn wanderer will not own me;
' 'Tis grown a rebel, to be rul'd no longer;
' Scorns the indulgent bofom, that firft lull'd it;
' And, like a difobedient child, difdains
' The foft authority of *Belvidera.*
' *Jaff.*' There was a time——
Bel. Yes, yes, there was a time,
When *Belvidera*'s tears, her cries, and ferrows,

B 3   Were

Were not defpis'd; when, if fhe chanc'd to figh,
Or look but fad——there was indeed a time,
When *Jaffier* would have ta'en her in his arms,
Fas'd her declining head upon his breaft,
And never left her, till he found the caufe.
' But let her now weep feas;
' Cry, till fhe rend the earth; figh, till fhe burft
' Her heart afunder; ftill he bears it all,
' Deaf as the wind, and as the rocks unfhaken.
   ' *Jaff.* Have I been deaf? Am I that rock unmov'd,
' Againft whofe root tears beat, and fighs are fent
' In vain? Have I beheld thy forrows calmly!
' Witnefs againft me, Heavens, have I done this?
' Then bear me in a whirlwind back again,
' And let that angry dear one ne'er forgive me.
' Oh! thou too rafhly cenfureft of my love;
" Couldft thou but think how I have fpent this night,
' Dark, and alone, no pillow to my head,
' Reft in my eyes, nor quiet in my heart,
' Thou wouldft not, *Belvidera*, fure thou wouldft not
' Talk to me thus; but like a pitying angel,
' Spreading thy wings, come fettle on my breaft,
' And hatch warm comforts there, ere forrows freeze it.
   ' *Bel.* Why then, poor mourner, in what baleful corner
' Haft thou been talking with that witch, the night?
' On what cold ftone haft thou been ftretch'd along,
' Gathering the grumbling winds about thy head,
' To mix with theirs the accent of my woes?
' Oh! now I find the caufe my love forfakes me:
' I am no longer fit to bear a fhare
' In his concernments. My weak female virtue
' Muft not be trufted: 'Tis too frail and tender.'
   Jaff. O *Portia*, *Portia*! What a foul was thine!
   Bel. That *Portia* was a woman; and when *Brutus*,
Big with the fate of *Rome*, (Heav'n guard thy fafety!)
Conceal'd from her the labours of his mind;
She let him fee her blood was great as his,
Flow'd from a fpring as noble, and a heart
Fit to partake his troubles as his love.
Fetch, fetch that dagger back, the dreadful dower
Thou gav'ft laft night in parting with me; ftrike it
Here to my heart; and, as the blood flows from it,
Judge if it run not pure as *Cato*'s daughter's.
   ' *Jaff.* Thou art too good, and I indeed unworthy,
                        ' Unworthy

' Unworthy so much virtue. Teach me how
' I may deserve such matchless love as thine,
' And see with what attention I'll obey thee.
   ' *Bel.* Do not despise me : that's the all I ask.
   ' *Jaff.* Despise thee ! Hear me——
   ' *Bel.* Oh ! thy charming tongue
' Is but too well acquainted with my weakness ;
' Knows, let it name but love, my melting heart
' Dissolv s within my breast ; till with clos'd eyes
' I reel into thy arms, and all's forgotten.
   ' *Jaff.* What shall I do ?
   ' *Bel.* Tell me ; be just, and tell me,
' Why dwells that busy cloud upon thy face ?
' Why am I made a stranger ? Why that sigh,
' And I not know the cause ? Why, when the world
' Is wrapp'd in rest, why chuses then my love
' To wander up and down in horrid darkness,
' Loathing his bed, and these desiring arms ?
' Why are these eyes blood-shot with tedious watching ?
' Why starts he now, and looks as if he wish'd
' His fate were finish'd ? Tell me, ease my fear ;
' Lest, when we next time meet, I want the power
' To search into the sickness of thy mind,
' But talk as wildly then, as thou look'st now.'
   Jaff. O *Belvidera !*
   Bel. Why was I last night deliver'd to a villain ?
   Jaff. Ha ! a villain ?
   Bel. Yes, to a villain ! Why at such an hour
Meets that assembly, all made up of wretches,
' That look as hell had drawn them into league ?'
Why, I in this hand, and in that a dagger,
Was I deliver'd with dreadful ceremonies ?
To you, sir, and to your honour I bequeath her,
And with her this : Whene'er I prove unworthy——
You know the rest—then strike it to her heart.
Oh ! why's that rest conceal'd from me ? Must I
Be made the hostage of a hellish trust ?
For such I know I am ; that's all my value.
But, by the love and loyalty I owe thee,
I'll free thee from the bondage of these slaves ;
Straight to the senate, tell 'em all I know,
All that I think, all that my fears inform me.
   Jaff. Is this the *Roman* virtue ; this the blood
That boasts its purity with *Cato*'s daughter ?
      .   B 4   Would

Would she have e'er betray'd her *Brutus*?

Pri. No:

For *Brutus* trusted her——Wert thou so kind,

What would not *Belvidera* suffer for thee?

  Jaff. I shall undo myself, and tell thee all.

' *Bel.* Look not upon me as I am, a woman,

' But as a bone, thy wife, thy friend; who long

' Has had admission to thy heart, and there

' Study'd the virtues of thy gallant nature.

' Thy constancy, thy courage, and thy truth,

' Have been my daily lesson: I have learn'd 'em.

' And, bold as thou, can suffer or despise

' The worst of fates for thee, and with thee share 'em.

  ' *Jaff.* O, thou divinest power! look down, and hear

' My prayers! instruct me to reward this virtue!'

Yet think a little, ere thou tempt me further;

Think I've a tale to tell will shake thy nature,

Melt all this boasted constancy thou talk'st of,

Into vile tears and despicable sorrows:

Then, if thou should'st betray me!——

  Bel. Shall I swear?

  Jaff. No, do not swear: I would not violate

Thy tender nature with so rude a bond;

But as thou hop'st to see me live my days,

And love thee long, lock this within thy breast:

I've bound myself, by all the strictest sacraments,

Divine and human——

  Bel. Speak!

  Jaff. To kill thy father——

  Bel. My father!

  Jaff. Nay, the throats of the whole senate

Shall bleed, my *Belvidera*. He amongst us,

That spares his father, brother, or his friend,

Is damn'd, ' How rich and beauteous will the face

' Of ruin look, when these wide streets run blood!

' I, and the glorious partners of my fortune,

' Shouting, and striding o'er the prostrate dead,

' Still to new waste; whilst thou, far off in safety,

' Smiling, shalt see the wonders of our daring;

' And, when night comes, with praise and love receive

  ' me.'

  Bel. Oh!

  Jaff. Have a care, and shrink not even in thought:

For if thou do'st——

Bel.

Bel. I know it; thou wilt kill me.
Do, ſtrike this ſword into this boſom: lay me
Dead on the earth, then thou will be ſafe.
Murder my father! Tho' his cruel nature
Has perſecuted me to my undoing;
Driven me to baſeſt wants; can I behold him,
With ſmiles of vengeance, butcher'd in his age?
The ſacred fountain of my life deſtroy'd?
And canſt thou ſhed the blood that gave me being?
Nay, be a traitor too, and ſell thy country?
Can thy great heart deſcend ſo vilely low,
Mix with hir'd ſlaves, bravoes, and common ſtabbers,
' Noſe-ſlitters, alley-lurking villains!' join
With ſuch a crew, and take a ruffian's wages,
To cut the throats of wretches as they ſleep?

Jaff. Thou wrong'ſt me, *Belvidera!* I've engag'd
With men of ſouls; fit to reform the ills
Of all mankind: there's not a heart amongſt them
But's ſtout as death, yet honeſt as the nature
Of man firſt made, ere fraud and vice were faſhions.

Bel. What's he, to whoſe curs'd hands laſt night thou
          gav'ſt me?
Was that well done! Oh! I could tell a ſtory,
Would rouze thy lion heart out of its den,
And make it rage with terrifying fury.

Jaff. Speak on, I charge thee.

Bel. O my love! if e'er
Thy *Belvidera's* peace deſerv'd thy care,
Remove me from this place. Laſt night! laſt night!

Jaff. Diſtract me not, but give me all the truth.

Bel. No ſooner wert thou gone, and I alone,
Left in the power of that old ſon of miſchief;
No ſooner was I laid on my ſad bed,
But that vile wretch approach'd me, looſe, ' unbutton'd,
' Ready for violation:' Then my heart
Throbb'd with its fears: Oh, how I wept and ſigh'd!
And ſhrunk and trembled! wiſh'd in vain for him
That ſhould protect me! Thou, alas! wert gone.

Jaff. Patience, ſweet Heav'n, till I make vengeance
     ſure.

Bel. He drew the hideous dagger forth, thou gav'ſt him,
And, with upbraiding ſmiles, he ſaid, *Behold it:*
This is the pledge of a falſe huſband's love:
And in my arms then preſs'd, and would have claſp'd me;

But with my cries, I fear'd his coward heart,
Till he withdrew, and mutter'd vows to hell.
These are thy friends! with these thy life, thy honour,
Thy love, all stak'd, and all will go to ruin.

Jaff. No more: I charge thee keep this secret close.
Clear up thy sorrows; look as if thy wrongs
Were all forgot, and treat him like a friend,
As no complaint were made. No more; retire,
Retire, my life, and doubt not of my honour;
I'll heal his failings, and deserve thy love.

Bel. Oh! should I part with thee, I fear thou wilt
In anger leave me, and return no more.

Jaff. Return no more! I would not live without thee
Another night, to purchase the creation.

Bel. When shall we meet again?

Jaff. Anon, at twelve
I'll steal myself to thy expecting arms:
Come like a travell'd dove, and bring thee peace.

Bel. Indeed!

Jaff. By all our loves.

Bel. 'Tis hard to part:
But sure no falshood ever look'd so fairly.
Farewell; remember twelve.   [*Exit.*

Jaff. Let Heav'n forget me,
When I remember not thy truth, thy love.
' How curs'd is my condition, tofs'd and jostled
' From every corner! Fortune's common fool,
' The jest of rogues, an instrumental ass,
' For villains to lay loads of shame upon,
' And drive about just for their ease and scorn.'

Enter Pierre.

Pier. Jaffier.

Jaff. Who calls?

Pier. A friend, that could have wish'd
T'have found thee otherwise employ'd. What, hunt
A wife on the dull soil! Sure a staunch husband
Of all hounds is the dullest. Wilt thou never,
Never be wean'd from caudles and confections?
What feminine tales hast thou been list'ning to,
Of unair'd shirts, catarrhs, and tooth-ach, got
By thin-sol'd shoes? Damnation! that a fellow,
Chosen to be a sharer in the destruction
Of a whole people, should sneak thus into corners
To waste his time, and fool his mind with love.

                                        Jaff.

Jaff. May not a man then trifle out an hour
With a kind woman, and not wrong his calling?
  Pier. Not in a cause like ours.
  Jaff. Then, friend, our cause
Is in a damn'd condition: for I'll tell thee,
That canker-worm, call'd lechery, has touch'd it;
'Tis tainted vilely. Would'st thou think it? *Renault*
(That mortify'd old wither'd winter rogue)
Loves simple fornication like a priest;
I found him out for watering at my wife;
He visited her last night, like a kind guardian:
Faith, she has some temptation, that's the truth on't.
  Pier. He durst not wrong his trust.
  Jaff. 'Twas something late though,
To take the freedom of a lady's chamber.
  Pier. Was she in bed?
  Jaff. Yes, faith! in virgin sheets,
White as her bosom, *Pierre*, dish'd neatly up,
Might tempt a weaker appetite to taste.
Oh! how the old fox stunk, I warrant thee,
When the rank fit was on him.
  Pier. Patience guide me!
He's us'd no violence?
  Jaff. No, no; out on't, violence!
Play'd with her neck; brush'd her with his grey beard;
Struggl'd and touz'd; tickl'd her till she squeak'd a little,
May be, or so—but not a jot of violence—
  Pier. Damn him.
  Jaff. Ay, so say I: but hush, no more on't,
All hitherto is well, and I believe
Myself no monster yet: ' tho' no man knows
' What fate he's born to.' Sure it is near the hour
We all should meet for our concluding orders:
Will the ambassador be here in person?
  Pier. No, he has sent commission to that villain *Re-*
To give the executing charge: [*nault,*
I'd have thee be a man, if possible,
And keep thy temper; for a brave revenge
Ne'er comes too late.
  Jaff. Fear not, I am as cool as patience.
' Had he compleated my dishonour, rather
' Than hazard the success our hopes are ripe for,
' I'd bear it all with mortifying virtue.'
  Pier. He's yonder, coming this way thro' the hall;

His

His thoughts seem full.

Jaff. Prithee retire and leave me
With him alone: I ll put him to some trial;
See how his rotten part will bear the touching.

Pier. Be careful then.   [*Exit.*

Jaff. Nay, never doubt, but trust me.
What, be a devil, take a damning oath
For shedding native blood! Can there be a sin
In merciful repentance? Oh, this villain!

Enter Renault.

Ren. Perverse and peevish: What a slave is man
To let his itching flesh thus get the better of him!
Dispatch the fool her husband—that were well.
Who's there?

Jeff. A man.

Ren. My friend, my near ally,
The hostage of your faith, my beauteous charge, is very

Jeff. Sir, are you sure of that?   [well.
Stands she in perfect health? Beats her pulse even;
Neither too hot nor cold?

Ren. What means that question?

Jaff. Oh! women have fantastic constitutions,
Inconstant in their wishes, always wavering,
And never fixt. Was it not boldly done
Even at first sight, to trust the thing I lov'd
(A tempting treasure too) with youth so fierce
And vigorous as thine? but thou art honest.

Ren. Who dare accuse me?

Jff. Curs'd be he that doubts
Thy virtue! I have try'd it, and declare,
Were I to chuse a guardian of my honour,
I'd put it in thy keeping; for I know thee.

Ren. Know me!

Jff. Ay, know thee. There's no falshood in thee;
Thou look'st just as thou art. Let us embrace.
Now would'st thou cut my throat, or I cut thine.

Ren. You dare not do't.

Jff. You lye, sir.

Ren. How!

Jaff. No more,
'Tis a base world, and must reform, that's all.

Enter Spinosa, Theodore, Elliot, Revillido, Durand,
Bramveil, *and the rest of the conspirators.*

Ren. Spinosa, Theodore, you are welcome.

Spin. You are trembling, sir.   *Ren.*

Ren. 'Tis a cold night, indeed ; I am aged ;
Full of decay and natural infirmities.   [*Pier. re enters.*
We shall be warm, my friends, I hope, to-morrow.

   Pier. 'Twas not well done ; thou should'st have strok'd
And not have gall'd him,   [him,

   Jaff. Damn him, let him chew on't.
Heav'n ! Where am I ? beset with cursed fiends,
That wait to damn me ! What a devil's man,
When he forgets his nature —— hush, my heart.

   Ren. My friends, 'tis late : are we assembled all ?
' Where's *Theodore ?*

   ' *Theod.* At hand.

   ' *Ren.* *Spinosa.*

   ' *Spin.* Here.

   ' *Ren.* *Bramveil.*

   ' *Bram.* I am ready.

   ' *Ren.* *Durand* and *Brabe.*

   ' *Dur.* Command us.
' We are both prepar'd.'

   Omnes. All ; all.

   Ren. ' *Mezzana, Revillido.*
' *Ternon, Retrosi :*' Oh ! you're brave men, I find
Fit to behold your fate, and meet her summons.
To-morrow's rising sun must see you all
Deck'd in your honours.   Are the soldiers ready ?

   Pier. All ; all.

   Ren. You, *Durand*, with your thousand, must possess
St. *Mark's* ; you, captain, know your charge already ;
'Tis to secure the ducal palace : ' You,
' *Brabe*, with an hundred more, must gain the *Secque :*
' With the like number, *Bramveil*, to the *Procurati.*'
Be all this done with the least tumult possible,
'Till in each place you post sufficient guards :
Then sheathe your swords in every breast you meet,

   Jaff. Oh, reverend cruelty ! damn'd bloody villain.

   Ren. During this execution, *Durand*, you
Must in the midst keep your battalia fast ;
And, *Theodore*, be sure to plant the cannon
That may command the street ; ' whilst *Revillido*,
' *Mezzana, Ternon,* and *Retrosi* guard you.'
This done, we'll give the general alarm,
Apply petards, and force the ars'nal gates ;
Then fire the city round in several places,
Or with our cannon (if it dare resist)

                                             Batter

Batter to ruin. But above all, I charge you
Shed blood enough ; ſpare neither ſex nor age,
Name nor condition : if there lives a ſenator
After-to morrow, though the dulleſt rogue
That e'er ſaid nothing, we have loſt our ends.
If poſſible, let's kill the very name
Of ſenator, and bury it in blood.

Jaff. Mercileſs, horrid ſlave—Ay, blood enough !
Shed blood enough, old *Renault !* how thou charm'ſt me !

Ren. But one thing more and then farewel, till fate
Join us again, or ſep'rate us for ever :
Firſt let's embrace. Heav'n knows who next ſhall thus
Wing ye together : but let us all remember,
We wear no common cauſe upon our ſword.
Let each man think, that on his ſingle virtue
Depends the good and fame of all the reſt ;
Eternal honour, or perpetual infamy.
' Let us remember, through what dreadful hazards
' Propitious fortune hitherto has led us :
' How often on the brink of ſome diſcovery
' Have we ſtood tottering, yet ſtill kept our ground
' So well, that the buſieſt ſearcher ne'er could follow
' Thoſe ſubtle tracks, which puzzled all ſuſpicion ?'
You droop, ſir.

Jaff. No ; with moſt profound attention
I've heard it all, and wonder at thy virtue.

Ren. ' Tho' there be yet few hours 'twixt them and
' Are not the ſenate lull'd in full ſecurity,   [ruin,
' Quiet and ſatisfy'd, as fools are always ?
' Never did ſo profound repoſe fore-run
' Calamity ſo great. Nay, our good fortune
' Has blinded the moſt piercing of mankind,
' Strengthen'd the fearfulleſt, charm'd the moſt ſuſpect-
' Confounded the moſt ſubtle ; for we live,   [ful,
' We live, my friends, and quickly ſhall our lives
' Prove fatal to theſe tyrants.' Let's conſider,
That we deſtroy oppreſſion, avarice,
A people nurs'd up equally with vices
And loathſome luſts, which nature moſt abhors,
And ſuch as without ſhame ſhe cannot ſuffer.

Jaff. O *Belvidera !* take me to thy arms,
And ſhew me where's my peace, for I have loſt it. [*Exit.*

Ren. Without the leaſt remorſe then, let's reſolve
With fire and ſword t'exterminate theſe tyrants ;

' And

' And when we shall behold these curs'd tribunals
' Stain'd by the tears and sufferings of the innocent,
' Burning with flames rather from Heav'n than ours,
' The raging, furious, and unpitying soldier
' Pulling his reeking dagger from the bosoms
' Of gasping wretches; death in every quarter;
' With all that sad disorder can produce
' To make a spectacle of horror; then,
' Then let us call to mind, my dearest friends,
' That there is nothing pure upon the earth;
' That the most valu'd things have most alloys,
' And that in change of all those vile enormities,'
Under whose weight this wretched country labours,
The means are only in our hands to crown them.

    Pier. And may those powers above, that are propitious
To gallant minds record this cause, and bless it!

    Ren. Thus happy, thus secure of all we wish for,
Should there, my friends, be found among us one
False to this glorious enterprize, what fate,
What vengeance, were enough for such a villain?

    Ell. Death here without repentance, hell hereafter.

    Ren. Let that be my lot, if as here I stand,
Lifted by fate among her darling sons,
Tho' I had one only brother, dear by all
The strictest ties of nature; ' tho' one hour
' Had given us birth, one fortune fed our wants,
' One only love, and that but of each other,
' Still fill'd our minds:' could I have such a friend
Join'd in this cause, and had but ground for fear
He meant foul play; may this right hand drop from me,
If I'd not hazard all my future peace,
And stab him to the heart before you. Who,
Who would do less? Would'st thou not, *Pierre*, the same?

    Pier. You've singled me, sir, out for this hard question,
As if 'twere started only for my sake?
Am I the thing you fear? Here, here's my bosom,
Search it with all your swords. Am I a traitor?

    Ren. No: but I fear your late commended friend
Is little less. Come, sirs, 'tis now no time
To trifle with our safety. Where's this *Jaffier*?

    Spin. He left the room just now, in strange disorder.

    Ren. Nay there is danger in him: I observ'd him;
During the time I took for explanation,
He was transported from most deep attention

To a confusion which he could not smother.
' His looks grew full of sadness and surprize,
' All which betray'd a wavering spirit in him,
' That labour'd with reluctancy and sorrow.'
What's requisite for safety must be done
With speedy execution; he remains
Yet in our power: I, for my own part, wear
A dagger——

    Pier. Well.

    Ren. And I could with it——

    Pier. Where?

    Ren. Bury'd in his heart.

    Pier. Away! we're yet all friends.
No more of this! 'twill breed ill blood among us.

    Spin. Let us all draw our swords, and search the house,
Pull him from the dark hole where he sits brooding
O'er his cold fears, and each man kill his share of him.

    Pier. Who talks of killing? Who's he'll shed the blood
That's dear to me? Is't you? or you, sir?
What, not one speak! how you stand gaping all
On your grave oracle, your wooden god there!
Yet not a word! then, sir, I'll tell you a secret;
Suspicion's but at best a coward's virtue.   [*To* Ren.

    Ren. A coward——   [*Handles his sword.*

    Pier. Put up thy sword, old man;
Thy hand shakes at it. Come, let's heal this breach;
I am too hot: we yet may all live friends.

    Spin. Till we are safe, our friendship cannot be so.

    Pier. Again! Who's that?

    Spin. 'Twas I.

    Theod. And I.

    Ren. And I.

    Om. And all.

    ' *Ren.* Who are on my side?

    Spin. ' Every honest sword.'
Let's die like men, and not be sold like slaves.

    Pier. One such word more, by Heav'n, I'll to the senate,
And hang ye all like dogs, in clusters.
Why weep your coward swords half out their shells?
Why do you not all brandish them like mine?
You fear to die, and yet dare talk of killing.

    Ren. Go to the senate, and betray us, haste!
Secure thy wretched life; we fear to die
Less than thou dar'st be honest.

                       Pier.

Pier. That's rank falfhood.
Fear'ft thou not death ? Fie, there's a knavifh itch
In that falt blood, an utter foe to fmarting.
Had *Jaffier*'s wife prov'd kind, he'd ftill been true.
Faugh—how that ftinks !
Thou die ! thou kill my friend ! or thou ! or thou !
' With that lean wither'd face !'
Away, difperfe all to your feveral charges,
And meet to-morrow where your honour calls you.
I'll bring the man, whofe blood you fo much thirft for,
And you fhall fee him venture for you fairly—
Hence ! hence, I fay.   [*Exit* Renault *angrily*.
   Spin. I fear we have been to blame,
And done too much.
   ' *Theed.* 'Twas too far urg'd againft the man you lov'd.
   ' *Rev.* Here take our fwords, and crufh them with your
   Spin. Forgive us, gallant friend.   [feet.
   Pier. Nay, now you've found
The way to melt, and caft me as you will.
' I'll fetch this friend, and give him to your mercy:
' Nay, he fhall die, if you will take him from me.
' For your repofe, I'll quit my heart's beft jewel ;
' But would not have him torn away by villains,
' A fpiteful villainy.
   ' *Spin.* No, may you both
' For ever live, and fill the world with fame.'
   Pier. ' Now ye're too kind.'   Whence arofe all this
            difcord ?
Oh, what a dangerous precipice have we 'fcap'd !
How near a fall was all we'd long been building !
What an eternal blot had ftain'd our glories,
If one, the braveft and the beft of men,
Had fall'n a facrifice to rafh fufpicion,
Butcher'd by thofe, whofe caufe he came to cherifh !
' Oh! could you know him all, as I have known him ;
' How good he is, how juft, how true, how brave,
' You would not leave this place till you had feen him ;
' Humbled yourfelves before him, kifs'd his feet,
' And gain'd remiffion for the worft of follies.'
Come but to-morrow, all your doubts fhall end,
And to your loves me better recommend,
That I've preferv'd your fame, and fav'd my friend.
                                 [*Exeunt*.

                    A C T

A C T IV.

S C E N E *the* Rialto.

Enter Jaffier *and* Belvidera.

Jaff. WHERE doſt thou lead me? Ev'ry ſtep I move,
   Methinks I tread upon ſome mangled limb
Of a rack'd friend. O, my charming ruin!
Where are we wandering?
 Bel. To eternal honour.
You do a deed ſhall chronicle thy name
Among the glorious legends of thoſe few
That have ſav'd ſinking nations. Thy renown
Shall be the future ſong of all the virgins,
Who by thy piety have been preſerv'd
From horrid violation. Every ſtreet
Shall be adorn'd with ſtatues to thy honour:
And at thy feet this great inſcription written,
Remember him that propp'd the fall of Venice.
 Jaff. Rather, remember him, who, after all
The ſacred bonds of oaths, aud holier friendſhip,
In fond compaſſion to a woman's tears,
Forgot his manhood, virtue, truth, and honour,
To ſacrifice the boſom that reliev'd him.
Why wilt thou damn me?
 Bel. O inconſtant man!
How will you promiſe; how will you deceive!
Do, return back, replace me in my bondage,
Tell all thy friends how dangerouſly thou lov'ſt me,
And let thy dagger do its bloody office.
' O! that kind dagger. *Jaffier*, how't will look
' Struck thro' my heart, drench'd in my blood to th'hilt;
' Whilſt theſe poor dying eyes, ſhall with their tears
' No more torment thee; then thou wilt be free:'
Or, if thou think'ſt it nobler, let me live,
Till I'm a victim to the hateful luſt
Of that infernal devil, ' that old fiend,
' That's damn'd himſelf, and would undo mankind.'
Laſt night, my love!
 Jaff. Name it not again:
It ſhews a beaſtly image to my fancy,
Will wake me into madneſs. ' Oh, the villain!
' That durſt approach ſuch purity as thine

           ' On

' On terms fo vile :' Deftruction, fwift deftruction,
Fall on my coward head, ' and make my name
' The common fcorn of fools, if I forgive him :
' If I forgive him ! If not revenge
' With utmoft rage, and moft unftaying fury,
' Thy fufferings, thou dear darling of my life.'
  Bel. Delay no longer then, but to the fenate,
And tell the difmal'ft ftory ever utter'd :
Tell 'em what bloodfhed, rapines, defolations,
Have been prepar'd : how near's the fatal hour.
Save thy poor country, fave the reverend blood
Of all its nobles, which to morrow's dawn
Muft elfe fee dead. ' Save the poor tender lives
' Of all thofe little infants, which the fwords
' Of murderers are whetting for, this moment.
' Think thou already hear'ft their dying fcreams ;
' Think that thou fee'ft their fad diftracted mothers,
' Kneeling before thy feet, and begging pity :
' With torn difhevel'd hair and ftreaming eyes,
' Their naked mangled breafts befmear'd with blood ;
' And even the milk, with which their fondled babes
' Softly they hufh'd, dropping in anguifh from 'em :
' Think thou feeft this, and then confult thy heart.
  ' *Jaff.* Oh !
  ' *Bel.* Think too, if you lofe this prefent minute,
' What miferies the next day brings upon thee :
' Imagine all the horror of that night ;
' Murder and rapine, wafte and defolation,
' Confus'dly raging :' Think what then may prove
My lot ; the ravifher may then come fafe,
And, 'midft the terror of the public ruin,
Do a damn'd deed ; ' perhaps may lay a train
' To catch thy life : then where will be revenge,
' The dear revenge that's due to fuch a wrong ?'
  Jaff. By all Heav'n's powers, prophetic truth dwells
    in thee ;
For every word thou fpeak'ft ftrikes thro' my heart,
' Like a new light, and fhews it, how't has wander'd.'
Juft what thou'ft made me, take me, *Belvidera*,
And lead me to the place where I'm to fay
This bitter leffon ; where I muft betray
My truth, my virtue, conftancy, and friends.
Muft I betray my friend ? Ah ! take me quickly ;
Secure me well before that thought's renew'd ;

If I relapse once more, all's lost for ever.

Bel. Hast thou a friend more dear than *Belvidera?*

Jaff. No; thou'rt my soul itself; wealth, friendship, honour;

All present joys, and earnest of all future,
Are summ'd in thee. 'Methinks when in thy arms,
' Thus leaning on thy breast, one minute's more
' Than a long thousand years of vulgar hours.
' Why was such happiness not given me pure?
' Why dash'd with cruel wrongs, and bitter warnings?'
Come, lead me forward, now, like a tame lamb
To sacrifice. Thus, in his fatal garlands
Deck'd fine and pleas'd, the wanton skips and plays,
Trots by th' enticing flatt'ring priestess' side,
And much transported with its little pride,
Forgets his dear companions of the plain;
'Till, by her bound, he's on the altar lain,
Yet then too hardly bleats, such pleasure's in the pain.

Enter Officer and six Guards.

Off. Stand! who goes there?

Bel. Friends.

' *Jaff.* Friends, *Belvidera!* Hide me from my friends:
' By Heav'n, I'd rather see the face of hell,
' Than meet the man I love.'

Off. But what friends are you?

Bel. Friends to the senate, and the state of *Venice.*

Off. My orders are to seize on all I find
At this late hour, and bring 'em to the council,
Who are now sitting.

Jaff. Sir, you shall be obey'd.
' Hold, brute, stand off! none of your paws upon me.'
Now the lot's cast, and, fate, do what thou wilt.

[*Exeunt guarded.*

SCENE, *the Senate house.*
Where appear sitting the Duke of Venice, Priuli,
Antonio, *and eight other Senators.*

Duke. Antony, Priuli, senators of *Venice,*
Speak, why are we assembled here this night?
What have you to inform us of, concerns
The state of *Venice'* honour, or its safety?

Pri. Could words express the story I've to tell you,
Fathers, these tears were useless, these sad tears
That fall from my old eyes; but there is cause
We all should weep, tear off these purple robes,

And

And wrap ourſelves in ſackcloth, ſitting down
On the ſad earth, and cry aloud to Heav'n :
Heav'n knows, if yet there be an hour to come
Ere *Venice* be no more.

All Sen. How!

Pri. Nay, we ſtand
Upon the very brink of gaping ruin.
Within this city's form'd a dark conſpiracy
To maſſacre us all, our wives and children,
Kindred and friends, our palaces and temples
To lay in aſhes : nay, the hour too fix'd ;   [ment,
The ſwords, for aught I know, drawn e'en this mo-
And the wild waſte begun. From unknown hands
I had this warning ; but, if we are men,
Let's not be tamely butcher'd, but do ſomething
That may inform the world, in after-ages,
Our virtue was not ruin'd, tho' we were. [*A noiſe without.*
Room, room, make room for ſome priſoners ——

' *Sen.* Let's raiſe the city.'

          Enter Officer and Guards.

Duke. Speak there. What diſturbance ?

Off. Two priſoners have the guards ſeiz'd in the ſtreet,
Who ſay, they come to inform this reverend ſenate
About the preſent danger.

          Enter Jaffier *and Officer.*

All. Give 'em entrance—Well, who are you ?

Jaff. A villain.

Ant. ' Short and pithy :'
The man ſpeaks well.

Jaff. Would every man, that hears me,
Would deal ſo honeſtly, and own his title.

Duke. 'Tis rumour'd, that a plot has been contriv'd
Againſt the ſtate ; and you've a ſhare in't too.
If you are a villain, to redeem your honour
Unfold the truth, and be reſtor'd with mercy.

Jaff. Think not, that I to ſave my life came hither ;
I know its value better ; but in pity
To all thoſe wretches, whoſe unhappy dooms
Are fix'd and ſeal'd. You ſee me here before you,
The ſworn and covenanted foe of *Venice :*
But uſe me as my dealings may deſerve,
And I may prove a friend.

Duke. The ſlaves capitulates ;
Give him the tortures.

Jaff. That you dare not do :
Your fear won't let you, nor the longing itch
To hear a ſtory which you dread the truth of :
Truth, which the fear of ſmart ſhall ne'er get from me,
Cowards are fear'd with threat'ning ; boys are whipt
Into confeſſions : but a ſteady mind
Acts of itſelf, ne'er aſks the body counſel.
Give him the tortures !—name but ſuch a thing
Again, by Heav'n I'll ſhut theſe lips for ever.
Not all your racks, your engines, or your wheels,
Shall force a groan away, that you may gueſs at.

   ' *Ant.* A bloody-minded fellow, I'll warrant ;
' A damn'd bloody-minded fellow.'

   Duke. Name your conditions.

   Jaff. For myſelf full pardon,
Befides the lives of two and twenty friends,
Whoſe names are here enroll'd —Nay, let their crimes
Be ne'er ſo monſtrous, I muſt have the oaths
And ſacred promiſe of this reverend council,
That in a full aſſembly of the ſenate
The thing I ſwear be ratify'd. Swear this,
And I'll unfold the ſecret of your danger.

   ' *All.* We'll ſwear.'

   Duke. Propoſe the oath.

   Jaff. By all the hopes
You have of peace and happineſs hereafter,
Swear.

   ' *All.* We all ſwear.

   ' *Jaff.* To grant me what I've aſk'd,
' Ye ſwear ?'

   All. We ſwear.

   Jaff. And, as ye keep the oath,
May you, and your poſterity be bleſs'd,
Or curs'd for ever,

   All. Elſe be curs'd for ever.

   Jaff. Then here's the liſt, and with't the full diſcloſe
Of all that threatens you.   [*Delivers a paper.*
Now, fate, thou haſt caught me.

   ' *Ant.* Why, what a dreadful catalogue of cut-throats
' is here ! I'll warrant you, not one of theſe fellows but
' has a face like a lion. I dare not ſo much as read
' their names over.'

   Duke. Give order that all diligent ſearch be made
To ſeize theſe men, their characters are public.

                            The

The paper intimates their rendezvous
To be at the houſe of the fam'd *Grecian* courtezan,
Call'd *Aquilina*; ſee the place ſecur'd.

  ' *Ant.* What, my Nicky Nacky! hurry durry!
' Nicky Nacky, in the plot—I'll make a ſpeech.
' Moſt noble ſenators,
' What headlong apprehenſions drive you on,
' Right noble, wife, and truly ſolid ſenators,
' To violate the laws and rights of nations?
' The lady is a lady of renown;
' 'Tis true, ſhe holds a houſe of fair reception,
' And, tho' I ſay't myſelf, as many more
' Can ſay, as well as I——
  ' 2 *Sen.* My lord, long ſpeeches
' Are frivolous here, when dangers are ſo near us.
' We all well know your intereſt in that lady;
' The world talks loud on't.
  ' *Ant.* Verily I have done;
' I ſay no more.
  ' *Duke.* But, ſince he has declar'd
' Himſelf concern'd, pray, captain, take great caution
' To treat the fair one as becomes her character;
' And let her bed-chamber be ſearch'd with decency.'
You, *Jaffier*, muſt with patience bear till morning
To be our priſoner.
  Jaff. Would the chains of death
Had bound me ſafe, ere I had known this minute.
' I've done a deed will make my ſtory hereafter
' Quoted in competition with all ill ones:
' The ſtory of my wickedneſs ſhall run
' Down thro' the low traditions of the vulgar,
' And boys be taught to tell the tale of *Jaffier*.'
  Duke. Captain, withdraw your priſoner.
  Jeff. Sir, if poſſible,
Lead me where my own thoughts themſelves may loſe me;
Where I may doze out what I've left of life,
Forget myſelf, and this day's guilt and falchood.
Cruel remembrance, how ſhall I appeaſe thee?
                      [*Exit guarded.*

  Off. [*without.*] More traitors; room, room, make
  Duke. How's this, guards?   [room there.
Where are our guards? Shut up the gates, the treaſon's
Already at the doors.
            Enter Officer.
  Off. My lords, more traitors,   Seiz'd

Seiz'd in the very act of consultation ;
Furnish'd with arms and instruments of mischief.
Bring in the prisoners.

    Enter Pierre, Renault, Theodore, Elliot, Revellido,
        and other conspirators, in fetters.

    Pier. You, my lords, and fathers,
(As you are pleas'd to call yourselves) of *Venice* ;
If you sit here to guide the course of justice,
Why these disgraceful chains upon the limbs
That have so often labour'd in your service ?
Are these the wreaths of triumph ye bestow
On those, that bring you conquest home, and honours ?
    Duke. Go on ; you shall be heard, sir.
    ' *Ant.* And be hang'd too, I hope.'
    Pier. Are these the trophies I've deserv'd, for fighting
Your battles with confederated powers ?
When winds and seas conspir'd to overthrow you,
And brought the fleets of *Spain* to your own harbours ;
And you, great Duke, shrunk trembling in your palace,
And saw your wife, the *Adriatic*, plough'd,
Like a lewd whore, by bolder plows than yours ;
Stepp'd not I forth, and taught your loose *Venetians*
The task of honour, and the way of greatness ?
Rais'd you from your capitulating fears
To stipulate the terms of su'd-for peace ?
And this my recompence ! If I'm a traitor,
Produce my charge ; or shew the wretch that's base
And brave enough to tell me I'm a traitor.
    Duke. Know you one *Jaffier ?*   [*Consp. murmur.*
    Pier. Yes, and know his virtue.
His justice, truth, his general worth, and sufferings
From a hard father, taught me first to love him.
    Duke. See him brought forth.
            Enter Jaffier *guarded.*
    Pier. My friend too bound ! nay then
Our fate has conquer'd us, and we must fall.
Why droops the man whose welfare's so much mine,
They're but one thing ? These reverend tyrants, *Jaffier,*
Call us traitors. Art thou one, my brother ?
    Jaff. To thee I am the falsest, veriest slave,
That e'er betray'd a generous, trusting friend,
And gave up honour to be sure of ruin.
All our fair hopes, which morning was t' have crown'd,
Has this curs'd tongue o'erthrown.

                        Pier.

E.Edwards ad viv del.   Published 1 Dec.r 1776, by T.Lowndes & Partners.   Collyer sculp.

Mr BENSLEY in the Character of PIERRE

Who's he disputes the Judgment of the Senate
Presumptuous Rebel!———

Act 4 Sc 2

Pier. So, then all's over:
Venice haſt loſt her freedom, I my life.
No more!

Duke. Say; will you make confeſſion
Of your vile deeds, and truſt the ſenate's mercy?

Pier. Curs'd be your ſenate : curs'd your conſtitution:
The curſe of growing factions and diviſions,
Still vex your councils, ſhake your public ſafety,
And make the robes of government you wear
Hateful to you, as theſe baſe chains to me.

Duke. Pardon, or death?

Pier. Death! honourable death!

Ren. Death's the beſt thing we aſk, or you can give.
No ſhameful bonds, but honourable death.

Duke. Break up the council. Captain, guard your
  priſoners.
Jaffier, you're free, but theſe muſt wait for judgment.
        Ex. all the ſenators.

Pier. Come, where's my dungeon? Lead me to my
It will not be the firſt time I've lodg'd hard [ſtraw:
To do the ſenate ſervice.

Jaff. Hold one moment.

Pier. Who's he diſputes the judgment of the ſenate?
Preſumptuous rebel—on—   [*Strikes* Jaff.

Jaff. By Heaven, you ſtir not!
I muſt be heard ; I muſt have leave to ſpeak.
Thou haſt diſgraced me, *Pierre,* by a vile blow:
Had not a dagger done thee nobler juſtice?
But uſe me as thou wilt, thou canſt not wrong me,
For I am fallen beneath the baſeſt injuries:
Yet look upon me with an eye of mercy,
With pity and with charity behold me ;
' Shut not thy heart againſt a friend's repentance:'
But, as there dwells a godlike nature in thee,
Liſten with mildneſs to my ſupplications.

Pier. What whining monk art thou? what holy cheat,
That would ſt incroach upon my credulous ears,
And cant'ſt thus vilely? Hence! I know thee not;
' Diſſemble and be naſty.' Leave, hypocrite.

Jaff. Not know me, *Pierre!*

Pier. No, know thee not! What art thou?

Jaff. *Jaffier,* thy friend, thy once-lov'd valu'd friend!
Tho' now deſervedly ſcorn'd, and us'd moſt hardly.

Pier. Thou, *Jaffier!* thou, my once-lov'd valu'd friend!
      C   By

By Heav'ns, thou ly'ft; the man fo call'd, my friend,
Was generous, honeft, faithful, juft, and valiant;
Noble in mind, and in his perfon lovely;
Dear to my eyes, and tender to my heart:
But thou, a wretched, bafe, falfe, worthlefs coward,
Poor, even in foul, and loathfome in thy afpect;
All eyes muft fhun thee, and all hearts deteft thee.
Prithee avoid; nor longer cling thus round me,
Like fomething baneful, that my nature's chill'd at.

   Jaff. I have not wrong'd thee, by thefe tears I have not.
'But ftill am honeft, true, and, hope too, valiant;
'My mind ftill full of thee, therefore ftill noble.
'Let not thy eyes then fhun me, nor thy heart
'Deteft me utterly. Oh! look upon me,
'Look back, and fee my fad, fincere fubmiffion!
'How my heart fwells, as e'en 'twould burft my bofom;
'Fond of its goal, and labouring to be at thee.
'What fhall I do? what fay, to make thee hear me?'

   Pier. Haft thou not wrong'd me? Dar'ft thou call
'That once-lov'd, valu'd friend of mine,   [thyfelf
And fwear thou haft not wrong'd me? Whence thefe
     chains?
Whence the vile death which I may meet this moment?
Whence this difhonour, but from thee, thou falfe one?

   Jaff. All's true; yet grant one thing, and I've done
   Pier. What's that?   [afking.
   Jaff. To take thy life, on fuch conditions
The council have propos'd: thou, and thy friends,
May yet live long, and to be better treated.

   Pier. Life! afk my life! confefs! record myfelf
A villain, for the privilege to breathe,
And carry up and down this curfed city,
A difcontented and repining fpirit,
Burthenfome to itfelf, a few years longer;
To lofe it, may be, at laft, in a lewd quarrel
For fome new friend, treacherous and falfe as thou art!
No, this vile world and I have long been jangling,
And cannot part on better terms than now,
When only men, like thee, are fit to live in't.

   Jaff. By all that's juft——

   Pier. Swear by fome other power,
For thou haft broke that facred oath too lately.

   Jaff. Then, by that hell I merit, I'll not leave thee,
Till, to thyfelf at leaft, thou'rt reconcil'd,

However

However thy refentment deal with me.

Pier. Not leave me!

Jaff. No; thou fhalt not force me from thee.
Ufe me reproachfully, and like a flave;
Tread on me, buffet me, heap wrongs on wrongs
On my poor head; I'll bear it all with patience
Shall weary out thy moft unfriendly cruelty:
Lie at thy feet, and kifs 'em, tho' they fpurn me;
Till wounded by my fufferings, thou relent,
And raife me to thy arms, with dear forgivenefs.

Pier. Art thou not——

Jaff. What?

Pier. A traitor?

Jaff. Yes.

Pier. A villain?

Jaff. Granted.

Pier. A coward, a moft fcandalous coward;
Spiritlefs, void of honoui; one who has fold
Thy everlafting fame for fhamelefs life!

Jaff. All, all, and more, much more: my faults are
numberlefs.

Pier. And would'ft thou have me live on terms like
Bafe, as thou'rt falfe——   [thine?

Jaff. No; 'tis to me that's granted:
The fafety of thy life was all I aim'd at,
In recompence for faith and truft fo broken.

Pier. I fcorn it more, becaufe preferv'd by thee;
And, as when firft my foolifh heart took pity
On thy misfortunes, fought thee in thy miferies,
Reliev'd thy wants, and rais'd thee from the ftate
Of wretchednefs, in which thy fate had plung'd thee,
To rank thee in my lift of noble friends;
All I receiv'd, in furety for thy truth,
Were unregarded oaths, and this, this dagger,
Given with a worthlefs pledge, thou fince haft ftol'n:
So I reftore it back to thee again;
Swearing by all thofe powers which thou haft violated,
Never from this curs'd hour, to hold communion,
Friendfhip, or intereft, with thee, tho' our years
Were to exceed thofe limited the world.
Take it—farewel—for now I owe thee nothing.

Jaff. Say, thou wilt live then.

Pier. For my life, difpofe it
Juft as thou wilt, becaufe 'tis what I'm tir'd with.

Jaff.

Jaff. O *Pierre!*

Pier. No more.

Jaff. My eyes won't lose the fight of thee,
But languish after thine, and ake with gazing.

Pier. Leave me—Nay, then thus, thus I throw thee
   from me;
And curses, great as is thy falshood, catch thee. [*Ex.*

 Jaff. Amen.
He's gone, my father, friend, preserver;
And here's the portion he has left me:
      [*Holds the dagger up.*
This dagger. Well remember'd! with this dagger,
I gave a folemn vow of dire importance;
Parted with this, and *Belvidera* together.
Have a care, mem'ry, drive that thought no farther:
No, I'll esteem it, as a friend's last legacy;
Treasure it up, within this wretched bosom,
Where it may grow acquainted with my heart,
That, when they meet, they start not from each other.
So, now for thinking—A blow, call'd traitor, villain,
Coward, dishonourable coward; fough!
' Oh! for a long found sleep, and so forget it.'
Down, busy devil.

    Enter Belvidera.

 Bel. Whither shall I fly?
Where hide me and my miseries together?
Where's now the *Roman* constancy I boasted?
Sunk into trembling fears and desperation,
Not daring to look up to that dear face
Which us'd to smile, even on my faults; but, down,
Bending these miserable eyes to earth,
Must move in penance, and implore much mercy.

 Jaff. Mercy! kind Heav'n has surely endless stores
Hoarded for thee, of blessings yet untasted:
' Let wretches, loaded hard with guilt, as I am,
' Bow with the weight, and groan beneath the burthen,
' Creep with a remnant of that strength they've left
' Before the footstool of that Heav'n they've injur'd.'
O, *Belvidera!* I am the wretched'st creature [me;
E'er crawl'd on earth. ' Now, if thou'st virtue, help
' Take me into thy arms, and speak the words of peace
' To my divided soul, that wars within me,
' And raises every sense to my confusion:
' By Heav'n, I'm tottering on the very brink
            ' Of

'	Of peace; and thou art all the hold I've left.
'	*Bel.* Alas! I know thy forrows are moſt mighty:
'	I know thou'ſt cauſe to mourn, to mourn, my *Jaffier*,
'	With endleſs cries, and never-ceaſing wailing:
'	Thou'ſt loſt——
'		*Jaff.* Oh! I have loſt what can't be counted;'
My friend too, *Belvidera*, that dear friend,
Who, next to thee, was all my health rejoic'd in,
Has us'd me like a ſlave, ſhamefully us'd me:
'Twould break thy pitying heart to hear the ſtory.
'	What ſhall I do? Reſentment, indignation,
'	Love, pity, fear, and mem'ry how I've wrong'd him,
'	Diſtract my quiet, with the very thought on't,
'	And tear my heart to pieces in my boſom.'
	Bel. What has he done?
'		*Jaff.* Thou'dſt hate me, ſhould I tell thee.
'		*Bel.* Why?　　　　　　　　　　　[bear it:
'	*Jaff.* Oh! he has us'd me! yet, by Heav'n, I
'	He has us'd me, *Belvidera!* but firſt ſwear,　　　[terly,
'	That when I've told thee, thou wilt not loath me ut-
'	Tho' vileſt blots and ſtains appear upon me;
'	But ſtill, at leaſt with charitable goodneſs,
'	Be near me, in the pangs of my affliction;
'	Nor ſcorn me, *Belvidera*, as he has done.
'	*Bel.* Have I then e'er been falſe, that now I'm
		'	doubted?
'	Speak, what's the cauſe I'm grown into diſtruſt?
'	Why thought unfit to hear my love's complaining?
'		*Jaff.* Oh!
'		*Bel.* Tell me.
'		*Jaff.* Bear my failings, for they're many.
'	O my dear angel! in that friend, I've loſt
'	All my foul's peace; for every thought of him,
'	Strikes my ſenſe hard, and deads it in my brains!
'	Would'ſt thou believe it?
'		*Bel.* Speak.'
	Jaff. Before we parted,
Ere yet his guards had led him to his priſon,
Full of ſevereſt ſorrows for his ſufferings,
With eyes o'erflowing, and a bleeding heart,
'	Humbling myſelf, almoſt beneath my nature,'
As at his feet I kneel'd, and ſued for mercy,
'	Forgetting all our friendſhip, all the dearneſs,
'	In which we've liv'd ſo many years together,'

C 3　　　　　　　　　　　　　　　　Wi*th*

With a reproachful hand, he dafh'd a blow:
He ftruck me, *Belvidera!* by Heav'n, he ftruck me!
Buffeted, call'd me traitor, villain, coward.
Am I a coward? Am I villain? Tell me:
Thou'rt the beft judge, and mad'ft me, if I am fo?
Damnation! coward!

   Bel. Oh! forgive him, *Jaffier;*
And, if his fufferings wound thy heart already,
What will they do to-morrow?

   J. ff. Ah!

   Bel. To-morrow,
When thou fhalt fee him ftretch'd in all the agonies
Of a tormenting and a fhameful death;
His bleeding bowels, and his broken limbs,
Infulted o'er by a vile butchering villain;
What will thy heart do then? Oh! fure 'twill ftream,
Like my eyes now.

   Jaff. What means thy dreadful ftory?
Death, and to-morrow? broken limbs and bowels!
' Infulted o'er by a vile butchering villain!
' By all my fears, I fhall ftart out to madnefs
' With barely gueffing, if the truth's hid longer.'

   Bel. The faithlefs fenators, 'tis they've decreed,
They fay, according to our friends' requeft,
They fhall have death, and no ignoble bondage:
Declare their promis'd mercy all as forfeited:
Falfe to their oaths, and deaf to interceffion,
Warrants are pafs'd for public death to-morrow.

   Jaff. Death! doom'd to die! condemn'd unheard!
      unpleaded!

   Bel. Nay, cruel'ft racks and torments are preparing
To force confeffion from their dying pangs.
Oh! do not look fo terribly upon me!
How your lips fhake, and all your face diforder'd!
What means my love?

   Jaff. Leave me, I charge thee leave me! —— Strong
Wake in my heart.   [temptations

   Bel For what?

   Jaff. No more, but leave me.

   Bel. Why?

   Jaff. Oh! by Heav'n, I love thee with that fondnefs,
I would not have thee ftay a moment longer
Near thefe curs'd hands; are they not cold upon thee?
        [*Pulls the dagger half out of his bofom,*
              and puts it back again.

Bel. No, everlasting comfort's in thy arms.
To lean thus on thy breast, is softer ease
Than downy pillows, deck'd on leaves of roses.

Jaff. Alas! thou think'st not of the thorns 'tis fill'd
with:
Fly ere they gall thee. There's a lurking serpent
Ready to leap, and sting thee to the heart:
Art thou not terrify'd?

Bel. No.

Jaff. Call to mind
What thou hast done, and whither thou hast brought me.

Bel. Hah!   [mischief!

Jaff. Where's my friend? my friend, thou smiling
Nay, shrink not, now 'tis too late; ' thou should'st have fled
' When thy guilt first had cause;' for dire revenge
Is up, and raging for my friend. He groans!
Hark, how he groans! his screams are in my ears
Already; see, they've fix'd him on the wheel,
And now they tear him—Murder! perjur'd senate!
Murder—Oh!—Hark thee, traitress, thou hast done this!
Thanks to thy tears, and false persuading love.
How her eyes speak! oh, thou bewitching creature!
                              [*Feeling for his dagger.*
Madness can't hurt thee. Come, thou little trembler,
Creep even into my heart, and there lie safe;
'Tis thy own citadel—Hah—yet stand off,
Heav'n must have justice, ' and my broken vows
' Will sink me else beneath its reaching mercy.'
I'll wink, and then 'tis done——

B l. What means the lord
Of me, my life, and love? What's in thy bosom,
Thou grasp'st at so? ' Nay, why am I thus treated?
    ' [Jaffier *draws the dagger, and offers to stab her.*
' What wilt thou do?' Ah! do not kill me, *Jaffier:*
' Pity these panting breasts, and trembling limbs,
' That us'd to clasp thee when thy looks were milder,
' That yet hang heavy on my unpurg'd soul;
' And plunge it not into eternal darkness.'

Jaff. Know, *Belvidera,* when we parted last,
I gave this dagger with thee, as in trust,
To be thy portion if I e'er prov'd false.
On such condition was my truth believ'd:
But now 'tis forfeited, and must be paid for.
                              [*Offers to stab her again.*

Bel. Oh! merc·.   [*Kneeling.*
Jaff. Nay, no ſtruggling.
Bel. Now, then, kill me.
           [*Leaps on his neck, and kiſſes him.*
While thus I cling about thy cruel neck,
Kiſs thy revengeful lips, and die in joys
Greater than any I can gueſs hereafter.
   Jaff. I am, I am a coward, witneſs Heav'n,
Witneſs it, earth, and ev'ry being witneſs:
'Tis but one blow! yet, by immortal love,
I cannot longer bear a thought to harm thee,
          [*He throws away the dagger, and embraces her.*
The ſeal of Providence is ſure upon thee;
And thou wert born for yet unheard-of wonders.
Oh! thou wert either born to ſave or damn me.
By all the power that's given thee o'er my ſoul,
By thy reſiſtleſs tears and conquering ſmiles,
' By the victorious love that ſtill waits on thee;'
Fly to thy cruel father, ſave my friend,
Or all our future quiet's loſt for ever.
Fall at his feet, cling round his rev'rend limbs,
Speak to him with thy eyes, and with thy tears,
Melt his hard heart, and wake dead nature in him,
Cruſh him in th' arms, torture him with thy ſoftneſs;
Nor, till thy prayers are granted, ſet him free,
But conquer him, as thou haſt conquer'd me.   [*Exeunt.*

ACT V.

SCENE, *an apartment in* Priuli's *houſe.*

Enter Priuli *ſolus.*

WHY, cruel Heav'n, have my unhappy days
    Been lengthen'd to this ſad one? Oh! diſhonour,
And deathleſs infamy have fall'n upon me.
Was it my fault? Am I a traitor? No.
But then, my only child, my daughter wedded:
There my beſt blood runs foul, and a diſeaſe
Incurable has ſeiz'd upon my memory,
To make it rot and ſtink to after-ages.
' Curs'd be the fatal minute when I got her;
' Or wou'd that I'd been any thing but man,

                         ' And

' And rais'd an iſſue which would ne'er have wrong'd me.
' The miſe·ableſt creatures (man excepted)
' Are not the leſs eſteem'd, tho' their poſterity
' Degenerate from the virtues of their fathers:
' The vileſt beaſts are happy in their offspring,
' While only man gets traitors, whores, and villains,
' Curs'd be the name, and ſome ſwift blow from fate,
' Lay this head deep, where mine may be forgotten.'

     Enter Belvidera *in a long mourning veil.*

  Bel. He's there, my father, my inhuman father,
That for three years has left an only child,
Expos'd to all the outrages of fate,
And cruel ruin!—oh ——
  Pri. What child of ſorrow
Art thou, that com'ſt wrapt up in weeds of ſadneſs,
And mov'ſt as if thy ſteps were tow'rds a grave?
  Bel. A wretch who, from the very top of happineſs
Am fallen into the loweſt depths of miſery,
And want your pitying hand to raiſe me up again.
  ' *Pri.* Indeed thou talk'ſt as thou hadſt taſted ſorrows:
' Would I could help thee!
  ' *Bel.* 'Tis greatly in your power:
' The world too ſpeaks you charitable; and I,
' Who ne'er aſk'd alms before, in that dear hope,
' Am come a begging to you, ſir.
  ' *Pri.* For what?
  ' *Bel.* Oh! well regard me, is this voice a ſtrange one?
' Conſider too when beggars once pretend
' A caſe like mine, no little will content 'em.'
  Pri. What wouldſt thou beg for?
  Bel. Pity and forgiveneſs.   [*Throws up her veil.*
By the kind tender names of child and father,
Hear my complaints, and take me to your love.
  Pri. My daughter!
  Bel. Yes, your daughter, ' by a mother
' Virtuous and noble, faithful to your honour,
' Obedient to your will, kind to your wiſhes,
' Dear to your arms. By all the joys ſhe gave you,
' When in her blooming years ſhe was your treaſure,
' Look kindly on me! In my face behold
' The lineaments of her's you've kiſs'd ſo often,
' Pleading the cauſe of your poor caſt-off child.
  ' *Pri.* Thou art my daughter.
  ' *Bel.* Yes'—and you've oft told me,

       C 5.   With.

With smiles of love and chaste paternal kisses,
I'u much resemblance of my mother.
   ' *Pri.* Oh!
' I..dst thou inherited her matchless virtues,
' I'd too been bless'd.
   ' *Bel.* Nay, do not call to memory
' My disobedience; but let pity enter
' Into your heart, and quite efface th' impression.
' For could you think how mine's perplex'd with sadness,
' Fears and despairs distract the peace within me;
' Oh! you would take me into your dear, dear arms,
' Hover with strong compassion o'er your young one,
' To shelter me with a protecting wing
' From the black gather'd storm, that's just, just break-
   Pri. Don't talk thus.   [ing.'
   Bel. Yes, I must: and you must hear too.
I have a husband.
   Pri. Damn him.
   Bel. Oh! do not curse him.
He would not speak so hard a word towards you
On any terms, howe'er he deal with me.
   Pri. Ah! what means my child?
   ' *Bel.* Oh! there's but this short moment
' 'Twixt me and fate: yet send me not with curses
' Down to my grave; afford me one kind blessing
' Before we part: just take me into your arms,
' And recommend me with a prayer to Heav'n,   —
' That I may die in peace; and when I'm dead——
   ' *Pri.* How my soul's catch'd!
   ' *Bel.* Lay me, I beg you lay me
' By the dear ashes of my tender mother.
' She would have pity'd me, had fate yet spar'd her.
   ' *Pri.* By Heav'n, my aking heart forebodes much mis-
      ' chief!
' Tell me thy story, for I'm still thy father.
   ' *Bel.* No: I'm still contented.
   ' *Pri.* Speak.
   ' *Bel.* No matter.
   ' *Pri.* Tell me:
' By yon bless'd Heav'n, my heart runs o'er with fond-
   ' *Bel.* Oh!   [ness.
   ' *Pri.* Utter it.'
   ' *Bel.* Oh! my dear husband, my dear husband,
Carries a dagger in his once kind bosom,

To pierce the heart of your poor *Belvidera.*

Pri. Kill thee!

Bel. Yes, kill me. When he pafs'd his faith
And covenant againft your ftate and fenate,
He gave me up a hoftage for his truth :
With me a dagger, and a dire commiffion,
Whene'er he fail'd, to plunge it thro' this bofom.
I learnt the danger, chofe the hour of love
T' attempt his heart, and bring it back to honour.
Great love prevail'd, and blefs'd me with fuccefs !
He came, confefs'd, betray'd his deareft friends
For promif'd mercy. Now they're doom'd to fuffer,
Gall'd with remembrance of what then was fworn,
If they are loft, he vows t'appeafe the gods
With this poor life, and make my blood th' atonement.

Pri. Heav'ns !

' *Bel.* Think you faw what pafs'd at our laft parting ;
' Think you beheld him like a raging lion,
' Pacing the earth, and tearing up his fteps,
' Fate in his eyes, and roaring with the pain
' Of burning fury : think you faw his one hand
' Fix'd on my throat, while the extended other
' Grafp'd a keen threat'ning dagger : Oh ! 'twas thus
' We laft embrac'd, when, trembling with revenge,
' He dragg'd me to the ground, and at my bofom
' Prefented horrid death. Cry'd out, my friends,
' Where are my friends ? fwore, wept, rag'd, threaten'd,
            lov'd,
' For he yet lov'd, and that dear love preferv'd me
' To this laft trial of a father's pity.
' I fear not death ; but cannot bear a thought
' That dear hand fhould do th' unfriendly office,'
If I was ever then your care, now hear me ;
Fly to the fenate, fave the promis'd lives
Of his dear friends, ere mine be made a facrifice.

Pri. Oh, my heart's comfort !

Bel. Will you not, my father ?
Weep not, but anfwer me.

Pri. By Heav'n, I will.
Not one of them but what fhall be immortal.
Canft thou forgive me all my follies paft ?
I'll henceforth be indeed a father ; never,
Never more thus expofe, but cherifh thee,
Dear as the vital warmth that feeds my life.

Dear

Dear as thefe eyes that weep in fondnefs o'er thee:
Peace to thy heart.   Farewell.

Bel. Go, and remember,
'Tis *Belvidera's* life her father pleads for.   [*Ex. feverally.*

'*Enter* Antonio.

'Hum, hum, ha!

'Signor *Priuli*, my lord *Priuli*, my lord, my lord, my
'lord.   Now we lords love to call one another by our
'titles.   My lord, my lord, my lord,—Pox on him, I
'am a lord as well as he.   And fo let him fiddle.—I'll
'warrant him he's gone to the fenate-houfe, and I'll
'be there too, foon enough for fomebody.   Odd—
'here's a tickling fpeech about the plot; I'll prove
'there's a plot with a vengeance—would I had it with-
'out book; let me fee——

' 'Moft reverend fenators,

'That there is a plot, furely by this time no man that
'hath eyes or underftanding in his head will prefume to
'doubt; 'tis as plain as the light in the cucumber—no
'—hold there—cucumber does not come in yet—'tis
'as plain as the light in the fun, or as the man in the
'moon, even at noon day.   It is indeed a pumpkin-
'plot, which juft as it was mellow, we have gather'd,
'and now we have gather'd it, prepar'd and drefs'd it,
'fhall we throw it like a pickled cucumber out of the
'window?   No: that it is not only a bloody, horrid, ex-
'ecrable, damnable, and audacious plot; but it is as I
'may fo fay, a faucy plot: and we all know, moft reve-
'rend fathers, that what is fauce for a goofe is fauce for a
'gander: therefore, I fay, as thofe blood-thirfty-ganders
'of the confpiracy would have deftroy'd us geefe of the
'fenate, let us make hafte to deftroy them; fo I humbly
'move for hanging—Hah! hurry durry,—I think this
'will do; though I was fomething out at firft, about the
'fun and the cucumber.

'*Enter* Aquilina.

'*Aqui.* Good-morrow, fenator.

Ant. Nacky, my dear Nacky; morrow, Nacky; odd
'I am very brifk, very merry, very pert, very jovial—
'ha a a a a—kifs me, Nacky! how doft thou do, my lit-
'tle tory rory trumpet? Kifs me, I fay, huffy, kifs me.

'*Aqui.* Kifs me, Nacky! hang you, fir coxcomb;
'hang you, fir.

'*Ant.* Haity, taity, is it fo indeed? With all my

L   'heart,

' heart, faith—*Hey, then up go we.* Faith, *hey—'hen up*
' *go we,* dum dum derum dump.   [*fings.*

‘ *Aqui.* Signor.

‘ *Ant.* Madona.

‘ *Aqui.* Do you intend to die in your bed ?

‘ *Ant.* About threefcore years hence much may be
' done, my dear.

‘ *Aqui.* You'll be hang'd, Signor.

‘ *Ant.* Hang'd, fweet-heart ! prithee be quiet; hang'd
‘ quoth-a ; that's a merry conceit with all my heart ;
‘ why thou jok'it, Nacky ; thou art given to joking,
‘ I'll fwear. Well, 1 proteft, Nacky, nay I muft pro-
‘ teft, and will proteft, that I love joking dearly, man.
‘ And I love thee for joking, and I'll kifs thee for jo-
‘ king, and towfe thee for joking ; and odd, 1 have a
‘ devilifh mind to take thee afide about that bufinefs
‘ for joking too, odd I have ; and *Hey, then up we go,*
‘ dum dum derum dump.   [*fings.*

‘ *Aqui.* See you this, fir ?   [*Draws a dagger.*

‘ *Ant.* O laud, a dagger ! Oh, laud ! it is naturally
‘ my averfion, I cannot endure the fight on't ; hide it, for
‘ Heaven's fake ; I cannot look that way till it be gone
‘ —hide it, hide it, oh ! oh ! hide it.

‘ *Aqui.* Yes, in your heart I'll hide it.

‘ *Ant.* My heart ! what hide a dagger in my heart's
‘ blood !

‘ *Aqui.* Yes, in thy heart, thy throat, thou pamper'd
        devil ;
‘ Thou haft help'd to fpoil my peace, and I'll have ven-
        geance
‘ On thy curs'd life, for all the bloody fenate,
‘ The perjur'd faithlefs fenate. Where's my lord,
‘ My happinefs, my love, my god, my hero ?
‘ Doom'd by thy accurfed tongue, among the reft,
‘ T' a fhameful rack. By all the rage that's in me,
‘ I'll be whole years in murdering thee.

‘ *Ant.* Why, Nacky,
‘ Wherefore fo paffionate ? What have I done ? What's
‘ the matter, my dear Nacky ? Am not I thy love, thy
‘ happinefs, thy lord, thy hero, thy fenator, and every
‘ thing in the world, Nacky ?

‘ *Aqui.* Thou ! think'it thou, thou art fit to meet my
‘ To bear the eager clafp of my embraces ?   [joys:

‘ Give me *Pierre,* or——

                                          ‘ *Ant.*

' *Ant.* Why, he's to be hang'd, little Nacky;
' Truſs'd up for treaſon, and ſo forth, child.
  ' *Aqui.* Thou ly'ſt; ſtop down thy throat that helliſh
  ' ſentence,
' Or 'tis thy laſt : ſwear that my love ſhall live,
' Or thou'rt dead .
  ' *Ant.* Ah! h h h.
' *Aqui.* Swear to recall his doom ;
' Swear at my feet, and tremble at my fury.
  ' *Ant.* I do ! Now if ſhe would but kick a little bit ;
' one kick now, Ah! h h h.
  ' *Aqui.* Swear, or—
  ' *Ant.* I do, by theſe dear fragrant foots, and little
' toes, ſweet as e e e e, my Nacky, Nacky, Nacky,
' faith and troth.
  ' *Aqui.* How !
  ' *Ant.* Nothing but untie thy ſhoe-ſtrings a little, that's
' all, that's all, as I hope to live, Nacky, that's all, all.
  ' *Aqui.* Nay, then —
  ' *Ant.* Hold ; hold ; thy love, thy lord, thy hero,
' ſhall be preſerv'd and ſafe.
  ' *Aqui.* Or may this poniard
' Ruſt in thy heart.
  ' *Ant.* With all my ſoul.
  ' *Aqui.* Farewel.   [*Exit.*
  ' *Ant.* Adieu. Why, what a bloody-minded inve-
' terate, termagant ſtrumpet have I been plagued with !
' Oh ! h h ! yet no more ! nay then I die, I die— I'm
' dead already.   [*Stretches himſelf out.*'
      S C E N E, *changes to a Garden.   Enter* Jaffier.

Jaff. Final deſtruction ſeize on all the world.
Bend down, ye Heav'ns, and ſhutting round this earth,
Cruſh the vile globe into its firſt confuſion ;
' Scorch it with elemental flames, to one curs'd cinder,
' And all us little creepers in't, call'd men,
' Burn, burn to nothing : but let *Venice* burn
' Hotter than all the reſt : here kindle hell,
' Ne'er to extinguiſh ; and let ſouls hereafter
' Groan here, in all thoſe pains which mine feels now.'
                  Enter Belvidera.

Bel. My life ——   [*Meeting him.*
Jaff. My plague——   [*Turning from her.*
Bel. Nay, then I ſee my ruin.
If I muſt die !
  ' *Jaff.* No, death's this day too buſy ;
                                          ' Thy

‘ Thy father's ill-timed mercy came too late.
‘ I thank thee for thy labours though ; and him too :
‘ But all my poor, betray'd, unhappy friends,
‘ Have summons to prepare for fate's black hour ;
‘ And yet I live.
 ‘ *Bel.* Then be the next my doom :
‘ I see, thou haſt paſs'd my ſentence in thy heart,
‘ And I'll no longer weep, or plead againſt it,
‘ But with the humbleſt, moſt obedient patience,
‘ Meet thy dear hands, and kiſs 'em when they wound
‘ Indeed I am willing ; but I beg thee do it   [me.
‘ With ſome remorſe ; and when thou giv'ſt the blow,
‘ View me with eyes of a relenting love,
‘ And ſhew me pity, for 'twill ſweeten juſtice.
 ‘ *Jaff.* Shew pity to thee !
 ‘ *Bel.* Yes ; and when thy hands,
‘ Charg'd with my fate, come trembling to the deed,
‘ As thou haſt done a thouſand thouſand times
‘ To this poor breaſt, when kinder rage hath brought thee,
‘ When our ſtung hearts have leap'd to meet each other,
‘ And melting kiſſes ſeal'd our lips together :
‘ When joys have left me gaſping in thy arms :
‘ So let my death come now, and I'll not ſhrink from't.’
 Jaff. Nay, *Belvidera,* do not fear my cruelty,
Nor let the thoughts of death perplex thy fancy ;
But anſwer me to what I ſhall demand,
With a firm temper and unſhaken ſpirit.
 Bel. I will, when I've done weeping—
 Jeff. Fie, no more on't———
How long is't ſince that miſerable day
We wedded firſt ?
 Bel. Oh ! h h !
 Jaff. Nay, keep in thy tears,
Leſt they unman me too.
 Bel. Heav'n knows I cannot ?
The words you utter found ſo very ſadly,
The ſtreams will follow—
 Jaff. Come, I'll kiſs 'em dry then.
 Bel. But was't a miſerable day ?
 Jaff. A curs'd one.
 Bel. I thought it otherwiſe ; and you've often ſworn,
‘ In the tranſporting hours of warmeſt love,
‘ When ſure you ſpoke the truth, you've ſworn,' you
 Jaff. 'Twas a raſh oath.   [bleſs'd it.
             Bel.

Bel. Then why am I not curs'd too ?

Jaff. No, *Belvidera* ; by th' eternal truth,
I doat with too much fondness.

Bel. Still so kind !
Still then do you love me ?

Jaff. ' Nature in her workings
' Inclines not with more ardour to creation,
' Than I do now towards thee :' man ne'er was bless'd
Since the first pair met, as I have been.

Bel. Then sure you will not curse me ?

Jaff. No, I'll bless thee.
I came on purpose, *Belvidera*, to bless thee.
'Tis now, I think, three years, we've liv'd together.

Bel. And may no fatal minute ever part us,
Till reverend grown for age and love, we go
Down to one grave, as our last bed, together ;
There sleep in peace, till an eternal morning.

' *Jaff.* When will that be ?   [*Sighing.*

' *Bel.* I hope, long ages hence.

' *Jaff.* Have I not hitherto (I beg thee tell me
' Thy very fears) us'd thee with tender'st love ?
' Did e'er my soul rise up in wrath against thee ?
' Did I e'er frown, when *Belvidera* smil'd ?
' Or by the least unfriendly word, betray
' Abating passion ? Have I ever wrong'd thee ?

' *Bel.* No.

' *Jaff.* Has my heart, or have my eyes, e'er wander'd
' To any other woman ?

' *Bel.* Never, never—I were the worst of false ones,
' should I accuse thee.
' I own I've been too happy ; bless'd above
' My sex's charter.

Jaff. Did I not say, I came to bless thee ?

Bel. You did.

Jaff. Then hear me, bounteous Heav'n :
Pour down your blessings on this beauteous head,
Where everlasting sweets are always springing,
With a continual giving hand : let peace,
Honour, and safety, always hover round her ;
Feed her with plenty ; let her eyes ne'er see
A sight of sorrow, nor her heart know mourning :
Crown all her days with joy, her nights with rest,
Harmless as her own thoughts ; and prop her virtue,
To bear the loss of one that too much lov'd ;
And comfort her with patience in our parting !   *Bel.*

Bel. How! parting, parting!

Jaff. Yes, for ever parting;
I have sworn, *Belvidera*, by yon Heav'n,
That best can tell how much I lose to leave thee,
We part this hour for ever.

Bel. Oh! call back
Your cruel blessing; stay with me, and curse me.

' *Jaff.* No, 'tis resolv'd.

' *Bel.* Then hear me too, just Heav'n:
' Pour down your curses on this wretched head,
' With never-ceasing vengeance; let despair,
' Danger, and infamy, nay all, surround me;
' Starve me with wantings: let my eyes ne'er see
' A sight of comfort, nor my heart know peace;
' But dash my days with sorrow, nights with horrors,
' Wild as my own thoughts now, and let loose fury
' To make me mad enough for what I lose,
' If I must lose him. If I must! I will not.
' Oh! turn and hear me!'

Jaff. Now hold, heart, or never.

Bel. By all the tender days we've liv'd together,
' By all our charming nights, and joys that crown'd em.'
Pity my sad condition; speak, but speak.

Jaff. Oh! oh!

Bel. By these arms, that now cling round thy neck,
' By this dear kiss, and by ten thousand more,'
By these poor streaming eyes ——

Jaff. Murder! unhold me:
By th' immortal destiny that doom'd me
                                        [*Draws his dagger.*
To this curs'd minute, I'll not live one longer;
Resolve to let me go; or see me fall——

' *Bel.* Hold, sir, be patient.'

Jaff. Hark, the dismal bell   [*Passing bell tolls.*
Tolls out for death! I must attend its call too;
For my poor friend, my dying *Pierre*, expects me:
He sent a message to require I'd see him
Before he dy'd, and take his last forgiveness.
Farewel for ever.

Bel. Leave thy dagger with me,
Bequeath me something—Not one kiss at parting!
Oh! my poor heart, when wilt thou break?
                              [*Going out, looks backs at him.*

Jaff. Yet stay :-

We have a child, as yet a tender infant:
Be a kind mother to him when I'm gone;
Breed him in virtue, and the paths of honour,
But never let him know his father's story;
I charge thee guard him from the wrongs, my fate
May do his future fortune or his name.
Now—nearer yet—   [*Approaching each other.*
Oh! that my arms were riveted
Thus round thee ever! But my friends! my oath!
This, and no more.   [*Kisses her.*

    Bel. Another, sure another,
For that poor little one you've ta'en such care of,
I'll give't him truly.
    Jaff. So—now farewel.
    Bel. For ever?
    Jaff. Heav'n knows, for ever; all good angels guard
        thee.   [*Exit.*
    Bel. All ill ones sure had charge of me this moment.
Curs'd be my days, and doubly curs'd my nights,
' Which I must now mourn out in widow'd tears;
' Blasted by every herb, and fruit, and tree;
' Curs'd be the rain that falls upon the earth,
' And may the general curse reach man and beast.'
Oh! give me daggers, fire, or water:
How I could bleed, how burn, how drown, the waves
Huzzing and foaming round my sinking head,
Till I descended to the peaceful bottom!
Oh! there's all quiet, here all rage and fury:
The air's too thin, and pierces my weak brain;
I long for thick substantial sleep: Hell! hell!
Burst from the centre, rage and roar aloud,
If thou art half so hot, so mad as I am.
        Enter Priuli, *and Servants.*
' Who's there?   [*They seize her.*
  ' *Pri.* Run, seize, and bring her safely home;
' Guard her as you would life: alas, poor creature!
  ' *Bel.* What to my husband! then conduct me quickly;
' Are all things ready? Shall we die most gloriously;
' Say not a word of this to my old father:
' Murmuring streams, soft shades, and springing flow-
    ers!
' Lutes, laurels, seas of milk, and ships of amber.'
                   [*Exeunt.*

SCENE

SCENE, *opening, discovers a Scaffold, and a Wheel pre-*
par'd for the Execution of Pierre ; *then enter Officer,* Pierre,
and Guards, ' a Friar,' *Executioner, and a great Rabble.*
' *Off.* Room, room there—stand all by, make room
' for the prisoner.'
   Pier. My friend not yet come ?
' *Fri.* Why are you so obstinate ?
' *Pier.* Why are you so troublesome, that a poor
    wretch can't die in peace,
' But you, like ravens, will be croaking round him ?——
   ' *Fri.* Yet Heav'n——
   ' *Pier.* I tell thee Heav'n and I are friends :
' I ne'er broke peace with't yet, by cruel murders,
' Rapine, or perjury, or vile deceiving :
' But liv'd in moral justice towards all men :
' Nor am a foe to the most strong believers,
' Howe'er my own short-sighted faith confines me,
   ' *Fri.* But an all-seeing Judge——
   ' *Pier.* You say my conscience
' Must be my accuser ; I have search'd that conscience,
' And find no records there of crimes that scare me.
   ' *Fri.* 'Tis strange, you should want faith.
   ' *Pier.* You want to lead
' My reason blindfold, like a hamper'd lion,
' Check'd of its nobler vigour ; then when bated
' Down to obedient tameness, make it couch
'. And shew strange tricks, which you call your signs of
' So silly souls are gull'd, and you get money.   [faith :
' Away ; no more.   Captain, I'd have hereafter
' This fellow write no lies of my conversion,
' Because he has crept upon my troubled hours.'
              Enter Jaffier.
   Jaff. Hold : eyes be dry ;
Heart, strengthen me to bear
This hideous sight, and humble me.   Take
The last forgiveness of a dying friend,
Betray'd by my vile falsehood, to his ruin.
O *Pierre!*
   Pier. Yet nearer.
   Jaff. Crawling on my knees,
And prostrate on the earth let let me approach thee :
How shall I look up to thy injur'd face,
That always us'd to smile with friendship on me ?
It darts an air of so much manly virtue,

                  That

That I, methinks, look little in thy fight,
And stripes are fitter for me   than embraces.

Pier. Dear to my arms, tho' thou'st undone my fame,
I can't forget to love thee.   I'r'ythee, *Jaffier,*
Forgive that filthy blow my passion dealt thee;
I am now preparing for the land of peace,
And fain would have the charitable wishes
Of all good men like thee, to blefs my journey.

Jaff. Good! I am the vilest creature, worse than e'er
Suffer'd the shameful fate thou'rt going to taste of.
‘ Why was I sent for to be us'd thus kindly ?
‘ Call, call me villain, as I am! describe
‘ The foul complexion of my hateful deeds :
‘ Lead me to th' rack, and stretch me in thy stead,
· I've crimes enough to give it its full load,
‘ And do it credit : thou wilt but spoil the use on't,
‘ And honest men hereafter bear its figure
‘ About them, as a charm for treacherous friendship.'

Off. The time grows short, your friends are dead al-
Jaff. Dead !   {ready.
Pier. Yes, dead, *Jaffier;* they've all dy'd like men too,
Worthy their character.

Jaff. And what must I do ?
Pier. O *Jaffier!*
Jaff. Speak aloud thy burthen'd soul,
And tell thy troubles to thy tortur'd friend.

Pier. Friend ! Could'st thou yet be a friend, a gene-
rous friend,
I might hope comfort from thy noble sorrows.
Heav'n knows, I want a friend.

Jaff. And a kind one,
That would not thus scorn my repenting virtue,
Or think, when he's to die, my thoughts are idle,

Pier. No ! live, I charge thee, *Jaffier.*
Jaff. Yes, I will live :
But it shall be to see thy fall reveng'd,
At such a rate, as *Venice* shall long groan for.

Pier. Wilt thou ?
Jaff. I will, by Heav'n.
Pier. Then still thour't noble,
And I forgive thee.   Oh !—yet—shall I trust thee ?
Jaff. No ; I've been false already.
Pier. Do'st thou love me ?
Jaff. Rip up my heart, and satisfy thy doubtings.

Pier.

Pier. Curſe on this weakneſs.   [*He weeps.*

Jaff. Tears! Amazement! Tears!
I never ſaw thee melted thus before;
And know there's ſomething labouring in thy boſom,
That muſt have vent: tho' I'm a villain, tell me.

  Pier. See'ſt thou that engine?   [*Pointing to the*

  Jaff. Why?   [*Wheel.*

  Pier. Is't fit a ſoldier, who has liv'd with honour,
Fought nations quarrels, and been crown'd with conqueſt,
Be expos'd, a common carcaſe, on a wheel?

  Jaff. Hah!

  Pier. Speak! is't fitting?

  Jaff. Fitting!

  Pier. Yes; is't fitting?

  Jaff. What's to be done?

  Pier. I'd have thee undertake
Something that's noble, to preſerve my memory
From the diſgrace that's ready to attaint it.

  Offi. The day grows late, ſir.

  Pier. I'll make haſte. O *Jaffier!*
Tho' thou'ſt betray'd me, do me ſome way juſtice.

  Jaff. No more of that: thy wiſhes ſhall be ſatisfy'd;
I have a wife, and ſhe ſhall bleed; my child too
Yield up his little throat, and all
T' appeaſe thee——

[*Going away,* Pierre *holds him.*

  Pier. No—this—no more.   [*He whiſpers* Jaffier.

  Jaff. Hah! is't then ſo?

  Pier. Moſt certainly.

  Jaff. I'll do't.

  Pier. Remember.

  Offi. Sir.

  Pier. Come, now I'm ready.

[*He and* Jaffier *aſcend the Scaffold.*
Captain, you ſhould be a gentleman of honour;
Keep off the rabble, that I may have room
To entertain my fate, and die with decency.
Come.   [*Takes off his gown, Executioner prepares to*

  ' *Fri.* Son.   *bind him.*

  ' *Pier.* Hence, tempter.

  ' *Offi.* Stand off, prieſt.

  ' *Pier.* I thank you, ſir.'
You'll think on't?   [*To* Jaffier.

  Jaff. 'T won't grow ſtale before to-morrow.

Pier.

Pier. Now, Jaffier! now I'm going. Now—
            [*Executioner having bound him.*
Jaff. Have at thee,
Thou honest heart, then—here—   [*Stabs him.*
And this is well too.   [*Stabs himself.*
 ' *Fri.* Damnable deed !'
Pier. Now thou hast indeed been faithful.
This was done nobly—We have deceiv'd the senate.
Jaff. Bravely.
Pier. Ha, ha ha !——oh ! oh !   [*Dies.*
Jaff. Now, ye curs'd rulers,
Thus of the blood y'ave shed, I make libation,
And sprinkle it mingling.   May it rest upon you,
And all your race.   Be henceforth peace a stranger
Within your walls ; let plagues and famine waste
Your generations— O poor *Belvidera !*
Sir, I have a wife, bear this in safety to her,
A tok'n that with my dying breath I bless'd her,
And the dear little infant left behind me.
I'm sick——I m quiet.   [*Dies.*
 ' *Off.* Bear this news to the senate,
 ' And guard their bodies. till there's further orders.
 ' Heav'n grant I die so well.'   [*Scene shuts upon them.*
   Soft Music.   Enter Belvidera *distracted, led by two*
            of her Women, Priuli *and Servants.*
   Pri. Strengthen her heart with patience, pitying
        Heav'n.
   Bel. Come, come, come. come, come, nay, come to bed,
Pr'ythee, my love.   The winds ; hark how they whistle ;
And the rain beats : Oh ! how the weather shrinks me !
You are angry now, who cares ? Pish, no indeed,
Chuse then, I say you shall not go, you shall not,
Whip your ill-nature ; get you gone then ; Oh !
Are you return'd ? See, father, here's he's come again :
Am I to blame to love him ; O, thou dear one.
Why do you fly me ? Are you angry still then ?
Jaffier, where art thou ? Father, why do you do thus ?
Stand off, don't hide him from me. He's there some-
        where.
Stand off, I say : What gone ? Remember't, tyrant :
I may revenge myself for this trick, one day.
I'll do't—I'll do't.   ' *Renault's* a nasty fellow ;
 ' Hang him. hang him, hang him.'
                                Enter

Enter Officer.

Pri. News, what news?   [*Officer whispers* Priuli.

Off. Moſt ſad, ſir;
Jaffier, upon the ſcaffold, to prevent
A ſhameful death, ſtabb'd *Pierre*, and next himſelf:
Both fell together.

Pri. Daughter.

Bel. Ha! look there!
My huſband bloody, and his friend too! Murder!
Who has done this? Speak to me, thou ſad viſion;
On theſe poor trembling knees I beg it.   Vaniſh'd—
Here they went down—Oh, I'll dig, dig the den up!
You ſhan't delude me thus.   Hoa, *Jaffier, Jaffier!*
Peep up, and give me but a look.   I have him!
I've got him, father: Oh! ' now how I'll ſmuggle him?'
My love! my dear! my bleſſing! help me! help me!
They have hold on me, and drag me to the bottom.
Nay—now they pull ſo hard—farewel—   [*Dies.*

' *Maid.* She's dead;
' Breathleſs and dead.'

Pri. Oh! guard me from the ſight on't.
Lead me into ſome place that's fit for mourning;
Where the free air, light, and the chearful ſun,
May never enter: hang it round with black;
Set up one taper, that may light a day,
As long as I've to live: and there all leave me:
    Sparing no tears, when you this tale relate,
    But bid all cruel fathers dread my fate.

[*Exeunt omnes.*

E P I.

THE Text is done, and now for application,
  And when that's ended, pass your approbation.
Though the Conspiracy's prevented here,
Methinks I see another hatching there:
And there's a certain faction fain would sway,
If they had strength enough, and damn this play:
But this the author boldly bid me say,
If any take this plainness in ill part,
He's glad on't from the bottom of his heart.
Poets in honour of the truth should write,
With the same spirit brave men for it fight.
And though against him causeless hatred rise,
And daily where he goes of late he spies
The scowls of sullen and revengeful eyes;
'Tis what he knows, with much contempt, to bear,
And serves a cause too good to let him fear.
He fears no poison from an incens'd drab,
No ruffian's five-foot sword, nor rascal's stab;
Nor any other snares of mischief laid,
Not a Rose-Alley cudgel ambuscade,
From any private cause where malice reigns,
Or general pique all blockheads have to brains;
Nothing shall damn his pen, when truth does call,
No, not the * picture mangler at Guildhall.
The rebel tribe, of which that vermin's one,
Have now set forward, and their course begun;
  And while that prince's figure they deface,
    As they before had massacred his name,
  Durst their base fears but look him in the face,
    They'd use his person as they've us'd his fame:
A face in which such lineaments they read
Of that great martyr's, whose rich blood they shed,
That their rebellious hate they still retain,
And in his son would murder him again.
With indignation then let each brave heart
Rouze and unite, to take his injur'd part;
'Till royal love and goodness call him home,
And songs of triumph melt him as he come:
'Till Heav'n his honour and our peace restore,
And villains never wrong his virtue more.

    * He that cut the Duke of York's picture.

    F I N I S.

TAMERLANE·

A

TRAGEDY,

WRITTEN BY

N. ROWE, Esq;

Marked with the Variations in the

MANAGER's BOOK,

AT THE

Theatre-Royal in Drury-Lane.

———— *Magnus ad altum*
Fulminat Euphraten bello, victorque volentes
Per Populos dat jura, viamque affectat Olympo.

Virg. Georg.

————————

LONDON:

PRINTED for T. and W. LOWNDES, J. NICHOLS,
W. NICOLL, and S. BLADON.

M.DCC.LXXXIV,

☞ The Reader is defired to obferve, that the Paffages omitted in the Reprefentation at the Theatres are here preferved, and marked with inverted Commas; as at Line 16 in Page 9, to Line 9 in Page 11.

To the Right Honourable

W I L L I A M,

Lord Marquis of *Hartington,*

(Afterwards Duke of *Devonſhire.)*

My Lord,

EVERY bodv is now ſo full of buſineſs, that
things of this kind, which are gener lly taken
for the entertainment of leiſure hours o ly, l k like
impertinence and in erruption. I am ſure it is a reaſon why I ought to beg your Lordſhip's pardon, for
troubling you with this tragedy; nor but that poetry
has always been, and will itill be, the entertainment
of all w ſe men, that ave any delicacy in their knowledge: Yet, at ſo critical a juncture as this is, I muſt
confeſs, I think your Lordſhip ought to give intirely
into thoſe public affairs, which at this time ſe m to
demand you. It is that happy turn whic our
Lordſhip has to buſineſs, that right underſtandi g of
your country's intereſt, and that conſtant zeal to
purſue it, that juſt thinking, that ſtrong and perſuaſive e'ocution, that firm and generous reſolution,
which upon all occaſions you have ſhewn in parlia-
ments; and, to add that which is the crowning good
quality, your Lordſhip's continual adherence and
unſhaken loyalty to His preſent Majeſty, which m ke
you at this time ſo neceſſary to the public. I muſt
confeſs (tho' there's no part in your Lordſhip's character but what the world ſhould be fond of), I cannot help diſtinguiſhing the laſt inſtance very particularly. It is doing, methinks, ſuch a juſtice to
goodneſs, to greatneſs, and to right reaſon, that
poſterity will believe there could be no man of good
ſenſe, but what muſt have agreed with your Lordſhip
in it. When the next age ſhall read the hiſtory of
this, what excuſe can they make for thoſe who did

A 2   not

not admire a prince whofe life has been a feries of good offices dne to mankind? When they fhall reckon up his labours from the battle of Sneff, to fome g'orious action which fhall be his laft (and which I therefore hope is very far removed from the prefent time), will they ever believe that he could have been too well loved, or too faithfully ferved and defended? The gr-at things which he did before we had that immediate intereft in him, which we now ha, pily have, is a noble and juft fubject for panegyric; but as benefits done to others can never touch us fo fenfibly as thofe we receive ourfelves, tho' the actions may be equally great; fo, methinks, I can hardly have patience to run back to hi having fav'd his own country, when I confider he has fince done the fame for us; let that be fufficient to us, for all we can fay of him, or do for him. What dangers and difficulties has he not ftruggled through, for the honour and fafety of thefe kingdoms? 'Tis a common praife, and what every one fpeaks, to fay, he has continually expofed his life for his people: But there are fome things more particular in his character, fome tnings rarely found amongft the policies of princes; a zeal for religion, moderated by reafon, without the rage and fire of perfecution; a charitable compaffion for thofe who cannot be convinced, and an unalterable perfeverance in thofe principles of whofe truth he is fatisfied; a defire of war for the fake of peace, and of peace for the good and honour of his fubjects equally with his own; a pious care fo compofing factions, though to foment them might make him arbitrary; and a generous ambition, that only aims at power, to enable hm to do good to all the reft of the world. I might add here, that inviolable and religious obfervance of his royal word, which the teft part of the powers of Europe have fo frequently, and fo happily for themfelves, depended upon in the greateft emergencies; but as this virtue

tue is generally reckoned as no more than that common honefty which the meaneft man would blufh to be without, fo it can hardly claim a pl ce amongft the more particular excellences of a great prince. It were to be wifhed indeed, that the world we e honeft to fuch a degree, and that there were not that fcandalous defect of common morality. Certainly nothing can be more fhocking to humanity, to the peace and order of the world, no hing can approach nearer to that favage ftate of nature, in which every man is to eat his fellow if he can mafter him, than an avowed liberty of breaking through all the moft folemn engagemnts of public faith. 'Tis fome h ng that brands a man with an infamy which nothing can explain his meaning, he may proteft, and pretend to extenuate or wipe out ; but the world has generally too much indignation for the affront, to bear it at that eafy rate. Minifters and Secretaries of ftate m y difplay their own parts in memorials with as much pomp and flourifh as they pleafe : I fancy the common anfwer upon fuch occafion, will always be, " You have deceived us grofsly, and we ne t er can nor will truft you a y more." When this vice comes amongft men of the firft r nk, it is the more fhocking, and I could wifh there were none fuch to whofe charge it might be laid.

Some people (who do me a very great honour in it) have fancied, that, in the perfon of Tamerlane, I have alluded to the greateft character of the prefent age. I don't know whether I ought not to apprehend a great deal of danger from avowing a defign like th t: It may be a talk indeed worthy the greateft geniu , whi h this or any other time has produced; but therefore I ought not to ftand the fhock of a parallel, left it fhould be feen, 'to my difadvantage, how far the *Hero* has *tranfcended the poet's thought.* There are many features, it is true, in that great

A 3   man's

man's life not unlike his Majesty; his courage, his piety, his moderation, his justice, and his fatherly love of his people, but, above all, his hate of tyranny and oppression, and his zealous care for the common good of mankind, carry a large resemblance of him: Several incidents are alike in their stories; and there wants nothing to his Majesty but such a deciding victory as that by which Tamer'ane gave peace to the world: That is yet to come; but I hope we may reasonably expect it from the unanimity of the present Parliament, and so formidable a force as that unanimity will give life and vigour to.

If your Lordship can find any thing in this poem like a Prince, who is so justly the object of your Lordship's and indeed of the world's veneration, I persuade myself it will prevail with you to forgive every thing else that you find amiss: You will excuse the faults in writing, for the goodness of the intention. I hope too, your Lordship will not be displeased that I take this opportunity of renewing the honour which I formerly had, to be known to your Lordship and which gives me at once the pleasure of expressing those just and dutiful sentiments I have for his Majesty, and that strong inclination which I have always had to be thought,

My Lord,

Your Lordship's most obedient

humble Servant,

N. ROWE.

PROLOGUE.

OF all the Muse's various labours, none
   Have lasted longer, or have higher flown,
Than those that tell the fame by antient heroes won.
With pleasure Rome and great Augustus heard
"Arms and the man" sung by the Mantuan bard:
In spite of time, the sacred story lives,
And Cæsar and his empire still survives.
Like him (tho' much unequal to his fame)
Our author makes a pious prince his theme:
High with the foremost names in arms he stood,
Had fought and suffer'd, for his country's good,
Yet sought not fame, but peace in fields of blood.
Safe under him his happy people sate,
And griev'd, at distance, for their neighbours fate:
Whilst with success a Turkish monarch crown'd,
Like spreading flame, deform'd the nations round;
With sword and fire he forc'd his impious way
To lawless power, and universal sway;
Some abject states, for fear, the tyrant join,
- Others, for gold, their liberties resign,
And venal princes sold their right divine:
Till Heav'n, the growing evil to redress,
Sent Tamerlane, to give the world a peace.
The hero, rous'd, asserts the glorious cause,
And to the field the chearful soldier draws:
Around in crowds his valiant leaders wait,
Anxious for glory, and secure of fate;
Well pleas'd, once more, to venture on his side,
And prove that faith again, which had so oft been try'd.
The peaceful fathers, who in senates meet,
Approve an enterprize so just, so great;
While with their prince's arms, their voice thus join'd,
Gains half the praise of having sav'd mankind.
   Ev'n in a circle, where, like this, the Fair
Were met, the bright assembly did declare,
Their house, with one consent, were for the war;
Each urg'd her lover to unsheathe his sword,
And never spare a man who broke his word.
Thus fir'd, the brave on to the danger press;
Their arms were crown'd abroad with just success,
And blest at home with beauty, and with peace.

Dra-

Dramatis Personæ, 1784.

M E N.

	At Drury Lane.	At Covent Garden.
Tamerlane	Mr. SMITH.	Mr. HENDERSON.
Bajazet,	Mr. PALMER.	Mr. KEMBLE.
Axalla,	Mr. GRIST.	Mr. WHITFIELD.
Moneses,	Mr.	Mr. WROUGHTON.
Saratocles,	Mr. FARREN.	
Prince of Tanais,	Mr. WRIGHTEN.	
Omar,	Mr. HURST.	Mr. BOOTH.
Mirvan,	Mr. NORRIS.	Mr. FEARON.
Zama,	Mr. WRIGHT.	
Haly,	Mr. CHAPLIN.	Mr. I. BATES.
Dervise,	Mr. BRANSBY.	Mr. THOMPSON.

W O M E N.

Arpasia,	Miss YOUNGE.	Mrs. BATES.
Selima.	Miss HOPKINS.	Mrs. KEMBLE.

Parthian *and* Tartar Soldiers, *Mutes belonging to* Bajazet, *other Attendants*

S C E N E, Tamerlane's *Camp, near* Angoria *in* Galatia.

ACT I. SCENE *before* Tamerlane's *tent.*

Enter the Prince of Tanais, Zama, *and* Mirvan.

Prince. HAIL to the fun! from whofe returning light
The chearful foldier's arms new luftre take,
To deck the pomp of battle. Oh, my friends!
Was ever fuch a glorious face of war?
See, from this height, how all Galatia's plains
With nations numberlefs are cover'd o'er;
Who, like a deluge, hide the face of earth,
And leave no object in the vaft horizon,
But glitt'ring arms and fkies.
    Zam. Our Afian world
From this important day expects a lord;
This day they hope an end of all their woes,
Of tyranny, of bondage, and oppreffion,
From our victorious emp'ror, Tamerlane.
    ' *Mir.*' Well has our holy Alha mark'd him out
' The fcourge of lawlefs pride, and dire ambition,
' The great avenger of the groaning world.
' Well has he worn the facred caufe of juftice
' Upon his profp'rous fword. Approving Heav'n
' Still crown'd the righteous warrior with fuccefs;
' As if it faid, Go forth, and be my champion,
' Thou, moft like me of all my works below.
    ' *Pr.* No luft of rule, the common vice of kings,
' No furious zeal, infpir'd by hot-brain'd priefts,
' Ill hid beneath religion's fpecious name,
' E'er drew his temp'rate courage to the field:
' But to redrefs an injur'd people's wrongs,
' To fave the weak one from the ftrong oppreffor,
' Is all his end of war. And when he draws
' The fword to punifh, like relenting Heav'n,
' He feems unwilling to deface his kind.
    ' *Mir.* So rich his foul in ev'ry virtuous grace,
' That, had not nature made him great by birth,
' Yet all the brave had fought him for their friend.
' The Chriftian prince, Axalla, nicely bred,
' In polifh'd arts of European courts,
' For him forfakes his native Italy,

A 5   ' And

‘ And lives a happy exile in his service.

    ‘ *Pr.* Pleas'd with the gentle manners of that prince,

‘ Our mighty lord is lavish to his friendship;

‘ Tho' Omar and the Tartar lords repine,

‘ And loudly tax their monarch as too partial.

    ‘ *Zam.* Ere the mid-hour of night, from tent to tent,

‘ Unweary'd, thro' the num'rous host he past,

‘ Viewing with careful eyes each sev'ral quarter;

‘ Whilst from his looks, as from Divinity,

‘ The soldiers took presage, and cry'd, Lead on,

‘ Great Alha, and our emperor, lead on,

‘ To victory and everlasting fame.’

    Mir. Hear you of Bajazet?

    Pr. Late in the evening

A slave of near attendance on his person

'Scap'd to our camp. From him we learn'd, the tyrant,

With rage redoubled, for the fight prepares;

Some accidental passion fires his breast

(Love, as 'tis thought, for a fair Grecian captive),

And adds new horror to his native fury.

‘ For five returning suns, scarce was he seen

‘ By any the most favour'd of his court,

‘ But in lascivious ease, among his women,

‘ Liv'd from the war retir'd; or else alone,

‘ In sullen mood, sat meditating plagues

‘ And ruin to the world; 'till yester morn,

‘ Like fire that lab'ring upwards rends the earth,

‘ He burst with fury from his tent, commanding

‘ All should be ready for the fight this day.

    ‘ *Zam.* I know his temper well, since in his court,

‘ Companion of the brave Axalla's embassy,

‘ I oft observ'd him proud, impatient

‘ Of aught superior, e'en of Heaven that made him.

‘ Fond of false glory, of the savage pow'r

‘ Of ruling without reason, of confounding

‘ Just and unjust, by an unbounded will;

‘ By whom religion, honour, all the bands

‘ That ought to hold the jarring world in peace,

‘ Were held the tricks of state, snares of wise princes,

‘ To draw their easy neighbours to destruction.

    ‘ *Mir.* Thrice, by our law and prophet has he sworn,

‘ By the world's Lord and Maker, lasting peace

‘ With our great master, and his royal friend

                      ‘ The

' The Grecian emperor ; as oft, regardlefs
' Of plighted faith, with moft unkingly bafenefs,
' Without a war proclaim'd or caufe pretended,
' Has ta'en th' advantage of their abfent arms,
' To wafte with fword and fire their fruitful fields :
' Like fome accurfed fiend, who, 'fcap'd from hell,
' Poifons the balmy air thro' which he flies,
' He blafts the bearded corn, and loaded branches,
' The lab'ring hind's beft hopes, and marks his way
     ' with ruin.'

Pr. But fee his fate ! The mighty Tamerlane
Comes, like the proxy of enquiring Heav'n,
To judge, and to redrefs.   [*Flourifh of trumpets.*

    Enter Tamerlane, *guards, and other attendants.*

Tam. Yet, yet a little, and deftructive Slaughter
Shall rage around, and mar this beauteous profpect.
Pafs but an hour, which ftands betwixt the lives
Of thoufands and eternity, what change
Shall hafty Death make in yon glitt'ring plain ?
Oh, thou fell monfter, War ! that in a moment
Lay'ft wafte the nobleft part of the creation,
The boaft and mafter-piece of the great Maker,
That wears in vain th' impreffion of his image,
Unprivileg'd from thee.
Health to our friends, and to our arms fuccefs !
     [*To the Prince,* Zama, *and* Mirvan.
Such as the caufe for which we fight deferves.

Pr. Nor can we afk beyond what Heaven beftows,
Preventing ftill our wifhes. See, great fir,
The univerfal joy your foldiers wear,
Omen of profp'rous battle.
Impatient of the tedious night, in arms
Watchful they ftood, expecting op'ning day ;
And now are hardly by their leaders held
From darting on the foe. ' Like a hot courfer,
' That bounding paws the mould'ring foil, difdaining
' The rein that checks him, eager for the race.'

Tam. Yes, prince, I mean to give a loofe to war.
This morn Axalla, with my Parthian horfe,
Arrives to join me. He who, like a ftorm,
Swept with his flying fquadrons all the plain
Between Angoria's walls and yon tall mountains,
That feem to reach the clouds ; and now he comes,

     A 6   Loaded

Loaden with spoils and conquest, to my aid.

[*Trumpets flourish.*

Zam. These trumpets speak his presence———
Enter Axalla, *who kneels to* Tamerlane.

Tam. Welcome! thou worthy partner of my laurels,
Thou brother of my choice, a band more sacred
Than nature's brittle tie. By holy friendship,
Glory and fame stood still for thy arrival;
My soul seem'd wanting in its better half,
And languish'd for thy absence; ' like a prophet,
' That waits the inspiration of his God.'

Ax. My emperor! My ever royal master!
To whom my secret soul more lowly bends,
Than forms of outward worship can express;
How poorly does your soldier pay this goodness,
Who wears his every hour of life out for you!
Yet 'tis his all, and what he has he offers;
Nor now disdain t' accept the gift he brings,
Enter Selima, Moneses, Stratocles, *prisoners*; guards,
mutes, &c.

This earnest of your fortune. See, my lord,
The noblest prize that ever grac'd my arms!
Approach, my fair———

Tam. This is indeed to conquer,
And well to be rewarded for thy conquest;
The bloom of op'ning flow'rs, unsully'd beauty,
Softness, and sweetest innocence she wears,
And looks like nature in the world's first spring.
But say, Axalla———

Sel. Most renown'd in war,   [*Kneeling to* Tam.
Look with compassion on a captive maid,
Tho' born of hostile blood; nor let my birth,
Deriv'd from Bajazet, prevent that mercy
Which every subject of your fortune finds.
War is the province of ambitious man,
Who tears the miserable world for empire;
Whilst our weak sex, incapable of wrong,
On either side claims privilege of safety.

Tam. [*Raising her.*] Rise, royal maid! the pride of
haughty pow'r
Pays homage, not receives it, from the fair.
Thy angry father fiercely calls me forth,
And urges me unwillingly to arms.

Yet,

Yet, though our frowning battles menace death
And mortal conflict, think not that we hold
Thy innocence and virtue as our foe.
Here, till the fate of Asia is decided,
In safety stay. To-morrow is your own.
Nor grieve for who may conquer, or who lose;
Fortune on either side shall wait thy wishes.

   Sel. Where shall my wonder and my praise begin?
From the successful labours of thy arms;
Or from a theme more soft and full of peace,
Thy mercy and thy gentleness? Oh, Tamerlane!
What can I pay thee for this noble usage,
But grateful praise? So Heaven itself is paid.
Give peace, ye Pow'rs above, peace to mankind;
Nor let my father wage unequal war
Against the force of such united virtues.   [*prospect*

   Tam. Heav'n hear thy pious wish!——But since our
Looks darkly on futurity, till Fate
Determine for us, let thy beauty's safety
Be my Axalla's care; in whose glad eyes
I read what joy the pleasing service gives him.
Is there amongst thy other pris'ners aught   [*To* Axalla.
Worthy our knowledge?

   Ax. This brave man, my lord,   [*Pointing to* Mon.
With long resistance held the combat doubtful.
His party, prest with numbers, soon grew faint,
And would have left their charge an easy prey;
Whilst he alone, undaunted at the odds,
Tho' hopeless to escape, fought well and firmly;
Nor yielded till, o'ermatch'd by many hands,
He seem'd to shame our conquest, whilst he own'd it.

   Tam. Thou speak'st him as a soldier should a soldier,
Just to the worth he finds. I would not war [*To* Mon.
With aught that wears thy virtuous stamp of greatness.
Thy habit speaks thee Christian—Nay, yet more,
My soul seems pleas'd to take acquaintance with thee,
As if ally'd to thine: perhaps 'tis sympathy
Of honest minds; like strings wound up in music,
Where, by one touch, both utter the same harmony.
Why art thou then a friend to Bajazet?
And why my enemy?

   Mon. If human wisdom
Could point out every action of our lives,
And say, Let it be thus, in spite of fate

Or partial fortune, then I had not been
The wretch I am.

　　Tam. The brave meet every accident
With equal minds.　Think nobler of thy foes,
Than to account thy chance in war an evil.

　　Mon. Far, far from that: I rather hold it grievous
That I was forc'd ev'n but to seem your enemy;
Nor think the basenefs of a vanquifh'd flave
Moves me to flatter for precarious life,
Or ill-bought freedom, when I fwear, by Heav'n,
Were I to choofe from all mankind a mafter,
It fhould be Tamerlane.

　　Tam. A noble freedom
Dwells with the brave, unknown to fawning fycophants,
And claims a privilege of being believ'd.
I take thy praife as earneft of thy friendfhip.

　　Mon. Still you prevent the homage I fhould offer.
Oh, royal fir! let my misfortunes plead,
And wipe away the hoftile mark I wore.
I was, when not long fince my fortune hail'd me,
Blefs'd to my wifh; I was the prince Moneíes,
Born and bred up to greatnefs: witnefs the blood,
Which, through fucceffive heroes veins, ally'd
To our Greek emperors, roll'd down to me,
Feeds the bright flame of glory in my heart.

　　Tam. Ev'n that, that princely tie, fhould bind thee
If virtue were not more than all alliance.　　[to me,

　　Mon. I have a fifter, Oh, fevere remembrance!
Our noble houfe's, nay, her fex's pride;
Nor think my tongue too lavifh, if I fpeak her
Fair as the fame of virtue, and yet chafte
As its cold precepts; wife beyond her fex
And blooming youth; foft as forgiving mercy,
Yet greatly brave and jealous for her honour:
Such as fhe was, to fay I barely lov'd her,
Is poor to my foul's meaning. From our infancy
There grew a mutual tendernefs between us,
Till not long fince her vows were kindly plighted
To a young lord, the equal of her birth.
The happy day was fix'd, and now approaching,
When faithlefs Bajazet (upon whofe honour,
In folemn treaty given, the Greeks depended)

　　　　　　　　　　　　　　　　　　　　With

With fudden war broke in upon the country,
Secure of peace, and for defence unready.

Tam. Let majefty no more be held divine,
Since kings, who are call'd gods, profane themfelves.

Mon. Among the wretches, whom that deluge fwept
Away to flavery, myfelf and fifter,
Then paffing near the frontiers to the court,
(Which waited for her nuptials) were furpris'd,
And made the captives of the tyrant's pow'r.
Soon as we reach'd his court, we found our ufage,
Beyond what we expected, fair and noble;
'Twas then the ftorm of your victorious arms
Look'd black, and feem'd to threaten, when he preft me
(By oft repeating inftances) to draw
My fword for him: but when he found my foul
Difdain'd his purpofe, he more fiercely told me,
That my Arpafia, my lov'd fifter's fate,
Depended on my courage fhewn for him.
I had long learnt to hold myfelf at nothing;
But for her fake, to ward the blow from her,
I bound my fervice to the man I hated.
Six days are paft, fince, by the fultan's order,
I left the pledge of my return behind,
And went to guard this princefs to his camp:
The reft the brave Axalla's fortune tells you.

Tam. Wifely the tyrant ftrove to prop his caufe,
By leaguing with thy virtue; but juft Heav'n
Has torn thee from his fide, and left him naked
To the avenging bolt that drives upon him.
Forget the name of captive, and I wifh
I could as well reftore that fair-one's freedom,
Whofe lofs hangs heavy on thee: yet ere night,
Perhaps, we may deferve thy friendfhip nobler;
Th' approaching ftorm may caft thy fhipwreck'd wealth
Back to thy arms: till that be paft, fince war
(Tho' in the jufteft caufe) is ever doubtful,
I will not afk thy fword to aid my victory,
Left it fhould hurt that hoftage of thy valour
Our common foe detains.

Mon. Let Bajazet
Bend to his yoke repining flaves by force;
You, fir, have found a nobler way to empire,
Lord of the willing world.

Tam.

' *Tam.* Oh, my Axalla!

' Thou haſt a tender ſoul, apt for compaſſion,

' And art thyſelf a lover and a friend.

' Does not this prince's fortune move thy temper?

   ' *Ax.* Yes, ſir, I mourn the brave Moneſes' fate,

' The merit of his virtue hardly match'd

' With diſadvent'rous chance: yet, prince, allow me,

' Allow me, from th' experience of a lover,

' To ſay, one perſon whom your ſtory mention'd

' (If he ſurvive) is far beyond you wretched:

' You nam'd the bridegroom of your beauteous ſiſter.

   ' *Mon.* I did. Oh, moſt accurſt!

   ' *Ax.* Think what he feels,

' Daſh'd in the fierceneſs of his expectation:

' Then, when th' approaching minute of poſſeſſion

' Had wound imagination to the height,

' Think if he lives!

   ' *Mon.* He lives! he does; 'tis true

' He lives! But how? To be a dog, and dead,

' Were paradiſe to ſuch a ſtate as his:

' He holds down life, as children do a potion,

' With ſtrong reluctance and convulſive ſtrugglings,

' Whilſt his misfortunes preſs him to diſgorge it.

   ' *Tam.* Spare the remembrance, 'tis an uſeleſs grief,

' And adds to the misfortune by repeating.

' The revolution of a day may bring

' Such turns, as Heav'n itſelf could ſcarce have promis'd,

' Far, far beyond thy wiſh: let that hope chear thee.'

Haſte, my Axalla, to diſpoſe with ſafety

The beauteous charge, and on the foe revenge

The pain which abſence gives; thy other care,

Honour and arms, now ſummon thy attendance.

Now do thy office well, my ſoul! Remember

Thy cauſe, the cauſe of Heaven and injur'd Earth.

O thou Supreme! if thy great ſpirit warms

My glowing breaſt, and fires my ſoul to arms,

Grant that my ſword, aſſiſted by thy pow'r,

This day may peace and happineſs reſtore,

That war and lawleſs rage may vex the world no more.

    [*Exeunt* Tamerlane, Moneſes, Stratocles, *prince of*

      Tanais, Zama, Mirvan, *and attendants.*

   Ax. The battle calls, and bids me haſte to leave thee;

Oh, Selima!——But let deſtruction wait.

                      Are

Are there not hours enough for blood and flaughter?
This moment fhall be love's, and I will waite it
In foft complainings, for thy fighs and coldnefs,
For thy forgetful coldnefs; even at Birza,
When in thy father's court my eyes firft own'd thee,
Fairer than light, the joy of their beholding,
Even then thou wert not thus.
 ' *Sel.* Art not thou chang'd,
' Chriftian Axalla? Art thou ftill the fame?
' Thofe were the gentle hours of peace, and thou
' The world's good angel, that didft kindly join
' Its mighty mafters in harmonious friendfhip:
' But fince thofe joys that once were ours are ioft,
' Forbear to mention 'em, and talk of war;
' Talk of thy conqueft and my chains, Axalla.
 ' *Ax.* Yet I will liften, fair, unkind, upbraider,
' Yet I will liften to thy charming accents,
' Altho' they make me curfe my fame and fortune,
' My laurel wreaths, and all the glorious trophies
' For whi h the valiant bleed—Oh, thou unjuft one!
' Doft thou then envy me this fmall return
' My niggard fate has made for all the mournings,
' For all the pains, for all the fleeplefs nights,
' That cruel abfence brings?
 ' *Sel.* Away, deceiver!
' I will not hear thy foothing. Is it thus
' That Chriftian lovers prove the faith they fwear?
' Are war and flavery the foft endearments
' With which they court the beauties they admire?
' 'Twas well my heart was cautious of believing
' Thy vows, and thy protefting. Know, my conqueror,
' Thy fword has vanquifh'd but the half of Selima;
' Her foul difdains thy victory.
 ' *Ax.* Hear, fweet Heav'n!
' Hear the fair tyrant, how fhe wrefts love's laws,
' As fhe had vow'd my ruin! What is conqueft?
' What joy have I from that but to behold thee,
' To kneel before thee, and with lifted eyes
' To view thee, as Devotion does a faint,
' With awful, trembling pleafure; then to fwear
' Thou art the queen and miftrefs of my foul?
' Has not ev'n Tamerlane (whofe word, next Heaven's,
' Makes fate at fecond-hand) bid thee difclaim

' Thy

' Thy fears? And dóst thou call thyfelf a flave,
' Only to try how far the fad impreffion
' Can fink into Axalla!
   ' *Sel.* Oh, Axalla!
' Ought I to hear you?
   ' *Ax.* Come back, ye hours,
' And tell my Selima what fhe has done!
' Bring back the time, when to her father's court
' .I came ambaffador of peace from Tamerlane;
' When, hid by confcious darknefs and difguife,
' I paft the dangers of the watchful guards,
' Bold as the youth who nightly fwam the Hellefpont:
' Then, then fhe was not fworn the foe of love;
' When, as my foul confeft its flame, and fued
' In moving founds for pity, fhe frown'd rarely,
' But, bluffing, heard me tell the gentle tale;
' Nay, ev'n confeft, and told me foftly, fighing,
' She thought there was no guilt in love like mine.'
   Sel. Young, and unfkilful in the world's falfe arts,
I fuffer'd love to fteal upon my foftnefs,
And warm me with a lambent guiltlefs flame:
Yes, I have heard thee fwear a thoufand times,
And call the confcious Pow'rs of heav'n to witnefs
The tend'reft, trueft, everlafting paffion.
But, Oh! 'tis paft: and I will charge remembrance
To banifh the fond image from my foul.
Since thou art fworn the foe of royal Bajazet,
I have refolv'd to hate thee.
   Ax. !s it poffible!
Hate is not in thy nature; thy whole frame
Is harmony, without one jarring atom.
Why doft thou force thy eyes to wear this coldnefs?
It damps the fprings of life. Oh! bid me die,
Much rather bid me die, if it be true,
That thou haft fworn to hate me.————
   Sel. Let life and death
Wait the decifion of the bloody field;
Nor can thy fate, my conqueror, depend
Upon a woman's hate. Yet, fince you urge
A power, which once perhaps I had, there is
But one requeft that I can make with honour.
   Ax. Oh, name it! fay!

Sel. Forego your right of war,
And render me this inftant to my father.

Ax. Impoffible!——The tumult of the battle,
That haftes to join, cuts off all means of commerce
Betwixt the armies.

Sel. Swear then to perform it,
Which way foe'er the chance of war determines,
On my firft inftance.

Ax. By the facred majefty
Of Heaven, to whom we kneel, I will obey thee ;
Yes, I will give thee this fevereft proof
Of my foul's vow d devotion ; I will part with thee,
('Thou cruel to command it!) I will part with thee,
As wretches that are doubtful of hereafter
Part with their lives, unwilling, loth, and fearful,
And trembling at futurity.   But is there nothing,
No fmall return that honour can afford,
For all this wafte of love ?

' *Sel.* The gifts of captives
' Wear fomewhat of conftraint ; and generous minds
' Difdain to give, where freedom of the choice
' Does but feem wanting

'*Ax.*' What! not one kind look?   [* *Trumpets.*
Then thou art chang'd indeed. * Hark, I am fummon'd,
And thou wilt fend me forth like one unblefs'd,
Whom fortune has forfaken, and ill fate
Mark'd for deftruction. ' Thy furprifing coldnefs
' Hangs on my foul, and weighs my courage down:
' And the firft feeble blow I meet fhall raze me
' From all remembrance :' nor is life or fame
Worthy my care, fince I am loft to thee.   [*Going*

Sel. Ha! Goeft thou to the fight ? ———

Ax. I do ——— Farewel ! ———

Sel. What! and no more! A figh heaves in my breaft,
And ftops the ftruggling accents on my tongue,
Elfe, fure, I fhould have added fomething more,
And made our parting fofter.

Ax. Give it way :
The niggard honour that affords not love
Forbids not pity ———

' *Sel.* Fate perhaps has fet
' This day the period of thy life and conquefts ;
' And I fhall fee thee borne at evening back

' A breath-

' A breathlefs corfe.——Oh! can I think on that,
' And hide my forrows?—No—they will have way,
' And all the vital air that life draws in
' Is render'd back in fighs.
   ' *Ax.* The murm'ring gale revives the drooping flame,
' That at thy coldnefs languifh'd in my breaft:
' So breathe the gentle zephyrs on the fpring,
' And waken every plant and od'rous flower,
' Which winter froft had blafted, to new life.
   ' *Sel.* To fee thee for this moment, and no more.—
' Oh! help me to refolve againft this tendernefs,
' That charms my fierce refentments, and prefents thee
' Not as thou art, mine and my father's foe,
' But as thou wert, when firft thy moving accents
' Won me to hear; when, as I liften'd to thee,
' The happy hours paft by us unperceiv'd,
' So was my foul fix'd to the foft enchantment.
   ' *Ax.* Let me be ftill the fame; I am, I muft be.'
If it were poffible my heart could ftray,
One look from thee would call it back again,
And fix the wanderer for ever thine.
   Sel. Where is my boafted refolution now?
                       [Sinking into his arms.
Oh, yes! thou art the fame; my heart joins with thee,
' And to betray me will believe thee ftill;
' It dances to the founds that mov'd it firft,
' And owns at once the weaknefs of my foul:
' So, when fome fkilful artift ftrikes the ftrings,
' The magic numbers roufe our fleeping paffions,
' And force us to confefs our grief and pleafure.'
Alas! Axalla, fay——doft thou not pity
My artlefs innocence, and eafy fondnefs?
Oh! turn thee from me, or I die with blufhing.
   Ax. No, let me rather gaze, for ever gaze,
And blefs the new-born glories that adorn thee;
' From every blufh, that kindles in thy cheeks,
' Ten thoufand little Loves and Graces fpring
' To revel in the rofes——'twill not be.'   *[Trumpets.*
This envious trumpet calls, and tears me from thee—
   Sel. My fears increafe, and doubly prefs me now:
I charge thee, if thy fword comes crofs my father,
Stop for a moment, and remember me.

                                    Ax.

Ax. Oh, doubt not but his life shall be my care,
Ev'n dearer than my own——

    Sel. Guard that for me too.

    Ax. Oh, Selima! thou hast restor'd my quiet,
The noble ardour of the war, with love
Returning, brightly burns within my breast,
And bids me be secure of all hereafter.
' So chears some pious saint a dying sinner
' (Who trembled at the thought of pains to come)
' With Heaven's forgiveness, and the hopes of mercy:
' At length, the tumult of his soul appeas'd,
' And every doubt and anxious scruple eas'd,
' Boldly he proves the dark, uncertain road,.   ⎫
' The peace, his holy comforter bestow'd,   ⎬
' Guides and protects him, like a guardian god.' [*Exit.*⎭

    Sel. In vain all arts a love sick virgin tries,
.Affects to frown, and seem severely wise,   ⎫
In hopes to cheat the wary lover's eyes: ⎬
If the dear youth her pity strives to move,   ⎭
And pleads, with tenderness, the cause of love!
Nature asserts her empire in her heart,
And kindly takes the faithful lover's part.
By love herself, and nature thus betray'd,   ⎫
No more she trusts in pride's fantastic aid,   ⎬
But bids her eyes confess the yielding maid.   ⎭

                        [*Exit* Selima, *guards following.*

A C T II. S C E N E, Tamerlaine's *camp.*

Enter Moneses.

Mon. THE dreadful business of the war is o'er;
        And Slaughter, that from yester' morn 'till
           even,
With giant steps, pass'd striding o'er the field,
Besmear'd and horrid with the blood of nations,
Now weary sits among the mangled heaps,
And slumbers o'er her prey ; while from this camp
The chearful sounds of victory and Tamerlane
Beat the high arch of heaven. ' Deciding Fate,
' That crowns him with the spoils of such a day,

                           ' Has

' Has giv'n it as an earneft of the world
' That fhortly fhall be his.'

Enter Stratocles.

My Stratocles!
Moft happily return'd; might I believe
Thou bring'ft me any joy?

Stra. With my beft diligence,
This night, I have enquir'd of what concerns you.
Scarce was the fun, who fhone upon the horror
Of the paft day. funk to the weftern ocean,
When, by permiffion from the prince Axalla,
I mixt among the tumult of the warriors
Returning from the battle : here a troop
Of hardy Parthians, red with honeft wounds,
Confeft the conqueft they had well deferv'd :
There a dejected crew of wretched captives,
' Sore with unprofitable hurts, and groaning
' Under new bondage,' followed fadly after
The haughty victor's heels. But that which fully
Crown'd the fuccefs of Tamerlane, was Bajazet,
Fall'n, like the proud archangel, from the height
Where once (ev'n next to majefty divine)
Enthron'd he fat, down to the vile defcent
And lownefs of a flave : but, Oh! to fpeak
The rage, the fiercenefs, and the indignation,
It bars all words, and cuts defcription fhort.

Mon. Then he is fall'n! that come, which on high
Portended ruin; he has fpent his blaze,
And fhall diftract the world with fears no more.
' Sure it muft bode me well ; for oft my foul
' Has ftarted into tumult at his name,
' As if my guardian angel took the alarm
' At the approach of fomewhat mortal to me.'
But fay, my friend, what hear'ft thou of Arpafia?
For there my thoughts, my every care is center'd.

Stra. Tho' on that purpofe ftill I bent my fearch,
Yet nothing certain could I gain, but this :
That in the pillage of the fultan's tent
Some women were made pris'ners, who this morning
Were to be offer'd to the emperor's view ;
Their names and qualities, tho' oft enquiring,
I could not learn.

Mon.

Mon. Then muſt my ſoul ſtill labour
Beneath uncertainty and anxious doubt,
The mind's worſt ſtate.　The tyrant's ruin gives me
But a half eaſe.
　　Stra. 'Twas ſaid, not far from hence
The captives were to wait the emperor's paſſage.
　　Mon. Haſte we to ſind the place.　Oh, my Arpaſia!
Shall we not meet ?　' Why hangs my heart thus heavy,
' Like death within my boſom ?　Oh, 'tis well,
' The joy of meeting pays the pangs of abſence,
' Elſe who could bear it ?'
When thy lov'd ſight ſhall bleſs my eyes again,
Then I will own, I ought not to complain,
Since that ſweet hour is worth whole years of pain.
　　　　　　　　　　[*Exeunt* Moneſes *and* Stratocles,

SCENE *the inſide of a magnificent tent.　Symphony of
　　　　　warlike muſic.*

Enter Tamerlane, Axalla, *Prince of* Tanais, Zama,
　　Mirvan, *ſoldiers, and other attendants.*

　　Ax. From this auſpicious day the Parthian name
Shall date its birth of empire, and extend,
Ev'n from the dawning Eaſt to utmoſt Thule,
The limits of its ſway.
　　Pr. Nations unknown
Where yet the Roman eagles never flew,
Shall pay their homage to victorious Tamerlane;
Bend to his valour and ſuperior virtue,
And own, that conqueſt is not given by chance,
But, bound by fatal and reſiſtleſs merit,
Waits on his arms.
　　Tam. It is too much: you dreſs me,
Like an uſurper. in the borrow'd attributes
Of injur'd Heaven.　Can we call conqueſt ours ?
Shall man, this pigmy, with a giant's pride,
Vaunt of himſelf, and ſay, Thus have I done this ?
Oh, vain pretence to greatneſs ! Like the moon,
We borrow all the brightneſs which we boaſt,
Dark in ourſelves and uſeleſs.　If that hand
That rules the fate of battles, ſtrike for us,
Crown us with fame, and gild our clay with honour,
　　　　　　　　　　　　　　　　　'Twere

'Twere moſt ungrateful to diſown the benefit,
And arrogate a praiſe which is not ours.

Ax. With ſuch unſhaken temper of the ſoul
To bear the ſwelling tide of proſp'rous fortune,
Is to deſerve that fortune : in adverſity,
The mind grows tough by buffeting the tempeſt,
Which, in ſucceſs diſſolving, ſinks to eaſe,
And loſes all her firmneſs.

Tam. Oh, Axalla!
Could I forget I am a man, as thou art ;
Would not the winter's cold, or ſummer's heat,
Sickneſs, or thirſt, and hunger, all the train
Of nature's clamorous appetites, aſſerting
An equal right in kings and common men,
Reprove me daily ?—No—If I boaſt of aught,
Be it, to have been Heaven's happy inſtrument,
The means of good to all my fellow-creatures :
This is a king's beſt praiſe.

Enter Omar.

Om. Honour and fame   [*Bowing to* Tamerlane.
For ever wait the emperor! May our prophet
Give him ten thouſand thouſand days of life,
And every day like this! The captive ſultan,
Fierce in his bonds, and at his fate repining,
Attends your ſacred will.

Tam. Let him approach.

Enter Bajazet *and other Turkiſh priſoners in chains, with a guard of ſoldiers.*

When I ſurvey the ruins of this field,
The wild deſtruction which thy fierce ambition
Has dealt among mankind, (ſo many widows
And helpleſs orphans has thy battle made,
That half our eaſtern world this day are mourners)
Well may I, in behalf of heav'n and earth,
Demand from thee atonement for this wrong,

Baj. Make thy demand to thoſe that own thy pow'r,
Know I am ſtill beyond it ; and tho' Fortune
(Curſe on that changeling deity of fools!)
Has ſtript me of the train and pomp of greatneſs,
That outſide of a king, yet ſtill my ſoul,
Fix'd high, and of itſelf alone dependent,
Is ever free and royal, and ev'n now,
As at the head of battle, does defy thee.

I know

I know what pow'r the chance of war has giv'n,
And dare thee to the ufe on't. This vile fpeeching,
This after-game of words, is what moft irks me;
Spare that, and for the reft 'tis equal all——
Be it as it may.

Tam. Well was it for the world,
When on their borders neighbouring princes met,
Frequent in friendly parle, by cool debates
Preventing wafteful war; fuch fhou'd our meeting
Have been, hadft thou but held in juft regard
The fanctity of leagues fo often fworn to.
Canft thou believe thy prophet, or, what's more,
That pow'r fupreme which made thee and thy prophet,
Will, with impunity, let pafs that breach
Of facred faith giv'n to the royal Greck?

Baj. Thou pedant talker! ha! art thou a king,
Poffefs'd of facred pow'r, Heav'n's darling attribute,
And doft thou prate of leagues, and oaths, and prophets?
I hate the Greek (perdition on his name!)
As I do thee, and would have met you both
As death does human nature, for deftruction.

Tam. Caufelefs to hate is not of human kind:
The favage brute that haunts in woods remote
And defart wilds, tears not the fearful traveler,
If hunger, or fome injury, provoke not.

Baj. Can a king want a caufe, when empire bids
Go on? What is he born for, but ambition?
It is his hunger, 'tis his call of nature,
The noble appetite which will be fatisfy'd,
And, like the food of Gods, make him immortal.

Tam. Henceforth I will not wonder we were foes,
Since fouls that differ fo by nature hate,
And ftrong antipathy forbids their union.

Baj. The noble fire that warms me, does indeed
Tranfcend thy coldnefs. I am pleas'd we differ,
Nor think alike.

Tam. No—for I think like Man,
Thou like a monfter, from whofe baleful prefence
Nature ftarts back; and tho' fhe fix'd her ftamp
On thy rough mafs, and mark'd thee for a man,
Now, confcious of her error, fhe difclaims thee,
As form'd for her deftruction.——
'Tis true, I am a king, as thou haft been:

B

Honour

Honour and glory too have been my aim ;
But tho' I dare face death, and all the dangers
Which furious war wears in its bloody front,
Yet would I chuse to fix my name by peace,
By juſtice, and by mercy ; and to raiſe
My trophies on the bleſſings of mankind :
Nor would I buy the empire of the world
With ruin of the people whom I ſway,
On-forfeit of my honour.

Baj. Prophet, I thank thee————
Damnation !—Couldſt thou rob me of my glory,
To dreſs up this tame king, this preaching derviſe ?
Unfit for war, thou ſhouldſt have liv'd ſecure
In lazy peace, and with debating ſenates
Shar'd a precarious ſceptre, ſat tamely ſtill,
And let bold factions canton out thy pow'r,
And wrangle for the ſpoils they robb'd thee of ;
Whilſt I (curſe on the power that ſtops my ardour !)
Would, like a tempeſt, ruſh amidſt the nations,
Be greatly terrible, and deal, like Alha,
My angry thunder on the frighted world.

Tam. The world !—'twould be too little for thy pride:
Thou wouldſt ſcale heav'n————

Baj. I would.—Away ! my ſoul
Diſdains thy conference.

Tam. Thou vain, raſh thing,
That, with gigantic inſolence, haſt dar'd
To lift thy wretched ſelf above the ſtars,
And mate with pow'r almighty: thou art fall'n !

Baj. 'Tis falſe ! I am not fall'n from aught I have
                been ;
At leaſt my ſoul reſolves to keep her ſtate,
And ſcorns to take acquaintance with ill fortune.

Tam. Almoſt beneath my pity art thou fall'n ;
Since, while th' avenging hand of Heav'n is on thee,
And preſſes to the duſt thy ſwelling ſoul,
Fool-hardy, with the ſtronger thou contendeſt.
To what vaſt heights had thy tumultuous temper
Been hurry'd, if ſucceſs had crown'd thy wiſhes !
Say, what had I to expect, if thou had'ſt conquer'd ?

Baj. Oh, glorious thought ! by Heav'n I will enjoy it,
Tho' but in fancy : imagination ſhall
Make room to entertain the vaſt idea.

O**b**!

Oh! had I been the mafter but of yefterday,
The world, the world had fe't me; and for thee,
I had us'd thee as thou art to me—a dog,
The object of my fcorn, and mortal hatred:
I would have taught thy neck to know my weight,
And mounted from that footftool to my faddle:
Then, when thy daily fervile tafk was done,
I would have cag'd thee for the fcorn of flaves,
'Till thou hadft begg'd to die; and ev'n that mercy
I had deny'd thee. Now thou know'ft my mind,
And queftion me no farther.

Tam. Well doft thou teach me
What juftice fhould exact from thee. Mankind,
With one confent, cry out for vengeance on thee;
Loudly they call to cut off this league-breaker,
This wild deftroyer from the face of earth.

Baj. Do it, and rid thy fhaking foul at once
Of its worft fear.

Tam. Why flept the thunder
That fhould have arm'd the idol deity,
And giv'n thee pow'r, ere yefter fun was fet,
To fhake the foul of Tamerlane. Hadft thou an arm
To make thee fear'd, thou fhouldft have prov'd it on me,
Amidft the fweat and blood of yonder field,
When thro' the tumult of the war I fought thee,
Fenc'd in with nations.

Baj. Curfe upon the ftars,
That fated us to different fcenes of flaughter!
Oh! could my fword have met thee——

Tam. Thou hadft then,
As now, been in my pow'r, and held thy life
Dependent on my gift—Yes, Bajazet,
I bid thee live—' fo much my foul difdains
' That thou fhouldft think I can fear aught but Heav'n:'
Nay more; couldft thou forget thy brutal fiercenefs,
And form thyfelf to manhood, I would bid thee
Live, and be ftill a king, that thou may'ft learn
What man fhould be to man, in war remembering
The common tie and brotherhood of kind.
This royal tent, with fuch of thy domeftics
As can be found, fhall wait upon thy fervice;
Nor will I ufe my fortune to demand

Hard terms of peace, but such as thou may'st offer
With honour, I with honour may receive.

[Tamerlane *signs to an officer, who unbinds* Bajazet.

Baj. Ha! say'st thou—no—our prophet's vengeance
blast me,
If thou shalt buy my friendship with thy empire.
Damnation on thee! thou smooth fawning talker!
Give me again my chains, that I may curse thee,
And gratify my rage: or, if thou wilt
Be a vain fool, and play with thy perdition,
Remember I'am thy foe, and hate thee deadly.
Thy folly on thy head!

Tam. Be still my foe.
Great minds, like Heav'n, are pleas'd in doing good,
'Tho' the ungrateful subjects of their favours
Are barren in return. ' Thy stubborn pride,
' That spurns the gentle office of humanity,
' Shall in my honour own, and thy despite,
' I have done as I ought.' Virtue still does
With scorn the mercenary world regard,
Where abject souls do good, and hope reward:
Above the worthless trophies men can raise,
She seeks not honours, wealth, nor airy praise, }
But with herself, herself the goddess pays.

[*Exeunt* Tamerlane, Axalla, *Prince of* Tanais, Mirvan, Zama, *and attendants.*

Baj. Come, lead me to my dungeon; plunge me
down
Deep from the hated sight of man and day;
Where, under covert of the friendly darkness,
My soul may brood, at leisure, o'er its anguish.

Om. Our royal master wou'd with noble usage,
Make your misfortunes light: he bids you hope——

Baj. I tell thee, slave, I have shook hands with hope,
And all my thoughts are rage, despair, and horror.
Ha! wherefore am I thus!—Perdition seize me!
But my cold blood runs shiv'ring to my heart,
A at lone phantom, that in dead of night,
With dreadful action, stalks around our beds.
The rage and fiercer passions of my breast
Are lost in new confusion.——

Enter Haly.

Ar asia !— ai !

Ha.

Ha. Oh, emperor! for whofe hard fate our prophet
And all the heroes of thy facred race
Are fad in Paradife, thy faithful Haly,
The flave of all thy pleafures, in this ruin,
This univerfal fhipwreck of thy fortunes,

Enter Arpafia.

Has gather'd up this treafure for thy arms:
Nor ev'n the victor, haughty Tamerlane,
(By whofe command once more thy flave beholds thee)
Denies this bleffing to thee, but with honour
Renders thee back thy queen, thy beauteous bride.

　　Baj. Oh! had her eyes with pity feen my forrows,
Had fhe the fondnefs of a tender bride,
Heav'n cou'd not have beftow'd a greater bleffing,
And love had made amends for lofs of empire.
But fee, what fury dwells upon her charms!
What lightning flafhes from her angry eyes!
With a malignant joy fhe views my ruin:
Even beauteous in her hatred, ftill fhe charms me,
And awes my fierce tumultuous foul to love.

　　Arp. And dar'ft thou hope, thou tyrant ravifher!
That heav'n has any joy in ftore for thee?
Look back upon the fum of thy paft life, ∙
Where tyranny, oppreffion, and injuftice,
Perjury, murders, fwell the black account;
Where loft Arpafia's wrongs ftand bleeding frefh,
Thy laft recorded crime. But Heav'n has found thee;
At length the tardy vengeance has o'erta'en thee.
My weary foul fhall bear a little longer
The pain of life, to call for juftice on thee:
That once complete, fink to the peaceful grave,
And lofe the memory of my wrongs and thee.

　　Baj. Thou rail'ft! I thank thee for it—Be perverfe,
And mufter all the woman in thy foul;
Goad me with curfes, be a very wife,
That I may fling off this tame love, and hate thee.

Enter Monefes.　　　　[Bajazet *ftarting.*

Ha! Keep thy temper, heart; nor take alarm
At a flave's prefence.

　　Mon. It is Arpafia!——Leave me, thou cold fear.
Sweet as the rofy morn fhe breaks upon me;
And forrow, like the night's unwholefome fhade,
Gives way before the golden dawn fhe brings.

B 3　　　　　　　　　　　　　　　　*Baj.*

Baj. [*Advancing towards him.*] Ha, Christian! Is it
well that we meet thus?
Is this thy faith?

Mn. Why does thy frowning brow
Put on this storm of fury? Is it strange
We should meet here, companions in misfortune,
The captives of one common chance of war?
Nor shouldst thou wonder that my sword has fail'd
Before the fortune of victorious Tamerlane,
When thou, with nations like the sanded shore,
With half the warring world upon thy side,
Couldst not stand up against this dreadful battle,
That crush'd thee with its shock. Thy men can witness,
These cowards that forsook me in the combat,
My sword was not inactive.

Baj. No——'Tis false:
Where is my daughter, thou vile Greek? Thou hast
Betray'd her to the Tartar; or even worse,
Pale with thy fear, didst lose her like a coward;
And, like a coward now, wouldst cast the blame
On fortune and ill stars.

Mon. Ha! said'st thou, like a coward?
What sanctity, what majesty divine
Hast thou put on, to guard thee from my rage,
That thus thou dar'st to wrong me?

Baj. Our, thou slave,
And know me for thy lord——

Mon. I tell thee, tyrant,
When in the pride of power thou sat'st on high,
When like an idol thou wert vainly worship'd
By prostrate wretches, born with slavish souls;
Ev'n when thou wert a king, thou wert no more
Nor greater than Moneses, born of a race
Royal and great as thine. What art thou now then?
The fate of war has set thee with the lowest;
And captives (like the subjects of the grave)
Losing distinction, serve one common lord.

Baj. Prav'd by this dog! Now give a loose to rage,
And curse thyself; curse thy false cheating prophet.
Ha! yet there's some revenge. Hear me, thou Christian!
Thou lef'st that sister with me: Thou impostor!
Thou boaster of thy honesty! Thou liar!
But take her to thee back.

2   Now

Now to explore my prison——if it holds
Another plague like this. The reftlefs damn'd
(If mufties lie not) wander thus in hell;
From fcorching flames to chilling frofts they run,
Then from their frofts to fires return again,
And only prove variety of pain.

[*Exeunt* Bajazet, Haly, Omar, *and guards.*

Arp. Stay, Bajazet. I charge thee, by my wrongs,
Stay and unfold a tale of fo much horror,
As only fits thy telling.——Oh, Monefes!

' *Mon.* Why doft thou weep? Why this tempeftuous
paffion,
' That ftops thy falt'ring tongue fhort on my name?
' Oh, fpeak! unveil this myftery of forrow,
' And draw the difmal fcene at once to fight.
' *Arp.* Thou art undone, loft, ruin'd, and undone!
' *Mon.* I will not think 'tis fo, while I have thee;
' While thus 'tis given to fold thee in my arms;
' For while I figh upon thy panting bofom,
' The fad remembrance of paft woes is loft
' *Arp.* Forbear to footh thy foul with flatt'ring thoughts
' Of evils overpaft, and joys to come:
' Our woes are like the genuine fhade beneath,
' Where fate cuts off the very hopes of day,
' And everlafting night and horror reign.'

Mon. By all the tendernefs and chafte endearments
Of our paft love, I charge thee, my Arpafia,
To eafe my foul of doubts! Give me to know,
At once, the utmoft malice of my fate!

Arp. Take then thy wretched fhare in all I fuffer,
Still partner of my heart! Scarce hadft thou left
The fultan's camp, when the imperious tyrant,
Soft'ning the pride and fiercenefs of his temper,
With gentle fpeech made offer of his love.
Amaz'd, as at the fhock of fudden death,
I ftarted into tears, and often urg'd
(Tho' ftill in vain) the difference of our faiths.
At laft, as flying to the utmoft refuge,
With lifted hands and ftreaming eyes, I own'd
The fraud, which when we firft were made his pris'ners,
' Confcious of my unhappy form, and fearing
' For thy dear life,' I forc'd thee to put on;
Thy borrow'd name of brother, mine of fifter;

Hiding

Hiding between that veil the nearer tie
Our mutual vows had made before the priest.
Kindling to rage at hearing of my story,
Then, be it so, he cry'd : Think'st thou thy vows,
Giv'n to a slave, sha'l bar me from thy beauties?
Then bade the priest pronounce the marriage rites :
Which he perform'd ; whilst, shrieking with despair,
I call'd in vain the Pow'rs of heav'n to aid me.

    Mon. Villain ! imperial villain !—Oh, the coward !
Aw'd by his guilt, tho' back'd by force and power,
He durst not, to my face, avow his purpose :
But, in my absence, like a lurking thief,
S ole on my treasure, and at once undid me.

    Arp. Had they not kept me from the means of death,
Forgetting all the rules of Christian suffering,
I had done a desp'rate murder on my soul,
Ere the rude slaves, that waited on his will,
Had forc'd me to his——

    Mon. Stop thee there, Arpasia,
And bar my fancy from the guilty scene !
Let not thought enter, lest the busy mind
Should muster such a train of monstrous images
As would distract me. Oh ! I cannot bear it.
Thou lovely hoard of sweets, where all my joys
Were treasur'd up, to have thee rifled thus !
' Thus torn untasted from my eager wishes !'
But I will have thee from him. Tamerlane
(The sovereign judge of equity on earth)
Shall do me justice on this mighty robber,
And render back thy beauties to Moneses.

    Arp. And who shall render back my peace, my honour,
The spotless whiteness of my virgin soul ?
Ah ! no, Moneses—Think not I will ever
Bring a polluted love to thy chaste arms :
I am the tyrant's wife. Oh, fatal title !
And, in the sight of all the saints, have sworn,
By honour, womanhood, and blushing shame,
To know no second bride-bed but my grave.

    ' *Mon.* I swear it must not be, since still my eye
' Finds thee as heav'nly white, as angel pure,
' As in the earliest hours of life thou wert :
' Nor art thou his, but mine ; thy first vow's mine,
' Thy soul is mine.——

                    ' *Arp.*

' *Arp.* Oh! think not, that the pow'r
' Of moſt perſuaſive eloquence can make me
' Forget I've been another's, been his wife.
' Now, by my bluſhes, by the ſtrong confuſion
' And anguiſh of my heart, ſpare me, Moneſes,
' Nor urge my trembling virtue to the precipice.'
Shortly, Oh! very ſhortly, if my ſorrows
Divine aright, and Heav'n be gracious to me,
Death ſhall diſſolve the fatal obligation,
' And give me up to peace, to that bleſt place
' Where the good reſt from care and anxious life.
   ' *Mon.* Oh, teach me, thou fair ſaint, like thee to
' Teach me, with hardy piety, to combat   [ſuffer!
' The preſent ills: inſtruct my eyes to paſs
' The narrow bounds of life, this land of ſorrow,
' And, with bold hopes, to view the realms beyond,
' Thoſe diſtant beauties of the future ſtate.
' Tell me, Arpaſia—ſay, what joys are thoſe
' That wait to crown the wretch who ſuffers here?
' Oh! tell me, and ſuſtain my failing faith.
   ' *Arp.* Imagine ſomewhat exquiſitely fine,
' Which fancy cannot paint, which the pleas'd mind
' Can barely know, unable to deſcribe it;
' Imagine 'tis a tract of endleſs joys
' Without ſatiety or interruption;
' Imagine, 'tis to meet and part no more.
   ' *Mon.* Grant, gentle Heav'n, that ſuch may be our
' Let us be bleſt together.—Oh, my ſoul!   [lot!
' Build on that hope, and let it arm thy courage
' To ſtruggle with the ſtorm that parts us now.
   ' *Arp.*' Yes. my Moneſes! now the ſurges riſe,
The ſwelling ſea breaks in between our barks,
And drives us to our fate on different rocks.
Farewell!——My ſoul lives with thee.——
   Mon. Death is parting,
'Tis the laſt ſad adieu 'twixt ſoul and body.
But this is ſomewhat worſe——My joy, my comfort,
All that was left in life, fleets after thee;
' My aching ſight hangs on thy parting beauties,
' Thy lovely eyes, all drown'd in floods of ſorrow.
' So ſinks the ſetting ſun beneath the waves,
' And leaves the traveller in pathleſs woods,
' Benighted and forlorn. ——Thus, with ſad eyes,

‘ Weſtward he turns, to mark the light's decay,
‘ Till, hav'ng loſt the laſt faint glimpſe of day,   ⎫
‘ Chearleſs, in darkneſs, he purſues his way.’   ⎬
                    [*Exeunt* Moneſes *and* Arpaſia ſeverally. ⎭

_____

ACT III. SCENE, *the inſide of the royal tent.*

Enter Axalla, Selima, *and women attendants.*

‘ *Ax.* CAN there be aught in love, beyond this
                         proof,
‘ This wond'rous proof, I give thee of my faith ?
‘ To tear thee from my bleeding boſom thus !
‘ To rend the ſtrings of life to ſet thee free,
‘ And yield thee to a cruel father's power,
‘ Foe to my hopes ! what canſt thou pay me back ?
‘ What but thyſelf, thou angel ! for this fondneſs ?
‘   *Sel.* Thou doſt upbraid me, beggar as I am,
‘ And urge me with my poverty of love.
‘ Perhaps thou think'ſt, 'tis nothing for a maid
‘ To ſtruggle through the niceneſs of her ſex,
‘ The bluſhes and the fears, and own ſhe loves :
‘ Thou think'ſt 'tis nothing for my artleſs heart
‘ To own my weakneſs, and confeſs thy triumph.
‘   *Ax.* Oh ! yes I own it ; my charm'd ears ne'er knew
‘ A ſound of ſo much rapture, ſo much joy.
‘ Not voices, inſtruments, not warbling birds,
‘ Not winds, not murm'ring waters join'd in concert,
‘ Not tuneful nature, not th' according ſpheres,
‘ Utter ſuch harmony, as when my Selima,
‘ With down-caſt looks and bluſhes, ſaid—I love.—
‘   *Sel.* And yet thou ſay'ſt, I am a niggard to thee.
‘ I ſwear the balance ſhall be held between us,
‘ And Love be judge, if after all the tenderneſs,
‘ Tears and confuſion of my virgin-ſoul,
‘ Thou ſhouldſt complain of aught, unjuſt Axalla !
‘   *Ax.* Why was I ever bleſt !—Why is remembrance
Rich with a thouſand pleaſing images
Of paſt enjoyments, ſince 'tis but to plague me ?
When thou art mine no more, what will it eaſe me
To think of all the golden minutes paſt,
To think that thou wert kind, and I was happy,
But, like an angel fall'n from bliſs, to curſe

                                                   My

My prefent ftate, and mourn the heav'n I've loft ?

Sel. Hope better for us both ; nor let thy fears,
Like an unlucky omen, crofs my way.
' My father, rough and ftormy in his nature,
' To me was always gentle, and, with fondnefs
' Paternal, ever met me with a bleffing.
' Oft, when offence had ftirr'd him to fuch fury,
' That not grave counfellors for wifdom fam'd,
' Nor hardy captains that had fought his battles,
' Prefum'd to fpeak, but ftruck with aweful dread
' Were hufh'd as death ; yet has he fmil'd on me,
' Kifs'd me, and bade me utter all my purpofe,
' Till with my idle prattle I had footh'd him,
' And won him from his anger.
  ' *Ax.* Oh ! I know
' Thou haft a tongue to charm the wildeft tempers.
' Herds would forget to graze, and favage beafts
' Stand ftill and lofe their fiercenefs, but to hear thee,
' As if they had reflection, and by reafon
' Forfook a lefs enjoyment for a greater.
' But, Oh ! when I revolve each circumftance,
' My Chriftian faith, my fervice clofely bound
' To Tamerlane, my mafter and my friend,
' Tell me, my charmer, if my fears are vain ?
' Think what remains for me, if the fierce fultan
' Should doom thy beauties to another's bed !'

Sel. 'Tis a fad thought ; but to appeafe thy doubts,
Here, in the aweful fight of Heav'n, I vow
No pow'r fhall e'er divide me from thy love,
Ev'n duty fhall not force me to be falfe.
My cruel ftars may tear thee from my arms,
But never from my heart ; ' and when the maids
' Shall yearly come with garlands of frefh flow'rs,
' To mourn with pious office o'er my grave,
' They fhall fit fadly down, and weeping tell
' How well I lov'd, how much I fuffer'd for thee ;
' And, while they grieve my fate, fhall praife my con-
    ' ftancy.'

Ax. But fee, the fultan comes !—' My beating heart
' Bounds with exulting motion ; hope and fear
' Fight with alternate conqueft in my breaft.
' Oh ! can I give her from me ? Yield her up ?

B 6   ' Now

' Now mourn, thou God of Love, fince Honour triumphs,
' And crowns his cruel altars with thy fpoils.'

Enter Bajazet.

Baj. To have a naufeous courtefy forc'd on me,
Spite of my will, by an infulting foe!
Ha! they would break the fiercenefs of my temper,
And make me fupple for their flavifh purpofe.
Curfe on their fawning arts! ' From Heav'n itfelf
' I would not, on fuch terms, receive a benefit,
' But fpurn it back upon the giver's hand.'

Sel. My lord! my royal father! | Sel. *comes forward,*
Baj. Ha! what art thou?   { *and kneels to* Baj.
What heavenly innocence! that in a form
So known, fo lov'd, haft left thy paradife,
For joy'efs prifon, for this place of woe!
Art thou my Selima?

Sel. Have you forgot me?
Alas, my piety is then in vain!
Your Selima, your daughter whom you lov'd,
The fondling once of her dear father's arms,
Is come to claim her fhare in his misfortunes;
' To wait and tend him with obfequious duty;
' To fit and weep for every care he feels;'
To help to wear the tedious minutes out,
To foften bondage, and the lofs of empire.

Baj. Now, by our prophet, if my wounded mind
Could know a thought of peace, it would be now:
E.'n from thy prating infancy thou wert
My joy, my little angel: fmiling comfort
Came with thee ftill to glad me. Now I'm curs'd
Ev'n in thee too. Reproach and infamy
Attend the Chriftian dog t' whom thou wert trufted.
To.fee thee here—'twere better fee thee dead!

Ax. Thus Tamerlane, to royal Bajazet,
With kingly greeting, fends: fince with the brave
(The bloody bus'nefs of the fight once ended)
Stern hate and oppofition ought to ceafe;
Thy queen already to thy arms reftor'd,
Receive this fecond gift, thy beauteous daughter;
And if there be aught farther in thy wifh,
Demand with honour, and obtain it freely.

Baj. Bear back the fulfome greeting to thy mafter;
Tell him, I'll none on't. Had he been a God,

All

All his omnipotence could not restore
My fame diminish'd, loss of sacred honour,
The radiancy of majesty eclips'd:
For aught besides, it is not worth my care;
The giver and his gifts are both beneath me.

Ax. Enough of war the wounded earth has known;
' Weary at length, and wasted with destruction,
' Sadly she rears her ruin'd head, to shew
' Her cities humbled, and her countries spoil'd,
' And to her mighty masters sues for peace.'
Oh, sultan! by the pow'r divine I swear,
With joy I would resign the savage trophies
In blood and battle gain'd, could I atone
The fatal breach 'twixt thee and Tamerlane;
And think a soldier's glory well bestow'd
To buy mankind a peace.

Baj. And what art thou,
That dost presume to mediate 'twixt the rage
Of angry kings?

Ax. A prince, born of the noblest,
And of a soul that answers to that birth,
That dares not but do well. Thou dost put on
A forc'd forgetfulness, thus not to know me,
A guest so lately to thy court, then meeting
On gentler terms.——

Sel. Could aught efface the merit
Of brave Axalla's name, yet when your daughter
Shall tell how well, how nobly she was us'd,
How light this gallant prince made all her bondage,
Most sure the royal Bajazet will own
That honour stands indebted to such goodness,
Nor can a monarch's friendship more than pay it.

Baj. Ha! know'st thou that, fond girl?—Go—'tis
        not well;
And when thou could'st descend to take a benefit
From a vile Christian, and thy father's foe,
Thou didst an act dishonest to thy race:
Henceforth, unless thou mean'st to cancel all
My share in thee, and write thyself a bastard,
Die, starve, know any evil, any pain,
Rather than taste a mercy from these dogs.

Sel. Alas, Axalla!

Ax. Weep not, lovely maid.!

                                        I swear,

I swear, ' one pearly drop from those fair eyes
' Would over-pay the service of my life !'
One sigh from thee has made a large amends
For all thy angry father's frowns and fierceness.

Baj. Oh, my curs'd fortune !—Am I fall'n thus low !
Dishonour'd to my face ! Thou earth-born thing !
Thou clod ! how hast thou dar'd to lift thy eyes
Up to the sacred race of mighty Ottoman,
Whom kings, whom e'en our prophet's holy offspring,
At distance have beheld ? And what art thou ?
What glorious titles blazon out thy birth ?
Thou vile obscurity ! ha !—say—thou base one.

Ax. Thus challeng'd, Virtue, modest as she is,
Stands up to do herself a common justice ;
To answer, and assert that in-born merit,
That worth, which conscious to herself she feels.
Were honour to be scann'd by long descent
From ancestors illustrious, I could vaunt
A lineage of the greatest, and recount
Among my fathers names of antient story,
Heroes and god-like patriots, who subdu'd
The world by arms and virtue, and, being Romans,
Scorn'd to be kings ; but that be their own praise :
Nor will I borrow merit from the dead,
Myself an undeserver. I could prove
My friendship such as thou might'st deign t' accept
With honour. when it comes with friendly office,
To render back thy crown and former greatness ;
' And yet e'en this, e'en all is poor, when Selima,
' With matchless worth, weighs down the adverse scale.'

Baj. To give me back what yesterday took from me,
Wou'd be to give like Heaven, when, having finish'd
This world (the goodly work of his creation),
He bid his favourite man be lord of all.
But this———

Ax. Nor is this gift beyond my pow'r.
Oft has the mighty master of my arms
Urg'd me with large ambition, to demand
Crowns and dominions from his bounteous pow'r :
'Tis true, I wav'd the proffer, and have held it
The worthier choice to wait upon his virtues,
To be the friend and partner of his wars,
Than to be Asia's lord. Nor wonder then,

If

If in the confidence of fuch a friendfhip,
I promife boldly, for the royal giver,
Thy crown and empire.

   Baj. For our daughter thus
Mean'ft thou to barter? Ha! I tell thee, Chriftian,
There is but one, one dowry thou canft give,
And I can afk, worthy my daughter's love.

   Ax. Oh! name the mighty ranfom; tafk my pow'r;
Let there be danger, difficulty, death,
T' enhance the price.

   Baj. I take thee at thy word.
Bring me the Tartar's head.

   Ax. Ha!

   Baj. Tamerlane's!
That death, that deadly poifon to my glory.

   Ax. Prodigious! Horrid!

   Sel. Loft! for ever loft!

   Baj. And could'ft thou hope to bribe me with aught elfe?
With a vile peace patch'd up on flavifh terms?
With tributary kingfhip?——No!——To merit
A recompence from me, fate my revenge.
The Tartar is my bane, I cannot bear him:
One heav'n and earth can never hold us both;
Still fhall we hate, and with defiance deadly
Keep rage alive, till one be loft for ever:
As if two funs fhould meet in the meridian,
And ftrive in fiery combat for the paffage.
Weep'ft thou, fond girl? Now, as thy king and father,
I charge thee, drive this flave from thy remembrance!
Hate fhall be pious in thee.   * Come and join
To curfe thy father's foes.   * [*Laying hold on her hand.*

   ' *Sel.* Undone for ever!
' Now, tyrant duty, art thou yet obeyed?
' There is no more to give thee. Oh, Axalla!'

   Bajazet *leads out* Selima, *fhe looking back on* Axalla.

   ' *Ax.* 'Tis what I fear'd; fool that I was t' obey!
' The coward Love, that could not bear her frown,
' Has wrought his own undoing. Perhaps e'en now
' The tyrant's rage prevails upon her fears:
' Fiercely he ftorms; fhe weeps, and fighs, and trembles,
' But fwears at length to think on me no more.
' He bade me take her.—But, Oh, gracious honour!
' Upon what terms? My foul yet fhudders at it,

                                  ' And

‘ And ſtands but half recover'd of her fright.
‘ The head of Tamerlane! monſtrous impiety!
‘ Bleed, bleed to death, my heart, be virtue's martyr.
‘ Oh, emperor! I own, I ought to give thee
‘ ſome nobler mark, than dying, of my faith.
‘ Then let the pains I feel my friendſhip prove,
‘ 'Tis eaſier far to die, than ceaſe to love.’ [Exit Axalla.

SCENE, Tamerlane's *camp.*

‘ *Enter ſeverally* Moneſes, *and* Prince *of* Tanais.

‘ *Mon.* If I not preſs untimely on his leiſure,
‘ You would much bind a ſtranger to your ſervice,
‘ To give me means of audience from the emperor.
‘ *Pr.* Moſt willingly ; tho' for the preſent moment
‘ We muſt intreat your ſtay; he holds him private.
‘ *Mon.* His council, I preſume ?
‘ *Pr.* No, the affair
‘ Is not of earth, but Heav'n—A holy man,
‘ (One whom our prophet's law calls ſuch) a derviſe,
‘ Keeps him in conference.
‘ *Mon.* Hours of religion,
‘ Eſpecially of princes, claim a reverence,
‘ Nor will be interrupted.
‘ *Pr.* What his buſ'neſs
‘ Imports we know not ; but with earneſt ſuit,
‘ This morn, he begg'd admittance. Our great maſter
‘ (Than whom none bows more lowly to high Heav'n)
‘ In reverend regard holds all that bear
‘ Relation to religion, and, on notice
‘ Of his requeſt, receiv'd him on the inſtant.
‘ *Mon.* We will attend his pleaſure.   [*Exeunt.'*
    Enter Tamerlane *and a* Derviſe.
Tam. Thou bring'ſt me thy credentials from the Higheſt,
From Alha and our Prophet. Speak thy meſſage,
It muſt import the beſt and nobleſt ends.
    Der. Thus ſpeaks our holy Mahomet, who has giv'n
To reign and conquer : Ill doſt thou repay   [thee
The bounties of his hand, unmindful of
The fountain whence thy ſtreams of greatneſs flow.
Thou haſt forgot high Heav'n, haſt beaten down
And trampled on religion's ſanctity.
                            Tam.

Tam. Now, as I'm a foldier and a king,
(The greatest names of honour) do but make
Thy imputation out, and Tamerlane
Shall do thee ample juftice on himfelf.
So much the facred name of Heaven awes me,
Could I fufpect my foul of harbouring aught
To its difhonour, I would fearch it ftrictly,
And drive th' offending thought with fury forth.

Der. Yes, thou haft hurt our holy prophet's honour,
By foftering the pernicious Chriftian fect;
Thofe, whom his fword purfu'd with fell deftruction,
Thou tak'ft into thy bofom, to thy councils;
They are thy only friends. The true believers
Mourn to behold thee favour this Axala.

Tam. I fear me, thou out-go'ft the prophet's order,
And bring'ft his venerable name to fhelter
A rudenefs ill-becoming thee to ufe,
Or me to fuffer. When thou nam'ft my friend,
Thou nam'ft a man beyond a monk's difcerning,
Virtuous and great, a warrior and a prince.

Der. He is a Chriftian; there our law condemns him,
Altho' he were ev'n all thou fpeak'ft, and more.

Tam. 'Tis falfe; no law divine condemns the virtuous,
For differing from the rules your fchools devife.
Look round, how Providence beftows alike
Sunfhine and rain, to blefs the fruitful year,
On different nations, all of different faiths;
And (tho' by feveral names and titles worfhip'd)
Heav'n takes the various tribute of their praife;
Since all agree to own, at leaft to mean,
One beft, one greateft, only Lord of all:
'Thus when he view'd the many forms of nature,
'He found that all was good, and beft the fair variety.'

Der. Moft impious and profane!——Nay, frown not,
Full of the prophet, I defpife the danger   [prince;
Thy angry power may threaten. I command thee
To hear and to obey; fince thus fays Mahomet:
Why have I made thee dreadful to the nations?
Why have I giv'n thee conqueft; but to fpread
My facred law ev'n to the utmoft earth,
And make my holy Mecca the world's worfhip?
Go on, and wherefoe'er thy arms fhall profper,
Plant there the prophet's name; with fword and fire

Drive

Drive out all other faiths, and let the world
Confess him only.

Tam. Had he but commanded
My sword to conquer all, to make the world
Know but one lord, the task were not so hard;
'Twere but to do what has been done already;
And Philip's son, and C. for did as much;
But to subdue th' unconquerable mind,
To make one reason have the same effect
Upon all apprehensions; to force this
Or this man just to think as thou and I do;
Impossible! unless souls were alike
In all, which differ now like human faces.

Der. Well might the holy cause be carried on,
If Musselmen did not make war on Musselmen.
Why hold'st thou captive a believing monarch?
Now, as thou hop'st to 'scape the prophet's curse,
Release the royal Bajazet, and join,
With force united, to destroy the Christians.

Tam. 'Tis well!—I've found the cause that mov'd thy.
What shallow politician set thee on,   [zeal.
In hopes to fright me this way to compliance?

Der. Our prophet only——

Tam. No—thou dost belie him,
Thou maker of new faiths! that dar'st to build
Thy fond inventions on religion's name.
Religion's lustre is, by native innocence,
Diviner, pure, and simple from all arts;
You daub and dress her like a common mistress,
The harlot of your fancies; and by adding
False beauties, which she wants not, make the world
Suspect her angel's face is foul beneath,
And wo not bear all lights.   Hence! I have found thee.

Der. I have but one resort. Now aid me, prophet! [*Aside.*
Yet I have somewhat further to unfold;
Our prophet speaks to thee in thunder—* thus——

[* *The Dervise draws a conceal'd dagger, and offers to
stab Tamerlane.*

Tam. No, villain, Heav'n is watchful o'er its wor-
          shipers,   [*Wresting the dagger from him.*
And blasts the murderer's purpose. Think, thou wretch!
Think on the pains that wait thy crime, and tremble
When I shall doom thee——

                                        Der.

Der. 'Tis but death at laſt ;
And I will ſuffer greatly for the cauſe
That urg'd me firſt to the bold deed.

Tam. Oh, impious!
Enthuſiaſm thus makes villains martyrs.
[*Pauſing.*] It ſhall be ſo—To die! 'twere a reward—
Now learn the difference 'twixt thy faith and mine:
Thine bids thee lift thy dagger to my throat ;
Mine can forgive the wrong, and bid thee live.
Keep thy own wicked ſecret, and be ſafe ;
If thou repent'ſt, I have gain'd one to virtue,
And am, in that, rewarded for my mercy ;
If thou continu'ſt ſtill to be the ſame,
'Tis puniſhment enough to be a villain.
Hence! from my ſight—It ſhocks my ſoul to think
That there is ſuch a monſter in my kind. [*Exit* Derviſe.
Whither will man's impiety extend?
Oh, gracious Heav'n! doſt thou withhold thy thunder,
When bold aſſaſſins take thy name upon 'em,
And ſwear they are the champions of thy cauſe?

Enter Moneſes.

Mon. Oh, Emperor! before whoſe awful throne
Th' afflicted never kneel in vain for juſtice, { *Kneeling*
Undone, and ruin'd, blaſted in my hopes, { *to* Tam.
Here let me fall before your ſacred feet,
And groan out my misfortunes, till your pity,
(The laſt ſupport and refuge that is left me)
Shall raiſe me from the ground, and bid me live.

Tam. Riſe, prince ; nor let me reckon up thy worth,
And tell how boldly that might bid thee aſk,
Leſt I ſhould make a merit of my juſtice,
The common debt I owe to thee, to all,
Ev'n to the meaneſt of mankind, the charter
By which I claim my crown, and Heav'n's protection.
Speak, then, as to a king, the ſacred name
Where pow'r is lodg'd, for righteous ends alone.

Mon. One only joy, one bleſſing, my fond heart
Had fix'd its wiſhes on, and that is loſt ;
That ſiſter, for whoſe ſafety my ſad ſoul
Endur'd a thouſand fears———

Tam. I well remember,
When, ere the battle join'd, I ſaw thee firſt,
With grief uncommon to a brother's love,

Thou

'Thou told'st a moving tale of her misfortunes,
Such as bespeak my pity. Is there aught
Thou canst demand from friendship? Ask, and have it.

Mon. First, Oh! let me intreat your royal goodness:
Forgive the folly of a lover's caution,
That forg'd a tale of folly to deceive you.
Said I, she was my sister?—Oh! 'tis false;
She holds a dearer interest in my soul,
' Such as the closest ties of blood ne'er knew;
' An interest, such as power, wealth, and honour,
' Can't buy, but love, love only, can bestow;'
She was the mistress of my vows, my bride,
By contract mine, and long ere this the priest
Had ty'd the knot for ever, had not Bajazet——

Tam. Ha! Bajazet!—If yet his pow'r withholds
The cause of all thy sorrows, all thy fears,
E'en gratitude for once shall gain upon him,
Spite of his savage temper, to restore her.
This morn a soldier brought a captive beauty,
Sad tho' she seem'd, yet of a form more rare,
By much the nobler spoil of all the field;
E'en Scipio, or a victor yet most cold,
Might have forgot his virtue at her sight.
Struck with a pleasing wonder, I beheld her,
Till, by a slave that waited near her person,
I learn'd she was the captive sultan's wife:
Strait I forbade my eyes the dangerous joy
Of gazing long, and sent her to her lord.

Mon. There was Moneses lost. Too sure my heart
(From the first mention of her wond'rous charms)
Presag'd it could be only my Arpasia.

Tam. Arpasia! did'st thou say?

Mon. Yes, my Arpasia.

Tam. Sure I mistake, or I fain would mistake thee;
I nam'd the queen of Bajazet; his wife.

Mon. His queen! his wife! He brings that holy title
To varnish o'er the monstrous wrongs he has done me.

Tam. Alas! I fear me, prince, thy griefs are just;
Thou art indeed, unhappy——

Mon. Can you pity me,
And not redress? *Oh, royal Tamerlane!   [*Kneeling.*
Thou succour of the wretched, reach thy mercy
To save me from the grave, and from oblivion;

Be

Be gracious to the hopes that wait my youth.
' Oh! let not sorrow blast me, left I wither,
' And fall in vile dishonour.' Let thy justice
Restore me my Arpasia ; give her back,
Back to my wishes, to my transports give her,
To my fond, restless, bleeding, dying bosom.
Oh! give her to me yet, while I have life
To bless thee for the bounty. Oh, Arpasia!

Tam. Unhappy, royal youth, why dost thou ask
What honour must deny ? Ha! is she not
His wife, whom he has wedded, whom enjoy'd?
And would'st thou have my partial friendship break
That holy knot, which ty'd once, all mankind
Agree to hold sacred and undissolvable ?
The brutal violence would stain my justice,
And brand me with a tyrant's hated name
To late posterity.

Mon. Are then the vows,
The holy vows we register'd in Heav'n,
But common air ?

Tam. Could thy fond love forget
The violation of a first enjoyment ? ————
But sorrow has disturb'd and hurt thy mind.

Mon. Perhaps it has, and like an idle madman,
That wanders with a train of hooting boys,
I do a thousand things to shame my reason.
Then let me fly, and bear my follies with me,
Far, far from the world's sight. Honour and fame,
Arms and the glorious war shall be forgotten ;
No noble found of greatness, or ambition,
Shall weak my drowsy soul from her dead sleep,
Till the last trump do summon.

Tam. Let thy virtue
Stand up and answer to these warring passions,
That vex thy manly temper. From the moment
When first I saw thee, something wond'rous noble
Shone thro' thy form, and won my friendship for thee,
Without the tedious form of long acquaintance;
Nor will I lose thee poorly for a woman.
Come, droop no more, thou shalt with me pursue
True greatness, till we rise to immortality.
Thou shalt forget these lesser cares, Moneses ;
Thou shalt, and help me to reform the world.

7   *Mon.*

Mon. ' So the good Genius warns his mortal charge
' To fly the evil fate that still pursues him,
' Till it have wrought his ruin.' Sacred Tamerlane,
Thy words are as the breath of angels to me.
But, oh! too deep the wounding grief is fix'd,
For any hand to heal.

    Tam. This dull despair,
Is the soul's lazines. Rouse to the combat,
And thou art sure to conquer. War shall restore thee,
The sound of arms shall wake thy martial ardour,
And cure this amorous sicknes of thy soul,
' Begun by sloth. and nurs'd by too much ease.
' The idle God of Love supinely dreams,
' Amidst inglorious shades and purling streams,
' In rosy fetters and fantastic chains,
' He binds deluded maids and simple swains ;
' With soft enjoyments wooes them to forget
' The hardy toils and labours of the great.
' But if the warlike trumpet's loud alarms
' To virtuous acts excite, and manly arms,
' The coward boy avows his abject fear,
' On silken wings sublime he cuts the air,
' Scar'd at the noble noise and thunder of the war.

       * " *The boy, fond Love,*
  " *Is nurs'd and bred in sloth, and too much ease* ;
  " *Near purling streams, in gloomy shades, he lies,*
  " *And loosely there, instructs his votaries,*
  " *Honour and active virtue to despise* ;
  " *But if the trumpets echo from afar,*
  " *On silken wings sublime he cuts the air,*
  " *Scar'd at the noise and clangor of the war.*"

                     [*Exeunt.*

ACT IV. SCENE, Bajazet's *tent.*

Enter Haly *and the* Dervise.

Haly. TO 'scape with life from an attempt like this,
      Demands my wonder justly.

    Der. True, it may ;
But 'tis a principle of his new faith ;
'Tis what his Christian favourites have inspir'd.

   * The lines in italics are now spoken at the Theatre, instead of
those between single commas.

                            Wha

Who fondly make a merit of forgiveneſs,
And give their foes a ſecond opportunity,
If the firſt blow ſhould miſs.—Failing to ſerve
The ſultan to my wiſh, and e'en deſpairing
Of further means t' effect his liberty,
A lucky accident retriev'd my hopes.

Ha. The prophet and our maſter will reward
Thy zeal in their behalf; but ſpeak thy purpoſe.

Der. Juſt ent'ring here I met the Tartar general,
Fierce Omar.

Ha. He commands, if I miſtake not,
This quarter of the army, and our guards.

Der. The ſame. By his ſtern aſpect, and the fires
That kindled in his eyes, I gueſs'd the tumult
Some wrong had rais'd in his tempeſtuous ſoul;
A friendſhip of old date had giv'n me privilege
To aſk of his concerns. In ſhort, I learn'd,
That burning for the ſultan's beauteous daughter,
He had begg'd her, as a captive of the war,
From Tamerlane; but meeting with denial
Of what he thought his ſervices might claim,
Loudly he ſtorms, and curſes the Italian,
As cauſe of this affront. I join'd his rage,
And added to his injuries the wrongs
Our prophet daily meets with from Axalla.
But ſee, he comes. Improve what I ſhall tell,
And all we wiſh is ours. [*They ſeem to talk together aſide.*
                    Enter Omar.

Om. No——if I forgive it,
Diſhonour blaſt my name! Was it for this
That I directed his firſt ſteps to greatneſs,
Taught him to climb, and made him what he is?
' When our great Cam firſt bent his eyes towards him,
' (Then petty prince of Parthia) and by me
' Perſuaded, rais'd him to his daughter's bed,
' Call'd him his ſon, and ſucceſſor of empire;'
Was it for this, that like a rock I ſtood
And ſtemm'd a torrent of our Tartar lords,
Who ſcorn'd his upſtart ſway? When Calibes,
In bold rebellion, drew e'en half the provinces
To his own cauſe, I, like his better angel,
Stood by his ſhaking throne, and fix'd it faſt;
And am I now ſo loſt to his remembrance,

That,

That, when I afk a captive, he fhall tell me,
She is Axalla's right, his Chriftian minion?

Der. Allow me, valiant Omar, to demand,
Since injur'd thus, why right you not yourfelf?
The prize you afk is in your power.

Om. It is,
And I will feize it, in defpite of Tamerlane
And that Italian dog.

Ha. What need of force,
When every thing concurs to meet your wifhes?
Our mighty mafter would not wifh a fon
Nobler than Omar. From a father's hand
Receive that daughter, which ungrateful Tamerlane
Has to your worth deny'd.

Om. Now by my arms,
It will be great revenge. What will your fultan
Give to the man that fhall reftore his liberty,
His crown, and give him pow'r to wreak his hatred
Upon his greateft foe?

Ha. All he can afk,
And far beyond his wifh————   [*Trumpets.*

Om. Thefe trumpets fpeak
The emperor's approach; he comes once more
To offer terms of peace. Retire within.
I will no farther—he grows deadly to me;
And curfe me, prophet, if I not repay
His hate, with retribution full as mortal.   [*Exeunt.*

S C E N E *draws, and difcovers* Arpafia *lying on a couch.*

S O N G.

To thee, Oh, gentle fleep, alone
   Is owing all our peace;
By thee our joys are heighten'd fhown,
   By thee our forrows ceafe.
The nymph, whofe hand, by fraud or force,
   Some tyrant has poffefs'd,
By thee, obtaining a divorce,
   In her own choice is blefs'd.
Oh, ftay! Arpafia bids thee ftay;
   The fadly weeping fair
Conjures thee, not to lofe in day
   The object of her care.

To grafp whofe pleafing form fhe fought,
   That motion chas'd her fleep;
Thus by ourfelves are oft'neft wrought
   The griefs for which we weep.

Arp. Oh, death! thou gentle end of human forrows,
Still muft my weary eye-lids vainly wake,
In tedious expectation of thy peace?
Why ftand thy thoufand thoufand doors ftill open,
To take the wretched in, if ftern religion
Guards every paffage, and forbids my entrance?—
Lucrece could bleed, and Portia fwallow fire,
When urg'd with griefs beyond a mortal fufferance;
But here it muft not be. Think then, Arpafia,
Think on the facred dictates of thy faith,
And let that arm thy virtue, to perform
What Cato's daughter durft not—Live, Arpafia,
And dare to be unhappy.
        Enter Tamerlane.
  Tam. When fortune fmiles upon the foldier's arms,
And adds e'en beauty to adorn his conqueft,
Yet fhe ordains, the fair fhould know no fears,
' No forrows to pollute their lovely eyes,
' But fhould be us'd e'en nobly, as herfelf,
' The queen and goddefs of the warrior's vows.'
Such welcome as a camp can give, fair Sultanefs,
We hope you have receiv'd; it fhall be larger,
And better as it may.
  Arp. Since I have borne
That miferable mark of fatal greatnefs,
I have forgot all difference of conditions;
Scepters and fetters are grown equal to me,
And the beft change my fate can bring is death.
  Tam. ' When forrow dwells in fuch an angel form,
' Well may we guefs that thofe above are mourners;
' Virtue is wrong'd, and bleeding innocence
' Suffers fome wond'rous violation here,
' To make the faints look fad.' Oh! teach my power
To cure thofe ills which you unjuftly fuffer,
Left Heav'n fhould wreft it from my idle hand,
If I look on, and fee you weep in vain.
  Arp. Not that my foul difdains the generous aid
Thy royal goodnefs proffers; but, Oh, emperor!

            C   It

It is not in my fate to be made happy;
Nor will I listen to the coz'ner, hope,
But stand resolv'd to bear the beating storm
That roars around me; safe in this alone,
That I am not immortal.— Tho' 'tis hard,
'Tis wond'rous hard, when I remember thee
(Dear native Greece!), and you, ye weeping maids,
That were companions of my virgin youth!
My noble parents! Oh, the grief of heart,
The pangs, that, for unhappy me, bring down
Their reverend ages to the grave with sorrow!
And yet there is a woe surpassing all:
Ye saints and angels, give me of your constancy,
If you expect I shall endure it long

Tam. Why is my pity all that I can give
To tears like yours? And yet I fear 'tis all;
Nor dare I ask what mighty loss you mourn,
Lest honour should forbid to give it back.

Arp. No, Tamerlane, nor did I mean thou should'st.
But know (tho' to the weakness of my sex
I yield these tears) my soul is more than man.
Think, I am born a Greek, nor doubt my virtue;
' A Greek! from whose fam'd ancestors of old
' Rome drew the patterns of her boasted heroes.'
They must be mighty evils that can vanquish
A Spartan courage, and a Christian faith.

Enter Bajazet.

Baj. To know no thought of rest! to have the mind
Still ministering fresh plagues, as in a circle,
Where one dishonour treads upon another;
What know the fiends beyond it?—Ha! by hell,

[*Seeing* Arp. *and* Tam.

There wanted only this to make me mad.
Comes he to triumph here? to rob me of my love,
And violate the last retreat of happiness?

Tam. But that I read upon thy frowning brow,
That war yet lives, and rages in thy breast;
Once more (in pity to the suff'ring world)
I meant to offer peace.———

Baj. And mean'st thou too
To treat it with our empress; and to barter
The spoils which fortune gave thee for her favours?

Arp. What would the tyrant?   [*Aside.*
                                                  Baj.

Baj. Seek'ſt thou thus our friendſhip?
Is this the royal uſage thou didſt boaſt?

Tam. The boiling paſſion that diſturbs thy ſoul
Spreads clouds around, and makes thy purpoſe dark—
Unriddle what thy myſtic fury aims at.

Baj. Is it a riddle? Read it there explain'd;
There, in my ſhame. Now judge me thou, Oh, Prophet,
And equal Heav'n, if this demand not rage!
The peaſant-hind, begot and born to ſlavery,
Yet dares aſſert a huſband's ſacred right,
And guards his homely couch from violation:
And ſhall a monarch tamely bear the wrong
Without complaining?

Tam. If I could have wrong'd thee,
If conſcious virtue, and all-judging Heav'n,
Stood not between, to bar ungovern'd appetite,
What hinder'd, but, in ſpite of thee my captive,
I might have us'd a victor's boundleſs power,
And ſated every wiſh my ſoul could form?
But, to ſecure thy fears, know, Bajazet,
This is among the things I dare not do.　　　[ſent?

Baj. By hell, 'tis falſe! elſe wherefore art thou pre-
What cam'ſt thou for, but to undo my honour?
I found thee holding amorous parley with her,
Gazing and glotting on her wanton eyes,
And bargaining for pleaſures yet to come:
My life, I know, is the devoted price——
But take it, I am weary of the pain.

Tam. Yet, ere thou raſhly urge my rage too far,
I warn thee to take heed: I am a man,
And have the frailties common to man's nature;
The fiery ſeeds of wrath are in my temper,
And may be blown up to ſo fierce a blaze
As wiſdom cannot rule. Know, thou haſt touch'd me
E'en in the niceſt, tend'reſt part, my honour;
My honour! which, like pow'r, diſdains being queſtion'd;
Thy breath has blaſted my fair virtue's fame,
And mark'd me for a villain, and a tyrant.

A·p. And ſtand I here an idle looker-on,
To ſee my innocence murder'd and mangled
By barbarous hands, nor can revenge the wrong?
Art thou a man, and dar'ſt thou uſe me thus?　　[*To* Baj.
Haſt thou not torn me ·rom my native country,

From the dear arms of my lamenting friends,
From my foul's peace, and from my injur'd love?
Haft thou not ruin'd, blotted me for ever,
And driv'n me to the brink of black defpair?
And is it in thy malice yet to add
A wound more deep, to fully my white name,
My virtue?————

   Baj. Yes, thou haft thy fex's virtues,
Their affectation, pride, ill-nature, noife,
Pronenefs to change, e'en from the joy that pleas'd 'em:
So gracious is your idol, dear variety,
That for another love you would forego
An angel's form, to mingle with a devil's.
' Thro' ev'ry ftate and rank of men you wander,
' Till e'en your large experience takes in all
' The different nations of the peopled earth.'   [tribe
   arp. Why fought'ft thou not from thy own impious
A wife like one of thefe? ' For fuch thy race
' (If human nature brings forth fuch) affords.
' Greece, for chafte virgins fam'd, and pious matrons,
' Teems not with monfters like your Turkish wives,
' Whom guardian eunuchs, haggar'd and deform'd,
' Whom walls and bars make honeft by conftraint.'
Know, I deteft, like hell, the crime thou mention'ft:
Not that I fear or reverence thee, thou tyrant;
But that my foul, confcious of whence it fprung,
Sits unpolluted in its facred temple,
And fcorns to mingle with a thought fo mean.

   Tam. Oh, pity! that a greatnefs fo divine
Should meet a fate fo wretched, fo unequal.————
Though blind and wilful to the good that courts thee,
                      [*To* Bajazet.
With open-handed bounty Heav'n purfues thee,
And bids thee (undeferving as thou art,
And monftrous in thy crimes) be happy yet;
Whilft thou, in fury, doft avert the bleffing,
And art an evil Genius to thyfelf.

   Baj. No—Thou, thou art my greateft curfe on earth!
Thou, who haft robb'd me of my crown and glory,
And now purfu'ft me to the verge of life,
To fpoil me of my honour: Thou! thou hypocrite!
That wear'ft a pageant outfide fhew of virtue,

                                  To

To cover the hot thoughts that glow within!
Thou rank adulterer!

Tam. Oh,. that thou wert
The lord of all those thousands that lie breathless
On yonder field of blood, that I again
Might hunt the face of death and danger,
Thro' the tumultuous battle, and there force thee,
Vanquish'd and sinking underneath my arm,
To own thou hast traduc'd me like a villain.

Baj. Ha! does it gall thee, Tartar? By Revenge
It joys me much to find thou feel'st my fury.
Yes, I will echo to thee, thou adulterer!
Thou dost profane the name of king and soldier,
And, like a ruffian bravo, cam'st with force
To violate the holy marriage-bed.

Tam. Wert thou not shelter'd by thy abject state,
The captive of my sword, by my just anger,
My breath, like thunder, should confound thy pride,
And doom thee dead this instant with a word.   [not.

Baj. 'Tis false! my fate's above thee, and thou dar'st
Tam. Ha! dare not! Thou hast rais'd my pond'rous
And now it falls to crush thee at a blow.   [rage,
A guard there!—* Seize and drag him to his fate!

[* *Enter a guard, they seize* Bajazet.
Tyrant, I'll do a double justice on thee;
At once revenge myself, and all mankind.

Baj. Well dost thou, ere thy violence and lust
Invade my bed, thus to begin with murder:
Drown all thy fears in blood, and sin securely.

Tam. Away!

Arp. [*Kneeling.*] Oh, stay! I charge thee by renown;
By that bright glory thy great soul pursues,
Call back the doom of death!

Tam. Fair injur'd excellence,
Why dost thou kneel, and waste such precious pray'rs,
' As might e'en bribe the saints to partial justice,'
For one to goodness lost, who first undid thee,
Who still pursues, and aggravates the wrong?

Baj. By Alha! no——I will not wear a life
Bought with such vile dishonour.—Death shall free me
At once from infamy, and thee, thou traitress!

Arp. No matter, tho' the whistling winds grow loud,
And the rude tempest roars, 'tis idle rage;

Oh!

Oh! mark it not; but let thy steady virtue
Be constant to its temper. Save his life,
And save Arpasia from the sport of talkers.
Think how the busy, meddling world will toss
Thy mighty name about, in scurril mirth;
Shall brand thy vengeance, as a foul design,
And make such monstrous legends of our lives,
As late posterity shall blush in reading.

   Tam Oh, matchless virtue! Yes, I will obey;
Tho' laggard in the race, admiring yet,
I will pursue the shining path thou tread'st.
Sultan, be safe! Reason resumes her empire,
                       [*The guards release* Bajazet.
And I am cool again.——Here break we off,
Lest farther speech should minister new rage.
Wisely from dangerous passions I retreat,
To keep a conquest which was hard to get:
And, Oh! 'tis time I should for flight prepare,
A war more fatal seems to threaten there,
And all my rebel-blood assists the fair:
One moment more, and I too late shall find,
That Love's the strongest pow'r that lords it o'er the
      mind.   [*Exit* Tamerlane, *followed by the guards.*

   Baj. To what new shame, what plague am I reserv'd?
' Why did my stars refuse me to be warm,
' While yet my regal state stood unimpeach'd,
' Nor knew the curse of having one above me?
' Then too (altho' by force I grasp'd the joy)
' My love was safe, nor felt the rack of doubt.'
Why hast thou forc'd this nauseous life upon me?
Is it to triumph o'er me?——But I will,
I will be free; I will forget thee all;
The bitter and the sweet, the joy and pain,
Death shall expunge at once, and ease my soul.
Prophet, take notice, I disclaim thy paradise,
Thy fragrant bow'rs, and everlasting shades;
Thou hast plac'd woman there, and all thy joys are
     tainted.   '[*Exit* Bajazet.

   Arp. A little longer yet, be strong, my heart;
A little longer let the busy spirits
Keep on their chearful round.—It wo'not be!
' Love, sorrow, and the sting of vile reproach,
' Succeeding one another in their course,
                             ' Like

'Like drops of eating water on the marble,
'At length have worn my boasted courage down:
'I will indulge the woman in my soul,
'And give a loose to tears and to impatience.'
Death is at last my due, and I will have it.———
And see, the poor Moneses comes, to take
One sad adieu, and then we part for ever.

Enter Moneses.

Mon. Already am I onward of my way; ,
Thy tuneful voice comes like a hollow sound
At distance, to my ears. My eyes grow heavy,
And all the glorious lights of heav'n look dim;
'Tis the last office they shall ever do me,
To view thee once, and then to close and die.

Arp. Alas, how happy have we been, Moneses!
Ye gentle days, that once were ours, what joys
Did every chearful morning bring along!
No fears, no jealousies, no angry parents,
That for unequal births, or fortunes, frown'd:
But Love, that kindly join'd our hearts, to bless us,
Made us a blessing too to all besides.

Mon. Oh, call not thy remembrance back, Arpasia!
'Tis grief unutterable; 'tis distraction!
'But let this last of hours be peaceful sorrow!'
Here let me kneel, and pay my latest vows.
Be witness, all ye saints, thou Heav'n and Nature,
Be witness of my truth, for you have known it!
Be witness that I never knew a pleasure,
In all the world could offer, like Arpasia!
Be witness, that I liv'd but in Arpasia!
And, Oh, be witness, that her loss has kill'd me!

Arp. While thou art speaking, life begins to fail,
And ev'ry tender accent chills like death.
Oh! let me haste then, yet, ere day declines,
And the long night prevail, once more to tell thee
What, and how dear, Moneses has been to me.
What has he not been?—All the names of love,
Brothers, or fathers, husbands, all are poor:
Moneses is myself; in my fond heart,
E'en in my vital blood, he lives and reigns;
The last dear object of my parting soul
Will be Moneses; the last breath that lingers
Within my panting breast, shall sigh, Moneses.

C 4   *Mon.*

Mox. It is enough! Now to thy reſt, my ſoul,
The world and thou have made an end at once.

Arp. Fain wou'd I ſtill detain thee, hold thee ſtill :
Nor honour can forbid, that we together
Should ſhare the poor few minutes that remain :
I ſwear, methinks this ſad ſociety
Has ſomewhat pleaſing in it.—Death's dark ſhades
Seem, as we journey on, to loſe their horror ;
At near approach the monſters, form'd by fear,
Are vaniſh'd all, and leave the proſpect clear :
Amidſt the gloomy vale, a pleaſing ſcene,　　}
With flow'rs adorn'd, and never-fading green,　}
Inviting ſtands, to take the wretched in :　　　}
No wars, no wrongs, no tyrants, no deſpair,　　}
Diſturb the quiet of a place ſo fair,　　　　　}
But injur'd lovers find Elyſium there.   [*Exeunt.* }

    Enter Bajazet, Omar, Haly, *and the* Dervite.

  Baj. Now, by the glorious tomb that ſhrines our Pro-
By Mecca's ſacred temple, here I ſwear,   [phet,
Our daughter is thy bride! and to that gift
Such wealth, ſuch pow'r, ſuch honours will I add,
That monarchs ſhall with envy view thy ſtate,
And own thou art a demi-god to them.
Thou haſt given me what I wiſh'd, pow'r of revenge,
And when a king rewards, 'tis ample retribution.

  Om. Twelve Tartar lords, each potent in his tribe,
Have ſworn to own my cauſe, and draw their thouſands,
To-morrow, from th' ungrateful Parthian's ſide.
The day declining ſeems to yield to night,
Ere little more than half her courſe be ended.
In an auſpicious hour prepare for flight ;
The leaders of the troops thro' which we paſs,
Rais'd by my pow'r, devoted to my ſervice,
Shall make our paſſage ſecret and ſecure.

  Der. Already, mighty Sultan, art thou ſafe,
Since, by yon paſſing torches' light I gueſs,
To his pavilion Tamerlane retires,
Attended by a train of waiting courtiers.
All who remain within theſe tents are thine,
And hail thee as their lord.————
Ha ! the Italian prince,
With ſad Moneſes, are not yet gone forth.

Baj. Ha! with our queen and daughter!

Om. They are ours:
I mark'd the flaves who waited on Axalla;
They, when the emperor paft out, preft on,
And mingled with the crowd, nor mifs'd their lord:
He is your pris'ner, fir: I go this moment,
To feize, and bring him to receive his doom.

[*Exit* Omar.

Baj. Hafte, Haly, follow, and fecure the Greek:
Him too I wifh to keep within my power. [*Exit* Haly.

Der. If my dread lord permit his flave to fpeak,
I would advife to fpare Axalla's life,
'Till we are fafe beyond the Parthian's power:
Him, as our pledge of fafety, may we hold;
And, could you gain him to affift your flight,
It might import you much.

Baj. Thou counfell'ft well;
And tho' I hate him (for he is a Chriftian,
And to my mortal enemy devoted),
Yet, to fecure my liberty and vengeance,
I wifh he now were ours.

Der. ———And fee! they come!
Fortune repents; again fhe courts your fide,
And, with this firft fair offering of fuccefs,
She wooes you to forget her crime of yefterday.

Enter Omar *with* Axalla *prifoner,* Selima *following weeping.*

Ax. I wo' not call thee villain; 'tis a name
Too holy for thy crime.   To break thy faith,
And turn a rebel to fo good a mafter,
Is an ingratitudë unmatch'd on earth.
The firft revolting angel's pride could only
Do more than thou haft done.   Thou copieft well,
And keep'ft the black original in view.

Om. Do rage, and vainly call upon thy mafter
To fave his minion.   My revenge has caught thee,
And I will make thee curfe that fond prefumption
That fet thee on to rival me in aught.

Baj. Chriftian, I hold thy fate at my difpofal!
One only way remains to mercy open;
Be partner of my flight, and my revenge,
And thou art fafe.   The other choice is death.

Om. What means the Sultan?

C 5

Der.

Der. I conjure you, hold————

Your rival is devoted to destruction :   [*Aside to* Omar.

Nor would the Sultan now defer his fate,

But for our common safety.—Listen further. *Whispers.*

Ax. Then briefly thus. Death is the choice I make ;

Since, next to Heav'n, my master and my friend

Has interest in my life, and still shall claim it.

Baj. Then take thy wish—Call in our mutes !

Sel. My father,

If yet you have not sworn to cast me off,

And turn me out, to wander in misfortune ;

If yet my voice be gracious in your ears ;

If yet my duty and my love offend not ;

Oh, call your sentence back, and save Axalla.

Baj. Rise, Selima! The slave deserves to die,

Who durst, with sullen pride, refuse my mercy :

Yet, for thy sake, once more I offer life.

Sel. Some angel whisper to my anxious soul,

What shall I do to save him.——' Oh, Axalla !

' Is it so easy to thee, to forsake me ?

' Canst thou resolve, with all this cold indifference,

' Never to see me more ? To leave me here

' The miserable mourner of thy fate,

' Condemn'd to waste my widow'd virgin youth,

' My tedious days and nights, in lonely weeping,

' And never know the voice of Comfort more ?

' *Ax.* Search not too deep the sorrows of my breast :

' Thou say'st, I am indifferent and cold :

' Oh ! is it possible my eyes should tell

' So little of the fighting storm within ?

' Oh, turn thee from me ; save me from thy beauties ;

' Falshood and ruin all look lovely there.

' Oh ! let my lab'ring soul yet struggle thro'——

' I will—I would resolve to die, and leave thee.

' *Baj.* Then let him die !—He trifles with my favour.

' I have too long attended his resolves.

' *Sel.* Oh ! stay a minute, yet a minute longer ; [*To* Baj.

' A minute is a little space in life.

' There is a kind consulting in his eyes,

' And I shall win him to your royal will.'

Oh, my Axalla ! seem but to content—'*To* Axalla *aside.*

Unkind and cruel, will you then do nothing ?

I find I am not worth thy least of cares.

                                                    Ax.

Ax. Oh! labour not to hang difhonour on me!
I could bear ficknefs, pain, and poverty,
'Thofe mortal evils, worfe than death, for thee.
But this—It has the force of Fate againft us,
And cannot be.

Sel. See, fee. Sir! he relents;   [*To* Bajazet.
Already he inclines to own your caufe.
A little longer, and he is all yours.

Baj. Then mark. how far a father's fondnefs yields.
'Till midnight I defer the death he merits,
And give him up, 'till then, to thy perfuafion.
If by that time he meets my will, he lives;
If not, thyfelf fhall own he dies with juftice.

Ax. 'Tis but to lengthen life upon the rack.
I am refolv'd already.

Sel. Oh! be ftill,
Nor rafhly urge a ruin on us both;
'Tis but a moment more I have to fave thee.
Be kind. aufpicious Alha, to my pray'r;
More for my love, than for myfelf, I fear;
Neglect mankind a while, and make him all thy care!
                              [*Exeunt* Axalla *and* Selima.

Baj. Monefes——is that dog fecur'd?

Om. He is.

Baj. 'Tis well—My foul perceives returning greatnefs,
As nature fee's the fpring. Lightly fhe bounds,
And fhakes difhonour, like a burthen, from her,
Once more imperial, aweful, and herfelf.
So, when of old. Jove from the Titans fled,   }
Ammon's rude front his radiant face bely'd,   }
And all the majefty of Heav'n lay hid.   }
At lenth, by fate, to pow'r divine reftor'd,   }
His thunder taught the world to know its lord!   }
The God grew terrible again, and was again ador'd }
                                   [*Exeunt.*

ACT V. SCENE Bajazet's *tent*.

Arp. SURE 'tis a horror more than darkneſs brings,
    That ſits upon the night! Fate is abroad;
Some ruling fiend hangs in the duſky air,
And ſcatters ruin, death, and wild diſtraction,
O'er all the wretched race of man below.
Not long ago, a troop of ghaſtly ſlaves
Ruſh'd in, and forc'd Moneſes from my ſight;
Death hung ſo heavy on his drooping ſpirits,
That ſcarcely could he ſay—Farewel—for ever!
And yet, methinks, ſome gentle ſpirit whiſpers,
Thy peace draws near, Arpaſia, ſigh no more!
And ſee, the king of terrors is at hand;
His miniſter appears.

Enter Bajazet *and* Haly.

Baj. [*Aſide to* Haly.] The reſt I leave
To thy diſpatch. For, Oh! my faithful Haly,
Another care has taken up thy maſter.
Spite of the high-wrought tempeſt in my ſoul,
Spite of the pangs which jealouſy has coſt me,
This haughty woman reigns within my breaſt:
' In vain I ſtrive to put her from my thoughts,
' To drive her out, with empire and revenge.
' Still ſhe comes back, like a retiring tide,
' That ebbs a while, but ſtrait returns again,
' And ſwells above the beach.'

Ha. Why wears my lord
An anxious thought for what his pow'r commands?
When, in an happy hour, you ſhall, ere long,
Have borne the empreſs from amidſt your foes,
She muſt be yours, be only and all yours.

Baj. On that depends my fear. Yes, I muſt have her;
I own, I will not, cannot go without her.
' But ſuch is the condition of our flight,
' That, ſhould ſhe not conſent, 'twould hazard all
' To bear her hence by force. Thus I reſolve then,
' By threats and pray'rs, by every way, to move her;
' If all prevail not, force is left at laſt;
' And I will ſet life, empire, on the venture,
' To keep her mine.—Be near to wait my will.

[*Exit* Haly.
When

When laft we parted, 'twas on angry terms;
Let the remembrance die, or kindly think
That jealous rage is but a hafty flame,
That blazes out, when love too fiercely burns.

Arp. For thee to wrong me, and for me to fuffer,
Is the hard leffon that my foul has learnt,
And now I ftand prepar'd for all to come:
Nor is it worth my leifure to diftinguifh
If love or jealoufy commit the violence:
Each have alike been fatal to my peace,
Confirming me a wretch, and thee a tyrant.

Baj. Still to deform thy gentle brow with frowns,
And fti'l to be perverie, it is a manner
Abhorrent from the foftnefs of thy fex:
Women, like fummer ftorms, a while are cloudy,
Burft out in thunder, and impetuous fhow'rs;
But ftrait the fun of beauty dawns abroad,
And all the fair horizon is ferene.

Arp. Then, to retrieve the honour of my fex,
Here I difclaim that changing and inconftancy:
To thee I will be ever as I am.

Baj. Thou fay'ft I am a tyrant; think fo ftill,
And let it warn thy prudence to lay hold
On the good hour of peace, that courts thee now.
Souls form'd like mine brook being fcorn'd but ill.
Be well advis'd, and profit by my patience;
It is a fhort-liv'd virtue.

Arp. Turn thy eyes
Back on the ftory of my woes, Barbarian!
Thou that haft violated all refpects
Due to my fex and honour of my birth!
Thou brutal ravifher, ' that haft undone me,
' Ruin'd my love!' Can I have peace with thee?
Impoffible! Firft heav'n and hell fhall join;
They only differ more.

Baj. I fee, 'tis vain
To court thy ftubborn temper with endearments.
Refolve, this moment, to return my love,
And be the willing partner of my flight,
Or, by the Prophet's holy law, thou dieft.

Arp. And doft thou hope to fright me with the phantom
Death? 'Tis the greateft mercy thou canft give;
So frequent are the murders of thy reign,

One

One day scarce passing by unmark'd with blood,
That children, by long use, have learnt to scorn it.
Know, I did in to aid thy treach'rous purpose,
And, should'st thou dare to force me, with my cries
I will call Heav'n and Earth to my assistance.

Baj. Confusion! dost thou brave me? But my wrath
Shall find a passage to thy swelling heart,
And rack thee worse than all the pains of death.
That Grecian dog, the minion of thy wishes,
Shall be dragg'd forth, and butcher'd in thy sight;
Thou shalt behold him when his pangs are terrible,
Then, when he stares and gasps, and struggles strongly,
' E'en in the bitterest agony of dying,'
'Till thou shalt rend thy hair, tear out thy eyes,
And curse thy pride, while I applaud my vengeance.

Ax. Oh, fatal image! all my pow'rs give way,
And resolution sickens at the thought;
' A flood of passion rises in my breast,
' And labours fiercely upward to my eyes.'
Come, all ye great examples of my sex,
Chaste virgins, tender wives, and pious matrons;
' Ye holy martyrs, who, with wond'rous faith
' And constancy unshaken, have sustain'd
' The rage of cruel men, and fiery persecution;'
Come to my aid, and teach me to defy
The malice of this fiend! I feel, I feel
Your sacred spirit arm me to resistance.
Yes, tyrant, I will stand this shock of fate;
Will live to triumph o'er thee, for a moment,
Then die well pleas'd, and follow my Moneses.

Baj. Thou talk'st it well. But talking is thy privilege;
'Tis all the boasted courage of thy sex;
Tho', for thy soul, thou dar'st not meet the danger.

Ax. By all my hopes of happiness I dare!——
' My soul is come within her ken of heav'n;
' Charm'd with the joys and beauties of that place,
' Her thoughts and all her cares she fixes there,
' And 'tis in vain for thee to rage below.
' Thus stars shine bright, and keep their place above,
' Tho' ruling winds deform this lower world.'

Baj. This moment is the trial.

Ax. I dare!
This moment then shall shew I am a Greek,

And

And speak my country's courage in my suff'ring.

Baj. Here, Mercy, I disclaim thee! Mark me, trai-
My love prepares a victim to thy pride,   [tress!
And when it greets thee next, 'twill be in blood.

[*Ex Baj.*

Arp. My heart beats higher, and my nimble spirits
Ride swiftly thro' their purple channel's round.
' 'Tis the last blaze of life. Nature revives,
' Like a dim winking lamp, that flashes brightly
' With parting light, and straight is dark for ever.'
And see, my last of sorrows is at hand;
Death and Moneses come together to me;
As if my stars, that had so long been cruel,
Grew kind at last, and gave me all I wish.

Enter Moneses, *guarded by some mutes; others at-*
tending with a cup of poison, and a bow-string.

Mon. I charge ye, O ye ministers of fate!
Be swift to execute your master's will;
Bear me to my Arpasia; let me tell her,
The tyrant is grown kind. He bids me go,
And die beneath her feet. ' A joy shoots thro''
' My drooping breast; as often when the trumpet
' Has call'd my youthful ardour forth to battle,
' High in my hopes, and ravish'd with the sound,
' I have rush'd eager on amidst the foremost,
' To purchase victory, or glorious death.'

Arp. If it be happiness, alas! to die,
To lie forgotten in the silent grave,
To love and glory lost, and from among
The great Creator's works expung'd and blotted;
Then, very shortly, shall we both be happy:

Mon. There is no room for doubt; 'tis certain bliss.
The tyrant's cruel violence, thy loss,
Already seem more light; nor has my soul
One unrepented guilt upon remembrance,
To make me dread the justice of hereafter:
But, standing now on the last verge of life,
Boldly I view the vast abyss eternity,
Eager to plunge, and leave my woes behind me.

Arp. By all the truth of our past loves, I vow,
To die appears a very nothing to me.
' But, Oh. Moneses! should I not allow
' Somewhat to love, and to my sex's tenderness?'

This

This very now I could put off my being
Without a groan; but to behold thee die!——
Nature fhrinks in me at the dreadful thought,
Nor can my conftancy fuftain this blow.

Mon. Since thou art arm'd for all things after death,
Why fhould the pomp and preparation of it
Be frightful to thy eyes? There's not a pain,
Which age or ficknefs brings, the leaft diforder
That vexes any part of this fine frame,
But's full as grievous. All that the mind feels
Is much, much more.—And fee, I go to prove it.

*Enter a mute; he figns to the reft, who proffer a
bow-ftring to* Monefes.

Arp. Think, ere we part!

Mon. Of what?

Arp. Of fomething foft,
Tender and kind, of fomething wond'rous fad.
Oh, my full foul!

Mon. My tongue is at a lofs;
Thoughts crowd fo faft, thy name is all I've left,
My kindeft, trueft, deareft, beft Arpafia!

[*The mutes ftruggle with him.*

Arp. I have a thoufand thoufand things to utter,
A thoufand more to hear yet. Barbarous villains!
Give me a minute. Speak to me, Monefes!

Mon. Speak to thee? 'Tis the bufinefs of my life,
'Tis all the ufe I have for vital air.
Stand off, ye flaves! To tell thee that my heart
Is full of thee; that even, at this dread moment,
My fond eyes gaze with joy and rapture on thee;
Angels, and light itfelf, are not fo fair——

Enter Bajazet, Haly, *and attendants.*

Baj. Ha! wherefore lives this dog? Be quick, ye
And rid me of the pain. [flaves!

Mon. For only death,
And the laft night can fhut out my Arpafia.

[*The mutes ftrangle* Monefes.

Arp. Oh, difmal! 'tis not to be borne! Ye moralifts!
Ye talkers! what are all your precepts now?
Patience! Diftraction! Blaft the tyrant, blaft him,
Avenging lightnings! Snatch him hence, ye fiends!
Love! Death! Monefes! ' Nature can no more;
' Ruin is on her, and fhe finks at once. [*She finks down.*

' *Baj.*

' *Baj.* Help, Haly, raife her up, and bear her out.

' *Ha.* Alas! fhe faints.

' *Arp.* No, tyrant, 'tis in vain.

' Oh! I am now beyond thy cruel pow'r;

' The peaceful flumber of the grave is on me:

' E'en all the tedious day of life I've wander'd,

' Bewilder'd with misfortunes:

' At length 'tis night, and I have reach'd my home.

' Forgetting all the toils and troubles paft,

' Weary I'll lay me down and fleep, till——Oh!'

[*She dies.*

Baj. Fly, ye flaves,
And fetch me cordials. No, fhe fhall not die!
Spite of her fullen pride, I'll hold-in life,
And force her to be bleft againft her will.

Ha. Already 'tis beyond the power of art;
For fee, a deadly cold has froze the blood,
The pliant limbs grow ftiff, and lofe their ufe,
And all the animating fire is quench'd:
E'en beauty too is dead; an afhy pale
Grows o'er the rofes; the red lips have loft
Their fragrant hue, for want of that fweet breath
That bleft 'em with its odours as it paft.

Baj. Can it be poffible? Can rage and grief,
Can love and indignation be fo fierce,
So mortal in a woman's heart? Confufion!
Is fhe efcap'd then? What is royalty,
If thofe that are my flaves, and fhould live for me,
Can die, and bid defiance to my power?

Enter the Dervife.

Der. The valiant Omar fends to tell thy greatnefs
The hour of flight is come, and urges hafte;
Since he defcries, near Tamerlane's pavilion,
Bright troops of crowding torches, who from thence,
On either hand, ftretch far into the night,
And feem to form a fhining front of battle.
Behold, e'en from this place thou may'ft difcern them.

[*Looking out.*

Baj. By Alha, yes! they caft a day around 'em,
And the plain feems thick fet with ftars, as heav'n.
Ha! or my eyes are falfe, they move this way;
'Tis certain fo. Fly, Haly, to our daughter.

[*Exit* Haly.

Let

Let some secure the Christian prince Axalla:
We will begone this minute.

Enter Omar.

Om. Lost! undone!

Baj. What mean'st thou?

Om. All our hopes of flight are lost.
Mirvan and Zama, with the Parthian horse,
Enclose us round, they hold us in a toil.

Baj. Ha! whence this unexpected curse of chance?

Om. Too late I learnt, that early in the night
A slave was suffer'd, by the princess' order,
To pass the guard. I clove the villain down
Who yielded to his flight; but that's poor vengeance.
That fugitive has rais'd the camp upon us,
And unperceiv'd, by favour of the night,
In silence they have march'd to intercept us.

Baj. My daughter! Oh, the traitress!

Der. Yet, we have
Axalla in our power; and angry Tamerlane
Will buy his fav'rite's life on any terms.

Om. With those few friends I have left for a while
Can face their force: if they refuse us peace,
Revenge shall sweeten ruin, ' and 'twill joy me,
' To drag my foe down with me in my fall.' [*Exit Om.*

Enter Haly, *with* Selima *captive.*

Ba. See where she comes with well-dissembled inno-
With truth and faith so lovely in her face,   [cence;
As if she durst e'en disavow the falsehood.——
Hop'st thou to make amends with trifling tears,
For my lost crown, and disappointed vengeance?
Ungrateful Selima! thy father's curse!
Bring forth the minion of her foolish heart;
He dies this moment.——

Ha. Would I could not speak
The crime of fatal love! The slave who fled,
By whom we are undone, was that Axalla.

Baj. Ha! say'st thou?

Ha. Hid beneath that vile appearance,
The princess found a means for his escape.

Sel. I am undone! e'en nature has disclaim'd me!
My father! have I lost you all? My father.

Baj. Talk'st thou of nature, who hast broke her bands!
Thou art my bane, thou witch, thou infant parricide!

But

Barralet ad viv del.   Walker sculp.

Mr. PALMER as BAJAZET and

But I will study to be strangely cruel;
I will forget the folly of my fondness;
Drive all the father from my breast; now snatch thee,
Tear thee to pieces, drink thy treacherous blood,
And make thee answer all my great revenge!
Now, now, thou traitress!   [*Offers to kill her.*
    Sel. Plunge the poignard deep!   [*She embraces him.*
The life my father gave shall hear his summons,
And issue at the wound——' Start not to feel
' My heart's warm blood gush out upon your hands;'
Since from your spring I drew the purple stream,
And I must pay it back if you demand it.   [weakness!
    Baj. Hence, from my thoughts, thou soft relenting
Hast thou not giv'n me up a prey? betray'd me?
    Sel. Oh, not for worlds! not e'en for all the joys,
Love, or the Prophet's paradise, can give!
' Amidst the fears and sorrows of my soul,'
Amidst the thousand pains of anxious tenderness,
I made the gentle, kind Axalla swear,
Your life, your crown, and honor should be safe.
    Baj. Away! my soul disdains the vile dependence!
No, let me rather die, die like a king!
Shall I fall down at the proud Tartar's foot,
And say, Have mercy on me? Hark! they come! [*Shout.*
Disgrace will overtake my ling'ring hand;
Die then! Thy father's shame, and thine, die with thee.
                        [*Offers to kill her.*
    Sel. For Heav'n, for pity's sake!
    Baj. No more, thou trifler!
                    [*She catches hold of his arm.*
Ha! dar'st thou bar my will? Tear off her hold!
    Sel. What, not for life! Should I not plead for life,
' When nature teaches e'en the brute creation
' To hold fast that, her best, her noblest gift?'
Look on my eyes, which you so oft have kiss'd,
And swore they were your best-lov'd queen's, my mo-
Behold 'em now, streaming for mercy, mercy!   [ther's;
Look on me, and deny me, if you can!
' 'Tis but for life! beg. Is that a boon
' So hard for me t' obtain, or you to grant?'
Oh, spare me! spare your Selima, my father!
    Baj. A lazy sloth hangs on my resolution:
It is my Selima!—Ha! What, my child!

                                And

And can I murder her?—Dreadful imagination!
Again they come! I leave her to my foes!   [*Shouts.*
And shall they triumph o'er the race of Bajazet!
Die, Selima! Is that a father's voice?
Rouse, rouse, my fury! Yes, she dies the victim
To my lost hopes. Out, out, thou foolish nature!
Justly she shares the ruin she has made.
Seize her, ye * slaves! and strang e her this moment!
                                        [* *To the mutes.*

Sel. Oh, let me die by you! Behold my breast!
I wo'not shrink! Oh, save me but from these!
    Baj. Dispatch.   [*The mutes seize her.*
    Sel. But for a moment, while I pray
That Heav'n may guard my royal father.
    Baj. Dogs!
    Sel. That you may only bless me, ere I die.   [*Shout.*
    Baj. Ye tedious villains, then the work is mine.
[*As* Bajazet *runs at* Selima, *with his sword, enter* Ta-
    merlane, Axalla, *&c.* Axalla *gets between* Bajazet *and*
    Selima, *whilst* Tamerlane *and the rest drive* Bajazet
    and the mutes off the stage.]
    Ax. And am I come to save thee? Oh, my joy!
' Be this the whitest hour of all my life;'
This one success is more than all my wars,
The noblest, dearest glory of my sword.
    Sel. Alas, Axalla! Death has been around me;
My coward soul still trembles at the fright,
And seems but half secure, e'en in thy arms.
    Ax. Retire, my fair, and let me guard thee forth:
Blood and tumultuous slaughter are about us,
' And danger in her ugliest form is here;'
Nor will the pleasure of my heart be full,
·'Till all my fears are ended in thy safety.
                        [*Exeunt* Axalla *and* Selima.
Enter Tamerlane, *the prince of* Tanais, Zama, Mirvan, *and*
    soldiers; with Bajazet, Omar, *and the Dervise prisoners.*
    Tam. Mercy at length gives up her peaceful sceptre,
And Justice sternly takes her turn to govern:
'Tis a rank world, and asks her keenest sword,
To cut up villainy of monstrous growth.
Zama, take care, that with the earliest dawn
Those traitors meet the fate their treason merits!
                    [*Pointing to* Omar *and the Dervise.*
                                            For

For thee, thou ty ant ! [*To Baj.*] whose oppreſſive violence
His ruin'd thoſe thou ſhould'ſt protect at home ;
‘ Whoſe wars, whoſe ſlaughters, whoſe aſſaſſinations,
‘ (hat baſeſt thirſt of blood ! that ſin of cowards !)
‘ Whoſe faith ſo often giv'n and always violated,
‘ Have been th' offence of Heav'n and plague of earth,’
What puniſhment is equal to thy crimes ?
The doom, thy rage deſign'd for me, be thine :
Clos'd in a cage. like ſome deſtructive beaſt,
I'll have thee borne about, in public view,
A great example of that righteous vengeance
That waits on cruelty and pride like thine.

Baj. It is beneath me to decline my fate ;
I ſtand prepar'd to meet thy utmoſt hate ;
Yet think not, I will long thy triumph ſee :
None want the means, when the ſoul dares be free.
I'll curſe thee with my laſt, my parting breath,
And keep the courage of my life in death ;
Then boldly venture on that world unknown ;
It cannot uſe me worſe than this has done.

[*Exit* Bajazet, *guarded.*

Tam. Behold the vain effects of earth-born pride,
That ſcorn'd Heaven's laws, and all its pow'r defy'd,
That could the hand which form'd it firſt forget,
And fondly ſay, I made myſelf be great !
But juſtly thoſe above aſſert their ſway, ⎫
And teach e'en Kings what homage they ſhould pay, ⎬
Who then rule beſt, when mindful to obey. ⎭

[*Exeunt omnes.*

E P I L O G U E.

TOO well we ſaw what muſt have been our fate, ⎫
  When harmony with beauty join'd, of late, ⎬
Threaten'd the ruin of our ſinking ſtate ; ⎭
Till you, from whom our being we receive,
In pity bid your own creation live :
With moving ſounds you kindly drew the fair,
And fix'd, once more, that ſhining circle here :
The lyre you bring is half Apollo's praiſe ;
Be ours the taſk to win and wear his bays.

7

Thi

Thin houses were before so frequent to us,
We wanted not a project to undo us;
We seldom saw your honours, but by chance,
As some folks meet their friends of Spain and France:
'Twas verse decay'd, or politics improv'd,
That had estrang'd you thus from what you lov'd.
Time was, when busy faces were a jest,
When wit and pleasure were in most request;
When chearful theatres with crowds were grac'd;
But those good days of poetry are past;
Now four reformers in an empty pit,
With table-books, as at a lecture, sit,
To take notes, and give evidence 'gainst wit.
Those who were once our friends, employ'd elsewhere,
Are busy now in settling peace and war:
With careful brows, at Tom's and Will's they meet,
And ask who did elections lose or get——
Our friend has lost it——Faith I'am sorry for't,
He's a good man, and ne'er was for the court;
He to no government will sue for grace,
By want of merit safe against a place,
By spite a patriot made, and sworn t' oppose
All who are uppermost, as England's foes:
Let whig or tory, any side prevail,
Still 'tis his constant privilege to rail.
Another, that the tax and war may cease,
Talks of the duke of Anjou's right, and peace:
And, from Spain's wise example, is for taking
A viceroy of the mighty monarch's making;
Who should all rights and liberties maintain,
And English laws by learn'd dragoons explain.
　Come leave these politics, and follow wit;
Here, uncontroll'd you may in judgement sit;
We'll never differ with a crowded pit:
We'd take you all, e'en on your own conditions,
Think you great men, and wond'rous politicians;
And if you slight the offers which we make you,
No Brentford princes will for statesmen take you.

A

T R A G E D Y.

WRITTEN BY

· Mr. AMB. PHILIPS.

Marked with the Variations in the

M A N A G E R's   B O O K,

AT THE

𝕿𝖍𝖊𝖆𝖙𝖗𝖊-𝕽𝖔𝖞𝖆𝖑 𝖎𝖓 𝕮𝖔𝖛𝖊𝖓𝖙𝕲𝖆𝖗𝖉𝖊𝖓.

L O N D O N:

Printed for W. Lowndes, W. Nicoll, and
S. Bladon.

M,DCC,LXXXVI,

*** The Reader is defired to obferve, that the Paffages omitted in the Reprefentation at the Theatres, are here preferved, and marked with inverted Commas; as in line 3 to 6, page 15.

HER GRACE THE

DUCHESS of MONTAGUE.

MADAM,

THIS Tragedy, which I do myfelf the honour to dedicate to your Grace, is formed upon an original which paffes for the moft finifhed piece, in this kind of writing, that has ever been produced in the *French* language. The principal action and main diftrefs of the play, is of fuch a nature, as feems more immediately to claim the patronage of a lady; and when I confider the great and fhining characters of antiquity that are celebrated in it, I am naturally directed to infcribe it to a perfon, whofe illuftrious father has, by a long feries of glorious actions, (for the fervice of his country, and in defence of the liberties of *Europe*) not only furpaffed the generals of his own time, but equalled the greateft heroes of former ages. The name of *Hector* could not be more ter-

A 2   rible

rible to the *Greeks*, than that of the Duke of *Marlborough* has been to the *French*.

The refined taste you are known to have in all entertainments for the diversion of the public, and the peculiar life and ornament your presence gives to all assemblies, was no small motive to determine me in the choice of my patroness. The charms that shine out in the person of your Grace, may convince every one, that there is nothing unnatural in the power which is ascribed to the beauty of *Andromache*.

The strict regard I have had to decency and good manners throughout this work, is the greatest merit I pretend to plead in favour of my presumption; and is, I am sensible, the only argument that can recommend it most effectually to your protection.

I am, with the greatest respect,

MADAM,

Your Grace's most humble,

And most obedient servant,

AMB. PHILIPS.

PREFACE.

IN all the works of genius and invention, whether in verse or prose, there are, in general, but three manners of style; the one sublime, and full of majesty; the other, simple, natural, and easy; and the third, swelling, forced, and unnatural. An injudicious affectation and sublimity, is what has betrayed a great many authors into the latter; not considering that real greatness in writing, as well as in manners, consists in an unaffected simplicity. The true sublime does not lie in strained metaphors and the pomp of words, but rises out of noble sentiments and strong images of nature; which will always appear the more conspicuous, when the language does not swell to hide and overshadow them.

These are the considerations that have induced me to write this Tragedy in a style very different from what has been usually practised among us in poems of this nature. I have had the advantage to copy after a very great master, whose writings are deservedly admired in all parts of *Europe*, and whose excellencies are too well known to the men of letters in this nation, to stand in need of any farther discovery of them here. If I have been able to keep up to the beauties of Monsieur *Racine*, in my attempts, and to do him no prejudice in the liberties I have taken frequently to vary from so great a poet, I shall have no reason to be dissatisfied with the labour it has cost me to bring the completest of his works upon the *English* stage.

I shall trouble my reader no farther, than to give him some short hints relating to this play, from the preface of the *French* author. The following lines of *Virgil* mark out the scene, the action, and the our principal actors in this Tragedy, together with their distinct characters; excepting that of *Hermione*, whose rage and jealousy is sufficiently painted in the *Andromache* of *Euripides*.

Littoraque

Littoraque Epiri legimus, portuque subimus
Chaonio, et celsam Buthroti ascendimus urbem—
Solemnes cum forte dapes, et tristia dona
Libabat cineri Andromache, manesque vocabat
Hectoreum ad tumulum, viridi quem cespite inanem,
Et geminas, causam lacrymis, sacraverat Aras—
Dejecit vultum, et demissa voce locuta est :
O felix una ante alias Priameia virgo,
Hostilem ad tumulum, Trojæ sub mœnibus altis
Jussa mori! quæ sortitus non pertulit ullos,
Nec victoris heri tetigit captiva cubile.
Nos patria incensa, diversa per æquora vectæ,
Stirpis Achilleæ fastus, juvenemque superbum,
Servitio enixæ tulimus, qui deinde secutus
Ledæam Hermionem, Lacedæmonisque Hymenæos—
Ast illum, ereptæ magno inflammatus amore
Conjugis, et scelerum furiis agitatus Orestes
Excipit incautam patriasque obtruncat ad aras.

VIRG. Æn. Lib. iii.

The great concern of *Andromache*, in the *Greek* poet, is
for the life of *Molossus*, a son she had by *Pyrrhus*. But it
is more conformable to the general notion we form of that
princess, at this great distance of time, to represent her
as the disconsolate widow of *Hector*, and to suppose her
the mother only of *Astyanax*. Considered in this light,
no doubt, she moves our compassion much more effectually, than she could be imagined to do in any distress for
a son by a second husband.

In order to bring about this beautiful incident, so ne-
cessary to heighten in *Andromache* the character of a tender
mother, an affectionate wife, and a widow full of veneration for the memory of her deceased husband, the life
of *Astyanax* is indeed a little prolonged beyond the term
fixed to it by the general consent of the ancient authors.
But so long as there is nothing improbable in the suppo-
sition, a judicious critic will always be pleased when he
finds a matter of fact (especially so far removed in the
dark and fabulous ages) falsified, for the embellishment
of a whole poem.

PRO-

PROLOGUE.

SINCE fancy by itself is loose and vain,
   The wise by rules that airy power restrain:
They think those writers mad, who at their ease
Convey this house and audience where they please;
Who nature's stated distances confound,
And make this spot all soils the sun goes round:
'Tis nothing, when a fancied scene's in view,
To skip from Covent-Garden to Peru.

   But Shakspeare's self transgrest; and shall each elf,
Each pygmy genius, quote great Shakspeare's self!
What critic dares prescribe what's just and fit,
Or mark out limits for such boundless wit!
Shakspeare could travel thro' earth, sea, and air,
And paint out all the powers and wonders there.
In barren deserts he makes nature smile,
And gives us feasts in his enchanted isle.
Our author does his feeble force confess,
Nor dares pretend such merit to transgress;
Does not such shining gifts of genius share,
And therefore makes propriety his care.
Your treat with studied decency he serves;
Not only rules of time and place preserves,
But strives to keep his character intire,
With French correctness, and with British fire.

   This piece, presented in a foreign tongue,
When France was glorious, and her monarch young,
An hundred times a crowded audience drew,
An hundred times repeated, still was new.

   Pyrrhus, provok'd, to no wild rants betray'd,
Resents his generous love so ill repaid;
Does like a man resent, a prince upbraid.
His sentiments disclose a royal mind,
Nor is he known a king from guards behind.

   Injur'd Hermione demands relief,
But not from heavy narratives of grief:
In conscious majesty her pride is shewn;
Born to avenge her wrongs, but not bemoan.

   Andromache——If in our author's lines,
As in the great original she shines,
Nothing but from barbarity she fears;
Attend with silence, you'll applaud with tears.

Dramatis Personæ, 1786.

M E N.	At Drury-Lane.	At Covent-Garden.
Pyrrhus, *son of Achilles, and King of Epirus, in love with* Hermione	Mr. Palmer.	Mr. Pope.
Andromache, *but betrothed to* Hermione	—	Mr. W. Palmer.
Phœnix, *Counsellor to* Pyrrhus	Mr. Packer.	Mr. Holman.
Orestes, *son of* Agamemnon, *Ambassador from the Greeks to* Pyrrhus, *in love with* Hermione	Mr. Smith.	
Pylades, *friend to* Orestes, *separated from him in a storm, driven on the coast of Epirus, and detained by contrary winds in the court of* Pyrrhus	Mr. Barrymore.	Mr. Davies.

W O M E N.

	At Drury-Lane.	At Covent-Garden.
Andromache, Hector's *widow, captive to* Pyrrhus, *and mother to* Astyanax	Miss Kemble.	Mrs. Wells.
Cephisa, *confidant to* Andromache	Miss Tidswell.	Mrs. Morton.
Hermione, *daughter to* Menelaus *and* Helen, *betrothed to* Pyrrhus	Mrs. Siddons.	Miss Brunton.
Cleone, *confidant to* Hermione	Miss Collins.	Miss Stuart.

Attendants on Pyrrhus *and* Orestes, &c.

The SCENE, *a Great Hall in the Court of* Pyrrhus, *at* Buthrotos, *the capital City of* Epirus.

ACT I.

Enter Oreſtes, Pylades, *and Attendants.*

Oreſ. O *Pylades!* what's life without a friend!
At ſight of thee my gloomy ſoul cheers up,
My hopes revive, and gladneſs dawns within me.
After an abſence of ſix tedious moons,
How could I hope to find my *Pylades,*
My joy, my comfort! on this fatal ſhore!
Even in the court of *Pyrrhus?* in theſe realms,
Theſe hated realms, ſo croſs to all my wiſhes.
O, my brave friend! may no blind ſtroke of fate
Divide us more, and tear me from myſelf.

Pyl. O prince! O my *Oreſtes!* O my friend!—
Thus let me ſpeak the welcome of my heart [*Embracing.*
Since I have gain'd this unexpected meeting,
Bleſt be the powers that barr'd my way to *Greece,*
And kept me here! ever ſince the unhappy day
When warring winds (*Epirus* full in view)
Sunder'd our barks on the loud ſtormy main.

Oreſ. It was, indeed, a morning full of horror!

Pyl. A thouſand boding cares have rack'd my ſoul
In your behalf. Often, with tears, I mourn'd
The fatal ills, to which your life's involv'd;
And grudg'd you dangers which I could not ſhare.
I fear'd to what extremities the black deſpair
That prey'd upon your mind, might have betray'd you,
And left the Gods, in pity to your woes,
Should hear your pray'rs, and take the life you loath'd.
But now with joy I ſee you!———The retinue,
And numerous followers that ſurround you here,

Speak better fortunes, and a mind difpos'd
To relifh life.

Oreſ. Alas! my friend, who knows
The deſtiny, to which I ſtand reſerv'd!
I come in ſearch of an inhuman fair;
And live or die, as ſhe decrees my fate.

Pyl. You much ſurprife me, prince!—I thought you
   cur'd
Of your unpity'd, unſuccefsful paſſion.
Why, in *Epirus*, ſhould you hope to find
Hermione lefs cruel, than at *Sparta?*
I thought her pride, and the diſdainful manner
In which ſhe treated all your conſtant ſufferings,
Had broke your fetters, and aſſur'd your freedom:
Aſham'd of your repulfe, and ſlighted vows,
You hated her; you talk'd of her no more:
Prince, you deceiv'd me.

Oreſ. I deceiv'd myſelf.
Do not upbraid the unhappy man that loves thee.
Thou know'ſt I never hid my paſſion from thee;
Thou ſaw'ſt it, in its birth, and in its progreſs;
And when, at laſt, the hoary King, her father,
Great *Menelaus*, gave away his daughter,
His lovely daughter, to the happy *Pyrrhus,*
Th' avenger of his wrongs, thou ſaw'ſt my grief,
My torture, my defpair; ' and how I dragg'd,
' From ſea to ſea, a heavy chain of woes.'
O *Pylades!* my heart has bled within me,
To ſee thee, preſt with ſorrows not thy own,
Still wand'ring with me, like a baniſh'd man,
Watchful, and anxious for thy wretched friend,
To temper the wild tranfports of my mind,
And ſave me from myſelf.

Pyl. Why thus unkind?
Why will you envy me the pleaſing taſk
Of generous love, and ſympathizing friendſhip?

Oreſ. Thou miracle of truth!—But hear me on.
When in the midſt of my difaſtrous fate,
I thought how the divine *Hermione,*
Deaf to the vows, regardlefs of my plaints,
Gave up herſelf, and all her charms, to *Pyrrhus;*

Thou

Thou may'ft remember, I abhorr'd her name,
Strove to forget her, and repay her fcorn.
I made my friends, and even myfelf, believe
My foul was freed. Alas! I did not fee,
That all the malice of my heart was love.
Triumphing thus, and yet a captive ftill,
In *Greece* I landed, and in *Greece* I found
The affembled princes all alarm'd with fears,
In which their common fafety feem'd concern'd.
I join'd them: for I hop'd that war and glory
Might fill my mind, and take up all my thoughts;
And that my fhatter'd foul, impair'd with grief,
Once more would reaffume its wonted vigour,
And every idle paffion quit my breaft.

   Pyl. The thought was worthy *Agamemnon*'s fon:

   Oref. But fee the ftrange perverfenefs of my ftars,
Which throws me on the rock I ftrove to fhun!
The jealous chiefs, and all the ftates of *Greece*,
With one united voice complain of *Pyrrhus;*
That now, forgetful of the promife giv'n,
And mindlefs of his godlike father's fate,
Aftyanax he nurfes in his court;
Aftyanax, the young, furviving hope   ·
Of ruin'd *Troy; Aftyanax,* defcended
From a long race of kings—great *Hector*'s fon.

   Pyl. A name ftill dreadful in the ears of *Greece!*
But, prince, you'll ceafe to wonder, why the child
Lives thus protected in the court of *Pyrrhus,*
When you fhall hear, the bright *Andromache,*
His lovely captive, charms him from his purpofe:
The mother's beauty guards the helplefs fon.

   Oref. Your tale confirms what I have heard; and hence
Spring all my hopes. Since my proud rival wooes
Another partner to his throne and bed,
Hermione may ftill be mine. Her father,
The injur'd *Menelaus,* thinks already
His daughter flighted, and th' intended nuptials
Too long delay'd. I heard his loud complaints
With fecret pleafure; and was glad to find
Th' ungrateful maid neglected in her turn,
And all my wrongs aveng'd in her difgrace.

                        Pyl.

Pyl. Oh, may you keep your juſt reſentments warm!

Orʒ. Reſentments! O my friend, too ſoon I found
    grew not out of hatred. I am betray'd:
I praᵗⁱⁱfe on myſelf, and fondly plot
My own undoing. Goaded on by love,
I canvaſs'd all the ſuffrages of *Greece;*
And here I come, their ſworn ambaſſador,
To ſpeak their jealouſies, and claim this boy.

    Pyl. *Pyrrhus* will treat your embaſſy with ſcorn,
Full of *Achilles,* his redoubted ſire;
Pyrrhus is proud, impetuous, headſtrong, fierce;
Made up of paſſions: will he then be ſway'd,
And give to death the ſon of her he loves?

    Oreſ. Oh, would he render up *Hermione,*
And keep *Aſtynax,* I ſhould be bleſt!
He muſt; he ſhall: *Hermione* is my life,
My ſoul, my rapture!————I'll no longer curb
The ſtrong deſire that hurries me to madneſs:
I'll give a looſe to love; I'll bear her hence;
I'll tear her from his arms; I'll———O, ye Gods!
Give me *Hermione,* or let me die!——
But tell me, *Pylades,* how ſtand my hopes?
Is *Pyrrhus* ſtill enamour'd with her charms?
Or doſt thou think he'll yield me up the prize,
The dear, dear prize, which he has raviſh'd from me!

    Pyl. I dare not flatter your fond hopes ſo far;
The King, indeed, cold to the *Spartan* Princeſs,
Turns all his paſſion to *Andromache,*
Hector's afflicted widow. But in vain,
With interwoven love and rage, he ſues
The charming captive, obſtinately cruel.
Oft he alarms her for her child, confin'd
Apart; and when her tears begin to flow,
As ſoon he ſtops them, and recals his threats.
Hermione a thouſand times has ſeen
His ill-requited vows return to her;
And takes his indignation all for love.
What can be gather'd from a man ſo various?
He may, in the diſorder of his ſoul,
Wed her he hates, and puniſh her he loves.

                      Oreſ.

Oref. But tell me, how the wrong'd *Hermione*
Brooks her flow nuptials, and difhonour'd charms?

Pyl. Hermione would fain be thought to fcorn
Her wavering lover, and difdain his falfhood;
But, fpite of all her pride and confcious beauty,
She mourns in fecret her neglected charms,
And oft has made me privy to her tears;
Still threatens to be gone, yet ftill fhe ftays,
And fometimes fighs, and wifhes for *Oreftes.*

Oref. Ah, were thofe wifhes from her heart, my friend,
I'd fly in tranfport——   [*Flourifh within.*

Pyl. Hear!——The King approaches
To give you audience. Speak your embaffy
Without referve: urge the demands of *Greece;*
And in the name of all her kings, require
That *Hector's* fon be given into your hands.
Pyrrhus, inftead of granting what they afk,
To fpeed his love, and win the *Trojan* dame,
Will make it merit to preferve her fon.
But, fee: he comes!

Oref. Meanwhile, my *Pylades,*
Go, and difpofe *Hermione* to fee
Her lover, who is come thus far, to throw
Himfelf, in all his forrows, at her feet. [*Exit* Pylades.

Enter Pyrrhus, Phœnix, *and Attendants.*

Before I fpeak the meffage of the *Greeks,*
Permit me, fir, to glory in the title
Of their ambaffador; fince I behold
Troy's vanquifher, and great *Achilles'* fon,
Nor does the fon rife fhort of fuch a father:
If *Hector* fell by him, *Troy* fell by you.
But what your father never would have done,
You do. You cherifh the remains of *Troy;*
And, by an ill-tim'd pity, keep alive
The dying embers of a ten year's war.
Have you fo foon forgot the mighty *Hector?*
The *Greeks* remember his high brandifh'd fword,
That fill'd their ftate with widows and with orphans;
For which they call for vengeance on his fon.
Who knows what he may one day prove? Who knows
                                        But

But he may brave us in our ports, and, fill'd
With *Hector*'s fury, set our fleets on blaze?
You may, yourself, live to repent your mercy.
Comply, then, with the *Grecians'* just demands;
Satiate their vengeance, and preserve yourself.

   Pyr. The *Greeks* are for my safety more concern'd
Than I desire. I thought your kings were met
On more important counsel. When I heard
The name of their ambassador, I hop'd
Some glorious enterprize was taking birth.
Is *Agamemnon*'s son dispatch'd for this?
And do the *Grecian* chiefs, renown'd in war,
A race of heroes, join in close debate,
To plot an infant's death?—What right has *Greece*
To ask his life? Must I, must I alone,
Of all her scepter'd warriors, be deny'd
To treat my captive as I please? Know, prince,
When *Troy* lay smoking on the ground, and each
Proud victor shar'd the harvest of the war,
Andromache, and this her son were mine;
Were mine by lot. And who shall wrest them from me?
Ulysses bore away old *Priam*'s queen;
Cassandra was your own great father's prize:
Did I concern myself in what they won?
Did I send embassies to claim their captives?

   Oref. But, sir, we fear for you, and for ourselves.
Troy may again revive, and a new *Hector*
Rise in *Astyanax*. Then think betimes——

   Pyr. Let dastard souls be timorously wise:
But tell them, *Pyrrhus* knows not how to form
Far fancy'd ills, and dangers out of sight.

   Oref. Sir, call to mind the unrivall'd strength of *Troy*,
Her walls, her bulwarks, and her gates of brass;
Her kings, her heroes, and embattled armies!

   Pyr. I call them all to mind; and see them all
Confus'd in dust; all mixt in one wide ruin;
All but a child, and he in bondage held.
What vengeance can we fear from such a *Troy*?
If they have sworn to extinguish *Hector*'s race,
Why was their vow for twelve long months deferr'd?
Why was he not in *Priam*'s bosom slain?

He

He fhould have fall'n among the flaughter'd heaps,
Whelm'd under *Troy*. His death had then been juft,
' When age and infancy, alike in vain,
' Pleaded their weaknefs ; when the heat of conqueft,
' And horrors of the fight, rouz'd all our rage,
' And blindly hurry'd us thro' fcenes of death.'
My fury then was without bounds ; but now,
My wrath appeas'd, muft I be cruel ftill ?
And, deaf to all the tender calls of pity,
Like a cool murderer, bathe my hands in blood ?
An infant's blood ?—No, prince—Go, bid the *Greeks*
Mark out fome other victim ; my revenge
Has had its fill. What has efcap'd from *Troy*
Shall not be fav'd to perifh in *Epirus*.

Oref. I need not tell you, fir, *Aftyanax*
Was doom'd to death in *Troy;* nor mention how
The crafty mother fav'd her darling fon.
The *Greeks* do now but urge their former fentence :
Nor is't the boy, but *Hector* they purfue :
The father draws their vengeance on the fon—
The father, who fo oft in *Grecian* blood
Has drench'd his fword—the father, whom the *Greeks*
May feek e'en here ——Prevent them, fir, in time.

Pyr. No! let them come ; fince I was born to wage
Eternal wars. Let them now turn their arms
On him who conquer'd for them. Let them come,
And in *Epirus* feek another *Troy*.
'Twas thus they recompenc'd my godlike fire ;
Thus was *Achilles* thank'd. But, prince, remember,
Their black ingratitude then coft them dear. .

Oref. Shall *Greece* then find a rebel fon in *Pyrrhus ?*
Pyr. Have I then conquer'd to depend on *Greece ?*
Oref. Hermione will fway your foul to peace,
And mediate 'twixt her father and yourfelf.
Her beauty will enforce my embaffy.

Pyr. Hermione may have her charms, and I
May love her ftill, tho' not her father's flave.
I may, in time, give proofs that I'm a lover,
But never muft forget that I'm a king.
Meanwhile, fir, you may fee fair *Helen's* daughter :
I know how near in blood you ftand ally'd.

That

That done, you have my anfwer, prince. The *Greeks*,
No doubt, expect your quick return.
      [*Exeunt* Oreftes, *and Attendant.*
Phœn. Sir, do you fend your rival to the princefs?
Pyr. I am told that he has lov'd her long.
Phœn. If fo,
Have you not caufe to fear the fmother'd flame
May kindle at her fight, and blaze a-new;
And fhe be wrought to liften to his paffion?
Pyr. Ay, let them, *Phœnix*, let them love their fill!
Le them go hence; let them depart together:
Together let them fail for *Sparta;* all my ports
Are open to them both. From what conftraint,
What irkfome thoughts, fhould I then be reliev'd!
Phœn. But, fir——
Pyr. I fhall another time, good *Phœnix*,
Unbofom to thee all my thoughts—For, fee,
Andromache appears.   [*Exit* Phœnix.
   Enter Andromache, *and* Cephifa.
May I, madam,
Flatter my hopes fo far as to believe
You come to feek me here?
Andr. This way, fir, leads
To thofe apartments where you guard my fon.
Since you permit me, once a-day, to vifit
All I have left of *Hector* and of *Troy*,
I go to weep a few fad moments with him.
I have not yet to-day embrac'd my child;
I have not held him in my widow'd arms.
Pyr. Ah, madam! fhould the threats of *Greece* prevail,
You'll have occafion for your tears, indeed!
Andr. Alas! what threats? What can alarm the *Greeks?*
There are no *Trojans* left.
Pyr. Their hate to *Hector*
Can never die: the terror of his name
Still fhakes their fouls, and makes them dread his fon.
Andr. A mighty honour for victorious *Greece*,
To fear an infant, a poor friendlefs child!
Who fmiles in bondage, nor yet knows himfelf
The fon of *Hector*, and the flave of *Pyrrhus.*
            Pyr.

Pyr. Weak as he is, the *Greeks* demand his life,
And fend no lefs than *Agamemnon*'s fon
To fetch him hence.
   Andr. And, fir, do you comply
With fuch demands!——This blow is aim'd at me.
How fhould the child avenge his flaughter'd fire?
But, cruel men! they will not have him live
To cheer my heavy heart, and eafe my bonds.
I promis'd to myfelf in him a fon,
In him a friend, a hufband, and a father.
But I muft fuffer forrow heap'd on forrow,
And ftill the fatal ftroke muft come from you.
   Pyr. Dry up thofe tears; I muft not fee you weep;
And know, I have rejected their demands.
The *Greeks* already threaten me with war;
But, fhould they arm, as once they did, for *Helen*,
And hide the *Adriatic* with their fleets;
Should they prepare a fecond ten-years fiege,
And lay my towers and palaces in duft;
I am determined to defend your fon,
And rather die myfelf than give him up.
But, madam, in the midft of all thefe dangers,
Will you refufe me a propitious fmile?
Hated of *Greece*, and preft on every fide,
Let me not, madam, while I fight your caufe,
Let me not combat with your cruelties,
And count *Andromach* amongft my foes.
   Andr. Confider, fir, how this will found in *Greece!*
How can fo great a foul betray fuch weaknefs?
Let not men fay, fo generous a defign
Was but the tranfport of a heart in love.
   Pyr. Your charms will juftify me to the world.
   Andr. How can *Andromache*, a captive queen,
O'erwhelm'd with grief, a burden to herfelf,
Harbour a thought of love? Alas! what charms
Have thefe unhappy eyes, by you condemn'd
To weep for ever.——Talk of it no more.——
To reverence the misfortunes of a foe;
To fuccour the diftreft; to give the fon
To an afflicted mother; to repel
Confederate nations, leagu'd againft his life;

Unbrib'b

Unbrib'd by love, unterrify'd by threats,
To pity, to protect him: thefe are cares,
Thefe are exploits worthy *Achilles's* fon.

Pyr. Will your refentments, then, endure for ever!
Muft *Pyrrhus* never be forgiven?——"Tis true,
My fword has often reek'd in *Phrygian* blood,
And carry'd havoc thro' your royal kindred;
But you, fair princefs, amply have aveng'd
Old *Priam's* vanquifh'd houfe; and all the woes
I brought on them, fall fhort of what I fuffer.
We both have fuffer'd in our turns, and now
Our common foes fhall teach us to unite.

Andr. Where does the captive not behold a foe?

Pyr. Forget the term of hatred, and behold
A friend in *Pyrrhus.* Give me but to hope,
I'll free your fon, I'll be a father to him;
Myfelf will teach him to avenge the *Trojans.*
I'll go in perfon to chaftife the *Greeks,*
Both for your wrongs and mine. Infpir'd by you,
What would I not atchieve? Again fhall *Troy*
Rife from its afhes: this right arm fhall fix
Her feat of empire, and your fon fhall reign.

Andr. Such dreams of greatnefs fuit not my condition:
His hopes of empire perifh'd with his father.
No; thou imperial city, ancient *Troy,*
Thou pride of *Afia,* founded by the Gods!
Never, Oh never, muft we hope to fee
Thofe bulwarks rife, which *Hector* could not guard!—
Sir, all I wifh for is fome quiet exile,
Where far from *Greece* remov'd, and far from you,
I may conceal my fon, and mourn my hufband.
Your love creates me envy. Oh, return!
Return to your betroth'd *Hermione.*

Pyr. Why do you mock me thus? you know, I cannot.
You know my heart is yours; my foul hangs on you;
You take up every wifh: my waking thoughts,
And nightly dreams, are all employ'd on you.
'Tis true, *Hermione* was fent to fhare
My throne and bed; and would with tranfport hear
The vows which you neglect.

Andr.

Andr. She has no *Troy*,
No *Hector* to lament : she has not loft
A hufband by your conquefts.   Such a hufband!
('Tormenting thought!) whofe death alone has made
Your fire immortal · *Pyrrhus* and *Achilles*,
Are both grown great by my calamities.

Pyr. Madam, 'tis well!   'Tis very well!   I find,
Your will muft be obey'd ; imperious captive.
It fhall.   Henceforth I blot you from my mind :
You teach me to forget your charms ; to hate you :
For know, inhuman beauty, I have lov'd
Too well to treat you with indifference.
'Think well upon it ; my diforder'd foul
Wavers between th' extreme of love and rage :
I have been too tame ; I will awake to vengeance !
The fon fhall anfwer for the mother's fcorn.
The *Greeks* demand him, nor will I endanger
My realms, to pleafure an ungrateful woman.

Andr. Then he muft die ! alas, my fon muft die !
He has no friend, no fuccour left, befide
His mother's tears, and his own innocence.

Pyr. Go, madam, vifit this unhappy fon.
The fight of him may bend your ftubborn heart,
And turn to foftnefs your unjuft difdain.
I fhall once more expect your anfwer.   Go ;
And think, while you embrace the captive boy,
Think, that his life depends on your refolves.
                    [*Exeunt* Pyrrhus, *and Attendants.*

Andr. I'll go ; and in the anguifh of my heart,
Weep o'er my child—If he muft die, my life
Is wrapt in his ; I fhall not long furvive.
'Tis for his fake that I have fuffer'd life,
Groan'd in captivity, and out-liv'd *Hector.*
Yes, my *Aftyanax*, we'll go together !
Together to the realms of night we'll go !
There to thy ravifh'd eyes thy fire I'll fhew,
And point him out among the fhades below.

                                    }
                              [*Exeunt.*

                    A C T

ACT II.

Enter Hermione *and* Cleone.

Her. WELL, I'll be rul'd, *Cleone:* I will see him:
      I have told *Pylades* that he may bring him;
But truſt me, were I left to my own thoughts,
I ſhould forbid him yet.

    Cleo. And why forbid him?
Is he not, madam, ſtill the ſame *Oreſtes?*
Oreſtes, whoſe return you oft have wiſh'd?
The man whoſe ſufferings you ſo late lamented,
And often prais'd his conſtancy and love?

    Her. That love, that conſtancy, ſo ill requited,
Upbraids me to myſelf. I bluſh to think
How I have us'd him, and would ſhun his preſence.
What will be my confuſion, when he ſees me
Neglected and forſaken, like himſelf!
Will he not ſay, is this the ſcornful maid?
The proud *Hermione?* that tyranniz'd
In *Sparta's* court, and triumph'd in her charms?
Her inſolence at laſt is well repaid.
I cannot bear the thought.

    Cleo. You wrong yourſelf
With unbecoming fears. He knows too well
Your beauty and your worth. Your lover comes not
To offer inſults, but repeat his vows,
And breathe his ardent paſſion at your feet.
But, madam, what's your royal father's will?
What orders do your letters bring from *Sparta?*

    Her. His orders are, if *Pyrrhus* ſtill delay
The nuptials, and refuſe to ſacrifice
This *Trojan* boy, I ſhould with ſpeed embark,
And with their embaſſy return to *Greece.*

    Cleo. What would you more? *Oreſtes* comes in time
To ſave your honour. *Pyrrhus* cools apace:
Prevent his falſhood, and forſake him firſt.
I know you hate him; you have told me ſo.

                           Her.

Her. Hate him! My injur'd honour bids me hate him.
The ungrateful man, to whom I fondly gave
My virgin heart; the man I lov'd so dearly;
The man I doated on! O, my *Cleone!*
How is it possible I should not hate him!

Cleo. Then give him over, madam. Quit his court,
And with *Orestes*——

Her. No! I must have time
To work up all my rage! To meditate
A parting full of horror! My revenge
Will be but too much quicken'd by the traitor.

Cleo. Do you then wait new insults, new affronts?
To draw you from your father! Than to leave you!
In his own court to leave you—for a captive!
If *Pyrrhus* can provoke you, he has done it.

Her. Why dost thou heighten my distress? I fear
To search out my own thoughts, and sound my heart.
Be blind to what thou see'st: Believe me cur'd:
Flatter my weakness; tell me I have conquer'd;
Think that my injur'd soul is set against him;
And do thy best to make me think so too.

Cleo. Why would you loiter here, then?

Her. Let us fly!
Let us be gone! I leave him to his captive:
Let him go kneel, and supplicate his slave.
Let us be gone!—But what if he repent?
What, if the perjur'd prince again submit,
And sue for pardon? What, if he renew
His former vows?—But, Oh, the faithless man!
He slights me! drives me to extremities!—However,
I'll stay, *Cleone*, to perplex their loves:
I'll stay, till, by an open breach of contract,
I make him hateful to the *Greeks*. Already
Their vengeance have I drawn upon the son;
The second embassy shall claim the mother:
I will redouble all my griefs upon her.

Cleo. Ah, madam! whither does your rage transport
you?
Andromache, alas! is innocent.
A woman plung'd in sorrow, dead to love,
And when she thinks of *Pyrrhus,* 'tis with horror.

Her.

Her. Would I had done fo, too!—He had not then
Betray'd my eafy faith.——But I, alas!
Difcover'd all the fondnefs of my foul;
I made no fecret of my paffion to him,
Nor thought it dangerous to be fincere.
My eyes, my tongue, my actions fpoke my heart.

Cleo. Well might you fpeak without referve, to one
Engag'd to you by folemn oaths and treaties.

Her. His ardour, too, was an excufe to mine:
With other eyes he faw me then!——*Cleone,*
Thou may'ft remember, every thing confpir'd
To favour him: my father's wrongs aveng'd;
The *Greeks* triumphant; fleets of *Trojan* fpoils;
His mighty fire's, his own immortal fame;
His eager love—all, all confpir'd againft me!
—But I have done—I'll think no more of *Pyrrhus.*
Oreftes wants not merit, and he loves me.
My gratitude, my honour, both plead for him;
And if I've power o'er my heart, 'tis his.

Cleo. Madam, he comes——

Her. Alas! I did not think
He was fo near! I wifh I might not fee him.

Enter Oreftes.

How am I to interpret, fir, this vifit?
Is it a compliment of form, or love?

Oref. Madam, you know my weaknefs. 'Tis my fate
To love unpity'd; to defire to fee you;
And ftill to fwear each time fhall be the laft.
My paffion breaks thro' my repeated oaths,
And every time I vifit you, I'm perjur'd.
Even now, I find my wounds all bleed afrefh;
I blufh to own it, but I know no cure.
I call the Gods to witnefs, I have try'd
Whatever man could do, (but try'd in vain)
To wear you from my mind. Thro' ftormy feas,
And favage climes, in a whole year of abfence,
I courted dangers, and I long'd for death.

Her. Why will you, prince, indulge this mournful tale
It ill becomes the ambaffador of *Greece,*
To talk of dying, and of love. Remember
The kings you reprefent: fhall their revenge

Be

Be difappointed by your ill-tim'd paffion?
Difcharge you. embaffy—'tis not *Oreftes*
The *Greeks* defire fhould die.

Oref. My embaffy
Is at an end; for *Pyrrhus* has refus'd
To give up *Hector*'s fon.   Some hidden power
Protects the boy.

Her. Faithlefs, ungrateful man!   [*Afide.*

Oref. I now prepare for *Greece ;* but, e'er I go,
Would hear my final doom pronounc'd by you——
What do I fay?—I do already hear it!
My doom is fixt: I read it in your eyes.

Her. Will you then ftill defpair? be ftill fufpicious?
What have I done? wherein have I been cruel?
'Tis true, you find me in the court of *Pyrrhus ;*
But 'twas my royal father fent me hither.
And who can tell, but I have fhar'd your griefs?
Have I ne'er wept in fecret?—never wifh'd
To fee *Oreftes ?*——

Oref. Wifh'd to fee *Oreftes !*
O joy! O ecftacy! My foul's intranc'd!
O charming princefs! O tranfcendant maid!
My utmoft wifh!——Thus, thus let me exprefs
My boundlefs thanks!——I never was unhappy——
Am I *Oreftes ?*——

Her. You are *Oreftes :*
The fame unalter'd, generous, faithful lover;
The prince whom I efteem, whom I lament,
And whom I fain would teach my heart to love.

Oref. Ay, there it is!—I have but your efteem,
While *Pyrrhus* has your heart.

Her. Believe me, prince,
Were you as *Pyrrhus,* I fhould hate you!

Oref. No!——
I fhould be bleft! I fhould be lov'd as he is!——
Yet all this while I die by your difdain,
While he neglects your charms, and courts another.

Her. And who has told you, prince, that I'm neglected?
Has *Pyrrhus* faid—— (Oh, I fhall go diftracted!)
Has *Pyrrhus* told you fo? or is it you

Who·

Who think thus meanly of me?—Sir, perhaps,
All do not judge like you!—

   Oref. Madam, go on!
Infult me ftill; I'm us'd to bear your fcorn.

   Her. Why am I told how *Pyrrhus* loves or hates?
—Go, prince, and arm the *Greeks* againft the rebel;
Let them lay wafte his country, raze his towns,
Deftroy his fleets, his palaces—himfelf!——
Go, prince, and tell me then how much I love him.

   Oref. To haften his deftruction, come yourfelf;
And work your royal father to his ruin.

   Her. Meanwhile, he weds *Andromache!*

   Oref. Ah, princefs!
What is't I hear?

   Her. What infamy for *Greece*,
If he fhould wed a *Phrygian*, and a captive?

   Oref. Is this your hatred, madam?—'Tis in vain
To hide your paffion; every thing betrays it:
Your looks, your fpeech, your anger, nay, your filence;
Your love appears in all; your fecret flame
Breaks out the more, the more you would conceal it.

   Her. Your jealoufy perverts my meaning ftill,
And wrefts each circumftance to your difquiet;
My very hate is conftrued into fondnefs.

   Oref. Impute my fears, if groundlefs, to my love.

   Her. Then hear me, prince. Obedience to a father
Firft brought me hither; and the fame obedience
Detains me here, till *Pyrrhus* drive me hence,
Or my offended father fhall recal me.
Tell this proud king, that *Menelaus* fcorns
To match his daughter with a foe of *Greece:*
Bid him refign *Aftyanax*, or me.
If he perfifts to guard the hoftile boy,
Hermione embarks with you for *Sparta.*

                [*Exeunt* Hermione, *and* Cleone.

   Oref. Then is *Oreftes* bleft! My griefs are fled!
Fled like a dream!—Methinks I tread in air!
Pyrrhus enamour'd of his captive queen,
Will thank me, if I take her rival hence—
He looks not on the princefs with my eyes!
Surprifing happinefs!—unlook'd for joy!

                               Never

'Never let love defpair!—The prize is mine!
'Be fmooth, ye feas, and ye propitious winds,
Breathe from *Epirus* to the *Spartan* coafts!
I long to view the fails unfurl'd!——But, fee!
Pyrrhus approaches in a happy hour.

          Enter Pyrrhus, *and* Phœnix.

   Pyr. I was in pain to find you, prince.   My warm
Ungovern'd temper, would not let me weigh
'The importance of your embaffy, and hear
You argue for my good.——I was to blame.
I fince have pois'd your reafons: and I thank
My good allies: their care deferves my thanks.
You have convinc'd me, that the weal of *Greece*,
My father's honour, and my own repofe,
Demand that *Hector*'s race fhould be deftroy'd.
I fhall deliver up *Aftyanax*,
And you yourfelf fhall bear the victim hence.

   Oref. If you approve it, fir, and are content
To fpill the blood of a defencelefs child,
The offended *Greeks*, no doubt, will be appeas'd.

   Pyr. Clofer to ftrain the knot of our alliance,
'I have determin'd to efpoufe *Hermione*.
You come in time to grace our nuptial rites:
'In you the kings of *Greece* will all be prefent,
And you have right to perfonate her father,
As his embaffador, and brother's fon.
Go, prince, renew your vifit; tell *Hermione*,
To-morrow I receive her from your hands.

   Oref. [*Afide.*] O change of fortune! Oh, undone
      Oreftes!   [*Exit.*

   Pyr. Well, *Phœnix!* Am I ftill a flave to love?
What think'ft thou now? Am I myfelf again?

   Phœn. 'Tis as it fhould be; this difcovers *Pyrrhus;*
Shews all the hero: now you are yourfelf—
The fon, the rival of the great *Achilles!*
Greece will applaud you, and the world confefs
Pyrrhus has conquer'd *Troy* a fecond time!

   Pyr. Nay, *Phœnix*, now I but begin to triumph;
I never was a conqueror till now!
Believe me, a whole hoft, a war of foes,
May fooner be fubdu'd than love. Oh, *Phœnix!*

            B   What

What ruin have I fhunn'd? The *Greeks* enrag'd,
Hung o'er me like a gathering ftorm, and foon
Had burft in thunder on my head; while I
Abandon'd duty, empire, honour, all,
To pleafe a thanklefs woman!——One kind look
Had quite undone me!

   Phæn. O, my royal mafter!
The Gods, in favour to you, made her cruel.

   Pyr. Thou faw'ft with how much fcorn fhe treated me!
When I permitted her to fee her fon,
I hop'd it might have work'd her to my wifhes.
I went to fee the mournful interview,
And found her bath'd in tears, and loft in paffion.
Wild with diftrefs, a thoufand times fhe call'd
On *Hector*'s name: and when I fpoke in comfort,
And promis'd my protection to her fon,
She kifs'd the boy, and call'd again on *Hector*:
‘ Then ftrain'd him in her arms, and cry'd, 'tis he!
‘ 'Tis he himfelf! his eyes, his every feature!
‘ His very frown, and his ftern look already!
‘ 'Tis he—'tis my lov'd lord, whom I embrace!'
Does fhe then think that I preferve the boy,
To foothe and keep alive her flame for *Hector?*

   Phæn. No doubt, fhe does; and thinks you favour'd
      in it;
But let her go, for an ungrateful woman!

   Pyr. I know the thoughts of her proud ftubborn heart:
Vain of her charms, and infolent in beauty,
She mocks my rage; and when it threatens loudeft,
Expects 'twill foon be humbled into love.
But we fhall change our parts, and fhe fhall find
I can be deaf like her, and fteel my heart.
She is *Hector*'s widow; I, *Achilles*' fon!
Pyrrhus is born to hate *Andromache.*

   Phæn. My royal mafter, talk of her no more;
I do not like this anger. Your *Hermione*
Should now engrofs your thoughts. 'Tis time to fee her;
'Tis time you fhould prepare the nuptial rites,
And not rely upon a rival's care:
It may be dangerous.

   Pyr. But tell me, *Phænix,*

Doft

Doſt thou not think, the proud *Andromache*
Will be enrag'd, when I ſhall wed the princeſs?

Phæn. Why does *Andromache* ſtill haunt your thoughts?
What is't to you, be ſhe enrag'd or pleas'd?
Let her name periſh—think of her no more.

Pyr. No, *Phænix!*—I have been too gentle with er,
I have check'd my wrath, and ſtifled my reſentment:
She knows not yet to what degree I hate her.
Let us return——I'll brave her to her face:
I'll give my anger its free courſe againſt her.
Thou ſhalt ſee, *Phænix*, how I'll break her pride!

Phæn. Oh, go not, ſir!—There's ruin in her eyes!
You do not know your ſtrength; you'll fall before her.
Adore her beauty, and revive her ſcorn.

Pyr. That were, indeed, a moſt unmanly weakneſs!
Thou doſt not know me, *Phænix*.

Phæn. Ah, my prince!
You are ſtill ſtruggling in the toils of love.

Pyr. Canſt thou then think, I love this woman ſtill?
One who repays my paſſion with diſdain!
A ſtranger, captive, friendleſs and forlorn;
She and her darling ſon within my power;
Her life a forfeit to the *Greeks:* yet I
Preſerve her ſon; would take her to my throne:
Would fight her battles, and avenge her wrongs;
And all this while ſhe treats me as her foe!

Phæn. You have it in your power to be reveng'd.

Pyr. Yes—and I'll ſhew my power! I'll give her cauſe
To hate me! her *Aſtyanax* ſhall die——
What tears will then be ſhed! How will ſhe then
In bitterneſs of heart reproach my name!
Then, to complete her woes, will I eſpouſe
Hermione——'Twill ſtab her to the heart!

Phæn. Alas, you threaten like a lover ſtill!

Pyr. *Phænix*, excuſe this ſtruggle of my ſoul;
'Tis the laſt effort of expiring love.

Phæn. Then haſten, ſir, to ſee the *Spartan* princeſs,
And turn the bent of your deſires on her.

Pyr. Oh! 'tis a heavy taſk to conquer love,
And wean the ſoul from her accuſtom'd fondneſs.
But, come——A long farewel to *Hector's* widow.

'Tis

'Tis with a secret pleasure I look back,
And see the many dangers I have pass'd.
The merchant, thus, in dreadful tempests tost,
Thrown by the waves on some unlook'd-for coast,
Oft turns, and sees, with a delighted eye,
Midst rocks and shelves, the broken billows fly!
And, while the outrageous winds the deep deform,
Smiles on the tumult, and enjoys the storm.   [*Exeunt.*

A C T   III.

Enter Pylades *and* Orestes.

Pyl. FOR Heaven's sake, sir, compose your ruffled
mind,   .
And moderate your rage!
    Oref. No, *Pylades!*
This is no time for counsel.—I am deaf.
Talk not of reason! I have been too patient.
Life is not worth my care. My soul grows desperate.
I'll bear her off, or perish in the attempt.
I'll force her from his arms——By Heaven, I will!
    Pyl. Well, 'tis agreed, my friend——We'll force her
hence,
But still consider, we are in *Epirus.*
The court, the guards, *Hermione* herself,
The very air we breathe, belongs to *Pyrrhus.*
Good Gods! what tempted you to seek her here?
    Oref. Lost to myself, I knew not what I did!
My purposes were wild. Perhaps I came
To menace *Pyrrhus*, and upbraid the woman.
    Pyl. This violence of temper may prove fatal.
    Oref. It must be more than man to bear these shocks,
These outrages of fate, with temper.
He tells me, that he weds *Hermione*,
And will to-morrow take her from my hand!—
My hand shall sooner tear the tyrant's heart.—
    Pyl. Your passion blinds you, sir; he's not to blame.
Could you but look into the soul of *Pyrrhus*,
Perhaps you'll find it tortur'd like your own.
                                              Oref.

Oref. No, *Pylades!*—'tis all defign.——His pride,
To triumph over me, has chang'd his love.
The fair *Hermione*, before I came,
In all her bloom of beauty, was neglected.
Ah, cruel Gods! I thought her all my own!
She was confenting to return to *Sparta:*
Her heart, divided betwixt rage and love,
Was on the wing to take its leave of *Pyrrhus.*
She heard my fighs, fhe pitied my complaints,
She prais'd my conftancy—The leaft indifference
From this proud king, had made *Oreftes* happy!

   Pyl. So your fond heart believes!——

  ' *Oref.* Did I not fee
' Her hate, her rage, her indignation rife,
' Againft the ungrateful man?
  ' *Pyl.* Believe me, prince,
' 'Twas then fhe lov'd him moft. Had *Pyrrhus* left her,
' She would have form'd fome new pretext to ftay.'
Take my advice——Think not to force her hence;
But fly yourfelf from her deftructive charms.
Her foul is link'd to *Pyrrhus*—' Were fhe yours,
' She would reproach you ftill, and ftill regret
' Her difappointed nuptials.—'
  Oref. Talk no more!
I cannot bear the thought! She muft be mine!
Did *Pyrrhus* carry thunder in his hand,
I'd ftand the bolt, and challenge all his fury,
Ere I refign *Hermione*——By force
I'll fnatch her hence, and bear her to my fhips:
Have we forgot her mother *Helen's* rape?

  Pyl. Will then, *Oreftes* turn a ravifher,
And blot his embaffy?
  Oref. O, *Pylades!*
My grief weighs heavy on me—'twill diftract me!
' O leave me to myfelf!——Let not thy friendfhip
' Involve thee in my woes. Too long already,
' Too long haft thou been punifh'd for my crimes.
' It is enough, my friend!——It is enough!
' Let not thy generous love betray thee farther.'
The Gods have fet me as their mark, to empty
Their quivers on me.—Leave me to myfelf,

                                Mine

Mine be the danger, mine the enterprize.
All I request of thee, is to return,
And in my place convey *Phœnix*
(As *Pyrrhus* has consented) into *Greece*.
Go, *Pylades*——

Pyl. Lead on, my friend, lead on!
Let us bear off *Hermione!*   No toil,
No danger can deter a friend——Lead on!
Draw up the *Greeks*, summon your num'rous train;
The ships are ready, and the wind sits fair:
There eastward lies the sea; the rolling waves
Break on those palace-stairs.   I know each pass,
Each avenue and outlet of the court.
This very night we'll carry her on board.

Orest. Thou art too good!—I trespass on thy friend-
        ship:
But, Oh! excuse a wretch, whom no man pities,
Except thyself: one, just about to lose
The treasure of his soul: ' whom all mankind
' Conspire to hate, and one who hates himself.'
When will my friendship be of use to thee?

Pyl. The question is unkind.—But now, remember
To keep your counsels close, and hide your thoughts;
Let not *Hermione* suspect——No more——
I see her coming, sir——

Orest. Away, my friend;
I am advis'd; my all depends upon it.   [*Exit* Pylades.
            Enter Hermione, *and* Cleone.

Orest. Madam, your orders are obey'd; I have seen
Pyrrhus, my rival; and have gain'd him for you.
The king resolves to wed you.

Her. So I am told;
And, farther, I am inform'd, that you, *Orestes*,
Are to dispose me for the intended marriage.

Orest. And are you, madam, willing to comply?
' *Her.* Could I imagine *Pyrrhus* lov'd me still?
' After so long delays, who would have thought
' His hidden flames would shew themselves at last,
' And kindle in his breast, when mine expir'd?
' I can suppose, with you, he fears the *Greeks*;

                                            ' That

That it is intereſt, and not love, directs him;
‘ And, that my eyes had greater power o’er you.
  ‘ Oreſ. No, princeſs, no! it is too plain he loves you.
‘ Your eyes do what they will, and cannot fail
‘ To gain a conqueſt, where you wiſh they ſhould.’
  Her. What can I do, alas! my faith is promis’d:
Can I refuſe what is not mine to give?
A princeſs is not at her choice to love;
All we have left us is a blind obedience:
And yet you ſee how far I had comply’d,
And made my duty yield to your entreaties.
  Oreſ. Ah, cruel maid! you knew—but I have done.
All have a right to pleaſe themſelves in love.
I blame you not. ’Tis true, I hop’d—but you
Are miſtreſs of your heart, and I’m content.
’Tis fortune is my enemy, not you.
. But, madam, I ſhall ſpare your farther pain
On this uneaſy theme, and take my leave.   [Exit.
  Her. Cleone, couldſt thou think he’d be ſo calm?
  Cleo. Madam, his ſilent grief ſits heavy on him.
He is to be pitied.   His too eager love
Has made him baſy to his own deſtruction.
His threats have wrought this change of mind in Pyrrhus.
  Her. Doſt thou think Pyrrhus capable of fear?
Whom ſhould the intrepid Pyrrhus fear?   The Greeks?
Did he not lead their harraſs’d troops to conqueſt,
When they deſpair’d, when they retir’d from Troy,
And fought for ſhelter in their burning fleets?
Did he not then ſupply his father’s place?
No, my Cleone, he is above conſtraint;
He acts unforc’d; and where he weds, he loves.
  Cleo. Oh, that Oreſtes had remain’d in Greece!
I fear to-morrow will prove fatal to him.
  Her. Wilt thou diſcourſe of nothing but Oreſtes?
Pyrrhus is mine again!——Is mine for ever!
Oh, my Cleone, I am wild with joy!
Pyrrhus, the bold, the brave, the godlike Pyrrhus!
—Oh, I could tell thee numberleſs exploits,
And tire thee with his battles.——Oh, Cleone——
  Cleo. Madam, conceal your joy—I ſee Andromache—
She weeps, and comes to ſpeak her ſorrows to you.
                    B 4   Her.

Her. I would indulge the gladnefs of my heart!
Let us retire—Her grief is out of feafon.
            Enter Andromache, *and* Cephifa.
    Andr. Ah, madam! whither, whither do you fly?
Where can your eyes behold a fight more pleafing
'Than *Hector's* widow, fuppliant and in tears?
I come not an alarm'd, a jealous foe,
'To envy you the heart your charms have won—
'The only man I fought to pleafe, is gone;
Kill'd in my fight, by an inhuman hand.
Hector firft taught me love; which my fond heart
Shall ever cherifh, till we meet in death.
But, Oh, I have a fon!—And you, one day,
Will be no ftranger to a mother's fondnefs:
But Heaven forbid that you fhould ever know
A mother's forrow for an only fon.
Her joy, her blifs, her laft furviving comfort!
When every hour fhe trembles for his life!
Your power o'er *Pyrrhus* may relieve my fears.
Alas, what danger is there in a child,
Sav'd from the wreck of a whole ruin'd empire?
Let me go hide him in fome defert ifle:
You may rely upon my tender care
'To keep him far from perils of ambition:
All he can learn of me will be to weep!
    Her. Madam, 'tis eafy to conceive your grief;
But, it would ill become me to folicit
In contradiction to my father's will:
'Tis he who urges to deftroy your fon.
Madam, if *Pyrrhus* muft be wrought to pity,
No woman does it better than yourfelf.
If you gain him, I fhall comply, of courfe.
                    [*Exeunt* Hermione, *and* Cleone.
    Andr. Didft thou not mind with what difdain fhe fpoke?
Youth and profperity have made her vain;
She has not feen the fickle turns of life.
    Ceph. Madam, were I as you, I'd take her counfel;
I'd fpeak my own diftrefs: one look from you
Will vanquifh *Pyrrhus*, and confound the *Greeks*——
See, where he comes——Lay hold on this occafion.
                                        Enter

Enter Pyrrhus, *and* Phœnix.

Pyr. Where is the princefs?—Did you not inform me
Hermione was here ?   [*To* Phœnix.

Phœn. I thought fo, fir.

Andr. Thou feeft what mighty power my eyes have
    on him !   [*To* Cephifa.

Pyr. What fays fhe, *Phœnix ?*

Andr. I have no hope left !

Phœn. Let us be gone—*Hermione* expects you.

Ceph. For Heaven's fake, madam, break this fullen
    filence.

Andr. My child's already promis'd !——

Ceph. But not given.

Andr. No! no!——my tears are vain!—His doom is
    fixt !

Pyr. See if fhe deigns to caft one look upon us !
Proud woman !

Andr. I provoke him by my prefence.
Let us retire.

Pyr. Come, let us fatisfy
The *Greeks,* and give them up this *Phrygian* boy.

Andr. Ah, fir, recal thofe words——What have you
    faid !
If you give up my fon, Oh, give up me !—
You, who fo many times have fworn me friendfhip :
Oh, Heavens !—will you not look with pity on me ?
Is there no hope ? Is there no room for pardon ?

Pyr. Phœnix will anfwer you—My word is paft.

Andr. You, who would brave fo many dangers for me,

Pyr. I was your lover then—I now am free.
To favour you, I might have fpar'd his life ;
But you would ne'er vouchfafe to afk it of me.
Now 'tis too late.

Andr. ' Ah, fir, you underftood
' My tears, my wifhes, which I durft not utter,
' Afraid of a repulfe.' Oh, fir, excufe
The pride of royal blood, that checks my foul,
And knows not how to be importunate.
You know, alas! I was not born to kneel,
To fue for pity, and to own a mafter.

Pyr. No! in your heart you curfe me ! you difdain

                    B 5   My

My generous flame, and scorn to be oblig'd!
'This very son, this darling of your soul,
'Would be less dear, did I preserve him for you.
'Your anger, your aversion, fall on me;
'You hate me more than the whole league of *Greece*:'
But I shall leave you to your great resentments.
Let us go, *Phœnix*, and appease the *Greeks*.

Andr. Then let me die! and let me go to *Hector*.

Ceph. But, madam———

Andr. What can I do more? The tyrant
Sees my distraction, and insults my tears. [*To* Ceph.
—Behold, how low you have reduc'd a queen!
These eyes have seen my country laid in ashes,
My kindred fall in war, my father slain,
My husband dragg'd in his own blood, my son
Condemn'd to bondage, and myself a slave;
Yet, in the midst of these unheard-of woes,
'Twas some relief to find myself your captive;
And that my son, deriv'd from ancient kings,
Since he must serve, had *Pyrrhus* for his master.
When *Priam* kneel'd, the great *Achilles* wept:
I hop'd I should not find his son less noble:
I thought the brave were still the more compassionate.
Oh, do not, sir, divide me from my child!—
If he must die——

Pyr. Phœnix, withdraw a while. [*Exit* Phœnix.

Pyr. Rise, madam—Yet you may preserve your son.
I find, whenever I provoke your tears,
I furnish you with arms against myself.
I thought my hatred fixt before I saw you.
Oh, turn your eyes upon me while I speak!
And see if you discover in my looks
An angry judge, or an obdurate foe.
Why will you force me to desert your cause?
In your son's name, I beg we may be friends;
'Let me entreat you to secure his life!
'Must I turn suppliant for him?' Think, Oh think,
'Tis the last time, you both may yet be happy!
I know the ties I break, the foes I arm;
I wrong *Hermione*; I send her hence;
And with her diadem I bind your brows.

Consider

Confider well; for 'tis of moment to you!
Choofe to be wretched, madam, or a queen.
' My foul, confum'd with a whole year's defpair,
' Can bear no longer thefe perplexing doubts;
' Enough of fighs and tears, and threats I've try'd;
' I know, if I'm depriv'd of you, I die:
' But Oh, I die, if I wait longer for you!'
I leave you to your thoughts.   When I return,
We'll to the temple—'There you'll find your fon;
And there be crown'd, or give him up for ever.   [*Exit.*
   Ceph. I told you, madam, that in fpite of *Greece,*
You would o'er-rule the malice of your fortune.
   Andr. Alas, *Cephifa,* what have I obtain'd!
Only a poor fhort refpite for my fon.
   Ceph. You have enough approv'd your faith to *Hector;*
To be reluctant ftill would be a crime.
He would himfelf perfuade you to comply.
   Andr. How!——wouldft thou give me *Pyrrhus* for a
     hufband?
   Ceph. Think you 'twill pleafe the ghoft of your dead
     hufband,
That you fhould facrifice his fon?   Confider,
Pyrrhus once more invites you to a throne;
Turns all his power againft the foes of *Troy,*
Remembers not *Achilles* was his father;
Retracts his conqueft, and forgets his hatred.
   Andr. But how can I forget it!—how can I
Forget my *Hector,* treated with difhonour;
Depriv'd of funeral rites, and vilely dragg'd,
A bloody corpfe, about the walls of *Troy!*
Can I forget the good old king his father,
Slain in my prefence—at the altar flain!
Which vainly, for protection, he embrac'd.
Haft thou forgot that dreadful night, *Cephifa,*
When a whole people fell!   Methinks I fee
Pyrrhus enrag'd, and, breathing vengeance, enter
Amidft the glare of burning palaces:
I fee him hew his paffage thro' my brothers,
And, bath'd in blood, lay all my kindred wafte.
Think, in this fcene of horror, what I fuffer'd!
This is the courtfhip I receiv'd from *Pyrrhus;*

And this the husband thou wouldst give me! No,
We both will perish first! I'll ne'er consent.

Ceph. Since you resolve *Astyanax* shall die,
Haste to the temple, bid your son farewel.
Why do you tremble, madam?

Andr. O *Cephisa!*
Thou hast awaken'd all the mother in me.
How can I bid farewel to the dear child,
The pledge, the image of my much-lov'd lord!
' Alas, I call to mind the fatal day,
' When his too forward courage led him forth
' To seek *Achilles.*

' *Ceph.* Oh, the unhappy hour!
' 'Twas then *Troy* fell, and all her Gods forsook her.
' *Andr.* That morn, *Cephisa*, that ill-fated morn,
' My husband bid thee bring *Astyanax* ;
' He took him in his arms ; and, as I wept,
' My wife, my dear *Andromache*, said he,
' (Heaving with stifled sighs to see me weep)
' What fortune may attend my arms, the Gods
' Alone can tell. To thee I give the boy ;
' Preserve him as the token of our loves ;
' If I should fall, let him not miss his sire
' While thou surviv'st ; but by thy tender care,
' Let the son see that thou didst love his father.
' *Ceph.* And will you throw away a life so precious?
' At once extirpate all the *Trojan* line?
' *Andr.* Inhuman king! What has he done to suffer?
' If I neglect your vows, is he to blame?
' Has he reproach'd you with his slaughter'd kindred!
' Can he resent those ills he does not know?—
Put, Oh! while I deliberate, he dies.
No, no, thou must not die, while I can save thee :
Oh! let me find out *Pyrrhus*—Oh, *Cephisa!*
Do you go find him.

Ceph. What must I say to him?

Andr. Tell him I love my son to such excess—
But dost thou think he means the child shall die?
Can love rejected turn to so much rage?

Ceph. Madam, he'll soon be here : resolve on something.

Andr. Well then, assure him—

                                        Ceph.

Ceph. Madam, of your love?

Andr. Alas, thou know'ft that is not in my power.
O my dead Lord! Oh, *Priam*'s royal houfe!
Oh, my *Aftyanax!* at what a price
Thy mother buys thee!—Let us go.

Ceph. But whither?
And what does your unfettled heart refolve?

Andr. Come, my *Cephifa*, let us go together,
To the fad monument which I have rais'd
To *Hector*'s fhade ; where, in their facred urn,
The afhes of my hero lie inclos'd,
The dear remains which I have fav'd from *Troy*;
There let me weep, there fummon to my aid,
With pious rite, my *Hector*'s awful fhade ;
Let him be witnefs to my doubts, my fears ;
My agonizing heart, my flowing tears :
Oh! may he rife in pity from his tomb,
And fix his wretched fon's uncertain doom. [*Exeunt.*

A C T   IV.

‘ *Enter* Andromache, *and* Cephifa.

‘ *Ceph.* BLEST be the tomb of *Hector*, that infpires
‘ Thefe pious thoughts : or is it *Hector*'s felf,
‘ That prompts you to preferve your fon! 'Tis he
‘ Who ftill prefides o'er ruin'd *Troy*; 'Tis he
‘ Who urges *Pyrrhus* to reftore *Aftyanax*.
‘ *Andr.* *Pyrrhus* has faid he will ; and thou haft heard
‘ him
‘ Juft now renew the oft-repeated promife.
‘ *Ceph.* Already, in the tranfports of his heart,
‘ He gives you up his kingdoms, his allies,
‘ And thinks himfelf o'erpaid for all in you.
‘ *Andr.* I think I may rely upon his promife ;
‘ And yet my heart is over-charg'd with grief.
‘ *Ceph.* Why fhould you grieve ? You fee he bids de-
‘ fiance
‘ To all the *Greeks*; and, to protect your fon
‘ Againft their rage, has plac'd his guards about him ;
‘ Leaving -

' Leaving himfelf defenceless, for his fake.
' But, madam, think, the coronation pomp
' Will foon demand your prefence in the temple:
' 'Tis time you lay afide thefe mourning weeds.
    ' *Andr.* I will be there; but firft would fee my fon.
    ' *Ceph.* Madam, you need not now be anxious for him,
' He will be always with you, all your own,
' To lavifh the whole mother's fondnefs on him.
' What a delight to train beneath your eye,
' A fon, who grows no longer up in bondage;
' A fon in whom a race of kings revives:
' But, madam, you are fad, and wrapt in thought,
' As if you relifh'd not your happinefs.
    ' *Andr.* Oh, I muft fee my fon once more, *Cephifa!*
    ' *Ceph.* Madam, he now will be no more a captive;
' Your vifits may be frequent as you pleafe.
' To-morrow you may pafs the live-long day—
    ' *Andr.* To-morrow! Oh, *Cephifa!*—But, no more!
' *Cephifa,* I have always found thee faithful:
' A load of care weighs down my drooping heart.
    ' *Ceph.* Oh! that 'twere poffible for me to eafe you!
    ' *Andr.* I foon fhall exercife thy long-try'd faith.—
' Meanwhile I do conjure thee, my *Cephifa,*
' Thou take no notice of my prefent trouble;
' And, when I fhall difclofe my fecret purpofe,
' That thou be be punctual to perform my will.
    ' *Ceph.* Madam, I have no will but yours. My life
' Is nothing, balanc'd with my love to you.
    ' *Andr.* I thank thee, good *Cephifa,* my *Aftyanax*
' Will recompence thy friendfhip to his mother.
' But, come; my heart's at eafe: affift me now
' To change this fable habit.—Yonder comes
' *Hermione;* I would not meet her rage.   [*Exeunt.*'
            Enter Hermione, *and* Cleone.
    Cleo. This unexpected filence, this referve,
This outward calm, this fettled frame of mind,
After fuch wrongs and infults, much furprize me!
You, who before could not command your rage,
When *Pyrrhus* look'd but kindly on his captive;
How can you bear unmov'd, that he fhould wed her,
And feat her on a throne which you fhould fill?

                                    I fear

I fear this dreadful ftillnefs in your foul!—
'Twere better, madam——
 Her. Have you call'd *Oreftes?*
 Cleo. Madam, I have; his love is too impatient
Not to obey with fpeed the welcome fummons.
His love-fick heart o'erlooks his unkind ufage:
His ardour's ftill the fame—Madam, he's here.
    Enter Oreftes.
 Oref. Ah, madam, is it true? does then *Oreftes*
At length attend you by your own commands?
What can I do—
 Her. Oreftes, do you love me?
 Oref. What means that queftion, princefs? Do I love
  you?
My oaths, my perjuries, my hopes, my fears,
My farewel, my return—all fpeak my love.
 Her. Avenge my wrongs, and I believe them all.
 Oref. It fhall be done—My foul has catch'd th' alarm,
We'll fpirit up the *Greeks*—I'll lead them on:
Your caufe fhall animate our fleets and armies,
Let us return; let us not lofe a moment,
But urge the fate of this devoted land:
Let us depart.
 Her. No, prince, let us ftay here!
I will have vengeance here—I will not carry
This load of infamy to *Greece,* nor truft
The chance of war to vindicate my wrongs.
Ere I depart, I'll make *Epirus* mourn.
If you avenge me, let it be this inftant;
My rage brooks no delay; hafte to the temple,
Hafte, prince, and facrifice him.
 Oref. Whom?
 Her. Why, *Pyrrhus.*
 Oref. Pyrrhus! Did you fay *Pyrrhus?*
 Her. You demur.—
Oh fly! be gone! give me not time to think—
Talk not of laws—he tramples on all laws—
Let me not hear him juftify'd—away!
 Oref. You cannot think I'll juftify my rival.
Madam, your love has made him criminal.
You fhall have vengeance; I'll have vengeance too:
           But

But let our hatred be profeft and open :
Let us alarm all *Greece*, denounce a war;
Let us attack him in his ftrength, and hunt him down
By conqueft : Should I turn bafe affaffin,
'Twould fully all the kings I reprefent.
    Her. Have not I been difhonour'd ? fet at nought ?
Expos'd to public fcorn ?—And will you fuffer
The tyrant, who dares ufe me thus, to live ?
Know, prince, I hate him more than once I lov'd him.
The Geds alone can tell how once I lov'd him ;
Yes, the falfe, perjur'd man, I once did love him ;
And, fpite of all his crimes and broken vows,
If he fhould live, I may relapfe—who knows
But I to-morrow may forgive his wrongs ?
    Oref. Firft let me tear him piece-meal—he fhall die.
But, madam, give me leifure to contrive
The place, the time, the manner of his death ;
Yet I'm a ftranger in the court of *Pyrrhus ;*
Scarce have I fet my foot within *Epirus.*
When you enjoin me to deftroy the prince.
It fhall be done this very night.
    Her. But now,
This very hour, he weds *Andromache ;*
The temple fhines with pomp ; the golden throne
Is now prepar'd ; the joyful rites begin ;
My fhame is public——Oh, be fpeedy, prince !
My wrath's impatient—*Pyrrhus* lives too long !
Intent on love, and heedlefs of his perfon,
He covers with his guards the *Trojan* boy.
Now is the time : affemble all your *Greeks ;*
Mine fhall affift them ; let their fury loofe :
Already they regard him as a foe.
Begone, *Oreftes*—kill the faithlefs tyrant ;
My love fhall recompence the glorious deed.
    Oref. Confider, madam——
    Her. You but mock my rage !
I was contriving how to make you happy.
Think you to merit by your idle fighs,
And not atteft your love by one brave action ?
Go, with your boafted conftancy ! and leave
Hermione to execute her own revenge.

                        I blufh

I blufh to think how my too eafy faith
Has twice been baffled in one fhameful hour!

Oref. Hear me but fpeak!—you know I'll die to ferve
you!

Her. I'll go myfelf: I'll ftab him at the altar;
Then drive the poniard, reeking with his blood,
Thro' my own heart. In death we fhall unite.
Better to die with him, than live with you!

Oref. That were to make him bleft, and me more
wretched.
Madam, he dies by me——Have you a foe,
And fhall I let him live? My rival, too?
Ere yon meridian fun declines, he dies;
And you fhall fay that I deferve your love.

Her. Go, prince; ftrike home! and leave the reft to
me;
Let all your fhips ftand ready for our flight. [*Exit* Oref.

Cleo. Madam, you'll perifh in this bold attempt.

Her. Give me my vengeance, I'm content to perifh.
I was to blame to truft it with another:
In my own hands it had been more fecure.
Oreftes hates not *Pyrrhus* as I hate him.
' I fhould have thruft the dagger home; have feen
' The tyrant curfe me with his parting breath,
' And roll about his dying eyes, in vain,
' To find *Andromache*, whom I would hide.'
Oh, would *Oreftes*, when he gives the blow,
Tell him he dies my victim!—Hafte, *Cleone;*
Charge him to fay, *Hermione's* refentment,
Not thofe of *Greece*, have fentenc'd him to death.
Hafte, my *Cleone!* My revenge is loft,
If *Pyrrhus* knows not that he dies by me!

Cleo. I fhall obey your orders——But I fee
The king approach—Who could expect him here?

Her. O fly! *Cleone*, fly! and bid *Oreftes*
Not to proceed a ftep before I fee him. [*Exit* Cleone.

Enter Pyrrhus.

Pyr. Madam, I ought to fhun an injur'd princefs:
Your diftant looks reproach me: and I come
Not to defend, but to avow my guilt.
Pyrrhus will ne'er approve his own injuftice,

Nor

Nor form excuses while his heart condemns him.
‘ I might perhaps alledge, our warlike fires,
‘ Unknown to us, engag’d us to each other,
‘ And join’d our hearts by contract, not by love ;
‘ But I detest such cobweb arts, I own
‘ My father’s treaty, and allow its force.
‘ I sent ambassadors to call you hither ;
‘ Receiv’d you as my queen ; and Lop’d my oaths
‘ So oft renew’d, might ripen into love.
‘ The Gods can witness, madam, how I fought
‘ Against *Andromache*’s too fatal charms !
‘ And still i wish I had the power to leave
‘ This *Trojan* beauty, and be just to you.’
Discharge your anger on this perjur’d man !
For I abhor my crime ! and should be pleas’d
To hear you speak your wrongs aloud : No terms,
No bitterness of wrath, nor keen reproach,
Will equal half the upbraidings of my heart.

   Her. I find, fir, you can be sincere : you scorn
To act your crimes with fear, like other men.
A hero should be bold ; above all laws ;
Be bravely false, and laugh at solemn ties.
To be perfidious shews a daring mind !
And you have nobly triumph’d o’er a maid !
To court me—to reject me—to return—
Then to forsake me for a *Phrygian* slave—
To lay proud *Troy* in ashes—then to raise
The son of *Hector*, and renounce the *Greeks*,
Are actions worthy the great soul of *Pyrrhus !*

   Pyr. Madam, go on : Give your resentment birth,
And pour forth all your indignation on me.

   Her. ’Twould please your queen, should I upbraid your
      falshood ;
Call you perfidious, traitor, all the names
That injur’d virgins lavish on your sex ;
I should o’erflow with tears, and die with grief,
And furnish out a tale to soothe her pride ;
But, fir, I would not over-charge her joys.
If you would charm *Andromache*, recount
Your bloody battles, your exploits, your slaughters,
Your great atchievements in her father’s palace.

                            She

She needs muſt love the man, who fought ſo bravely,
And in her ſight ſlew half her royal kindred!
Pyr. With horror I look back on my paſt deeds!
I puniſh'd *Helen's* wrongs too far; I ſhed
Too much of blood: But, madam, *Helen's* daughter
Should not object thoſe ills the mother cauſ'd.
However, I am pleas'd to find you hate me—
I was too forward to accuſe myſelf—
The man who ne'er was lov'd, can ne'er be falſe.
Obedience to a father brought you hither;
And I ſtood bound by promiſe to receive you:
But our deſires were different ways inclin'd;
And you, I own, were not oblig'd to love me.
Her. Have I not lov'd you, then! perfidious man!
For you I ſlighted all the *Grecian* princes;
Forſook my father's houſe; conceal'd my wrongs,
When moſt provok'd; would not return to *Sparta,*
In hopes that time might fix your wavering heart.
I lov'd you when inconſtant; and even now,
Inhuman king! that you pronounce my death,
My heart ſtill doubts, if I ſhould love, or hate you—
But, Oh, ſince you reſolve to wed another,
Defer your cruel purpoſe till to-morrow,
That I may not be here to grace her triumph!
This is the laſt requeſt I e'er ſhall make you—
See, if the barbarous prince vouchſafes an anſwer!
Go, then, to the lov'd *Phrygian;* hence! begone!
And bear to her thoſe vows that once were mine:
Go, in defiance to the avenging Gods!
Begone! the prieſt expects you at the altar—
But, tyrant, have a care I come not thither.   [*Exit.*
    Enter Phœnix.
Phœn. Sir, did you mind her threats? your life's in
        danger:
There is no trifling with a woman's rage.
The *Greeks* that ſwarm about the court, all hate you;
Will treat you as their country's enemy,
And join in her revenge: Beſides, *Oreſtes*
Still loves her to diſtraction.   Sir, I beg——
Pyr. How, *Phœnix,* ſhould I fear a woman's threats?
A nobler paſſion takes up all my thoughts:
                                    I muſt

I muſt prepare to meet *And.omache.*
Do thou place all my guards about her ſon:
If he be ſafe, *Pyrrhus* is free from fear.   [*Exit.*

   Phœn. Oh, *Pyrrhus!* Oh, what pity 'tis, the Gods,
Who fill'd thy ſoul with every kingly virtue,
Form'd thee for empire and conſummate greatneſs,
Should leave thee ſo expos'd to wild deſires,
That hurry thee beyond the bounds of reaſon!   [*Flouriſh.*
‘ Such was *Achilles*, generous, fierce, and brave;
‘ Open, and undeſigning; but impatient,
‘ Undiſciplin'd, and not to be controul'd.
‘ I fear this whirl of paſſion, this career,
‘ That over-bears reflection and cool thought—
‘ I tremble for the event!'——But ſee, the queen,
Magnificent in royal pride, appears.
I muſt obey, and guard her ſon from danger.   [*Exit.*

        Enter Andromache, *and* Cephiſa.

   Ceph. Madam, once more you look and move a queen,
Your ſorrows are diſpers'd, your charms revive,
And every faded beauty blooms anew.

   Andr. Yet all is not as I could wiſh, *Cephiſa.*

   Ceph. You ſee the king is watchful o'er your ſon;
Decks him with princely robes, with guards ſurrounds
    him.
Aſtyanax begins to reign already.

   Andr. *Pyrrhus* is nobly minded; and I fain
Would live to thank him for *Aſtyanax:*
'Tis a vain thought.—However, ſince my child
Has ſuch a friend, I ought not to repine.

   Ceph. ‘ Theſe dark unfoldings of your ſoul perplex me.
‘ What meant thoſe floods of tears, thoſe warm embraces,
‘ As if you bid your ſon adieu for ever.'
For Heaven's ſake, madam, let me know your griefs.
If you diſtruſt my faith——

   Andr. That were to wrong thee.
Oh, my *Cephiſa!* This gay, borrow'd air,
This blaze of jewels, and this bridal dreſs,
Are but mock trapppings, to conceal my woe:
My heart ſtill mourns; I ſtill am *Hector's* widow.

   Ceph. Will you then break the promiſe giv'n to *Pyrrhus,*
Blow up his rage again, and blaſt your hopes?

                            Andr.

Andr. I thought, *Cephifa*, thou hadſt known thy miſ-
treſs.
Couldſt thou believe I would be falſe to *Hector?*
Fall off from ſuch a huſband! Break his reſt,
And call him to this hated light again,
To ſee *Andromache* in *Pyrrhus'* arms!
' Would *Hector*, were he living, and I dead,
' Forget *Andromache*, and wed her foe?'
    Ceph. I cannot gueſs what drift your thoughts purſue;
But, Oh, I fear there's ſomething dreadful in it!
Muſt then *Aſtyanax* be doom'd to die,
And you to linger out a life in bondage?
    ' *Andr.* Nor this, nor that, *Cephiſa*, will I bear.
' My word is paſt to *Pyrrhus*, his to me;
' And I rely upon his promis'd faith.
' Unequal as he is, I know him well:
' *Pyrrhus* is violent, but he's ſincere,
' And will perform beyond what he has ſworn.
' The *Greeks* will but incenſe him more; their rage
' Will make him cheriſh *Hector*'s ſon.
    ' *Ceph.* Ah, madam!
' Explain theſe riddles to my boding heart.
    ' *Andr.* Thou mayſt remember, for thou oft haſt heard
        ' me
' Relate the dreadful viſion which I ſaw,
' When firſt I landed captive in *Epirus.*
' That very night, as in a dream I lay,
' A ghaſtly figure, full of gaping wounds,
' His eyes aglare, his hair all ſtiff with blood,
' Full in my ſight thrice ſhook his head, and groan'd.
' I ſoon diſcern'd my ſlaughter'd *Hector*'s ſhade;
' But, Oh, how chang'd! Ye Gods, how much unlike
' The living *Hector!*—Loud he bid me fly!
' Fly from *Achilles'* ſon! then ſternly frown'd,
' And diſappear'd : Struck with the dreadful ſound,
' I ſtarted, and awak'd.
    ' *Ceph.* But did he bid you
' Deſtroy *Aſtyanax?*
    ' *Andr.* *Cephiſa*, I'll preſerve him;
' With my own life, *Cephiſa*, I'll preſerve him.
                                        ' Ceph.

' *Ceph.* What may thefe words, fo full of horror,
   ' mean ?'
Andr. Know then the fecret purpofe of my foul :
Andromache will not be falfe to *Pyrrhus*,
Nor violate her facred love to *Hector.*
This hour I'll meet the king ; the holy prieft
Shall join us, and confirm our mutual vows.
This will fecure a father to my child :
·That done, I have no farther ufe for life :
This pointed dagger, this determin'd hand,
Shall fave my virtue, and conclude my woes.
   ' *Ceph.* Ah, madam! recollect your fcatter'd reafon;
' This fell defpair ill fuits your prefent fortunes.
   · *Andr.* No other ftratagem can ferve my purpofe—
' This is the fole expedient, to be juft
· To *Hector*, to *Aftyanax*, to *Pyrrhus.*
' I foon fhall vifit *Hector*, and the fhades
' Of my great anceftors.'——*Cephifa*, thou
Wilt lend a hand to clofe thy miftrefs' eyes.
   Ceph. Oh, never think that I will ftay behind you!
Andr. No, my *Cephifa*; I muft have thee live.
' Remember, thou didft promife to obey,
' And to be fecret, wilt thou now betray me ?
' After thy long, thy faithful fervice, wilt thou
' Refufe my laft commands, my dying wifh ?
' Once more I do conjure thee, live for me!
   ' *Ceph.* Life is not worth my care when you are gone.
' *Andr.*' I muft commit into thy faithful hands
All that is dear and precious to my foul ;
Live, and fupply my abfence to my child.
All that remains of *Troy;* a future progeny
Of heroes, and a diftant line of kings,
In him, is all iutrufted to thy care.
   ' *Ceph.* But, madam, what will be the rage of *Pyrrhus*,
' Defrauded of his promis'd happinefs?
   ' *Andr.* That will require thy utmoft fkill : Obferve
' The firft impetuous onfets of his grief :
' Ufe every artifice to keep him ftedfaft.
' Sometimes with tears thou mayft difcourfe of me ;
' Speak of our marriage ; let him think I lov'd him ;
                                          ' Tell

DISTREST MOTHER.

G. Sherwin del. & sculp.

Mrs HARTLEY in the Character of ANDROMACHE.

This Pointed Dagger, this determin'd Hand,
shall save my Virtue, and conclude my Woes.

Tell him my foul repos'd itfelf on him,
‘ When I refign'd my fon to his protection.’
  Ceph. Oh for a fpirit to fupport my grief!
Is there aught more, before you go for ever?
  Andr. Oh, my *Cephifa!* my fwoln heart is full!
I have a thoufand farewels to my fon——
But tears break in!—Grief interrupts my fpeech!—
My foul o'erflows in fondnefs!—Let him know
I dy'd to fave him—and would die again.
Seafon his mind with early hints of glory;
Make him acquainted with his anceftors;
Trace out their fhining ftory in his thoughts:
Dwell on the exploits of his immortal father;
And fometimes let him hear his mother's name.
‘ Let him reflect upon his royal birth
‘ With modeft pride—*Pyrrhus* will prove a friend—
‘ But let him know he has a conqueror's right.’
He muft be taught to ftifle his refentments,
And facrifice his vengeance to his fafety.
Should he prove headftrong, rafh, or unadvis'd,
He then will fruftrate all his mother's virtue,
Provoke his fate, and I fhall die in vain.
  Ceph. Alas, I fear I never fhall outlive you!
  Andr. No more—thy tears, *Cephifa*, will betray me;
Affume a cheerful look—But ftill remember——
                    [*Flourifh within.*
Hark how the trumpet, with its fprightly notes,
Proclaims th' appointed hour, and calls us hence:
Hector, I come, once more a queen, to join thee!
Thus the gay victim, with frefh garlands crown'd,
Pleas'd with the facred fife's enlivening found,
Thro' gazing crowds, in folemn ftate proceeds;
And, dreft in fatal pomp, magnificently bleeds.

A C T   V.

Hermione *alone*.

WHAT have I done? Where am I? Where is
     Pyrrhus?
Ye Gods! what mean thefe horrors?—I'm undone!
                                My

My foul is on the rack !——I cannot bear it !——
Why do I wander, like fome guilty ghoft ?
What brought me to this place ? What keeps me here ?
The court of *Pyrrhus* has no room for me !
Do I ftill doubt, if I fhould love or hate him ?
Hard-hearted man ! how unconcern'd he left me !
Did he once figh ? beftow one pitying look ?
Once fhed a tear ? or fpeak one foft, kind word ?
Did he fo much as feign one moment's forrow,
To calm my grief, and mitigate his falfhood ?——
Why am I ftill thus anxious for his life ?
Why do I ftart at his impending fate ?
Shall he then live ? Shall the bafe traitor live
To laugh at my diftrefs ? No, let him perifh !
Be quick, *Oreftes !*——Execute my orders !
Alas ! my orders ! Oh, prepofterous guilt !
Can I decree the death of him I love ?
Was it for this my foul delighted in him ?
Was it for this I left my father's court ?
Have I then crofs'd fo many realms and feas
To murder *Pyrrhus ?*

Enter Cleone.

Oh, *Cleone,* help me !
What have I done ? Is *Pyrrhus* yet alive ?
What fay'ft thou ?—Anfwer me—Where is the king ?

Cleo. Madam, I faw the cruel prince fet forward,
Triumphant in his looks, and full of joy.
Still as he walk'd, his ravifh'd eyes were fix'd
On the fair captive ; while thro' fhouting crowds
She pafs'd along with a dejected air,
And feem'd to mourn her *Hector* to the laft.

Her. Infulting tyrant ! I fhall burft with rage !——
But fay, *Cleone,* didft thou mark him well ?
Was his brow fmooth ? Say, did there not appear
Some fhade of grief ? fome little cloud of forrow
Did he not ftop ? Did he not once look back ?
Didft thou approach him ? Was he not confounded ?
Did he not——Oh, be quick, and tell me all !

Cleo. Madam, the tumult of his joy admits
No thought but love. Unguarded he march'd on,

'Midft

'Midſt a promiſcuous throng of friends and foes,
His cares all turn upon *Aſtyanax*,
Whom he has lodg'd within the citadel,
Defended by the ſtrength of all his guards.

Her. Enough!—He dies!—The traitor!——Where's
Oreſtes?

Cleo. He's in the temple, with his whole retinue.

Her. Is he ſtill reſolute? Is he ſtill determin'd?

Cleo. Madam, I fear——

Her. How!—Is *Oreſtes* falſe?
Does he betray me, too?

Cleo. A thouſand doubts
Perplex his ſoul, and wound him with remorſe;
His virtue and his love prevail by turns.
He told me *Pyrrhus* ſhould not fall ignobly—
Pyrrhus, the warlike ſon of great *Achilles*.
He dreads the cenſure of the *Grecian* ſtates;
Of all mankind, and fears to ſtain his honour.

Her. Poor tim'rous wretch! 'tis falſe! he baſely fears
To cope with dangers, and encounter death:
'Tis that he fears.—Am I bright *Helen*'s daughter?
To vindicate her wrongs all *Greece* conſpir'd;
For her confederate nations fought, and kings were ſlain;
Troy was o'erthrown, and a whole empire fell.
My eyes want force to raiſe a lover's arm
Againſt a tyrant that has dar'd to wrong me!

Cleo. Madam, like *Helen*, truſt your cauſe to *Greece*.

Her. No; I'll avenge myſelf, I'll to the temple;
I'll overturn the altar, ſtab the prieſt;
I'll hurl deſtruction, like a whirlwind, round me!
They muſt not wed! they muſt not live! they ſhall not!
Let me be gone—I have no time to loſe—
Stand off! hold me not! I am all diſtraction!
O *Pyrrhus!* tyrant! traitor! thou ſhalt bleed.

Enter Oreſtes.

Oreſ. Madam, 'tis done: your orders are obey'd:
The tyrant lies expiring at the altar.

Her. Is *Pyrrhus* ſlain?—

Oreſ. Even now he gaſps in death.
Our *Greeks*, all undiſtinguiſh'd in the crowd,

C

Flock'd

Flock'd to the temple, and difpers'd themfelves
On every fide the altar : I was there :
Pyrrhus obferv'd me with a haughty eye,
And, proud to triumph over *Greece* in me,
From his own brows he took the diadem,
And bound it on the temples of his captive.
Receive, faid he, my crown; receive my faith,
Mine and my people's fovereign reign for ever,
From this bleft hour, a father to your fon ;
I'll fcourge his foes : henceforward he be ftyl'd
The *Trojan* king : ' I fwear it at the altar,
' And call the Gods to ratify my vows.'
His fubjects with loud acclamations fhook
The fpacious dome ! our *Greeks*, enrag'd, cry'd out
Revenge ! revenge ! broke thro' the thronging prefs,
And ruſh'd tumultuous on the unguarded king.
' Their eager fury left no work for me.'
Pyrrhus awhile oppos'd their clafhing fwords,
And dealt his fatal blows on every fide,
With manly fiercenefs ; till oppreft by numbers,
Streaming with blood, all over gafh'd with wounds,
He reel'd, he groan'd, and at the altar fell.—
Hafte, madam ; let us fly ! hafte to our fhips !
They lie unmoor'd—Our friends attend us there.
 Her. What have they done !
 Oref. Madam, forgive their rage.
I own your vengeance had been more complete
Had *Pyrrhus* fall'n by me ; and had he known,
Hermione chaftis'd him by my arm
 Her. Peace, monfter, peace !—Go! tell thy horrid tale
To favages, and howl it out in deferts.
Wouldft thou impute to me thy barbarous guilt ?
Me wouldft thou make th' accomplice of thy crimes !
Hence, to thy *Greeks !* and boaft thy foul exploits !
My foul abhors them ! I difclaim the deed !
Begone ! I knew thee not, thou fell barbarian !
What had he done ? What could provoke thy madnefs
To affafinate fo great, fo brave a man ?
Who fet thee on ?
 Oref. Oh, grant me patience, Heaven !   With

With your own lips did you not curfe the tyrant,
Pronounce his death, and urge me to deftroy him?
Her. What if, tranfported by my boundlefs paffion,
I could not bear to fee him wed another,
Were you t' obey a jealous woman's phrenzy?
You fhould have div'd into my inmoft thoughts:
My heart, tho' full of rage, was free from malice;
And all my anger was excefs of love.
Why did you take me at my word? You faw
The ftruggles of my foul; you heard me rave;
You fhould have queftion'd me a thoufand times,
Yet ftill have doubted, and have queftion'd on,
Before you ventur'd on a life fo precious.

    Oref. Hear me but fpeak—Heaven knows, againft my
    will——

    Her. Why did you not return? Why not confult me
A fecond time? and, undetermin'd ftill,
Again return, and ftill find new delays?
What had your rafh officious *Greeks*, dire blood hounds!
To do with my revenge? What drew you hither?
To bring on me the vengeful woes that haunt you?
Are thefe the fruits of your detefted love?
Your fatal embaffy, your hateful prefence.
Drove *Pyrrhus* to my rival, and deftroys
Both him and me.—He might have lov'd me ftill,
Had you ne'er interpos'd.—Avaunt! begone!
And leave me in *Epirus.*—I renounce
My friends, my country, *Greece*, and all mankind:
But chiefly I renounce thee! monfter, thee!   [*Exit.*

    Oref. Am I awake? where am I? Soft, my foul;
Be not too rafh.——Was that *Hermione?*
Why fhould her anger thunder againft me?
Was not this blood fhed all by her command?—
I am indeed a moft outrageous monfter!
A ruffian, murderer, a bafe affaffin!
And all to pleafe a falfe ungrateful woman.
Henceforward, let the laws of nature ceafe;
And let the pale that fevers right and wrong,
Things facred and profane, be broken down;
Gods in their temples, kings upon their thrones,

        Are

Are not in safety while *Orestes* lives.
Oh, never more shall my torn mind be heal'd,
Nor taste the gentle comforts of repose!
A dreadful band of gloomy cares surround me,
And lay strong siege to my distracted soul.

    Enter Pylades, attended by Greeks.

 Pyl. Haste, prince; let us be gone: 'tis death to stay.
Andromache reigns queen: she gives the alarm,
And vows revenge upon the foes of *Pyrrhus.*
The people arm and muster in the streets:
Our *Greeks* will not be able long to guard
The palace gates, and to secure our flight.
We must be speedy, sir.

 Oreſ. You may depart,
My friends—*Hermione* and I remain.——
Her cruelty has quite undone me!—' Go,
' And leave me to myself—I'll find her out.'

 Pyl. Alas, unhappy princess!—She's no more;
' Forget her, sir, and save yourself with us.'

 Oreſ. Hermione no more!—O, all ye powers!

 Pyl. Full of disorder, wildness in her looks,
With hands expanded, and dishevell'd hair,
Breathless and pale, with shrieks she sought the temple;
In the mid-way she met the corpse of *Pyrrhus;*
She startled at the sight; then, stiff with horror,
Gaz'd frightful! Waken'd from the dire amaze,
She rais'd her eyes to Heaven with such a look
As spoke her sorrows, and reproach'd the Gods;
Then plung'd a poniard deep within her breast,
And fell on *Pyrrhus,* grasping him in death.

 Oreſ. I thank you, Gods—I never could expect
To be so wretched!—You have been industrious
To finish your decrees; to make *Orestes*
A dreadful instance of your power to punish;
I'm singled out to bear the wrath of Heaven.

 Pyl. You hazard your retreat by these delays.
The guards will soon beset us. Your complaints
Are vain, and may be fatal.

 Oreſ. True, my friend:
And therefore 'twas I thank'd the bounteous Gods,

          My

My fate's accomplish'd.—I shall die content.
Oh, bear me hence—Blow, winds!

Pyl. Let us be gone.

Orest. The murder'd lovers wait me—Hark, they call!
Nay, if your blood still reeks, I'll mingle mine:
One tomb will hold us all.

Pyl. Alas! I fear
His raving will return with his misfortunes.

Orest. I am dizzy!—Clouds!—Quite lost in utter dark-
ness!
Guide me, some friendly pilot, thro' the storm.
I shiver! Oh, I freeze!—So—Light returns;
'Tis the grey dawn——See, *Pylades!* behold!——
I am encompass'd with a sea of blood!——
The crimson billows!—Oh! my brain's on fire!

Pyl. How is it, sir?—Repose yourself on me.

Orest. Pyrrhus, stand off!—What wouldst thou?—How
he glares!
What envious hand has clos'd thy wounds?——Have at
thee.
It is *Hermione* that strikes—Confusion!
She catches *Pyrrhus* in her arms.—Oh, save me!
How terrible she looks!—She knits her brow!
She frowns me dead; she frights me into madness!
Where am I?—Who are you?

Pyl. Alas, poor prince!
' Help to support him.—How he pants for breath!'

Orest. This is most kind, my *Pylades*—Oh, why,
Why was I born to give thee endless trouble?

Pyl. All will go well—He settles into reason.

Orest. Who talks of reason? Better to have none,
Than not enough.—Run, some one, tell my *Greeks*
I will not have them touch the king—Now—now!
I blaze again!—See there—Look where they come;
A shoal of furies—How they swarm about me!
My terror!—Hide me!—Oh, their snaky locks!
Hark, how they hiss!—See, see their flaming brands!
Now they let drive at me!——How they grin,
And shake their iron whips!—My ears! what yelling!
And see, *Hermione!*——she sets them on——

Thrust

Thrust not your scorpions thus into my bosom!
Oh!—I am stung to death!—Dispatch me soon!
There—take my heart, *Hermione!*—Tear it out!
Disjoint me!—kill me!—Oh, my tortur'd soul!

Pyl. Kind Heaven, restore him to his wonted calm!
Oft have I seen him rave, but never thus—
Quite spent!—Assist me, friends, to bear him off.
Our time is short: should his strong rage return,
'Twould be beyond our power to force him hence.
Away, my friends!—I hear the portal open.   [*Exeunt.*

Enter Phoenix, *attended by Guards.*

Phœn. All, all are fled!——*Orestes* is not here!——
Triumphant villains!—The base, giddy rabble,
Whose hands should all have been employ'd with fire,
To waste the fleet, flock'd round the dying princess:
And, while they stand agaze, the *Greeks* embark.
Oh, 'tis too plain!——This sacrileg'ous murder
Was autheriz'd.——Th' ambassador's escape
Declares his guilt.——Most bloody embassy!
Most unexampled deeds!—Where, where, ye Gods,
Is majesty secure, if in your temples
You give it no protection!——See, the queen.

[*A flourish of trumpets.*

Enter Andromache, *and* Cephisa, *with Attendants.*

Andr. Yes, ye inhuman *Greeks!* the time will come
When you shall dearly pay your bloody deeds!
How should the *Trojans* hope for mercy from you.
When thus you turn your impious rage on *Pyrrhus;*
Pyrrhus, the bravest man in all your league;
The man, whose single valour made you triumph.

[*A dead march behind.*

Is my child there?——
Ceph. It is the corps of *Pyrrhus;*
The weeping soldiers bear him on their shields.
Andr. Ill-fated prince! too negligent of life!
And too unwary of the faithless *Greeks!*
Cut off in the fresh rip'ning prime of manhood,
E'en in the prime of life; thy triumphs new,
And all thy glories in full blossom round thee!
The very *Trojans* would bewail thy fate.

Ceph.

Ceph. Alas, then, will your forrows never end!

Andr. Oh, never, never!—While I live, my tears
Will never ceafe; for I was born to grieve.——
Give prefent orders for the fun'ral pomp :   [*To* Phœn.
Let him be rob'd in all his regal flate;
Place round him every fhining mark of honour;
And let the pile that confecrates his afhes,
Rife like his fame, and blaze above the clouds.

           [*Exit* Phœnix. *A flourifh of trumpets.*

Ceph. The found proclaims th' arrival of the prince,
The guards conduct him from the citadel.

Andr. With open arms I'll meet him!—O, *Cephifa!*
A fpringing joy, mixt with a foft concern,
A pleafure, which no language can exprefs,
An ecftafy, that mothers only feel,
Plays round my heart, and brightens up my forrow,
Like gleams of funfhine in a low'ring fky.

Tho' plung'd in ills, and exercis'd in care,
Yet never let the noble mind defpair.
When preft by dangers, and befet with foes,
The Gods their timely fuccour interpofe ;
And when our virtue finks, o'erwhelm'd with grief,
By unforefeen expedients brings relief.

                    [*Exeunt omnes.*

AND OF THE FIFTH ACT.

EPILOGUE.

SPOKEN BY ANDROMACHE.

I Hope you'll own, that with becoming art,
I've play'd my game, and topp'd the widow's part.
My spouse, poor man, could not live out the play,
But dy'd commodiously on wedding-day,
While I, his relict, made, at one bold fling,
Myself a princess, and young Sty a king.

You, ladies, who protract a lover's pain,
And hear your servants sigh whole years in vain;
Which of you all would not on marriage venture,
Might she so soon upon her jointure enter?

'Twas a strange 'scape! had Pyrrhus liv'd till now,
I had been finely hamper'd in my vow.
To die by one's own hand, and fly the charms
Of love and life in a young monarch's arms!
'Twere an hard fate——ere I had undergone it,
I might have took one night—to think upon it.

But why, you'll say, was all this grief exprest
For a first husband, laid long since at rest?
Why so much coldness to my kind protector?
——Ah, ladies! had you known the good man Hector—
Homer will tell you, (or I'm misinform'd)
That when enrag'd, the Grecian camp he storm'd;
To break the ten-fold barriers of the gate,
He threw a stone of such prodigious weight
As no two men could lift, not even of those
Who in that age of thundering mortals rose;
——It would have sprain'd a dozen modern beaux.

At length, howe'er, I laid my weeds aside,
And sunk the widow in the well-dress'd bride.
In you it still remains to grace the play,
And bless with joy my coronation day;
Take then, ye circles of the brave and fair,
The fatherless and widow to your care.

F I N I S.